OUTLAWS AND HIGHWAYMEN

The Cult of the Robber in England from the
Middle Ages to the Nineteenth Century

GILLIAN SPRAGGS

PIMLICO

Published by Pimlico 2001

2 4 6 8 10 9 7 5 3 1

First published in Great Britain by
Pimlico 2001

Pimlico
Random House, 20 Vauxhall Bridge Road,
London SW1V 2SA

Random House Australia (Pty) Limited
20 Alfred Street, Milsons Point, Sydney,
New South Wales 2061, Australia

Random House New Zealand Limited
18 Poland Road, Glenfield,
Auckland 10, New Zealand

Random House (Pty) Limited
Endulini, 5a Jubilee Road, Parktown 2193, South Africa

The Random House Group Limited Reg. No. 954009
www.randomhouse.co.uk

A CIP catalogue record for this book
is available from the British Library

ISBN 0–7126–6479–3

Papers used by Random House are natural,
recyclable products made from wood grown in sustainable forests;
the manufacturing processes conform to the environmental
regulations of the country of origin

Typeset by Deltatype Ltd, Birkenhead, Merseyside
Printed and bound in Great Britain by
Mackays of Chatham PLC

To Leo Salingar

Contents

Acknowledgements

The research for this book began at the University of Cambridge in the second half of the 1970s, while I was working on a study of Falstaff that formed part of a PhD thesis on 'Rogues and Vagabonds in English Literature, 1552–1642'. That thesis was supervised by Leo Salingar, to whose teaching and scholarly example I owe a lasting debt. I also profited from the teaching of Keith Wrightson, who introduced me to the disciplines of academic social history, in the process giving me a lifelong taste for historical writing. The idea of a book on the literature and history of the English highway robber was one that was already beginning to take shape before I submitted my thesis. In those years, Jane Hitchcot was a continual source of stimulating suggestions and comments.

The curse of the independent scholar is isolation, but in my case this has been greatly mitigated over the last decade by the welcome I have been given in the English Department at Loughborough University. I should like to take this opportunity to record my appreciation and thanks, and, in particular, to thank the many members of that department, past and present, from whom I have received personal encouragement.

I should like to thank the staffs of the British Library, Cambridge University Library, Leicester University Library, the Pilkington Library of Loughborough University, the English Faculty Library, Cambridge and Angel Row Library, Nottingham. My thanks are also due to Martin Butler and Helen Phillips, for providing me with information, and Malcolm Hornsby, of Antiquarian and Second-hand Books, Loughborough, who has kindly allowed me to reproduce an illustration from his first edition of *Barnaby Rudge*.

Martyn Bennett, Stella Brooks, Sam Eaton, Catie Gill, Alison Hennegan, Ilid Landry, Laurie Marks, Marion Shaw, Mog Singer and Diana Wallace have all read sections of this book in draft. I am extremely grateful to them for their comments and suggestions.

Acknowledgements

Throughout the writing of this book and for many of the years of research that preceded it, Mog Singer has given me unstinting encouragement and every kind of support. I also owe a very great deal to the encouragement and work of Meg Davis, my friend and agent, without whom this project might never have come to fruition. Finally, I should like to thank Will Sulkin, who commissioned the book for Pimlico, and Jörg Hensgen, who has been a most supportive and helpful editor.

Note

The orthography of some of the passages quoted in this book has been slightly modernised for ease of reading. Any thorn character occurring in a Middle English passage has been changed to *th*; all yogh characters have been changed as appropriate to *y*, *g* or *gh*. In Middle and Early Modern English, consonantal *i* has been changed to *j*. Likewise, consonantal *u* has been changed to *v*; where *v* represents a vowel, it has been changed to *u*. 'Long s' has been replaced by *s*. Contractions have been silently expanded.

In a few cases the punctuation has been slightly altered for clarity; where this has been done, it has been recorded in the notes.

All translations into Modern English of originals in Latin or Anglo-French are by the author.

Robbery is a felony by the Common law, committed by a violent assault, upon the person of another, by putting him in fear, and taking from his person his money or other goods of any value whatsoever.

. . .

. . . that which is taken in his presence, is in law taken from his person.

Edward Coke, *The Third Part of the Institutes of the Laws of England* (a. 1634)

A romantic interest . . . attached, and perhaps still attaches, to the names of freebooters of this class [highwaymen]. The vulgar eagerly drank in tales of their ferocity and audacity, of their occasional acts of generosity and good nature, of their amours, of their miraculous escapes, of their desperate struggles, and of their manly bearing at the bar and in the cart. . . . In these anecdotes there is doubtless a large mixture of fable; but they are not on that account unworthy of being recorded; for it is both an authentic and an important fact that such tales, whether false or true, were heard by our ancestors with eagerness and faith.

Thomas Babington Macaulay, *The History of England* (1849)

I knew a very wise man . . . [who] believed if a man were permitted to make all the ballads, he need not care who should make the laws of a nation.

Andrew Fletcher of Saltoun, *An Account of a Conversation Concerning a Right Regulation of Governments* (1704)

1

Introduction: the Cult of the Robber

During the reign of George II, a visitor from France, the Abbé Le Blanc, wrote home to a friend about an incident that had happened to an English gentleman he had met. This man had been held up on the highway by Dick Turpin, at that time the most famous robber in England. Forcing his victim to yield by firing a pistol, 'The highwayman took his money, his watch and his snuff-box, leaving him only two shillings to continue his journey. Before he left him, he required his word of honour that he would not cause him to be pursued, nor inform against him before a justice; which being given, they both parted very courteously.' The following year, they once again came face to face, this time at the Newmarket races. Remaining true to his word, the gentleman made no move to have Turpin arrested, and when the highwayman offered him a bet, he accepted, 'and had the lucky fortune to win it. Mr. Turpin, smitten with his generous behaviour, paid him honestly the money he had won, and was very sorry that the trifling affair, which had happen'd between them, did not permit them to drink together.'

Such conduct, the Frenchman said, is 'here thought very genteel' (or gentlemanly). But he himself takes a different view, finding it ridiculous and bizarre. In an otherwise well-regulated country, it is a scandal that no one can travel on the roads without running the risk of being robbed. Yet the English people he meets treat it very much as a joke. Some are even proud of it. 'There are some Englishmen not less vain in boasting of the address of their highwaymen, than of the bravery of their troops.' And he adds: 'a noted thief is a kind of hero, in high repute among the populace'.[1]

Le Blanc's irritation and puzzlement are understandable. At the time of his visit, in the late 1730s, England was the greatest commercial nation in the world. Its public culture stressed the importance of civilised behaviour and polite manners. An immoderate admiration for armed robbers must have seemed, on the face of it, an unlikely national trait. What the abbé probably did not know is that the attitudes he describes had already had an extremely long history. For centuries, England had been a notorious place for robberies, especially for robberies on the highway. And for much of that time, the English had taken a strange sort of pride in boasting about their robbers.

The note is first struck plainly in the later fifteenth century, by Sir John Fortescue, a former Chief Justice of the King's Bench. During the 1470s, after a lifetime of involvement in public affairs, he wrote a short treatise, *The Governance of England*, in which he presented his conclusions on the best way to achieve stable government. Among the matters he found it relevant to discuss were the relative courage of the English and the French. The standard he chose to judge this by is remarkable: he argues that the English were obviously the braver nation because English robbers were bolder than French robbers. According to him, it was quite common in England for three or four robbers to attack and rob six or seven honest men. In France, though, a band of robbers would never attack unless they were very much in the majority. As a result, he claims, far more Englishmen than Frenchmen were hanged each year for robbery:

> . . . it is right selde that Ffrenchmen be hanged ffor robbery, ffor thai have no hartes to do so terable an acte. Ther bith therfore mo men hanged in Englande in a yere ffor robbery and manslaughter, then ther be hanged in Ffraunce ffor such maner of crime in vij yeres.

> . . . *it is very seldom that Frenchmen are hanged for robbery, for they have no hearts to do so terrible an act. There are therefore more men hanged in England in a year for robbery and manslaughter than are hanged in France for such manner of crime in seven years.*

And he continues with a side swipe at the Scots, who he says are very rarely hanged for robbery, though they are frequently hanged for stealing goods in the absence of the owner.

> But ther hartes serve hem not to take a manys gode, while he is present, and woll defende it . . . But the Englysh man is off another corage. Ffor yff he be pouere, and see another man havynge rychesse, wich mey be taken ffrom hym be myght, he will not spare to do so, but yff that pouere man be right trewe.

> *But their hearts serve them not to take a man's property while he is present, and will defend it . . . But the Englishman is of another courage. For if he should be poor and see another man having riches which may be taken from him by might, he will not spare to do so, unless that poor man should be very honest.*

Fortescue's comments have been often quoted for their curiosity value, but usually with only a sketchy sense of the context. What are the points he is making? That among the English, respect for other people's property is an uncommon virtue. That Englishmen are unusually prone to commit robbery, which is defined by him, in accordance with English common law, as taking goods by violence in the presence of the owner.[2] Fortescue takes it for granted that a primary cause of property crime is relative poverty. Indeed, his warm appreciation of the qualities of the English criminal finds its place in his treatise as part of an argument that the king's best security lies in refraining from excessive taxation. Some people, he says, have argued that if the common people of England were taxed to the point of extreme poverty, as they are in France, this will prevent them from rebelling. But this is a short-sighted view. Among other things, it leaves out of consideration the different national characters of the French and the English. It is not poverty that keeps the ordinary people of France from rising up but 'cowardisse and lakke off . . . corage, wich no Ffrenchman hath like unto a Englysh man'. Oppress the English with heavy taxes, and the people will be certain to rebel. Moreover, there will be far more thieves and robbers.

But in Fortescue's view, if poverty is the root cause of property crime, it takes more than poverty to make a robber. Unlike the sneak-thief, the robber encounters his victims face to face, and is prepared to risk his life fighting. A man who commits robbery must be brave as well as desperate, and bravery of that kind is a distinguishing characteristic of the English. When the English robber confronts his victim, Fortescue sees an icon of national courage and resistance.[3]

Whether the English, in the late Middle Ages or at any other time, were really more liable to commit robbery with violence than the French or the Scots is a question I cannot answer; it is unlikely that the evidence exists to make a comparison. But it is certain that there was a widespread belief, lasting for centuries, that England was markedly crime-ridden, and there are many references to the frequency both of robberies and executions. One of the earliest attempts to analyse the problem in a systematic way was made by Sir Thomas More, in a dialogue that forms part of his Latin work *Utopia* (1516). Like Fortescue, More's traveller-sage, the character Hythlodaeus, has no doubt that the primary cause of property crime is poverty. Looking at English society in the early sixteenth century, he picks out three principal causes. First is the custom of the nobility in keeping large households of servingmen, who, since they have never been trained in a trade, have nothing to turn to but crime once they are out of a place. Second is the growing practice of enclosure for sheep farming, and the consequent eviction of tenants by greedy landlords, which is the cause of a huge increase in the numbers of vagrants. Last of all, Hythlodaeus criticises what he sees as habits of excessive consumption, and a widespread indulgence in expensive leisure activities such as drinking, gambling and spending time in brothels; with the result that there is a tendency for people at almost all levels in society to live beyond their means, and to resort to robbery when they are out of money. The accuracy of More's analysis is not at issue; this book is not a study of the causes of crime and poverty, but of images of the robber, ideas about robbery and robbers, and social attitudes towards them. What is of very great interest in this passage is what he says incidentally to his main argument.

More refuses to foster the notion that there are more robbers in England than in any other country – he includes a digression on the special problems of the French in this respect. But it is plain that he takes it for granted that becoming a robber is a course that is particularly likely to be adopted by certain sorts of men. His character Hythlodaeus suggests that many robberies were committed by men who had formerly been retainers in noble households. Men like this, he says, are not used to doing anything besides swaggering about with sword and buckler. Once they have been dismissed from service, they are sure to starve, 'unless they should devote themselves actively to robbery'.* Hythlodaeus's opponent in the dialogue, an unnamed English lawyer, responds to this by arguing that it is essential that the welfare of such men should be treated as of primary importance, because in time of war they make up the backbone of the army, being 'of a loftier and nobler spirit'† than artisans and peasants. To which Hythlodaeus replies that in that case, the lawyer might just as well have argued that for the sake of war it was necessary to encourage thieves, since, as he sardonically observes, 'Robbers do not make spiritless soldiers, nor are soldiers the most cowardly of robbers, so well are the occupations in harmony with each other.' He makes it clear that he has little respect for the lawyer's views, commenting a little further on that in general, artisans and peasants are not believed to be greatly cowed by 'the idle servants of the gentry', whose inactive way of life has made them soft and weak. Later, in another sly dig, he echoes his opponent's own words, when he returns once more to the problem of the cast-off servingman, who has, he says, nothing to turn to but begging, unless it is robbery, 'to which you may more easily persuade the noble spirits'.‡⁴

Hythlodaeus thinks that the men most likely to commit robbery are those trained to arms, like retainers and soldiers. The lawyer unequivocally admires such men, believing them essential to the national defence, and attributing to them 'nobler' spirits than are to be found among craftsmen

---

* *nisi strennue latrocinentur*

† *animi magis excelsi ac generosioris*

‡ *quod generosis animis persuadeas facilius*

4

and farmers. Hythlodaeus, however, makes no bones about regarding them as parasites – he more than once refers to them as 'idle' – and as altogether something of a social danger. To understand more fully what is at stake here, it is helpful to look at what More's Tudor translator, Ralph Robinson, made of some of these passages. Robinson's translation appeared in 1551. He wrote in the style approved by his contemporaries, never making one word do where he could use three or four, and the elegance and economy of More's Latin is quite lost in his translation. However, among its virtues is a certain explicitness. It is particularly interesting to see how he translates the expression 'noble spirit', *generosus animus*, once used by the lawyer as a quality attributed collectively to retainers, and later used by Hythlodaeus in the plural, as a mocking way of referring to such men. On the first occasion, the reference to 'men of loftier and nobler spirit' becomes, in Robinson, 'men of stowter stomackes, bolder spirites, and manlyer courages'. The thing that comes immediately to attention is that Robinson has introduced a whole new concept, absent in the Latin, of 'manliness' – inasmuch as they may be assumed to be tough and brave, noblemen's retainers are manly men, 'real men', a connection so obvious to Robinson that he has read it into a text where it isn't to be found. And this isn't the first point where he has smuggled it in without warrant from the Latin. Where Hythlodaeus speaks of out-of-service retainers devoting themselves 'actively', *strennue*, to robbery, Robinson says that such men '*manfullye* playe the theves' (my italics). (The word 'thief' here means robber, as it often does throughout most of the period covered by this book.) Courage is a proof of manhood; fighting is a proof of manhood; it would seem that even a willingness to commit robbery may be regarded as a proof of manhood. No doubt Robinson intends this ironically, in the spirit of his original, More. But this doesn't mean that he is not faithfully representing attitudes that prevailed, at least among certain sections, in the society he lived in; and in fact, there is good reason to suppose that he is representing such attitudes quite accurately.

When Robinson comes to translate the phrase 'noble spirits' as it is used by Hythlodaeus, it emerges as 'these gentell bloudes and stoute stomackes'.[5] 'Stout' means tough; a 'stout stomach' is a proud man, one who will not brook, stomach, put up with any mistreatment or oppression. But it is the term 'gentell bloudes' that I am most interested in at this point, because it makes very explicit connections that are certainly present in the Latin, between noblemen's retainers and gentle birth, between gentle birth and the courage that is expected of fighting-men, and between gentle birth and a propensity for robbery. The Latin word More uses, *generosus*, sometimes means, as one might expect, 'generous'; it also means 'noble', in the moral sense; but the underlying, root meaning is 'well-born'. More than once in the present passage More uses *generosus* to mean 'gentleman', and in any Latin document an Englishman of gentle status would usually have *generosus* written after his name.

In More's day and for a long time afterwards the nobility and gentry still liked to see themselves as a fighting elite, and the descendants of a fighting elite; conspicuous among the attributes that were supposed to have descended to them from their ancestors were courage, pride and a taste for fighting, besides qualities such as honesty and generosity. Employment in manual trades was felt to be beneath them, but gentle status was by no means incompatible with a place as a servant of the less menial type. Indeed, for a landless younger son, service in some great household was an accepted career both before and long after the time at which More was writing.

Utopia is in every way a provocative text, opening to challenge all sorts of assumptions that were widely taken for granted. As part of this challenging approach, More calls into question the social usefulness of the nobility: he terms them as well as their servants 'idle', and is scathing about their extravagance and greed and the social damage they do. By implication, he is not impressed by the assumption that these men must be indulged merely because their supposedly superior fighting qualities will be needed in time of war. And in making it plain that he regards the impoverished gentleman as particularly likely to turn robber, it is clear that he intends no commendation of their courage, but a further indictment of aristocratic rapaciousness and unscrupulousness.

More did not invent the gentleman robber. By his time, the phenomenon was already one of very long standing. In the next chapter we shall take a look at the Folville brothers, a bandit gang of the fourteenth century. The Folvilles were men of old family, the younger sons of a landed knight in Leicestershire. Brigand gentry of a similar stamp were not uncommon at the time.[6] Social conditions gradually changed, and with them attitudes to robbery. But for long after the ending of the Middle Ages, the gentleman robber continued to pursue his violent and precarious career. Commenting in 1587 on the prevalence of robbery in England, William Harrison thought that the chief culprits were 'young shifting gentlemen, which oftentimes do bear more port than they are able to maintain' – that is, young men of good family who lack proper resources and are living beyond their means. These, he says, engage in highway robberies and 'break into the wealthy men's houses'.[7] There are cases of real-life gentlemen robbers throughout the seventeenth century, and there are even a scattered few in the eighteenth century.

Sir Thomas More himself, though bred from citizen stock, was born to gentle status. However, he shows little sign of any special sympathy for the gentleman who felt himself driven to turn robber. Nevertheless, there is no doubt that such sympathy was widely felt. In Richard Head's novel *The English Rogue* (1665) a young man who joins a gang of highwaymen is advised that if he should ever be brought to trial, he should tell the judges 'that I was born a Gentleman, and well educated, but being a younger brother, I had not where withal allowed me for a subsistance, and rather then I would live beneath my birth, or disparage the stock from whence I came (here fetching a deep sigh, and looking very sadly) necessity constraining me to supply my wants, I fell into these wicked courses'. This, he is told, will make them pity him, and may even lead to a pardon.[8] The situation is fictional, but it is not therefore implausible. Later in this book we shall look more closely at the workings of the justice system in cases of highway robbery. For the time being, it is enough to note that the judges themselves will normally have been men of good family, and the kind of appeal that is being recommended to the robber recruit has been carefully calculated to gain their sympathy.

The solidarity of the well-born is one thing; but even poor commoners who turned robber won themselves a large measure of respect. In his book *A Politic Plat for the honour of the Prince* (1580), Robert Hitchcock writes of 'poor householders' living in the towns, 'who by their poverty are driven to bring up their youth idly', that is, without a trade. When such a young man is grown, he has no choice but to become a confidence man or a cutpurse, 'or else, if he be of courage, plain robbing by the wayside, which they count an honest shift for the time, and so come they daily to the gallows'. Only the 'base-minded' among them will stoop to begging: 'For the heart, mind, and value of a man is such, and his spirit is so great, that he will travel all the kingdoms of Princes to seek entertainment; rather than he will show his face to beg or crave relief of thousands of people, that be unworthy to unbuckle his shoes: and in his great want, will take with force and courage from them that hath, to serve his necessity; thinking it more happy to die speedily, than to live defamed and miserably.'[9] In view of this tribute to the robber ethos, it may not come as much of a surprise to learn that Hitchcock was not only a gentleman but also a soldier. However, although his expression of these sentiments is exceptionally eloquent, similar views may be found in many other places.

Robbery, then, was widely regarded as a way in which a mettlesome fellow might provide for himself while making a point about his manhood, while the penniless young gentleman who took a purse on the highway, or even burgled a house, was felt by many people to be showing the pride and courage that he had inherited from his ancestors. Considering the social endorsement of robbery that such attitudes indicate, it would not be at all surprising if observers were right in finding that Englishmen had a marked propensity to commit this kind of crime. Poverty alone does not make the criminal, any more than the inbred disposition of the individual; cultural

Pride ~ tradition

factors are immensely important. A few thoughtful commentators showed themselves fully aware of the influence of cultural attitudes on criminal activity. In a dialogue published in 1572, Thomas Wilson makes one of his characters, the Preacher, remark: 'Theaft is counted so horrible amongest some nations, that men commonly will rather sterve then steale, and here in England he that can robbe a man by the hygh waye is called a tall felowe.' Further down the page another speaker singles out robbery as one of the besetting sins of the Englishman, comparable to the pride of the Spaniards or the revengefulness of the Italians.[10] The Englishman who committed robbery acted in the knowledge that he was upholding a great national tradition.

More than a hundred years later, the note of admiration for the robber's fighting spirit rings out from a letter by John Verney, a baronet's younger son turned London merchant. 'A couple of highwaymen, having robbed a countryman and leaving him his horse, he pursued 'em with hue and cry which overtook them, but they being very stout fought their way through Islington and all the road along to this town's end, where after both their swords were broke in their hands and they unhorsed, they were seized and carried to Newgate. *'Tis great pity such men should be hanged.*'[11] In some people's eyes, sentiments of this kind were obvious subjects for satire. In 1613, the poet George Wither had scoffingly suggested that those who wanted to be taken for 'brave gallant men', to gain the esteem of 'the *Common people*' and win themselves 'an everlasting name', should take to the seas as pirates, or else, as robbers,

> well mounted keepe themselves on land,
> And bid our wealthy travellers to stand,
> Emptying their full cram'd bags; for that's a tricke
> Which sometimes wan renoune to cutting *Dicke*.
> But some may tell me, though that such,
> It doth not goe against their conscience much:
> And though there's boldnes showne in such a case,
> *Yet to be Tost at Tyburns a disgrace,*
> No, 'tis their credit, for the people then,
> Wil say, *'tis pitty, they were proper men.*[12]

'Cutting Dick', hero of a lost play, flourished from about 1600 to 1602.[13] (Many prominent highway robbers had only very brief careers in the public eye.) In effect, Wither is pointing towards a cult of the robber, with its fashionable heroes, its distinctive outlook and set of values, its own mystique and traditions. And though he doesn't mention it, it had its own literature, too, which played an important role in shaping and transmitting those values and traditions. In Wither's time, ballads, plays, anecdotes and

8

criminal biographies were already feeding the public appetite for tales and glamorous images of robber life, just as they were to do throughout the next century, and long beyond it. As Christopher Hill has recently speculated, popular literary forms can often provide insights that may otherwise be missed.[14] Certainly such material is invaluable in seeking to grasp and analyse the continually shifting elements of the robber cult.

One detail of Wither's satire that requires comment is the way he identifies the cult of the robber with 'the *Common people*'. It is they, he says, who are given to making heroes out of highwaymen, and turn up at Tyburn to watch them die. So far I have focused mainly on the part played by aristocratic values and codes of behaviour in encouraging an admiring attitude towards the violent robber. Wither is certainly right in indicating a mass popular following; but this hardly disproves my point, since in a traditional society aristocratic tastes and values are certain to influence the whole. It suits Wither's purpose as a moralising satirist to ignore the gentlemanly associations of robbery, and to damn the hero-worship of highwaymen as essentially low and vulgar. And no doubt that was how he saw it. A gentleman by birth himself, he speaks from the point of view of one who subscribes to a code of behaviour that we might call polite, civilised, 'gentlemanly' in the modern sense. Similar views on how a gentleman should think and behave had been around for a very long time. But the older, narrower outlook that judged a man and, above all, a gentleman on his show of pride and courage was still extremely influential. In Wither's time and for much later, the traditions of the gentleman robber continued to flourish, and many people of gentle breeding regarded robbers with a striking tolerance, and even with admiration.

As for the common people: for them, part of the mystique of robbery, and especially of highway robbery, was precisely its association with the gentry. It was, as we might say nowadays, a crime that had some class to it. So much so, that a poor boy who turned to robbery on the highway might see himself as bettering his status; even, as becoming a gentleman. This is quite explicitly stated by the reformed highwayman John Clavell in his verse pamphlet *A Recantation of An Ill Led Life* (1628). Himself of old gentry stock, he observes that some people regard becoming a highwayman as a 'gentle course' (that is, one suited to a man of good family), and sometimes gentlemen, out of necessity, have been known to commit the odd robbery. But many of those who rob on the highway are men of 'courser natures', ill-bred fellows from far down the social scale. In a passage rhetorically addressed to such men, he declares that it is not surprising that once they are embarked on a robber's career, they are reluctant to leave it:

> For you have got by this vild course of sinning
> A kinde of state, ne're knowne to your beginning;

9

And from attending others, are become
The principall', and best men in the roome,
Where (like the Asse in trappings) you doe awe
The silly beasts, that Beere and Claret draw;
For they you Captaines and Leivtenants call,
And tremble when a frowne you doe let fall,
For *Peerelesse* now your selves are Masters growne,
That in mans memorie were Foot-Boyes knowne . . .[15]

Like a gentleman, a highway robber does no manual work, and yet he has money in his pocket, he wears good clothes and rides a fine horse. People who don't know who he is respond to his outward appearance and treat him with respect as a 'Master', or gentleman. As for those who know his secret, such as the servants of some of the inns he frequents, these view him as a hero, and flatter him by addressing him with military titles. A hundred years later, in *The Beggar's Opera* (1728), John Gay satirised exactly the same sort of 'social climbing' in the character of the highwayman, Captain Macheath, who 'looks upon himself in the Military Capacity, as a Gentleman by his Profession'.[16] An army officer, whatever his origins, was generally conceded to be a gentleman by virtue of his rank and service.[17] Macheath feels that his violent confrontations on the highway entitle him to claim the same status.

According to Clavell, highway robbers took a pride in their way of life, and liked to be referred to as '*Knights of the Roades*', or at the very least, as '*High-way Lawyers*'. They did not think of themselves as criminals but as men of courage and honour who fully deserved to be admired. They believed that the public saw the matter in that light, too. In his chosen role as the exposer of the robbers' pretensions, Clavell describes this as a fantasy. He insists that only a wicked or an ignorant person could fail to recognise the truth of the robber's existence: that it is worthless and shows no proofs of genuine courage. Even so, he cannot conceal his awareness that in many people's eyes, the man who showed himself daring enough to rob on the highway acquired considerable kudos. Such was the prestige of the mounted robber that, as Clavell complains, some men would pretend to be highwaymen when they were not, and would boast in their cups about robberies they had never committed, purely in order to impress their hearers.[18]

Clavell implies that most of his old comrades had been menial servants before they took to robbery. We cannot necessarily take his remarks at face value. Written in jail, under threat of the gallows, his *Recantation* is very much a propaganda work, designed to win the approval of the authorities by debunking the highwayman's mystique. With this in mind, he might have chosen to exaggerate the proportion of former servants among the men who robbed on the roads. 'Foot-Boys' (or servant lads) weren't held in much respect. On the other hand, we have seen that over a hundred years earlier Sir Thomas More suggested that many robberies were the work of servingmen who had been dismissed by their masters; though it is true that More's observations refer less to menial servants than to the armed toughs with whom, in the early sixteenth century, a man of wealth and standing still expected to surround himself. More's comments on the subject, though provocatively expressed, are not entirely original. At least as far back as the middle of the thirteenth century, there was an expectation that in times when great men reduced their households, the attendants whom they dismissed would be likely to resort to robbery.[19]

A social problem that More does not mention was that of the retainer or servingman whose master paid him inadequate wages, or even none at all, leaving him to make up his income wherever he could – by tips, by bribes from those who were hoping for his master's patronage, and sometimes by frauds and property crimes, including robbery. Again, this abuse goes back at least as far as the mid-thirteenth century. Among those found to have been involved in a famous robbery that took place at Alton in Hampshire in 1248 were a number of men in King Henry III's own household. On their way to the gallows some of these men sent a message to the King, to protest that they had been driven to the crime by his failure to pay them their wages.[20] More than three centuries later, in the reign of Elizabeth, the Essex parson William Harrison, writing a chapter on crime and punishment for his *Description of England*, says of household servingmen that their 'wages cannot suffice so much as to find them breeches', as a result of which 'they are now and then constrained' to practise highway robbery, housebreaking and horse-theft.[21] It was hardly strange that servants were drawn to the robber's life. Their wages, when paid, were low and their job security poor. And a gentleman's servant of humble birth acquired the violent code of the gentry at the same time as he learned to imitate their manners.

This chapter began with Dick Turpin – no gentleman he, though capable, it seems, of living up to genteel behaviour when encountered at the races. If this episode really happened, it was probably in the spring of 1738, when Turpin's career as an active robber was more or less over. He had, in fact, just one more year to live before he was hanged at York in April 1739.[22] Nowadays, Turpin is the only highwayman whom most people in England remember by name, and there is a prevailing notion that the great age of the English robber took place in the eighteenth century. In the popular imagination, the highway robber is a figure on horseback in a three-cornered hat, who holds up a mailcoach with pistols. However, Turpin, as we have seen, is a fairly late arrival in the history of the English robber. And the glorification of the highwayman that Le Blanc found so astonishing in eighteenth-century England becomes more intelligible once it is placed in context and viewed as a survival from an earlier time. Rather than as the heyday of the robber, the eighteenth century might more reasonably be seen as a period of decadence and decline.

Nostalgia for the robbers of the past long predates the growth of the Turpin legend. In 1622 the boatman-poet John Taylor, who liked to be called the Water Poet, published a light-hearted pamphlet on the topic of thieves and thieving. Towards the end he included an appreciative roll-call of the robber heroes of popular English history:

> *England* still hath bin a fruitfull Land
> Of valiant *Thieves*, that durst bid true men stand.
> One *Bellin Dun*, a famous *Thiefe* surviv'd,
> From whom the towne of *Dunstable*'s deriv'd;
> And *Robin Hood* with little *John* agreed
> To rob the rich men, and the poore to feede.
>
> . . .
>
> Once the fift *Henry* could rob ex'lent well,
> When he was Prince of *Wales*, as Stories tell.
> Then Fryer *Tucke*, a tall stout *Thiefe* indeed,
> Could better rob and steale, then preach or read.[23]

For Taylor, the famous robbers of tradition are figures from the Middle Ages: Robin Hood, Prince Hal and the now forgotten Bellin Dun. And though his view of history may be founded on legend, it focuses unerringly on the time when the robber cult took shape: the centuries which we now label the 'medieval period'. If we are to seek for the great age of the robber, it is here that we should look, in a society in which violent conflict of one kind or another was a fairly common occurrence: wars abroad, rebellions and civil wars at home, and frequent skirmishing between members of competing families and interest groups. In this world not only courage but aggressiveness, the will to take violent action, were very much prized qualities in a man. Here, if anywhere, the national worship of the armed robber may begin to make some kind of sense.

2

Robbery in the Greenwood

In the very early years of the fourteenth century, a man whose name is lost to us wrote a poem in Anglo-Norman French. The choice of language tells us that he had had an education of the kind appropriate to a man of good family. The poem that he wrote reads like a song, a protest song. It is written in the voice of a man who feels that he has been deeply wronged, and allowing for a certain amount of fictionalising and dramatising, it is hard not to feel that the rage in these verses must arise from a real sense of grievance, whether personal to the poet, or expressed on behalf of a patron or circle. The poem is furiously critical of a newly devised approach to law enforcement: the institution by Edward I of royal commissions of trailbaston. Beginning in 1304, small groups of justices were sent into different regions of England with authority to investigate and punish cases of homicide, robbery, extortion and other violent offences. They were specifically instructed to prosecute not only the principals in such crimes, but also those who conspired with them: the people who received them in their houses, acted as their accomplices, shielded them from justice, or hired them as thugs. The measure was intended to reassert the King's authority and deal with a crisis in public order that had developed during his long campaigns abroad. It was supposed to protect the King's subjects and ensure the proper functioning of the justice system. But the voice we hear in the poem belongs to a frightened and angry man, who maintains that the trailbaston procedure has become a weapon in the hands of unscrupulous enemies who are seeking to destroy him.

He presents himself as a good subject of the King, whom he has served 'in peace and war'. He is not guilty of the charges that are being brought against him. Though he has been indicted for robberies and other offences, he is innocent; he has never been a robber, and if he has killed anyone, he says, 'it was certainly not through any will of my own'. Perhaps the poet meant this last protestation to be interpreted sceptically; but in the Middle

Ages most people took it for granted that there were times when killing might be forced on a man, in self-defence or to protect his rights. The poem makes most sense if it is intended to expose the predicament of an innocent man who has been trapped by false accusations in a terrifying legal machine. This is not a meek man. He utters violent threats against the jurors who have, he says, indicted him 'out of malice', as well as against two of the trailbaston judges, whom he attacks by name, and blames for being 'men of cruelty'. The implication is that they are biased. He admits, frankly, that his experiences are making him lose his sense of what is right; this is the effect of bad laws. He is particularly bitter about what he sees as the trailbaston commissioners' over-readiness to identify conspiracy where it does not exist. 'If I should be a companion [or, belong to an association] and have some skill in archery',* he says, one of his neighbours will accuse him of 'going shooting in the woods', that is, of poaching; if he has more knowledge of the law than his neighbours have, it will be assumed that he is untrustworthy, and is conspiring to subvert the legal system. He is afraid of going to jail, where the sheriff will expect a bribe 'for not putting me in a deep dungeon'. He takes it for granted that if he is tried in the trailbaston court, he will be found guilty and heavily fined, and he does not have the resources to pay. If he cannot pay the fine, he will be 'delivered over to death'. Then, as now, the penalty for non-payment of fines was imprisonment. His fear seems to be that he will rot in jail until he dies.

Rather than let this happen, he will take himself to the woods. To his original audience, the image that this would have evoked would not have been that of some scrubby little patch of woodland, such as survive in England today. During the Middle Ages, vast areas of countryside were still covered with mature forest, dense, virtually trackless, the haunt of boars and wolves. For a man in fear of the law, they were the traditional hideout. The speaker does not spell out the legal implications of going on the run like this; his audience would have grasped the point at once. What he intends to do is to allow himself to be outlawed, rather than turn up to stand trial. Outlawry was the eventual penalty imposed by the courts on a man who failed repeatedly to appear to answer a charge. His goods and chattels were confiscated by the Crown and any lands he might hold were forfeited to his lord. If he were captured, he would usually be brought before the justices, who on proof of his outlawry, without further trial, would order his execution. At the time this poem was written, it was still the case that anyone who chose might attempt his arrest, and if he resisted, might kill him without risking punishment. In effect, an outlaw was a man who had put himself outside the law's protection. But when the law is

---

* *Si je sei compagnoun e sache de archerye*

controlled by your enemies, and is being made the instrument of your destruction, then to go into outlawry may become the only choice. And it was not an irrevocable step. The speaker anticipates that the time will come when he will receive a pardon. His hope is not unreasonable. Many outlaws were successful in negotiating pardons from the Crown, and returned peaceably to a life within the law.[1]

The speaker's woodland bolt-hole is described in lyrical terms. He calls it 'the wood of Belregard', or 'Fair Appearance', a made-up name, suggestive of a place in a courtly romance. There, 'the nightingale sings every day without stopping'; in other words, it is always spring or early summer. It is easily recognisable as a variant version of the *locus amoenus*, or lovely landscape, more or less formal descriptions of which are a commonplace of medieval literature. In one stanza, he refers to Belregard as the 'vert bois', the green wood: in its English form, this phrase will reverberate throughout the later outlaw tales and poems. He advises everyone who is indicted by the court to come and join him there, 'for the common law is too unreliable'. In the shade of the woods, 'there is no false dealing nor any bad law'.[2]

The wood of Belregard is a place whose natural beauties are matched by the integrity and freedom of the life among its trees. But existence as an outlaw is not without its problems. One of the speaker's complaints is that now he is on the run he can no longer find a way to provide for himself. He does not state directly what he intends to do about this. Instead, he observes darkly that the shortcomings of trailbaston justice will force some people to turn to robbery who have never been robbers before. The irony of the situation is surely not lost on him, though he does not feel the need to stress it. The King ordained the trailbaston commissions as a measure to suppress robbers. But because the courts are unfairly administered, innocents like himself, accused of involvement in crimes in which they had no hand, are being left with no alternative but to embark on a career in robbery. He invites 'merchants and monks' to curse the people who set up the trailbaston, since 'for them the royal protection will not be worth a garlic-head, unless they hand over the coins without anything in exchange'.[3] From a robber's point of view, merchants and monks offered rich pickings; they feature as victims of robberies in legal records and chronicles, and also in tales of legendary outlaws.

The Outlaw's Song, as it is sometimes called, mentions four trailbaston judges by name. The same men are named in a commission for the south-western counties which was dated in April 1305 and remained current until February 1307. Beyond this, the original occasion for the poem cannot now be recovered. The author chose to write a lyric, not a narrative. He evokes a situation; insofar as he tells a story, he does so only in a truncated and indirect way. Moreover, the speaker's plight, though

15

feelingly lamented, is described in studiedly general terms. But the outspoken criticism of the trailbaston ordinance, the violent threats levelled against two of the judges, indicate that the circumstances under which it was written were quite specific. In a marked manner it points us towards history: towards particular social grievances and even towards personal enmities arising at a particular time and place.

Simultaneously, and with just as much insistence, it points us in another direction entirely: towards an established territory of the imagination. Angry though its tone may be, it is a carefully wrought literary work, in which the author articulates his concerns with trailbaston justice by giving a voice to the figure of the righteous outlaw and making creative use of the symbolism of the greenwood. The wood of Belregard is not a real place, and it is not intended to be mistaken for one. It stands for a cluster of symbols and ideas, and it draws a great deal of its substance from a cultural tradition of songs and tales about outlaw life.

Much of this material is lost, but enough survives to suggest that it was surprisingly various. The earliest extant narrative about an English outlaw is a Latin life of Hereward, famous for his guerrilla war against the Normans after the Conquest. This is nearly two centuries older than *The Outlaw's Song*. Many of its episodes and embedded stories are analogues to tales that were later told of other outlaw heroes. One such was the Marcher lord Fouke Fitz Waryn, whose three-year career as an outlaw, in the reign of King John, was the subject of a verse romance in Anglo-Norman French, composed in the late thirteenth century, just a decade or so before *The Outlaw's Song*. The original romance has disappeared; but a prose version survives, preserved, interestingly enough, in the same handwriting as *The Outlaw's Song*, although in a different manuscript.[4]

The compiler of these manuscripts seems to have had a taste for outlaw literature. The manuscript that has preserved *The Outlaw's Song* also contains two other lyric poems, both of them in English, in which the woodland refuge features as a theme. One, 'Lenten ys come with love to toune', is a spirited love song. Spring has come; everything makes love to its mate; women become astonishingly proud; if the speaker is rejected by one particular woman, he will abandon all these delights, 'ant wyht in wode be fleme' – and quickly become a fugitive in the wood. Here, as in *The Outlaw's Song*, the wood is a place apart, a refuge for a man disgusted with human cruelty and faithlessness – in this case, the hard-heartedness of the woman with whom he is in love. The perfunctory way in which the fugitive theme is treated indicates how conventional it had already become.

The other lyric, '*De Clerico et Puella*', is in dialogue form: a young scholar begs his beloved to run away with him. She tells him that her father and all her kinsfolk are lying in wait for him, day and night, and will kill him if they catch him in her bower. He describes how, for the sake of

16

her love, he has suffered innumerable wounds, far from his home and from other human beings, living in the woodland. At the thought of this, her heart is softened, and she promises to be his.[5] In this poem the woodland is a place of suffering and testing, and also of deep loneliness. There is a strong suggestion that it is the lover's hiding place from his murderous enemies, the girl's kin, and that he has been forced into outlawry as a result of their hostility.[6]

Despite the lyricism with which he describes the beauty and peacefulness of Belregard, the speaker in *The Outlaw's Song* also misses his family, and longs to go back to his home. But Belregard is as much a symbol for a dream of escape as an image of exile. In some respects the fantasy is almost Arcadian: of a place where winter never comes, where men deal fairly with each other. In this regard, it anticipates an enduring theme of the Robin Hood stories. More challengingly, the 'green wood of Belregard' is a place of refuge from which an innocent man, not reconciled to harsh treatment, may plan his vengeance on his enemies. The outlaw tale is an action genre, and revenge of one kind or another is often a central motive.

Though Belregard is an invented place, and though it was certainly inspired by earlier manifestations of the 'greenwood' theme in outlaw tales and songs, it draws a large measure of its imaginative force from real woods where real outlaws gathered. Some twenty-five years after *The Outlaw's Song* was written, the situation that is sketched in the poem found some curious echoes in a well-documented incident. A band of outlawed men, lurking in a wood, engineered a violent encounter with a trailbaston judge, against whom they had grounds for revenge. At any rate, this is the version of the episode that was recorded in a Latin chronicle by Henry of Knighton, a monk of Leicester Abbey:

> In 1331 the trailbaston judges sat throughout England, and many outlaws were made in every place. For this reason Richard de Willoughby, a king's justice, was taken prisoner after Christmas, while he was travelling towards Grantham, by Richard de Folville, rector of Teigh in Rutland, who was a wild and daring man, and prone to acts of violence. He was led into a nearby wood to a company of confederates and there, under compulsion, paid a ransom for his life of ninety marks, after swearing on oath that he would always comply with their instructions.[7]

The speaker in *The Outlaw's Song* threatens the cruel judges with violence; he says that 'if they were in my jurisdiction, they would not find a refuge', and he is graphic about the mutilations he would like to inflict on them, which he insists would be only justice.[8] Folville and his companions preferred to take their resentments out in money. Knighton seems to have been misinformed about the size of the ransom; at any rate, documents in the subsequent legal case state that the sum paid was actually 1,300 marks, and that during the kidnapping Willoughby was also robbed of goods worth £100.[9] All this was a small fortune by the standards of the time. However, according to Knighton, the crime was not a simple matter of profit, but an act of vengeance. He identifies its motive as arising from Willoughby's activities as a trailbaston judge, and the anger of men who had allowed themselves to be outlawed rather than put their faith in the justice of his courtroom. How far may we rely on Knighton's account? He was a local man. And if we find it suspicious that his story conforms so closely to an ideal pattern, in which the innocent outlaw takes his justified revenge on the corrupt representative of the law, we must still take account of the fact that he knew far more about the background to the episode than we shall ever retrieve from what remains of the written records.

The names of a number of Richard de Folville's associates on this occasion may be found in the documents of the legal case that was set in motion after Willoughby's release. Several of them were brothers of his: Eustace, Laurence, Walter and Robert de Folville. Though Knighton gives the chief part to Richard, one of the indictments in the case names his brother Eustace as the leader of the 'societas', the 'fellowship' or gang. He was the eldest of them: the second son of John de Folville, lord of the manors of Ashby Folville in Leicestershire and Teigh in Rutland. The first-born son of John de Folville was also named John; he had inherited his father's estates, and seems to have led a more or less blameless life. His younger brothers had first fallen foul of the law five years previously, in 1326, when they had taken part in the murder of Sir Roger Bellers, a substantial Leicestershire landholder and a royal official, while he was travelling to Leicester from his manor of Kirby Bellers.[10] Henry of Knighton chronicles this episode as well. He says that prior to the murder Bellers 'had inflicted threats and injustices' on Eustace and his brothers, and he adds that Bellers 'had been an oppressor of his neighbours, religious and others, because of his greed for their possessions'. As a monk of Leicester Abbey, Knighton may well have had direct knowledge of Bellers's predatory behaviour from the experience of his own community. At any rate, it is clear that he thinks that he is no loss to local society. His respect for the nerve shown by the murderers is evident when he states that Bellers 'was killed by three brothers, despite having with him a retinue of fifty'.[11]

Knighton is right that there were three Folvilles present at the murder: Eustace, Robert and Walter. However, the death blow was given by Ralph la Zouch, a member of another Leicestershire landed family. All were soon

18

outlawed. The Folvilles took refuge in Lincolnshire, where they committed a series of robberies. As the speaker in *The Outlaw's Song* comments:

> Some will become robbers who never used to be,
> Who dare not come to peace for fear of jail.
> They lack what it takes to keep them alive each day.[12]

However, early in 1327 Edward III succeeded to the throne and a general
pardon was announced. The four Folvilles who had been indicted for the
murder (who included Richard, the rector of Teigh, who had presumably
been an accessory) were able to buy themselves immunity from punishment in return for a payment to the Crown.[13] They did not go back to
peaceful ways. Between that time and the kidnapping four years later of Sir
Richard de Willoughby, the younger Folville brothers, separately and in
various combinations, were involved in a series of cases of murder,
robbery, extortion by threats and other violent crimes, varied only by a
short spell in the royal army in 1329, in consideration of which four of
them again received a pardon. But by the end of the following year several
of the brothers, including Eustace and Richard, were once again on the
run.[14] It is clear that when Knighton described Richard de Folville as
'prone to acts of violence' he was referring to a record of conspicuous
brutality. Priest though he was, Richard's violent career would have
surprised no one in his own time. The records reveal so many similar
thugs in holy orders that it has even been suggested that the astute
professional malefactor may well have regarded clerical status as a useful
qualification.[15] A cleric could not be executed; though he might be jailed.

As specialists in violence, the Folvilles sometimes joined forces with
men of similar experience and reputation, notably with a trio of Derbyshire
brothers, James, John and Nicholas Coterel. The Coterels and some of
their associates were among the gang who took part in the kidnapping of
Willoughby. At one time or another, many of the men involved in this
crime had had encounters with Willoughby in his capacity as a judge.[16] If
Knighton is right, they felt they had reason to be aggrieved with him, and
to seek for a means to be revenged. And if the Folvilles and their friends
were no innocents, still, Willoughby was hardly a paragon of judicial
virtue. He seems to have had a reputation for exceptional greed and
dishonesty. A few years later, he was put on trial for corruption, apparently
in response to a public outcry. No doubt the Folvilles and their supporters
saw a certain rough justice in appropriating the wealth of a judge who was
rumoured to have 'sold the laws as if they were oxen or cows'.[17]

The gang that kidnapped Willoughby is described in an indictment as
having been led by Eustace de Folville or, elsewhere in the same
document, by Eustace de Folville and James Coterel. However, the lion's

share of the 1,300 marks that Willoughby paid in ransom went to neither of these men. When the payment was shared out, Eustace and his brothers received 300 marks, and the Coterels a mere 40 marks. Behind the men of violence lurks a shadowy figure, perhaps several of them, the gang's protectors, who were no doubt involved in the crime's instigation and planning, in addition to giving practical help before and after it. In his study of the Coterel gang, John Bellamy fingers Sir Robert Touchet, who held land in several Midland counties. The share-out after the kidnapping took place on one of his manors, at Markeaton Park in Derbyshire. A local jury found that he and his brother Edmund, the parson of nearby Mackworth, had had knowledge of the ransoming and had given it their approval. These two stood in the role of patrons and supporters to the Coterel and Folville brothers. After the Coterels had been outlawed for murder, early in 1331, the Touchets more than once gave shelter to them. And at the time of the Willoughby kidnapping Eustace de Folville and two of his brothers were retainers in the Touchet household and wore their livery or household cognisance. Bellamy suggests, very plausibly, that a generous portion of Willoughby's ransom fell to the share of Sir Robert.[18]

If Bellamy is right, we have here something more than the problem, already an old one, of the underpaid or unwaged retainer who resorts to crime to put some extra money in his pocket. It is something different even from the problem of the professional robber who would attach himself as a retainer to some magnate in the hope that his lord would support his side of the case, if he should find himself in trouble with the law. The common term for this was 'maintenance', and there were a number of forms it could take, from heavy use of the lord's influence on the sheriff, jurors and justices, through bribery, to downright intimidation. This problem was a serious one in the later Middle Ages, and it was still a live issue in the sixteenth century. But Sir Robert Touchet was not simply a man who, for the sake of his own prestige, or because it suited him, was prepared to connive at the misdeeds of his servants. Touchet went out of his way to attract to his household some of the most violent outlaws who were at that time operating in the East Midlands.

Another accessory to the Willoughby kidnapping was Sir Robert de Vere, constable of Rockingham Castle in Northamptonshire. The sinister flavour of his management of this royal castle may be gathered from an indictment in another case, which details how bands of armed men, twenty or thirty in number, would visit him there, leaving secretly in the early hours. No one who brought provisions to the castle was allowed to enter, so that they should not be in a position to identify these visitors. Rockingham Castle stands near the meeting point of the boundaries of Northamptonshire, Leicestershire and Rutland, which made it an ideal bolt-hole. If the sheriff of one of these counties should come into view with a posse, any fugitives who were in the castle might escape into either of the neighbouring counties – and out of his jurisdiction.[19] Magnates of the stamp of Touchet and Vere were not unusual in the 1330s and 1340s. On several occasions in the latter decade the Commons petitioned the King in Parliament to take action over maintenance. A petition of 1348 is particularly eloquent: it speaks of 'robbers, bandits and other malefactors' who 'on foot and on horseback, travel and ride on the highway through all the land in divers places and commit larcenies and robberies'. Accordingly, the King is prayed 'to charge the great ones of the land that no such people should be maintained by them, either in secret or openly'.[20]

The ransoming of Willoughby, then, was a complex affair. Considering Willoughby's reputation, the Folvilles and their associates may well have felt, as Henry of Knighton implies, that their treatment of him had justifications. Knighton himself, monk though he was, conspicuously fails to condemn them. On the other hand, the involvement in the kidnapping of such entrepreneurs of violent crime as Sir Robert Touchet and Sir Robert de Vere disturbs the clean outlines that Knighton gave the episode in his chronicle. And the blood-stained careers of Richard and his brothers make them awkward candidates for the role of injured innocents. But violent and lawless though they were, Knighton was not alone in his admiration for the Folvilles. Something of a legend developed about their exploits, and this survived for at least a generation after they were dead. Richard died in about 1340, dragged out of his own church and beheaded by a band of armed men sent to arrest him. By the right of sanctuary, he ought to have been safe in there; but he and his followers had been firing arrows at his pursuers from inside, which no doubt made them angry enough not to care that they were committing sacrilege. His brother Eustace died in 1347.[21]

Thirty years later, we find the expression 'Folvilles' laws' in currency as a catchphrase. It occurs, in a striking context, in William Langland's great allegorical poem *Piers Plowman*. Among the gifts of the Holy Spirit that Grace distributes among mankind, such as intelligence, sound commercial instincts, skill in various crafts and a vocation to the life of prayer, is included the following:

> And some to ryde and to recovere that unrightfully was wonne;
> He wissed hem wynne it ageyne thorw wightnesse of handes,
> And fecchen it fro fals men with folvyles lawes.[22]

And some to ride and to recover what was wrongfully acquired; [Grace] taught them to win it again through the strength of their hands, and retrieve it from wicked men with Folvilles' laws.

Langland did not approve of robbers. Elsewhere in *Piers Plowman* we read of Robert the Robber, who repents, weeping that he has squandered all his booty, and has nothing left with which to make restitution, as the Church's teaching taught him he should do.[23] But by his day the popular imagination had smoothed away memory of the Folville brothers' more sordid offences. They were remembered only as Knighton had preferred to memorialise them, as men who, when it became necessary, 'took the law into their own hands' and rode out to right injustice with the force of arms. For Langland, strength of body, skill in arms, the resolve to employ violence were gifts from God. Like God's other gifts, they ought to be used for good, to take back from dishonest men what they have misappropriated from others. But the use of violence is not always wrong in itself. Human society needs men like the Folville brothers – or at least, like the Folvilles in their most famous and justifiable exploits, the killing of the unscrupulous land-grabber, Bellers, and the ransoming of Willoughby, the unjust judge.

We are used, these days, to a consensus morality that sanctions violence and the shedding of blood as at best a necessary evil. But in his own time, Langland's notion of strength in arms as a gift from God would have appeared unremarkable. It fits perfectly well with the traditional doctrine of the medieval Church about the roles within the Christian community of the various social estates. While churchmen preached and prayed, and labourers sweated so that everyone should eat, it was the task of the knights, the men trained to war, not only to defend the land from its enemies but also to keep the peace within it: to prevent wicked men from preying on the weak.[24] Nor did the Church necessarily disapprove of forcible expropriation, so long as the motive was acceptable. In *Dives and Pauper*, an exposition of the Ten Commandments written in the first decade of the fifteenth century, we read:

> . . . because of ryghtwysnesse man may takyn away anothir mannys good agenys his wil, as in ryghtful bataylye thingis that wern withholdyn unryghtfullyche ben takyn awey from hem that so unryghtfullyche withheldyn is, and they that fyghtyn ryghtfullyche mon takyn awey her goodys that fyghtyn agenys hem unryghtfullyche, so that they don it for ryghtwysnesse and nout for false covetyse . . . [25]

> . . . *in a righteous cause, a man may take away another man's property against his will, as for example in rightful battle things that have been wrongly withheld are taken away from those that withheld them thus wrongfully, and those that fight with right on their side may take away the property of those that wrongly fight against them, so long as they do it for righteousness' sake, and not for dishonest greed . . .*

The less conventional part of Langland's teaching comes with the invocation of 'folvyles lawes': the implication is that to police the community in a way that will be in accordance with God's will, a way that will be true to righteous principles, is liable to involve going outside the established procedures of the legal system and administering the rough justice of the outlaw. This, to say the least of it, tells us a great deal about the public image of the judicial process in the second half of the fourteenth century. Unless he had influential well-wishers, or money with which to bribe the officials, a man who found himself dispossessed of his property, or wronged in some other way, could not expect to find redress through the courts. All he had to rely on was strength and prowess in arms – his own or that of his friends. This sounds simply brutal and desperate, and it is, of course. Nevertheless, it is important to bear in mind that, as John Bellamy has pointed out, many people believed that to settle a dispute by taking up arms was to refer one's cause directly to the judgement of God.[26] This is one of the reasons why Knighton stresses the terrible odds the Folvilles had faced in their attack on Bellers. Their success in the teeth of a vastly superior force showed they had God on their side.

The studies conducted by Bellamy and his predecessor E. L. G. Stones into the lives and activities of the Folvilles and the Coterels shed a good deal of light on the institution of outlawry in the later Middle Ages, as well as on the careers of a certain kind of specialist in criminal violence. They also help to illuminate the workings of the society within which such men flourished. By most standards, even its own, it was often remarkably corrupt and lawless. In such a world, it is hardly surprising that for many men the legend of the righteous outlaw should have developed a huge emotional charge. In Henry of Knighton's slanted reports on the crimes of the Folville brothers, in the catchphrase that Langland picked out of popular speech, we witness something of the power of the legend to co-opt the exploits of real men and shape them to conform to its patterns.

3

The Outlaw Dispossessed

The main themes of the medieval outlaw legend are already visible in certain traditions about the careers of some of the Anglo-Saxon aristocracy in the years following the Norman Conquest. A passage in quite a late source, a mid-thirteenth-century Latin chronicle by Matthew Paris, describes their activities in terms that repay some attention. It occurs as part of a summary of the reign of William I. 'The English nobility and gentry were driven out from their possessions. Ashamed to beg, ignorant of how to dig, they and their sons and brothers took refuge in the woods. They robbed and raided rapaciously, but only when they were lacking in game or other victuals.'[1] Here we find the woodland refuge, and the poaching motif that was to become so prominent in the stories of Robin Hood and other outlaw heroes. Less familiar to us now, because not featured strongly in the Robin Hood corpus, is the idea of the outlaw band that is built around family ties.[2] Later in this chapter, we shall look at the Anglo-Norman romance of *Fouke le Fitz Waryn*, which has as its hero a historical outlaw of the early thirteenth century whose following included several of his brothers. The cases of the Folville and Coterel brothers provide further examples of outlaw gangs bound together by kinship, and there is other documentary evidence to suggest that similar associations were fairly common.[3]

One of the central themes of the outlaw legend is that of the man who is driven out of the secure place in society that has previously been his. Matthew Paris's summary account of the post-Conquest fugitives associates them with the related theme of the man born to inherit lands who is dispossessed of them by his enemies. This is a important element in the tales of Fouke Fitz Waryn and the later, wholly fictional, outlaw Gamelyn. It is also an essentially aristocratic concern. Once he has lost his lands, what can such a man do? Matthew Paris excuses the dispossessed English landowners for not having chosen to take up work as labourers, on the

24

grounds that they hadn't been trained to it. To beg for their living, as he says, would have shamed them. Evidently, a little robbery is nothing to blush for, though he is careful to stress that they only engaged in it at times of extremity. This is almost the earliest instance I have encountered of the notion, widely accepted for at least five centuries, that whereas it is shameful to beg, a man may turn robber and still keep his pride. It is no coincidence that it crops up in a specifically aristocratic connection.[4] The claim that these noble fugitives only engaged in robbery when other resources were lacking is plainly intended to increase sympathy for them and accord with the writer's own sense of what is acceptable. Matthew Paris, like Henry of Knighton, was a monk. The Church taught that while theft and robbery were sins, everyone was entitled to what he needed in order to keep him alive. In a case of extreme need, a person might take and use goods that belonged to someone else, whether secretly (as in theft) or openly (as a robber does), and in the eyes of God and the Church, no sin would have been committed. In such a situation all property became, in a moral sense, communal, as it had been in the beginning.[5] This doctrine left open a small but important space in which a tolerant attitude to the thief and the robber might flourish even among churchmen, who, as we shall see, were often very hostile to the cult of the armed criminal. There is one further point that stands out from Matthew Paris's account of the post-Conquest outlaws: he obviously doesn't think that poaching game for food is any sort of blot or crime at all, in spite of the rigorous Forest Laws which had been decreed by William the Conqueror and which were still very much in force in his own day.

Most of the English leaders who took to the wilderness in the years after the Conquest are shadowy figures: like the earls Edwin and Morcar, of whom the chronicler William of Malmesbury, writing in the next generation, tells us that they refused to come to open engagement with the Conqueror's forces, but 'disturbed the woodlands with covert robberies' until they were murdered through the treachery of their followers.[6] Only one has left a substantial legend: a man called Hereward, a thane, or well-born landholder below the rank of nobleman – Matthew Paris would probably have thought of him as a *generosus*, or gentleman. Twice Hereward made his mark on the history of his times: in 1070, when he and his men helped part of a Danish invasion force to sack Peterborough town and abbey, and in the year following, when he played a major part in the resistance of the Isle of Ely, an English outlaw stronghold, to a prolonged siege by the Normans. In the end, the rebel leaders (who included Earl Morcar) agreed to surrender to the King. Hereward alone refused to submit, and successfully led his followers in an escape.[7]

Almost the only other thing that is certain about the historical Hereward is that he was the kind of man about whom songs were sung and stories told. A generation after his death, many of the tales about him were gathered in a Latin prose narrative entitled *Gesta Herwardi Incliti Exulis et Milites* – 'The Exploits of Hereward the Celebrated Outlaw and Soldier'. This was written in the earlier part of the twelfth century, at some point after 1109. It is a curious piece of writing: part sober and plausible history, part wild romance. The author claims to have talked to some of Hereward's surviving comrades, but this has not saved him from making a major mistake in chronology. But if the history is muddled at best, the legend is vividly presented. For the author of the *Gesta Herwardi*, Hereward was a pattern hero, and his story was especially to be recommended to 'those who wish to follow the military profession'. His life offers examples of 'great spirited deeds' and of *liberalitas*, the kind of behaviour that befits a free man. So we are told that Hereward as a youth is handsome, courageous and generous, as a young man of gentle blood was supposed to be. Less attractively, he is also reckless, quarrelsome, violent and extravagant. His vices, of course, are his virtues, taken to extremes. The young man is restless; he likes to see action. He makes a considerable nuisance of himself, both to his parents and to the other people living in the neighbourhood. In the end his own father begs the King to banish him from the realm. However, unruly as he is, he does not disgrace himself in any irretrievable way. If he had been cowardly or mean, he would have shown himself unworthy of his ancestors; but his vices, like his virtues, are those of a well-born youth of spirit. In an aristocratic culture, they are easily pardoned.

Hereward is eighteen when he is banished. This, the Latin narrative says, is when he first acquires the byname *Exul*, 'the Exile', or 'the Outlaw'.[8] The king on the throne is still Edward the Confessor, and the Norman Conquest is a few years in the future. Hereward's chance to prove that violent young men can sometimes have their uses has not yet arrived. So he goes abroad. At this point he enters a romance landscape, in which a woman who is raped by a bear gives birth to a bear of human intelligence (Hereward kills it), and Cornwall (which had been part of England for two centuries) has an independent king of its own. Eventually, he returns to his own country, having gained a reputation as a soldier, and acquired the sort of equipment that every hero finds handy: a famous sword, which he has won through combat; a helmet and armour of a metal superior to steel; a horse of exceptional swiftness; and a wise and beautiful wife. Back in the real world, England has fallen to the forces of William of Normandy. Hereward arrives incognito at Bourne, in Lincolnshire, described in the *Gesta Herwardi* as his family home. He is told that his father's house is full of Normans, and the head of his younger brother is on a pole above the gate. He had been killed the day before Hereward's arrival, while protecting their mother, who is now a widow, from rape. That night, Hereward hears the Normans celebrating, and goes to the house. First, he takes down his brother's head. With the help of a single follower, whom he sets to guard the door, he kills the new lord and fifteen of his companions. Then he cuts their heads off, and sets them up where he had found his brother's.

From a hero of romance, Hereward has now become an outlaw avenger, in a setting recognisably close to eleventh-century England. He assembles a band of men and before long takes refuge in the woods. For a while, he and his followers join the defence of the Isle of Ely, a wild, inaccessible place, surrounded by marshes. Several of the English leaders had taken refuge there, including Earl Morcar, whose reputation as a raider is mentioned above. But the Conqueror lays siege to it with his armies until the rest of the defenders agree to submit. Hereward alone leads his men in an escape and returns to the woods. The *Gesta Herwardi* was almost certainly written by a monk of Ely. Its account of the siege is full and detailed. Moreover, the siege itself, and Hereward's part in it, is attested from other sources. But the *Gesta* is wrong on a crucial point. It says that shortly after the siege of Ely, Hereward and his men sacked the monastery and town of Peterborough. However, the monks of Peterborough recorded a different sequence of events, which is certainly the correct one. First Hereward and his men took part in the sack of Peterborough; then they and the invading Danes with whom they had joined forces carried off the loot to Ely.

The author of the *Gesta Herwardi* shows signs of embarrassment over the sack of Peterborough. He puts the best gloss on events that he can. He describes the raid as an act of revenge on the Norman abbot of Peterborough, whom Hereward had captured in a skirmish, and ransomed for a great sum. Before he had released the abbot, he had made him swear that he will no longer make war on him. But the abbot broke his oath and offered rewards to knights in his service to attack him. It is at this point that Hereward burns down Peterborough, kills the abbot and carries off the treasures from the church. Hereward's share in the looting of the abbey church is well attested, but the monk who wrote the *Gesta* balks at this act of sacrilege in his hero. In defiance of history, he has Hereward return the loot, in response to a threatening vision of St Peter. However, the mid-twelfth-century poet Geoffrey Gaimar, who had obviously heard a similar version of events, writes with approval of the sack of Peterborough in his Anglo-Norman verse chronicle, *L'Estoire des Engleis*. He says that Peterborough had broken faith with Hereward, and it was not wrong of him to seek vengeance.[9] This pattern of capture, broken faith and consequent revenge is found in later tales. When the thirteenth-century outlaw hero Fouke Fitz Waryn captures his enemy King John, he lets him go after he has sworn to return his inheritance; but the King cannot be trusted, and breaks his word. Likewise, when Robin Hood has the Sheriff of Nottingham in his power, he makes him swear an oath not to do him any harm, and to help any of his men whom he comes across. But the Sheriff's response is to lure him to Nottingham by proclaiming an archery contest, which turns out to be the cover for an ambush. Robin has the last word, when on their next encounter he shoots down the Sheriff on the streets of Nottingham and cuts off his head.[10] Henry of Knighton's account of the kidnapping of Sir Richard de Willoughby shows that it was not only legendary outlaws who were expected to extract oaths from their captives. No doubt, as he pursued the Folville brothers through the law, Willoughby justified himself with the same argument as King John does in *Fouke le Fitz Waryn*: that an oath compelled by force could not be held to bind.

The *Gesta Herwardi* makes the sack of Peterborough into a splendid tale. It culminates when Hereward and his men retreat from the town, only to lose their way in the woods on a night of storm. St Peter, appeased by the return of the abbey treasures, sends a huge white wolf to lead them to safety; and their way is lit by mysterious lights that attach themselves to their spears. More prosaic versions of the raid are given by the chroniclers of Peterborough Abbey itself. They say the raid was carried out before the Norman abbot imposed by King William had even arrived to take up his post; the ransom story, then, is a fiction. They remembered that before the Conquest Hereward had been a tenant of the abbey, a fact that is confirmed by the Domesday Book, the record of the great survey of land ownership conducted in 1086. They say that he represented the removal of the abbey's treasures as an act of loyalty, and as necessary to keep them from the Normans; but the monks and their men refused to yield them up to him, so he set fire to the abbey buildings in order to gain access.[11] An interesting slant on the incident is offered by William of Malmesbury, writing before 1125. It was from Malmesbury Abbey that King William translated the Norman abbot Turold to Peterborough. Turold was by more than one account an autocratic and martial figure, who surrounded himself with an entourage of knights. On William of Malmesbury's report, he was appointed to Peterborough specifically for this reason, as the abbey, 'because of its situation among the fens, was troubled by petty robbers,* led by a man called Hereward'. Turold was unpopular at Malmesbury; the King is reported to have said, 'Since he behaves more like a soldier than an abbot, I shall find an opposite number for him to fight.'[12] This story helps to account for Hereward's determination to steal a march on Turold by plundering the monastery before he and his knights could arrive.

For the author of the *Gesta Herwardi*, Hereward is a great soldier, a

---

* *a latrunculis*

model and inspiration; for William of Malmesbury, he is merely a bandit chief. Throughout the Middle Ages, the difference between a robber and a soldier was often purely a matter of point of view. A soldier hoped to enrich himself with plunder, and with the proceeds of ransoming prisoners.[13] Soldiers sometimes received no pay, or else were in arrears of pay, and in such cases they had little choice but to forage and loot as they went. A robber lived off his robberies, and sometimes by related crimes, such as kidnapping. Unless the cause he fought for was recognised as a just one, any soldier might be stigmatised as a robber.[14] Conversely, a robber might sincerely believe in the righteousness of his actions; might feel, indeed, that his position was closely analogous to that of a soldier fighting in a just war. The soldier, the robber, the outlaw: in medieval England, these figures have a tendency to slide in and out of one another. For men who were accustomed to the use of weapons, it was an easy matter to slip from one role to another.

Some of these men, like Hereward, were of aristocratic descent. The Latin for knight, *miles*, means soldier. Men of knightly family were normally trained to arms, and took pride in coming from a lineage of fighting-men, whose prestige they knew they were expected to uphold. Three centuries after Hereward, the Folville brothers, sons of a landed knight, sometimes lived like bandits, from robberies and the proceeds of kidnapping, and sometimes took service in the King's army.[15] In either case, they aimed to flourish by the arts of appropriating the property of others through professionally calculated violence.

As for William of Malmesbury's derogatory view of Hereward: it is conditioned by his belief that the Conquest of England was a justified war, since William of Normandy, and not Earl Harold, was the rightful heir to King Edward the Confessor.[16] For William of Malmesbury, Hereward was merely a rebel, who fought against the king whom God had appointed. Accordingly, his raiding was no better than robbery; it could not be counted as a legitimate taking of booty. The author of the *Gesta*, on the other hand, views Hereward as a local hero of more or less legendary standing, who fought as a man of old family should to regain the inheritance that was rightfully his.

Throughout the *Gesta Herwardi*, the narrative is highly episodic. Many of its motifs and stories are familiar from tales of later outlaws. Archery plays no more than a minor part in most of it, but there is one episode that shows Hereward himself as a champion archer, almost the equal of Robin Hood, when he fires a shot of startling force and accuracy at one of his chief enemies, who is only saved from death by his armour. Hereward is also a master of disguise. At one point during the siege of Ely he disguises himself as a fisherman and comes with a boat to help the Normans transport materials to build their siege works. At the end of the day he sets fire to the lot and escapes. Another episode tells how he disguises himself as a potter and goes as a spy to the King's court, where he wanders about selling pots. The story ends with violence, as the cooks try to rough up the supposed potter and he, resenting this, fights back, is taken into custody and has to cut his way out. He escapes on his famous mare Swallow, a beast of striking ugliness, who was given her name because of her speed and endurance. In the late fifteenth-century metrical narrative *Robin Hood and the Potter*, the outlaw likewise disguises himself as a potter and goes to sell pots in Nottingham, with a view to making trouble for the Sheriff.[17] Some of Hereward's companions have tales of their own. Wulfric the Heron once saved four brothers, innocent men, from execution, having first, it seems, persuaded the executioners that he was a harmless and ludicrous figure. Similar tales were later told of Robin Hood. Another Wulfric was nicknamed 'the Black' because he had once gone unrecognised among his enemies with his face smeared with charcoal and taking them by surprise, had killed ten of them single-handedly.[18] When Fouke Fitz Waryn kidnaps his enemy King John, he first disguises himself as a charcoal-burner, before tricking him and leading him astray.[19]

The *Gesta Herwardi* is the oldest surviving assemblage of stories about an English outlaw and his band. In it we glimpse a wealth of tales about men outside the law. It is unlikely that all or even most of these tales originated with the Hereward saga, any more than they disappeared from tradition when the hero himself began to be forgotten. No doubt these or similar stories had once been attached to the names of prominent outlaws and fugitives in earlier times. Certainly, the story of the daring leader who spies on the enemy camp in disguise was told by William of Malmesbury, first about Alfred the Great, at a time when he was heavily pressed by the Danes, and a couple of chapters later, with almost exactly the same details, about the Danish leader Anlaf. It is obvious that we are dealing with a traditional folk-tale motif.[20] With this in view, we can see that there is no reason to assume that the *Gesta Herwardi* itself was necessarily a direct source for either *Fouke le Fitz Waryn* or the later cycle of tales about Robin Hood. In the days before print, vernacular oral tradition was a far more powerful means of transmission than a written text in Latin which may not ever have been widely read. We know there were songs and tales about Hereward in English that have not come down to us and that probably never existed in written form. At least one other outlaw from the post-Conquest period also became a hero of popular stories: the Shropshire landowner Eadric the Wild, who fought against the Normans for several years from his power base in the West Midlands. However, there are only a few scattered indications as to what these tales were about.[21] Part of the importance of the *Gesta Herwardi* is its value as evidence for the content of a body of traditional material that has otherwise not survived. It shows us that feats of archery, fights against the odds, heroic rescues, cunning tricks and disguises were already the currency of outlaw stories three centuries before the date of the earliest extant tales of Robin Hood. Some of the stories of Hereward and his men continued to find echoes in tales of robbers and highwaymen up to the nineteenth century. Jack Sheppard, executed for robbery in 1724, was remembered for well over a century for his remarkable exploits as a jail-breaker. It would be good to know more about Hereward's companion Leofwin the Crafty, who earned his byname with his many escapes from captivity. A talent for daring escapes has always been one of the attributes that qualifies an otherwise run-of-the-mill law-breaker for the status of a legendary hero.[22] Another story told about Hereward and his men was that once, when they were being closely hunted by their enemies, they reversed the shoes on their horses' feet so as to confuse the pursuit. The same story is told of Fouke Fitz Waryn. But in the last years of the mounted robber the highwaymen of the Cotswolds are said to have found a way to improve this trick. They shod their horses with circular shoes.[23] As for Hereward's wonderful mare Swallow, she too had equally legendary successors, the most famous being the wholly imaginary Black Bess. This was the gallant horse that was assigned to Dick Turpin by Harrison Ainsworth in 1834, in his Gothic romance *Rookwood*, and that afterwards passed into popular tradition.[24]

The finale to the legend of Hereward the Outlaw comes in a choice of flavours. If we wish, we can follow the version in the *Gesta Herwardi*, in which King William ultimately agrees to restore his family estates to him, rather than that such a dangerous man should continue to live by raiding. After this, he serves the King faithfully for many years. There is evidence in the Domesday Book to suggest that something like this may have been the true end of the story. It exemplifies a pattern that was to be repeated many times, both in the careers of other historical outlaws and in tales of the outlaws of legend. Both Fouke Fitz Waryn and the fictional outlaw Gamelyn likewise receive royal pardons and return to live on their estates. However, Geoffrey Gaimar, in his *L'Estoire des Engleis*, records a variant tradition concerning Hereward's fate. He says that Hereward negotiated a truce with the King and was about to agree a permanent peace in return for promising to fight in William's wars in France. But Hereward's enemies among the Norman lords, furious at the prospect of his receiving the King's protection, attacked him in large numbers when he was unarmed and feasting. Even then, he could only be killed when four of them at once stabbed him from behind with lances. So in this version the great warrior comes to a violent end, murdered by cowardly assailants who take him unawares. The outlaw or robber hero very often meets his death as a result of some form of treachery. The legend of Robin Hood provides another such case: the outlaw dies when a nun, his relative, seduced by one of his enemies, allows the outlaw to bleed to death when he trusts her to perform a small piece of surgery.[25]

In his ground-breaking study *The Outlaws of Medieval England*, Maurice Keen once argued that the explanation of Hereward's lasting fame lay in his reputation as 'a native hero struggling against a hated conqueror', and he made the assumption that the primary audience for the stories were members of 'the conquered race'.[26] More recently, John Hayward has similarly characterised Hereward as 'an emblem of resistance to a foreign oppressor', but has acknowledged what he sees as 'an enigma': the appeal that his story plainly had for the Normans. Two of the earliest and fullest versions of the Hereward legend were both written by Normans: the poet-chronicler Geoffrey Gaimar and the author of the *Gesta Herwardi*, who was almost certainly an Ely monk with the Norman name of Richard. Hayward gives a partial answer to his own riddle by commenting on some of the characteristics of the Englishman that were guaranteed to rouse admiration even in his enemies: 'pride in his race, military skill and lack of physical fear'.[27] Hereward and his Norman adversaries shared very much the same aristocratic warrior code, in which these qualities were rated highly. So too were such attributes as open-handed generosity and the keeping of faith. When Hereward avenges his murdered brother, he keeps faith with him and with his family. But those who do not keep faith with Hereward himself, like the abbot of Peterborough in the *Gesta* account, are punished at his own hands. Generosity and faith-keeping are two of the most important qualities of the good lord. Hereward demonstrates his abilities as a leader by the way he attracts loyal followers, who are portrayed as minor heroes in their own right, and successfully leads them in battle, often against great odds.

Whatever tales of Hereward may have been circulating in the vernacular, the *Gesta Herwardi* itself was not written to console or encourage the beaten English. It was intended, as its author expressly says, for young men of the knightly class as an example of the life of a great soldier.[28] And though it seems obvious to us now to read it as a story about a patriotic freedom fighter, it is not clear that that is how the historical Hereward would have understood himself, nor does it seem to be quite in those terms that the early texts depict his activities. When Gaimar introduces Hereward as a leader of the English resistance, he does not speak of him as a patriot: he says, 'Normans had disinherited him'.[29] Tim Lundgren has pointed out that there are parallels to Hereward's outlaw career in the chronicle accounts of certain nobles who were outlawed earlier in the eleventh century, during the reign of Edward the Confessor. When Earl Aelfgar was outlawed in 1055, he raised troops in Ireland and Wales, allied himself with the King of North Wales, put to flight an

English army and sacked the cathedral and city of Hereford. 'And then when they had done the most damage,' says one of the Anglo-Saxon chronicles, drily, 'it was decided that it would be a good policy to revoke Earl Aelfgar's outlawry and give him back his earldom and everything that had been taken from him.'[30] Aelfgar's strategy seems to have been to force the King to reinstate him by causing so much trouble that this was seen as the preferable course. In much the same way, Hereward, finding himself disinherited, raised a small army, harried the fen country and helped to sack Peterborough. By demonstrating his capacity to make a nuisance of himself, he eventually brought William to negotiate a deal with him – a deal that involved his swearing fealty to the invader, and if Gaimar be believed, signing up to fight the King's wars. He behaved, in short, less like an English patriot than a shrewd and tough medieval aristocrat, engaged in a dispute over land with his overlord. Given a bit of bad luck, any landholder might have found himself in a similar situation. The Norman aristocracy would not have found it hard to feel a sympathetic interest in Hereward's predicament, to match their respect for the heroic persistence with which he upheld his rights.

Conflict with an overlord and a dispute about an inheritance lie at the heart of the story of Fouke Fitz Waryn. At one time this existed in at least three versions: an Anglo-Norman romance in verse of the late thirteenth century, a prose rendering of that romance, also in French, which was made at some point in the second or third decade of the fourteenth century, and a verse romance in English. Only the prose text survives.[31] *Fouke le Fitz Waryn* combines traditions about the history of the Fitz Waryn family with tales of outlaw life in the woods, some of which, as we have already seen, are similar to stories that are told or touched on in the *Gesta Herwardi*. The central situation, of the band of brothers who resist the persecutions of an unjust ruler, resembles that in a French *chanson de geste*, *Renaud de Montauban*. This story of the four sons of Duke Aymon who lead a fugitive life in the face of the hostility of King Charlemagne incorporates several motifs that are also found in outlaw and highwayman tales, and at least one episode in *Fouke le Fitz Waryn* is imitated from it directly.[32] Like Hereward in the *Gesta*, when Fouke travels overseas he generally finds himself in romance territory: he kills a dragon and later a giant. Nevertheless, there was a real Fouke Fitz Waryn, who lived into extreme old age and died in about 1258. The author of the original romance was spinning a story about a man whose living presence must have been still remembered. There is no doubt that he had access to authentic information about aspects of his hero's career.

The historical Fouke was a man of knightly rank, descended from several generations of Marcher lords on the Welsh borders. On the death of his father in 1198 he fell heir to the family holdings. A year later, King John had succeeded to the throne, and by the end of 1200, Fouke was in revolt. After roughly three years of outlawry, he and his followers, who included a couple of his brothers, made peace with the King and received a pardon. The romance explains this episode by reference to an old enmity between Fouke and John, dating back to when both were children. It states that the immediate cause of the trouble was Fouke's claim to Whittington Castle in Shropshire. At the time he came into his inheritance this was held by the Powys family, but it had once belonged to the Fitz Waryns. Seeing an opportunity to revenge their childhood quarrel, John denied Fouke's clear right to Whittington in favour of Sir Morys de Powys. In response to this abuse of royal power, Fouke and his brothers (he has four in the romance) repudiated their fealty to the King. This account of Fouke's motives may well be reasonably accurate. Certainly, the Fitz Waryn claim to Whittington is a matter of history. It had been recognised in 1195, during the lifetime of Fouke's father, but when Fouke offered King John £100 to have it confirmed, early in the year 1200, he found his offer disregarded. Instead, John accepted Morys de Powys's smaller offer of fifty marks. On Morys's death, a few months later, Whittington passed to his sons. But less than a year after Fouke had been pardoned, the King confirmed him in possession of Whittington 'as his right and inheritance'. Altogether, the timing of these events tends to substantiate the bones of the narrative that is related in *Fouke le Fitz Waryn*.[33]

More than half the romance is given over to stories of Fouke's time as an outlaw. He and his brothers move from wood to wood. While they are hiding in Wiltshire, in the forest of Braydon, they see a company of merchants travelling with a bodyguard. Fouke sends his brother John to question them, who demands 'in love' that they come to speak with 'his lord in the forest'. This piece of brigand courtesy, reminiscent of scenes in *A Gest of Robyn Hode*, fails to have the desired effect: John is assaulted and the outlaws attack, forcing the merchants to surrender. When Fouke cross-questions them, he learns that they are travelling as agents of the King, and the costly goods they are carrying all belong to him. Fouke plunders them, entertains them (again in a fashion that recalls Robin Hood) to a woodland dinner, and sends them on their way with an ironic message of thanks to the King. As in Knighton's account of the fleecing of Justice Willoughby, this is robbery as revenge and reparation. Here and elsewhere in the romance it is stated that Fouke never did any damage to anyone except King John and the knights who were loyal to him; but he is said to have pillaged John's property whenever he was able.[34] Making the point that Fouke never robbed anyone but the King is plainly felt to be important in establishing his image as a 'good' outlaw. It was legitimate to take booty from one's enemies, so long as one was fighting in a just war. Fouke's case against King John rested on the fact that by refusing him the lordship of Whittington, the King had denied him his rights in law. In Fouke's time, 'denial of justice' was widely recognised as lawful grounds for waging private war, even against one's overlord and king. To further emphasise the justice of Fouke's cause, King John is repeatedly shown as unfit to rule. Not only is he no respecter of law, but he is treacherous and murderous. When Fouke and his brothers leave the court, John immediately sends after them a large band of knights, with instructions to kill them on the spot, without even a pretence of proceeding against them in legal form.[35]

In order to stress the point that Fouke is very far from being a common sort of robber, the romance supplies him with a foil, in the shape of one Pieres de Brubyle, a knight of the Scottish border country. He, we are told, had gathered a band of debauched young men of good family and was in the habit of going round the area murdering and robbing merchants and other law-abiding people. Whenever he goes out robbing, he calls himself Fouke Fitz Waryn, so that Fouke receives the blame. But one day, Pieres and his men overrun the home of a wealthy knight, Robert Fitz Sampsoun, who has been in the habit of providing Fouke and his companions with a refuge. Fouke arrives to find them feasting in the hall, while Fitz Sampsoun and his household, including his wife, are lying bound on one side. The robbers are all wearing masks, and keeping up the pretence that Pieres is Fouke Fitz Waryn. Fouke, who has left his followers outside, terrifies them all into remaining still, then threatens to kill Pieres unless he binds the hands of each of his companions. Next, he makes him cut off their heads, and finally he beheads Pieres himself. Thus single-handedly Fouke vindicates his name and proves his outstanding courage. Meanwhile, the unprincipled robber, Pieres, who robs the innocent and hides behind a mask and a stolen name, shows that in spite of his gentle birth he is ignoble in every way, even to the point of being a craven coward.[36]

The conventions of the outlaw story provide the author of *Fouke le Fitz Waryn* with plenty of material: hairbreadth escapes and daring rescues, spying expeditions in disguise, varied by skirmishes with troops of knights sent out to hunt down Fouke and his brothers. At one point Fouke turns pirate, and plunders the English coast, always being careful, of course, to confine his ravages to Crown property. His strategy is that of Earl Aelfgar, though Fouke's depredations are on a smaller scale. He sets out to cause so much trouble that the King will be driven to rescind his outlawry and give him what he wants. Twice he captures John himself. On the first occasion, he decoys him into an ambush in Windsor Forest. 'Now I have you in my jurisdiction',* he says, and he tells him he will pass judgement on him, the same judgement that John would have passed on Fouke if he had been

---

* *ore je vous ay en mon bandon*

able to catch him. The use of legal language is deliberate. John has denied Fouke the justice of the royal courts; now Fouke, outside the law, is claiming the authority to try John in a court of his own. He swears that John shall die because of the way he has injured and disinherited Fouke himself and so many others. But when John begs for mercy, and promises to set matters right, Fouke spares him and sets him free. In effect, he grants the King a pardon: a reversal in roles whose irony goes very deep. Any judge might, after trial, sentence a man to death; but the granting of pardons was strictly a royal prerogative.[37] However, as soon as John is safe, he goes back on his word. When Fouke captures him for a second time, he prudently keeps six of John's knights as his hostages. On this occasion, a lasting peace is made. Fouke receives his lands back, and is given the lordship of Whittington.[38]

But the story doesn't end at this point. It follows Fouke into his later years, and tells us how in time he comes to repent all the killings he has committed and his other 'great crimes'. To obtain remission from Purgatory, he founds a priory in honour of the Virgin. In his old age, he is the subject of a miracle; like St Paul on the road to Damascus, he sees a great light. A voice tells him that he will be granted the privilege to suffer penance for his sins in this life rather than in Purgatory. After this, he is blind until his death. Fouke's repentance and divinely imposed penance are doubtless intended to be the final proof of his virtue. St Thomas Aquinas said of 'those who make a sinful use of the sword' that 'they are punished eternally, unless they repent'.[39] There are parallels in some related texts. Guy of Warwick, the subject of another Anglo–Norman romance, also repents in his later years, and more extravagantly than Fouke. So does the French hero Renaud de Montauban, the eldest of the four sons of Aymon. However, in the context of the English outlaw legend, Fouke's highly orthodox penitence marks him out. Although the legend of Robin Hood stresses the hero's devotion to hearing the mass, this is never viewed in the stories as conflicting in any way with his career of robbery and lawless violence, and he lives and dies a greenwood outlaw. Gamelyn, who features in the oldest surviving outlaw tale in the English language, resembles Fouke more closely, in that he eventually receives his inheritance and returns to a settled place in society. Despite the fact that while he is still an outlaw, he commits some spectacular murders, among them that of his own brother, the question of repentance is never raised in what, as we shall see, is a strikingly anti-clerical text.

Nevertheless, Fouke's repentance, at the end of a stirring life, foreshadows a pattern that later becomes very prominent in the age of popular print. In broadside ballads and chapbook biographies, the 'good' robber's ultimate repentance is a necessary stage in his story. But this we shall look at further in its place.

4

'I wil be Justice this day'

In *Fasciculus Morum*, a Latin handbook for preachers that was written in the early fourteenth century, there is a sardonic passage on robbers.

> Take note that among all nations the English may return thanks to God for a special privilege. For it is said that Ireland and Wales are overrun with robbers, who steal their neighbours' cows, oxen and other cattle, on account of which they are openly called 'robbers'. But in England – may God be praised – this is not the case. . . . Among us, gentlemen* are called 'shaveldours' and 'ryfelours'. For men of this kind break into the treasure-houses of the great, carry off property, drive away herds, plunder churchmen, nor does this touch their consciences; instead, they are hugely delighted when they can plunder an abbot, a prior or another monastic, and they say: 'Undoubtedly it was God's will that such a peasant, monk or friar encountered us today.' It seems to them that whatever they do, they do justly and with reason.† And so they do nothing for which they do not know how to come up with reasons that appear to be satisfactory, as a result of the lying way they disguise them and misrepresent them.[1]

This is the earliest text I have found that attributes to the English as a nation a distinctively tolerant attitude to robbers. The author is partly being ironic, of course: it is not the English in general but the English gentry who practise open robbery whenever they can, yet never give it its proper name, nor acknowledge that there is anything wrong with what they do. English ecclesiastics, and peasants, as well, are obviously likely to see the matter from a different point of view. At the time this passage was

---

* *generosi*

† *juste . . . et cum racione*

written, 'ryfelour' (from the verb 'to rifle') and 'shaveldour' were the very latest slang terms for a raider or robber.[2] The friar who wrote the handbook associates the use of such expressions with a particular outlook, one that sees the life of plunder as normal and right, and even as being sanctioned by God. For him, the refusal of these gentlemen robbers to use straightforward language to describe themselves is part of the misrepresentation in which they engage in order to justify their activities to themselves and others.

One element in the distinctive set of attitudes that the author of *Fasciculus Morum* associates with the 'shaveldours' is a spirit of violent hostility to the Church, and particularly to the monastic orders. It is not simply the case that they rob them because they are wealthy. They take a special delight in plundering churchmen. A similar outlook is found in some of the surviving early texts of the Robin Hood cycle. In *A Gest of Robyn Hode*, the outlaw instructs his men to target, among others, bishops, archbishops and abbots. Shortly afterwards, the abbot and high cellarer of St Mary's Abbey in York emerge as two of the villains of the piece, conspiring to strip a knight of his lands. Their punishment comes later on, when the cellarer, travelling through Barnsdale, is held up by Robin's men and robbed of a substantial sum. Robin's willingness to rob churchmen is presented side by side with his showy but idiosyncratic veneration for certain religious forms. He will never have dinner until he has heard three masses, for the Father, the Holy Ghost and the Virgin. To the last of these he has a special devotion, and he is even prepared to accept her as surety to a loan, and to treat the arrival of the cellarer of St Mary's with his chest of money as the Virgin's fulfilling her obligation.[3] Robber and outlaw though he is, Robin behaves in this tale as though he has God on his side, and whatever he does is treated as something done, in the words of *Fasciculus Morum*, 'justly and with reason'.

The Tale of Gamelyn is another outlaw story that is strongly anti-clerical in spirit. As we shall see, the hero shows an enthusiasm for robbing monastics that borders on the fanatical. It was written in a Midland county at some point during the middle decades of the fourteenth century: that is, during or shortly after the time that the Folville brothers were pursuing their wild careers.[4] Like the Hereward legend and *Fouke le Fitz Waryn*, *The Tale of Gamelyn* revolves round a stolen inheritance. It begins at the deathbed of a wealthy knight, Sir Johan of Boundys, who is concerned to make sure that Gamelyn, the youngest of his three sons, should inherit a proper share of his lands and property. Sir Johan explicitly rejects as unacceptable the prevalent custom of primogeniture, by which all of his lands would have passed to the eldest. In this respect, Gamelyn is much luckier than many younger brothers.[5] However, as soon as his father dies, the eldest son, Johan, takes charge of the boy. He plunders Gamelyn's inheritance for his own profit, neglects to look after his lands, and brings him up as a servant in his kitchen.

In more than one study of *The Tale of Gamelyn*, the hero has been described as a yeoman, a man of free birth but not of 'good' or gentle family.[6] This is to perpetrate a serious misreading. The point is emphasised by Gamelyn himself. When his brother calls him a 'gadeling', or 'fellow', with the implication that he is of low birth, he responds hotly:

> I am no worse gadeling, ne no worse wight,
> But born of a lady and geten of a knight.[7]

I am no worse a fellow, nor no worse a person, than born of a lady and begotten by a knight.

The confusion over Gamelyn's status seems to have arisen because of certain affinities between *The Tale of Gamelyn* and the stories of the medieval Robin Hood cycle. In addition to a marked hostility to churchmen, elements in common include a treacherous sheriff, fighting with staffs and a wrestling match. The fifteenth-century metrical tales of Robin Hood all describe the hero as a yeoman. We shall look in more detail at the implications of this in the next two chapters. But Gamelyn is of gentle family. This is important. For though Robin Hood is the most famous of all the outlaw heroes, he is in some ways an anomaly. The only others who are described as yeomen are Adam Bell and his comrades, in the metrical narrative that bears their names. There are plenty of yeomen and peasant robbers who feature in the legal records, but for several centuries the heroic outlaw and robber of literature and tradition is nearly always a man of high status. This stereotype is so powerful that in a number of sixteenth- and seventeenth-century texts Robin Hood himself is revamped from a yeoman into an earl.[8]

Gamelyn, then, comes from a knightly family – as does Fouke Fitz Waryn. However, while Fouke is educated at the royal court, Gamelyn, a male Cinderella, receives the training of a scullion. Although, as it turns out, he has absorbed some ideas about the way that a gentleman ought to behave, he has no pretensions to being a hero of chivalry. His favoured weapon is the plebeian staff, and the only element of the marvellous is his prodigious strength, his personal version of the Third Son's luck or special grace. The tale was intended for oral delivery; it introduces itself as a 'talking', and periodically enjoins its audience to listen.[9] Who that audience was, we do not know, except that it was potentially a wide one. But for a lot of the time the story reads like a wish-fulfilment fantasy for younger brothers, servingmen and underdogs in general.

Gamelyn himself has always been taken to be an imaginary figure. He has a name, but, unlike Robin Hood, no local habitation. The setting of his story, down-to-earth as it is, is simply some unnamed English shire, at a time not far distant from the date of the poem. The main action begins one day when Gamelyn is in his late teens. He has begun to realise how badly his brother has treated him. When Johan comes by and asks him if dinner is ready, Gamelyn tells him to cook it himself, and follows this up by cursing him for his predatory stewardship of Gamelyn's inheritance. Johan's response is to tell his men to come with cudgels and beat the boy senseless; but Gamelyn picks up a pestle – a fitting weapon for a kitchen hand – and lays about them till they back away. Not surprisingly. An illumination in the fourteenth-century Luttrell Psalter depicts a bearded male who is pounding the contents of a very large mortar with a sturdy pestle that is twice his own height.[10] In the hands of a man strong enough to wield it, it would be a terrifying weapon. Once it is clear that Gamelyn cannot be controlled through violence, his smooth-talking brother soothes him down. He promises to give Gamelyn his inheritance, but he is secretly plotting to get rid of him.

There is no obvious hint of parody in this poem, but it is very noticeable that the kind of romance episode that we find in *Fouke le Fitz Waryn* is here transposed into a much more everyday, rustic mode. In place of the knightly skirmishes, we have a scuffle with some cowardly servingmen. And next, in place of a formal knightly combat, Gamelyn goes to a wrestling match. His brother encourages him, in the hope he will get his neck broken. Gamelyn is pitted against a tough and dangerous champion, but his outstanding strength brings him the victory. When he goes back to his brother's house, he is accompanied by a crowd of admiring hangers-on. Johan's reaction is to order his porter to lock the gate, but this does not avail against the hulking Gamelyn, who simply kicks it in, breaks the porter's neck with his bare hands, and throws the unfortunate fellow down a well. Gamelyn then welcomes in his new friends with the suggestive words, 'we wiln be maistres heer and aske no man leve' (we will be the masters here, and ask no man's permission): very much a younger brother's, or a servant's, dream.[11] He treats them to a magnificent feast. It lasts for seven days and nights, but at the end of that time, his guests insist that they really must go home. His brother Johan has been hiding in a turret, but as soon as Gamelyn is alone he comes down and once again deceives him with his lying words. First, he wins Gamelyn's gratitude by promising to make him his heir. He then claims that when Gamelyn had thrown his porter down the well, he had sworn in his anger to have him bound hand and foot. In order to prevent his being forsworn – which would have dishonoured him – he asks Gamelyn to let himself be tied up. Gamelyn, still too trusting, agrees; only to find, of course, that Johan has not the least intention of ever setting him free. Instead, he fetters him to a post in the hall, and tells everyone who comes in that Gamelyn has gone mad.

After Gamelyn has been tied up without food for two days and nights, he begs one of the servingmen, Adam, the 'spenser' or pantryman, to unlock his fetters, promising to share his lands with him. This is an offer that Adam cannot resist; so as soon as Johan has gone to bed, he takes the keys, frees Gamelyn, and takes him to the pantry for some food and drink. However, Adam is keen, if possible, to see matters arranged peaceably. He tells Gamelyn that his brother is about to hold a feast of his own, to which he has invited a number of wealthy churchmen. He proposes that Gamelyn should put his fetters back on, and see if he can persuade the guests to have him set free. But if they will not, Adam has a plan to fall back on. The fetters will not, in fact, be locked; and Adam will keep a couple of staffs in a handy place, one for Gamelyn and one for him. This is how Gamelyn acquires his sidekick: no knight, nor even a man-at-arms, but an ordinary servingman, who helps him not from loyalty but on the promise of a substantial reward. But this is not inappropriate, for the kitchen servant Adam is in some ways a double of the scullion hero Gamelyn, and just as Gamelyn dreams of taking possession of his inheritance, now Adam, too, has in prospect the chance to become one of the landed gentry.

When the guests arrive for Johan's feast, Gamelyn invokes the crucified Christ in begging them to help him. Yet although these are men in holy orders, who ought to show compassion in Christ's name, all he gets back are hostile and spiteful responses. So Adam brings out the cudgels, and he and Gamelyn beat up the monastics, meanwhile making cheerful jokes about giving them absolution.[12] None of the laymen present will intervene, because in the violently anti-clerical world of the poem, it is a given fact that they all hate churchmen.[13] As for Johan, Gamelyn gives him a blow that breaks his backbone and in one of the story's moments of reversal, sets him in the fetters where he himself had sat. Then, while the monks and friars are carried home in carts, Gamelyn and Adam, who have evidently worked up a sweat, take the time for a wash. However, it is not long before the next scuffle: with twenty-four brash young men of the sheriff's household, who come to arrest them, but who run away quickly once Gamelyn and Adam start to knock them about. But when Gamelyn looks into the distance and sees the sheriff on his way with a very large posse, he and Adam decide it is time to drink a pledge to each other and make off to the wood.

Once they are among the trees, Adam is miserable; his clothes are getting ripped, and he is hungry and wishes he were back in his pantry. At this point they see a large band of 'yonge men' sitting having dinner. These are outlaws, of course, and the 'mayster outlawe' sends seven of his men to fetch these 'gestes' to him. Although *The Tale of Gamelyn* is older,

41

perhaps by more than a century, than any of the surviving Robin Hood narratives, this is a moment that closely resembles episodes in *A Gest of Robyn Hode*, in which anyone who travels through Robin's forest is likely to find themselves, willing or unwilling, a guest at his table.[14] When the seven young men accost Gamelyn and Adam, they tell them that they have been sent by the king of the outlaws. Gamelyn tells Adam that if the outlaw chief is 'hende [courteous] and come of gentil blood', he will give them food and drink and treat them well.[15] And so it proves. Robin Hood makes rich guests pay for their dinner; so too, presumably, might the outlaw king whom Gamelyn meets. But both of them treat poor men with courteous hospitality. In each case this is a sign that the outlaw chief possesses noble qualities. Generosity in the modern sense is an important mark of the man of gentle family (*generosus*). It is an attribute that is likely to commend itself most of all to retainers, servingmen and other dependants. Gamelyn has already demonstrated his own sound instincts for lavish hospitality with the seven-day feast to celebrate his win at wrestling.

Hearing of Gamelyn's exploits, the outlaw king makes him his deputy. Three weeks later, the king obtains a pardon and returns to his home, and Gamelyn becomes the 'maister outlawe' in his place.[16] The scullion boy has made himself a master of other men; he has the allegiance of the outlaws; but so long as he remains in the woods, he cannot make himself master of his inheritance. Meanwhile, his dishonest brother has become the county sheriff, and has arranged for Gamelyn to be officially declared outlaw. As a result, Gamelyn's lands have been forfeited. Gamelyn's response is to turn up in court at the next county assize and reproach his brother for his action. Not surprisingly, Johan has him arrested and thrown into jail to await judgement. At this point the second of Gamelyn's brothers comes into the story. Sir Ote, we learn, is a 'goode knight', and he is shocked at what Johan has done.[17] He bails Gamelyn out and takes him home. However, Gamelyn, as outlaw chief, feels a responsibility to make sure that matters are going well with his men. He tells Ote that he must go back to the woods. Ote is alarmed. A surety whose prisoner failed to appear for trial was usually fined, but in theory he might be punished in the place of the accused.[18] This is what Johan has threatened to do, and Ote, very reasonably, fears. But when Gamelyn promises to turn up in court, Ote agrees to trust him.

Hitherto, little has been said about Gamelyn's activities as an outlaw. As 'good' outlaws, Hereward and Fouke Fitz Waryn had lived by plundering their enemies. Since Hereward treated all Normans as his foes, and Fouke could feel justified in viewing any raid on Crown property as reparation for his treatment by the King, this gave both of them plenty of scope. Gamelyn's chief enemy is his brother Johan; but Johan is only a simple

knight with a modest holding of land. As the 'maister outlawe', Gamelyn
has to find the means to support a large following. And as a 'good' outlaw
in a story, he cannot engage in indiscriminate banditry, no matter what a
man like him might really have done in life. Instead, he confines himself to
robbing men in religious orders.

> Whyl Gamelyn was outlawed hadde he no cors;
> There was no man that for him ferde the wors,
> But abbotes and priours, monk and chanoun;
> On hem left he no-thing whan he mighte hem nom.[19]

While Gamelyn was an outlaw, he had no one's curse; there was no man that
for his sake was any the worse, apart from abbots and priors, monk and
canon; those he left with nothing whenever he was able to catch them.

An outlaw who does no one any harm is clearly a 'good' outlaw. Robbing
monks evidently does not count against this. After all, it has already been
established at Johan's feast that all monks, friars and canons are pitiless
wretches whom any decent layman is happy to see knocked around. As
their self-appointed scourge, Gamelyn seems to be balanced between two
roles: as an avenger in a personal quarrel and as an agent of correction of an
unpopular social group. Of course, the author of *Fasciculus Morum* (himself
a friar) would doubtless have viewed Gamelyn as just another rapacious
gentleman robber with an unjustified sense of his own righteousness.

Meanwhile, Gamelyn still has a problem to solve in the world outside
the woods; and while he has been terrorising monks, his brother the sheriff
has been bribing a jury to make sure that he will be hanged. However,
Gamelyn has begun to learn some caution. This time, he arrives at the
courtroom in company with his outlaw following. He sends Adam inside to
see how matters are proceeding, and Adam returns with the news that Sir
Ote is in fetters. The bribed jury have convicted him in Gamelyn's place
and the judge has passed sentence on him to hang. Adam in his anger
wants Gamelyn to kill everyone in the courtroom. This gives Gamelyn a
chance to establish himself, yet again, as a 'good' outlaw, no indiscriminate
killer.

> 'Adam,' seyde Gamelyn, 'we wiln nought don so,
> We wil slee the giltif and lat the other go.
> . . .
> Lat non scape at the dore; take, yonge men, yeme:
> For I wil be Justice this day, domes for to deme.'[20]

'Adam,' said Gamelyn, 'we will not do so. We will slay the guilty and let the

others go. . . . Let no one escape by the door; take, young men, care: for I will be the justice this day, judgements to give.'

Gamelyn enters the hall, frees Sir Ote, and orders the judge to leave his seat. When the judge ignores him, he hurls him over the bar and takes his place. Ote sits next to him, Adam at his feet in place of a clerk, and Gamelyn picks a jury from among his outlaws. Then they sit in judgement on the judge, the original jury, and his brother Johan, the sheriff, before hanging the whole lot outside the courtroom.

When Johan begs for mercy, reminding Gamelyn that they are brothers, Gamelyn replies, 'and thou were maister yit I schulde have wors' (if you were still master, I should have worse [treatment]).[21] Gamelyn has made himself his brother's master in a way that will permit no answering back. Of Johan, the narrative gleefully remarks: 'He was hanged by the nekke and nought by the purs'. To be 'hanged by the purse' was to be fined or buy a pardon.[22] Most men of Johan's standing could usually arrange pardons for offences for which a poorer man would be hanged. We have seen this system operating in the cases of those rather equivocal strongmen, the Folville brothers. One of the pleasures *The Tale of Gamelyn* offered to its audience is that of seeing a bad man of knightly status summarily and violently punished – an event that under the forms of law seems to have been quite rare.[23] Outlaw justice is more reliably retributive than the King's.

This is fortunate for Gamelyn, since not only is he still an outlaw, but he has now compounded his offences with some remarkably audacious lynchings in open defiance of the royal system of justice. However, when he and Sir Ote approach the King with their 'frendes', that is, by way of some influential go-betweens, they find no difficulty in making their peace. What is more, in evident appreciation of their integrity as judges, the King makes Ote a justice, and Gamelyn chief justice of the royal forest. All Gamelyn's outlaws are pardoned, too, 'And sitthen in good office the king hem hath y-pilt' (and then the king appointed them to good [profitable] offices).[24] And, of course, Gamelyn finally comes into possession of his inheritance. It is noticeable that nothing more is said about Adam the pantryman, nor are we told whether he ever received the promised share of Gamelyn's lands. A landed servingman of humble birth is, perhaps, a dream too many, one that is better not given too much emphasis. It might seem equally unlikely that a pardoned outlaw should receive an office of profit under the Crown, but there are a number of documented instances where precisely this took place. Several of the outlaws associated with the Folvilles and the Coterels benefited in this way. It seems to have been a deliberate device to give them employment and an income, in the hope that they would stay on the right side of the law. It often worked, too. Many a pardoned outlaw, like Gamelyn and Sir Ote, afterwards led a blameless life.[25]

The courtroom episode in *Gamelyn*, dramatic though it is, is not without analogues in both history and literature. In the first half of the fourteenth century there are a number of cases of justices, sheriffs and other court officials being attacked in court and of sessions being summarily terminated on the intervention of bands of armed men. There is even an instance, in Ipswich in 1344, where judicial proceedings were imitated in mockery by a crowd of hostile demonstrators.[26] Among the songs and tales of legendary and imaginary outlaws, we have already seen how Fouke Fitz Waryn adopts the legal terminology of 'jurisdiction' and 'judgement' when he seeks to intimidate the captured King John.[27] In *The Outlaw's Song*, too, the speaker uses similar language when he utters threats against his enemies among the trailbaston judges: 'if they were in my bailiwick',* he says, 'they would not find a refuge'.[28]

One of the most extraordinary documents associated with the green-wood tradition also uses a quasi-legal style. It is, in fact, a threatening letter, sent in 1336 by a professional enforcer on behalf of a client (an abbot, no less) to bully the Archbishop of York and his attorney into withdrawing their own candidate for a benefice so that the abbot might put in a man of his own. A sordid little quarrel; but the text of the letter, in Anglo-Norman French, the language of the law courts, touches the whole affair with fantasy. It is couched as though from king to subject; the strong-arm man awards himself the title of 'Lyonel, roi de la Route de Raveners', King of the Company of Plunderers, and signs off, 'Given at our castle of the North Wind in the Tower of the Vert' (or greenwood) 'in the first year of our reign'. If his intervention on behalf of the abbot is disregarded, he says, 'we shall instruct our sheriff of the north that he should make the great distress on you'. This is legal language. To make a distress was roughly equivalent to sending in the bailiffs: if a fine or debt was outstanding, a person's goods or land might be seized. What 'Lyonel' (aka Adam de Ravensworth) is intimating, in his colourful way, is that if the archbishop does not acquiesce, he will have his possessions plundered. At another point, Ravensworth threatens him with 'a thousand pounds damage from us and ours'. He speaks as though he commands a large band of robbers, but it is not clear whether this was true. It certainly seems unlikely that he really had a hideout in the greenwood, since as soon as enquiries were made, he was quickly arrested by the sheriff. What this document shows is that a real-life gangster might draw for his own ends on

---

* *en ma baylie*

the mystique of the outlaw-robbers of tradition. A feature of that tradition was the claim to operate an alternative system of authority and law.[29]

'It happith ofte they that were more worthy to be honged dampneth hem that beth lasse worthy' (it often happens that those who would be more deserving of being hanged condemn those who deserve it less). So lamented the preacher Thomas Wimbledon in 1387. Complaints against judges and jurors who took bribes or who were afraid to displease the powerful by giving verdicts against their interests crop up frequently in fourteenth- and fifteenth-century sermon writings. But the preachers were seldom activists; it was not part of their project; their task, as they understood it, was to touch men's consciences, by pointing to injustice, and warning of the wrath to come. At the Day of Doom, judge and felon alike must stand before the judgement seat of God.[30]

Not everyone had the patience to await God's final verdict. The outlaw legend offered a seductive alternative. At the point when law, rather than being a means to prevent oppression, has become oppression's instrument, the man who has embraced outlawry, who, faced with a corrupt system, has deliberately gone outside it, executes justice on the oppressors. Where property has been wrongly appropriated (a central issue in many of the stories) the outlaw implements 'folvyles lawes' in forcing its return. And where the guilty are sitting in judgement on the innocent, the strong arm of the outlaw effects a reversal, so that executive power and the will to judge fairly are once again on the same side, and the guilty are made to answer for their misdeeds.

In effect, to take over a courtroom, to pronounce and execute judgement in full legal form, is the ultimate claim to righteousness: to be acting, in the words of *Fasciculus Morum*, 'justly and with reason'. Gamelyn, we are told at the end of the tale, 'wrak him of his enemys and quitte hem here meede' (revenged himself on his enemies, and paid them their reward).[31] The second half of this line echoes a definition of justice that in one form or another is a favourite among medieval jurists and theologians: justice is the virtue that gives to each person what is rightly theirs.[32] The deviously murderous Johan, the venal judge and jury, who are ready, for a bribe, to hang the innocent Sir Ote: it is not unreasonable to argue that six foot of rope is exactly what they have merited. However, any orthodox cleric would have been bound to point out that Gamelyn's 'justice' is faulty on two important counts. First, in being motivated by vengeance, his intentions are wrong; as we might say, he lacks impartiality. Secondly, he has no authority for his judgements. From a strictly orthodox point of view, true justice proceeded from God, who deputed authority to the rightful ruler of the land, who in turn delegated power to try cases and pass sentences to his properly appointed judges.[33] In this way of thinking, outlaw justice is unauthorised, and so no justice at all. Gamelyn cannot rightly fill the judge's place; he can only usurp it. The author of *The Tale of Gamelyn* was not ignorant of this line of argument. Indeed, in one of his story's final twists, he implicitly acknowledges its force. When the King, after granting Gamelyn a pardon, goes on to make him a justice, there is a clear suggestion that he is vindicating Gamelyn's previous appearance on the judge's bench.

William Langland esteems 'folvyles lawes', the unofficial justice of the outlaw, as a gift of the Holy Spirit, though he condemns the crimes of Robert the Robber. The monastic chronicler Henry of Knighton shows a cautious sympathy for the Folville brothers in their role as outlaw-avengers. Another chronicler, Matthew Paris, writes about the English bandits of the post-Conquest period in terms that suggest that in his view it is not all that unreasonable that the gentleman who has no lands nor livelihood should commit the odd robbery now and again. But there are other voices from inside the medieval Church that are not at all indulgent to the outlaw, either as robber or avenger. At the start of this chapter I quoted at some length from the attack on robbers in *Fasciculus Morum*. This is not the only sermon text of the later Middle Ages to condemn robbers who think they have God on their side, bringing them aid. Murderers, too, are criticised for the same presumptuousness.[34] It is easy to understand how revenge killers might view themselves as the instruments of divinely sanctioned punishment.

The sermon-writers deplore what they see as England's excessive lawlessness, and the failure to punish crimes of violence, including robberies, murders and beatings. Writing in 1330 or just before it, the Dominican John de Bromyard, author of a huge and very influential handbook for preachers, states that on account of its 'false men', or as we would say, its criminals, 'the land has a scandalous reputation, even in foreign countries', and he condemns those lords who practise maintenance, giving such men their protection, so that no one dares to indict them or imprison them.[35] Another famous preacher, Thomas Brinton, who was Bishop of Rochester from 1373 to 1389, is extremely outspoken on these issues, deploring the fact that serious crime went largely uncontrolled. More than once he contrasts the state of affairs in other countries, where 'murderers and thieves are hanged by the neck together', with that in England, where 'for the most part they are hanged by the purse'.[36] And he is angry about cases in which 'a deliberate killer or especially famous robber . . . is arrested', only for his relatives to use their influence to have him set free. He represents them as saying, '[He is] of our blood; if justice should proceed against him, all our family would be shamefully dishonoured.' To this Brinton returns: 'To spare such men because of a blood-relationship would be to offend God and the law.'[37] This is an attack on aristocratic privilege. It is, by and large, the nobility and gentry who can raise the money for pardons, and who have the connections and clout to keep an arrested man from being hanged. Brinton's modern editor believes from the evidence of his will that he was 'of humble extraction'.[38] This would make good sense in the light of his social outlook.

All the evidence suggests that both the outlaw legend and the indulgence of the robber that flourished alongside it emerged in the context of aristocratic culture. The author of the *Gesta Herwardi* holds Hereward up as an example to aspiring military leaders. Fouke Fitz Waryn is a hero in a chivalric romance written for aristocrats in Anglo-Norman French. Gamelyn, certainly, is a rustic, untutored sort of gentleman – but he is a gentleman nevertheless, represented as open-handed, naturally warlike and a born leader of men. Meanwhile, it is members of the nobility and gentry who, in a phrase that becomes a commonplace, are 'ashamed to beg, and ignorant of how to dig', and who therefore will live by plunder if they have no other resources. There is an implication in this that a poor man's misdeeds are less deserving of tolerance. And indeed, Bishop Brinton expresses outrage at the fact that while 'a deliberate killer or a manifest thief who has been often allowed to go free' may be spared from execution if he or his friends pay a bribe, a boy may be hanged for thieving a few pears if he makes the mistake of stealing them from an influential lord.[39] Finally, the 'shaveldours' who rouse the indignation of the author of *Fasciculus Morum* by their self-righteous approach to robbing the clergy are specifically said to be members of the gentry – indeed, he goes so far as to imply that all English gentlemen share the same outlook and are tainted with the same kind of crimes. Why the enthusiasm for robbing clerics in particular? What is the source of the hostility towards churchmen that wells up in *The Tale of Gamelyn* and in some of the stories of the Robin Hood cycle?

The clergy who come to Johan's feast in *Gamelyn* expose themselves as pitiless and greedy, unwilling to displease their wealthy host by speaking up for an ill-treated orphan boy. In *A Gest of Robyn Hode*, the monks who are robbed have already been revealed as avaricious oppressors, hoping to foreclose on a loan so that they can turn a knight off his lands. The shortcomings of the clergy are criticised and satirised repeatedly in the literature of the fourteenth and fifteenth centuries. Again and again we encounter complaints about their greed, their worldliness, their lack of chastity. This probably helps to explain why the 'shaveldours' believed it was a righteous act to rob them. It is certainly part of the context in which a great many people plainly found pleasure in stories of wealthy churchmen humbled and plundered at the hands of robbers.

But I think there is more to it than this. The outlaw is always an ambiguous figure. On the one hand, the outlaw of legend is traditionally innocent of serious offences, hemmed in by dangerous and corrupt enemies, driven to take the law into his own hands as the only means of setting matters right. He is also, attractively, a protector to those with troubles of their own; a development that is already apparent when the outlaw king welcomes Gamelyn and Adam to his table, and that will become a key theme in *A Gest of Robyn Hode*. It is implicit, also, in Langland's reference to 'folvyles lawes': those who ride out to take back from dishonest men that which was wrongly appropriated are not likely, in the context of this particular passage, to be fighting for a purely private cause. On the other hand, both in legend and in real life, the outlaw is at best an avenger, and even those who admire him often make no bones about the fact that he depends for his subsistence on robbery and raiding. When we examine the well-documented case of the Folville brothers, we find men whose outlaw careers began with the murder of an oppressive local magnate. However, very soon they have become professional hard men, available to work for pay as specialists in illegal violence. At one point they were paid £20 to wreck a water-mill.[40] Such men were convenient tools; not the opponents of a corrupt system but the instruments of the people who operated it to their own advantage. When Sir Robert Touchet gave his livery to Eustace de Folville and two of his brothers, it was because it was useful to him to be seen to have such men in his following. The preacher John de Bromyard, a close contemporary of the Folvilles, speaks of 'dishonest men' who provide a refuge for 'robbers, murderers, fighters and dishonest rascals', protecting them from punishment. In return, these fellows will do 'whatever that great protector tells them, whether he wants anyone beaten, or plundered, or robbed, or murdered'.[41] In another place Bromyard says savagely, 'He who is able to bring in his following more robbers and murderers is the one who is master of all.'[42]

The sermon-writers and moral teachers are outspoken critics of such abuses and of the social conditions and attitudes that fostered them. More than this: even the idealised outlaw of legend took on a tarnished look when viewed in the mirror of orthodox Christian social teaching. The repentant robber would receive God's mercy, though he must first recompense his victims for what he has taken from them.[43] But there was no scope for glorifying the avenger or distinguishing 'good' robbers from bad. The revenger sins in wrath; the robber in avarice.[44] Any attempt to show their actions in a good light is sheer misrepresentation; it is inspired by the Devil, the Father of Lies.[45] I suggest that if the 'shaveldours' took a particular pleasure in robbing churchmen, it was partly because the Church was extremely critical of robbers, not least of robbers with pretensions to righteousness. The cleric-bashing of *The Tale of Gamelyn* reflects a clash of values that was already quite old at the time the poem was written. On the one side, there is the Church, preaching damnation to the murderer and the robber. On the other side, the outlaw-avenger, bringing death to his enemies, who is often the same man as the gentleman robber, convinced that taking other people's property by force was part of his right as a man of warlike spirit and ancestry.

5

The Robin Hood Tradition

The most famous of all the outlaw heroes is also one of the most shadowy. Almost the only thing that may be said with confidence about the original Robin Hood is that he was a deeply obscure figure, whose exploits, whatever these may have been, failed to catch the attention of any chronicler in his own times. His fame flourished among the people and surfaced slowly, filtering into the written record by way of proverbs and rhyming tales. Of the stories that have survived, even the earliest draw heavily on stock situations and traditional tale-types. In spite of many attempts, no one has identified much in them that might correspond to fact, nor managed to connect them convincingly with any of the various Robert or Robin Hoods whose lives have left documentary traces.[1]

The importance of Robin Hood lies in the legend, not in the lost circumstances of his life. But partly because its hero's identity has been so thoroughly mislaid, the legend has proved to be malleable; over the centuries it has been endlessly appropriated and reinvented. In Chapter One I quoted the Jacobean versifier John Taylor, whose summary of the outlaw's career, that he made a pact with Little John to rob the rich and feed the poor, will have raised few readers' eyebrows.[2] This is, after all, the thing that everybody knows about Robin Hood. However, when Taylor was writing, in 1622, it was a fairly recent development of a legend that was already very old. The theme had crystallised gradually. In his Latin chronicle *Historia Majoris Britanniae*, published in 1521, the Scotsman John Major assigned Robin Hood to the reign of Richard I. In a highly sympathetic account of the outlaw, he says: 'he did not steal the goods of the poor; as a matter of fact, he provided for them sumptuously with goods that he plundered from abbots'.[3] Major is drawing on some passages in the late medieval metrical tale, *A Gest of Robyn Hode*, which describe the outlaw as hospitable to poor travellers and, in particular, tell of his heroic generosity towards an impoverished knight.[4] In 1569, Major's description of Robin Hood was freely translated by Richard Grafton in his *Chronicle at large*. Out of his own head, apparently, Grafton added an important amplification; he said that Robin 'relieved and ayded' the poor 'with suche goodes as hee gate from the riche, which he spared not, namely the riche priestes, fat Abbottes, and the houses of riche Carles'.[5] By 'Carles' he meant churls, miserly fellows: men who ignored obligations to be hospitable and generous. Grafton's Robin Hood specialises in stealing not only from abbots but from the undeserving rich in general. But it was the poet William Warner who fixed the theme in the form in which it has become proverbial, in the second edition of his popular verse narrative *Albions England* (1589). In the inset story of Robin Hood, Warner says of the outlaw's followers that they 'tooke from rich to give the poore', whilst their leader would encourage them by demanding rhetorically, 'what juster life than ours?'[6] Warner has finally completed the process of turning the open-handed robber of medieval tradition into a principled figure engaged in a systematic project of redistribution from the rich to the poor.

The development has been enormously important. It has been taken up in nearly all the subsequent versions of the legend, and for very good reason. It has stamped it with a mark of distinction, and raised Robin Hood far above the ruck of common brigands. In modern times it has enabled Eric Hobsbawm, in an influential series of writings, to identify him as the archetype of the 'social bandit', a 'primitive rebel', who champions his people against oppression and engages in the redistribution of wealth out of an instinctive feeling for social justice.[7] This Robin Hood is an imaginatively and morally satisfying figure, who has had an enormous literary and cultural influence. But he is not to be found in any of the medieval texts. The Robin Hood of the original legend is a highway robber. He is usually represented as courteous and generous, at any rate to those who take his fancy, but he is a robber just the same.

One or two modern writers on the Robin Hood tradition have plainly found this troubling, to the extent that they have looked for ways to excuse and gloss over their hero's propensity for taking other men's goods. The most extreme exponent of this tactic is Joseph Falaky Nagy, who, noting that in several of the narratives the naked act of robbery is blandly expressed through euphemism – so that Robin commonly presents himself as collecting a debt, a toll, a payment for a meal – has leaped from this to the assertion that the outlaw is 'not really' a robber, and that he and his men 'Rarely . . . commit an outright act of theft'.[8] Nagy's comments are inaccurate as well as naively conceived, and spring from an ahistorical approach. In considering the early Robin Hood texts and documents, we should do well to remember Chief Justice Fortescue and his unembarrassed vaunting of the courageous English robber. Fortescue made his remarks in the second half of the fifteenth century: precisely the period, to judge from the evidence, when the popular enthusiasm for Robin Hood was at or near its height.

The earliest reference to Robin Hood as a hero of rhyming tales dates from the late 1370s. It is found in the 'B' text or first revision of Langland's religious allegory *Piers Plowman*. In a satirical passage, Sloth, an ill-educated parish priest, confesses that his knowledge of the Paternoster, the Latin text of the Lord's Prayer, is less than satisfactory. Instead, he says, he has learned 'rymes of Robyn hood', an admission that leaves him thoroughly exposed as a moral and intellectual inadequate.[9] Thirty-odd years later, an allusion in the dialogue *Dives and Pauper* shows an explicit hostility to the Robin Hood stories, while betraying their widespread popularity. Pauper, a mendicant preacher, deplores the fact that laymen would sooner hear 'a tale or a song of Robyn Hood' than hear mass or matins or a sermon.[10] The writers of the preaching tradition did not appreciate outlaw stories any more than they approved of robbers. Moreover, in the tales of the Robin Hood cycle, they recognised that they had a powerful rival for the attention of the people.

We cannot be certain how close the surviving tales may be to the songs and stories that were circulating in the late fourteenth century and the early decades of the fifteenth. At least one narrative is lost; we know of it only from a short Latin abstract made by a fifteenth-century chronicler.[11] Meanwhile, the oldest manuscript containing the text of a Robin Hood tale in English was compiled at the earliest in about 1450.[12] So the very oldest extant narrative poems exist only in versions that were current during the second half of the fifteenth century.

Already at this date the green-clad archer and his companions had begun to become established as favourite characters in the pageantry and drama that were popular forms of holiday entertainment. Three play-texts are still in existence, the earliest dating from about 1475, but these are very basic affairs, hardly more than excuses for a lot of mock fighting.[13] It is likely that much of the performance would have been improvised extempore, as the young men of the parish engaged in archery contests or went 'gathering' – collecting money among the crowds who turned out to see the fun.[14] This would have allowed for plenty of appropriate role playing, since, after all, relieving passers-by of their spare cash was one of the things for which Robin Hood's band was most famous. Certainly, a disapproving commentator in Elizabeth's reign complained that those who refused to pay up on these occasions could expect to be 'mocked and flouted at shamefully', and he says that in extreme cases they might even be ducked in water or 'carried upon a Cowlstaffe' – set astride a pole and carried about to be jeered at.[15] But it is unlikely that such rough treatment was typical. As a general rule, the 'gatherings' took place under very respectable auspices: they were organised, or at least countenanced, by the churchwardens, and the money that was collected was handed over to them. Some of it would be spent on a feast for the men who had played the parts of Robin Hood and his company, and the rest would be put towards the expenses of the parish.[16] This may offer another clue to the beginnings of the notion that Robin Hood 'took from the rich to give to the poor', since it was common for the parish authorities to pay out sums in charity to people who were in need.

It is fairly certain that festival occasions of this type came to be favourite times for singing or reciting the Robin Hood ballads and metrical tales. A ballad that has only survived in very late copies begins with an address to 'you gentlemen all . . . / That are in this bower within', which marks it plainly as written for delivery in the context of summertime revels.[17] The building of 'summer halls' or 'bowers' out of branches was a popular feature of the Robin Hood games and similar festivities.[18] Even the oldest tale in English, *Robin Hood and the Monk*, may show the influence of the holiday play-acting: the action begins at Whitsuntide, and Whitsun was the traditional time for Robin Hood plays and gatherings.[19] Again and again, the tales begin 'in summer', 'in a May morning', 'when leaves grow green'.[20] Unlike some of the other outlaws in poems and tales of the late Middle Ages, Robin and his men are never glimpsed contending with the rigours of a winter in the open.[21] They are inseparably associated with the landscape of early summer.

Just as much as the play-texts, the ballads and metrical tales are works designed for performance. Most of the people who enjoyed them would experience them not as private readers but as members of a group, listening to a recital by a minstrel or else by some amateur enthusiast like Langland's deadbeat priest. Who was it who formed the audience for the plays and tales? The Scottish chronicler Walter Bower, writing in the 1440s, said that it was the '*stolidum vulgus*', the stupid rabble, who made their holiday entertainment from 'comedies and tragedies' about Robin Hood and his men. He said that they preferred hearing minstrels chant tales on this subject more than on any other.[22] Records suggest that the plays and festival role playing flourished chiefly in an urban context, and most of all in certain market towns.[23] The reason for this may partly be that such places were relatively prosperous, and could find the money to mount such displays. The performers and the core audience at these events will have been mainly artisans. However, the legend was certainly capable of appealing much more widely. In 1473, a Norfolk knight, Sir John Paston, complained in a letter about the desertion of a servingman whom he had kept in his employment for three years 'to pleye Seynt Jorge and Robynhod and the shryff off Notyngham'.[24] Evidently the man was a talented actor, a leading figure in shows put on to amuse the Paston household.

By the early years of the next century, Robin Hood role plays were among the pastimes of the highest in the land. Early in 1510, the young King Henry VIII, with a company of twelve noblemen, 'came sodainly in a mornyng, into the Quenes Chambre' dressed in clothes of Kendal green, with swords and bucklers, bows and arrows, 'like out lawes, or Robyn Hodes men'.[25] No doubt to their amusement, they startled the Queen and her ladies quite a lot. On that occasion, the main part of the entertainment took the form of dancing, perhaps the fashionable morris dances which became closely associated with Robin Hood role playing.[26] A few years later, in 1515, the King was content to take a less active part. This time he and his queen, Catherine of Aragon, were out for a summertime ride when they encountered a company of two hundred bowmen, all clothed in green. Their leader, who introduced himself as Robin Hood, asked the King if he would like to view an archery display. Afterwards he invited the King and Queen 'to come into the grene wood, and to se how the outlawes lyve'. They were escorted to a version of the traditional summer hall, made out of boughs and decorated with flowers. This one, with a hall and two chambers in it, is likely to have been bigger and more elaborate than most. Here they were served with 'outlawes brekefastes' of venison (what else?). The 'outlaws' on this occasion were men of the King's Guard.[27] Part of the inspiration for this show certainly came from *A Gest of Robyn Hode*, in which Robin entertains an unspecified King Edward and his retinue to a feast and archery contest in the forest near Nottingham.[28] Henry VIII's meeting with the 'outlaws' took place at Shooters Hill in Kent, a spot on the main route from London to Dover that had long been notorious for robberies.[29] Clearly, someone had decided that this was the perfect setting for a staged encounter with a legendary robber chief.

The Robin Hood figure excited the imaginations of men of widely differing birth and status. However, when we look closely at the known enthusiasts for the legend, it soon becomes clear that they had certain things in common. When Henry VIII dressed himself up as an outlaw and came with his friends to surprise the Queen and her ladies, he was not yet nineteen, an active young man, who took part regularly in jousts and other martial sports and was particularly famous for his skill as an archer.[30] In 1473, Sir John Paston was aged about thirty-three and though he was not a boy any more, by the reckonings of his own time he would not reach his middle age for a couple more years. Moreover, it is clear from family correspondence that his closest relatives saw him as inclined to immaturity. He was a bachelor, happier, it seems, to play at courtship than to settle down. He was a jousting champion, but when, on one occasion, he expressed pride in his achievements, he received a dismissive response from his serious-minded brother, who plainly felt the whole business was a frivolous distraction. More creditably, perhaps, but not without a bearing on the present issue, Sir John was a man of military experience.[31]

At a very much lower social level, in places like Reading and Amersham, it was the 'lads' or 'young men' of the parish who took their bows and arrows, dressed themselves in green and went about 'to gather for Robin Hood'.[32] The bows and arrows were not necessarily for show: in some places the entertainment included an archery contest. In 1583, an Elizabethan looked back nostalgically on the annual Robin Hood 'game' of his youth, organised by the town with the purpose of encouraging 'young men' and 'stripplings' to learn how to shoot.[33] In Henry VIII's reign, and for a while afterwards, the advancement of archery was still felt to be crucially important for the national defence.[34] In addition to the archery contests, of course, there were the plays: very simple texts, basic chains of rhyming dialogue on which to hang bouts of archery, wrestling, sword-play or fighting with staves. The evidence is scattered, but the direction in which it points is pretty plain. The glamour of Robin Hood, peerless archer, poacher, robber, acknowledged leader of a band of tough young men, was experienced, as one might have expected, principally by men, by young men, by young men with a taste for archery and various kinds of weapon-play. No doubt many of them acquitted themselves well in the drinking that accompanied the day's festivities. 'Manly men', their contemporaries would have called them, and 'good fellows'. But of that I shall have more to say later.

One very striking aspect of the Robin Hood figure is its fluid and multiple nature. The Robin Hood of popular tradition was never a single entity. There is evidence, sketchy but very suggestive, that as early as the thirteenth century names such as 'Robehod' and 'Robynhod' had become nicknames used by or applied to particular individuals, some of whom, at any rate, were noteworthy for typical Robin Hood activities, such as robbery, archery or poaching. In this sense even the 'real' Robin Hood had a multiple existence.[35] By the time the Robin Hood role-playing games had become a popular feature of the summer festivities, every Whitsun saw a new crop of master outlaws, surrounded by uproarious bands, parading in the streets and greens of various towns and villages. Meanwhile, even the Robin Hood of the metrical tales is far from being a single unified figure. In *Robin Hood and the Potter*, which was written down in about 1500, the outlaw is a character out of farce: at first an unsuccessful robber, who even with sword and buckler turns out to be no match for the two-hand staff of the stalwart Potter, and then a trickster, who visits Nottingham using the Potter's gear and clothes as a disguise, and persuades the Sheriff to come to the forest with him, where he promises to show him Robin Hood. Of

56

course, once among the trees, Robin blows his horn and summons his men. It's a light-hearted tale throughout: the Sheriff comes to no great harm, just the loss of his horse and gear, and the mockery of his wife when he reaches home. As for the Potter, he is handsomely recompensed. But this Robin Hood, far from robbing only the rich, is prepared to attack even a craftsman travelling to market with his wares.[36]

The real hero of the oldest of these tales, *Robin Hood and the Monk*, is not Robin himself, who is captured early in the story, but his 'man' Little John, whose fidelity, daring and ingenuity bring about his escape. John's behaviour is the more admirable in that Robin, before his capture, has provoked him to a serious quarrel. The two outlaws were on their way to Nottingham, competing at archery as they went, and Robin, to his great disgust, had shot less well than his follower. This Robin is neither courteous nor generous but churlish, mean and a bad loser; he refuses to pay off a bet, calls John a liar and even hits him. John goes back to the forest, saying that he will leave his service, but when he hears of his master's capture, he forgets his anger and risks his life to save him. Robin's role in this tale is largely that of a foil to the best-known member of his band: the effect of his bad treatment of John is to throw the latter's loyalty into high relief.

As in *Robin Hood and the Potter*, the story turns on trickery and concealed identity, but in *Robin Hood and the Monk*, the outlaws show themselves very much more violent. When Robin is arrested, he kills twelve Nottingham men before his sword breaks. These are not men-at-arms, but ordinary townsfolk, armed, as the Potter was, with staves. The alarm has been raised by a monk, who hates Robin because he once robbed him of more than £100 (an enormous sum for the time). The monk is sent with letters to the King, to tell him of Robin's arrest; but he is held up on the road by Little John and Much the miller's son, who murder not only him but also his 'litull page, / Ffor ferd [fear] lest he wold tell'. Then they retrieve the letters and take them to the King, who, not knowing who they are, rewards them for their news, and sends them back to Nottingham with a warrant to fetch Robin. With the royal seal to vouch for them, they are allowed into the town, where the Sheriff receives them as King's messengers and treats them to a feast. But at night they make their way to the jail and set Robin free. During the course of the jail-break, Little John adds to the casual carnage by running his sword through the jailer. These are outlaws as heroic killers, men of their hands, reckless and ruthless. Their virtues are courage, and, on John's part, his exemplary loyalty.[37]

Typical of Robin in this and other tales is his religious devotion to the Virgin Mary and to the mass.[38] It is to hear the mass that Robin ventures into Nottingham, and he prays to Mary to bring him out again safely. After Robin's capture, the memory of his devotion to the Virgin is a comfort to

Little John, who takes it as a guarantee that his master will escape execution. He also says that Mary's power will assist him in intercepting the monk. In effect, he appeals for her intercession to help him carry out a murder. Many stories were told in devotional works of the Virgin's interventions on behalf of those who prayed to her regularly, even those who seemed to be least deserving. A particularly striking tale was that of the thief who was saved from hanging when 'the blessed Virgin sustained and hanged him up with her hands three days that he died not ne [nor] had no hurt'. His executioners took the point and let him go, whereupon he immediately entered a monastery.[39] Compared to this, Robin's rescue from the Sheriff's jail is a very modest sort of miracle. On the other hand, one feels that any competent preacher of the time would have pointed out that the author of *Robin Hood and the Monk* is lacking in his grasp of Christian principles. In this tale, Robin Hood is not only a robber but a homicide. However, his escape from jail prompts no thought of repentance in him, let alone of devoting himself to religion; instead, he returns to the carefree life of the greenwood to feast on stolen venison.[40]

The most elaborate of the surviving medieval tales, *A Gest of Robyn Hode*, is extant only in printed editions. In its present form it probably dates from the second half of the fifteenth century. The author has taken a number of shorter stories, most of which are otherwise lost, and combined them into a single ambitious narrative. One of the main threads of the plot concerns Robin's befriending of a knight, at first unnamed, but later in the poem called Sir Richard at the Lee, and the latter's subsequent involvement in the outlaws' affairs. Another traces the course of the feud between the outlaws and the Sheriff of Nottingham.

The knight comes into the narrative near the start, when he is held up by Robin's men on his way through Barnsdale. Told that a well-known outlaw is expecting him to dinner, he shows no anxiety. It shortly transpires that he has very little on him worth stealing. He explains that he has spent all he had to buy a pardon for his son, who has killed two men in a joust. He has even had to mortgage his lands to the abbot of St Mary's Abbey. Now the abbot is about to foreclose, and the knight expects to lose everything. Robin agrees to lend him the £400 that he needs to redeem his lands, although the only guarantor the knight can offer is the Virgin Mary. Later in the tale, the outlaws hold up one of the monks of St Mary's, the high cellarer, and rob him of twice the sum. When the knight comes to pay off his debt, Robin refuses to accept it, saying that he has been paid by Our Lady.

Meanwhile, Little John, whom Robin had seconded to the service of the knight, has since been begged off him by the Sheriff of Nottingham, who is impressed by John's prowess as an archer. John has given the Sheriff an assumed name and the Sheriff has no notion that his new retainer is a notorious outlaw. Little John enters the Sheriff's service with no good intentions and soon arranges with the cook, who turns out to be another tough fellow, that they will plunder the Sheriff's strong-room and take his money and plate to Robin. Immediately afterwards, John caps even this exploit by decoying the Sheriff into an ambush whilst he is hunting in the woods. He is forced to have dinner off his stolen silver plate and to spend an uncomfortable night beneath the trees. In the morning, Robin lets him go, after he has sworn an oath of friendship to the outlaws. However, his word turns out to be worth no more than King John's was, in the close analogue to this episode that occurs in *Fouke le Fitz Waryn*.[41]

Once the Sheriff is back in Nottingham, he announces an archery contest, with a silver arrow as the prize. Robin cannot resist the chance to compete, though he does take a very large bodyguard. As soon as he wins the contest, the Sheriff's men attack him, and the outlaws have to fight their way out. Little John is injured and they are forced to take refuge in the castle of the knight, who now has a name, Sir Richard at the Lee. After Sir Richard has refused to hand them over, the Sheriff goes to the King for a warrant to arrest Sir Richard and captures him when he rides out hawking. By this time the outlaws are back in the greenwood, and Sir Richard's wife rides to find them. Robin and his men intercept the Sheriff's posse in the Nottingham streets, kill the Sheriff and release Sir Richard. Now he, too, must take to the greenwood. His lands, of course, are confiscated.

With the Sheriff dead, the King himself comes to Nottingham, intending to capture Robin and Sir Richard. But he cannot track Robin down until he takes the advice that he and five of his knights should ride through the greenwood disguised as monks. Sure enough, they are held up, robbed and in accordance with Robin's custom, made to have dinner with him. Afterwards they are treated to the spectacle of an archery contest among the outlaws. But when Robin sees the King's face up close, he recognises him and kneels, and so do all the rest. The King grants them pardons, Sir Richard receives his lands back, and Robin is given a place at court in the King's service. With any other legendary outlaw, this would be the end of the story. However, after a while, Robin grows tired of life at court and makes an excuse to return to the greenwood, where he lives as an outlaw for a further twenty-two years. He is finally killed through the treachery of the prioress of 'Kyrkesly', his close relation, who betrays him to his enemy, her lover.

Lengthy and complex, *A Gest of Robyn Hode* is something more than a simple tale, and much more than a ballad. In effect, it amounts to an outlaw romance. It is in keeping with the genre that the Robin Hood figure is accorded many of the attributes that would be appropriate to a hero of chivalry. In the opening stanzas we are told that he is a proud outlaw, and the most courteous outlaw there ever was. He is devout, and hears mass every day, not just once (as enjoined by the rules of knighthood) but three times. He is honourable in his treatment of women, and will never attack a company in which a woman is travelling. And later, in his dealings with the knight, he shows himself to be conspicuously generous. All of these are qualities that are supposed to be characteristic of aristocrats, 'gentlemen of birth', and equally they are suited to the hero of a romance, who was in any case nearly always a prince, knight or baron.[42] But from the earliest stanzas of *A Gest of Robyn Hode*, and also in the two other early tales, the point is stressed that this is a hero who makes no pretensions to coming from an aristocratic family, but who is proud to declare himself a man of yeoman status.

Robin Hood's identity as a yeoman sets him apart not only from most of the heroes of romance but also from earlier outlaws of legend. Hereward, Fouke Fitz Waryn, the fictional Gamelyn, were all 'noble robbers' in a literal sense, gentlemen bandits, men of good family. In Robin Hood we have for the first time a heroic robber who is avowedly not of gentle birth. It has long been accepted that his status as a yeoman is an important clue to the cultural origins of the legend, the social group who stimulated its development, the audience for whom the tales were first composed.[43]

What did the term 'yeoman' convey to a late-medieval audience? A yeoman was originally an officer in a nobleman's household, below the rank of esquire, but higher than the grooms or menials. He was not of gentle blood, but nor was he a serf; he was freeborn, and his place was recognised as an honourable one. Yeomen officers of this kind often had skills as huntsmen and an association with the forest environment. Chaucer's Yeoman in the Prologue to *The Canterbury Tales* is the Knight's servant, but he is also a forester, skilled in woodcraft, wearing the huntsman's green clothing and carrying a horn. He also carries the bow that was both the mark of a huntsman and in wartime the yeoman's weapon par excellence. But although Chaucer's Yeoman is in some senses typical of his kind, the term 'yeoman' was already coming to have a wider range of reference, and to denote a status within society as well as a type of service within the noble household. It was being used increasingly to describe the social group of free landholders who were neither serfs nor gentry. In law, these were sometimes viewed as the equivalent of artisans; and artisans, too, came to be described as yeomen.[44] Yeomen of several of these types may be found in the early Robin Hood tales. In *A Gest*, Robin lends Little John to the impoverished knight, to be his servant and have a yeoman's place with him. Here, it is clear that service is the point. Similarly, the monk whom Little John, Much and Scarlock hold up on the high road is accompanied by 'two and fyfty wyght [strong] yonge yemen', who are his servants and bodyguard. But Robin, who is in no man's service, is also a yeoman. Little John describes him as 'a yeman of the forest', and Robin later applies the same description to himself and his men, adding in explanation, 'We lyve by our kynges dere'. These are yeomen as huntsmen and foresters, conceived of as an identity which is separable from that of servant.[45] In *Robin Hood and the Potter*, we have a third kind of yeoman in the Potter, who refers to himself as 'a pore yeman'. Since, like Robin, he is plainly not in service, this must be in reference to his standing in society, as a free man of a certain substance. Between him and Robin there would seem at first sight to be little in common, but after their fight Robin recognises him as a kindred spirit and offers him a 'ffelischepe', a fellowship or partnership, which the Potter gladly accepts.[46]

It was artisan yeomen of this last type, living in the towns, who took up the Robin Hood figure with relish and incorporated it into their holiday entertainments. *Robin Hood and the Potter* seems calculated to appeal to such an audience, and its affinity with the world of the municipal shows is suggested by the fact that, at some point before about 1560, it formed the basis of a play-text, written for performance at 'Maye games' or summer festivals.[47] An allusion thirty years later indicates that the Potter, flourishing his 'two handed staffe', was a well-recognised figure in the festival processions.[48]

The bones of that particular story are very old: in disguising himself as a potter to visit his enemy's stronghold, Robin Hood is following in the footsteps of Hereward and other outlaws of legend.[49] However, in this version, the potter who provides the disguise becomes a prominent character in his own right, a tough fighter, who shows himself more than a match for Robin, and gives him such a beating that Little John and the rest are forced to stop the fight. The Potter then follows his triumph with some pointed comments on Robin's lack of 'cortesey' in holding up 'a pore yeman' like himself. Robin accepts these strictures meekly, and hails them as an expression of 'god yemenrey', good 'yeomanry', proper yeomanlike behaviour.[50] Altogether, the scenario in these opening stanzas hugely flatters the craftsman at the expense of the outlaw chief. Moreover, though Robin Hood himself is unquestionably the hero of the rest of the tale, he achieves his exploits in disguise, in effect as a stand-in potter. It's as if he becomes the craftsman's wild alter ego, who takes crazy risks, behaves in flamboyant ways and runs rings round authority in the person of the Sheriff.

It has been argued that *Robin Hood and the Potter*, early though it is, already bears signs of a process by which the legend of the yeoman outlaw was adapted to the imaginative requirements of an artisan audience.[51] Certainly, the two other early tales show no sign of a special regard for the feelings of urban craftsmen. Earlier in this chapter, I mentioned that in

Robin Hood and the Monk, the cornered Robin cuts down twelve men from the posse of Nottingham citizens who turn out to arrest him. *A Gest of Robyn Hode* is not so bloodthirsty. However, after Robin, in the forest, has made his peace with the King, the two ride to Nottingham with their respective followings, all dressed alike in outlaw's green. This causes terror in the town: the Nottingham yeomen and their 'knaves' or servants, seeing an enormous band of outlaws on the way, anticipate a blood-bath and run for their lives. The moment is treated as humorous; there is a gleeful description of how even the crippled old women hop frantically away on their crutches. Meanwhile, the King is laughing his head off. The joke is not one that has been designed to pander to the pride of yeomen artisans.[52] These two tales, *Robin Hood and the Monk* and *A Gest of Robyn Hode*, are the oldest and most important. Since, as we have seen, they feature townsmen merely as the corpses who mark the hero's prowess or the cowards whose fleeing backs proclaim his bloody reputation, it doesn't seem likely that they were composed with an urban audience primarily in view.

Many years ago, in his book *The Outlaws of Medieval Legend*, Maurice Keen made a detailed case for arguing that Robin Hood was first and foremost a hero for the peasantry, the labourers and farmers. He identified the yeomanry with the most prosperous and independent section of this group, and interpreted the Robin Hood figure as a voice of social justice and a champion of the poor.[53] It's an attractive picture, and one that chimes with the now traditional notion of Robin Hood as the archetypal 'social bandit'. Unfortunately, there are a number of reasons why it doesn't fit the facts, as Keen himself has pointed out more recently. The existing tales of Robin Hood show no trace of the specific aspirations and grievances of the late-medieval peasantry. Issues such as manorial serfdom or unfair wage regulation are completely absent from them. Moreover, although Robin frequently features as a scourge of the dishonourable and greedy, the targets of his rough justice are either grasping monks or his inevitable enemy, the Sheriff of Nottingham. Dislike of sheriffs and of worldly clerics was widespread, and certainly wasn't restricted to any one social stratum.[54] In fact, as we have seen, Robin Hood's enthusiasm for robbing the clergy finds a close parallel in the attitudes attributed to the 'shaveldours', the gentlemen robbers described in *Fasciculus Morum*.[55] It is also the case that when the outlaw extends his help to a traveller who is down on his luck, as he does in *A Gest of Robyn Hode*, the man he befriends is not a serf, nor even a yeoman, but a knight, a man of higher status than his own. True, at an early point in the same tale Robin instructs his men not to rob or injure any 'husbonde', any husbandman or farmer. But leaving aside the fact that no highwayman ever grew rich by robbing small agriculturalists, this hardly shows a special identification with the peasantry. Preying on the

62

poor was against the laws of chivalry. As at many other points in this particular text, the outlaw is being made to conform to the behaviour expected of a hero of romance.

Originally, as we have seen, the term 'yeoman' signified an officer of middling rank within a noble household.[56] In his full-length study of the Robin Hood figure, the historian James Holt makes a strong case for his view that it was household officers of this kind who were the primary audience for the tales. He points out that several of the recurrent preoccupations in the stories of the Robin Hood corpus are with topics of particular importance to such men: the giving of 'livery', for instance, an identifying badge or garment, and 'fee', the payment that was made to a retainer. He also notes the stress laid on the outlaws' detailed knowledge of the rules of 'curteyse', courtesy, appropriate and mannerly behaviour. He suggests that these are indications that the tales were composed initially for performance within the households of the knights and the nobility, for the entertainment of their yeomen servants.[57] Holt's theory has not gone without challenge. When his book first appeared, it was reviewed at length by R. Barrie Dobson and John Taylor, the editors of a fine anthology of Robin Hood ballads and related material. On the basis of Holt's arguments, they were prepared to accept that performance within the feudal household had left its marks on the cycle. However, they were reluctant to give up entirely the notion of Robin Hood as in some sense a popular figure, a hero for the common man. They note the length of time (perhaps as long as two hundred years) that the legend was in process of taking shape before the earliest extant tales were written down. They argue for the possibility that the hero began as, to use their words, 'a figure of genuinely popular notoriety, later given a veneer of semi-courtly attributes'.[58] Perhaps this may have been so. It is a suggestion that is, in its nature, impossible to prove or disprove. Certainly, it is a weakness in Holt's argument that all the textual evidence he cites is drawn from *A Gest of Robyn Hode*, in which the hero is a far more courtly figure than in either of the two other early metrical tales. I believe that Holt is right that the earliest extant Robin Hood tales show signs of having been written to appeal to an audience of yeomen servitors. Moreover, I think there is additional evidence that may be brought to support his case, specifically from *Robin Hood and the Monk*, a text he and others have tended to neglect. On the other hand, the outlaw heroes who emerge from my reading of this text, as also from my reading of *A Gest of Robyn Hode*, are somewhat less courtly, much less conformist, more distinctively yeomanly as opposed to gentlemanly, than Holt's interpretation would make them. They are wilder altogether, in fact. They may even be felt to answer to Dobson and Taylor's dream of a 'popular' Robin Hood. But since this is about to lead us into a whole new topic, it seems a good idea to end this chapter and start another.

6

Good Fellows and Sworn Brothers

Of all the early Robin Hood narratives, *A Gest of Robyn Hode* is by far the most elaborate and impressive. As such, it has tended to draw to itself a very large share of the detailed historical and critical attention that has been paid to these tales. It is certainly a rewarding text to study, but for now I want to look more closely at the oldest vernacular tale of all, *Robin Hood and the Monk*. As I noted earlier, the true hero of this narrative is not Robin Hood himself but his equally famous companion, Little John. The central theme of this story is the relationship between master and man, and this is explored through the shifts and reversals in the relationship between these two principals.

At the start of the tale, John addresses Robin as 'my dere mayster'. He acknowledges himself subordinate, but in language that combines respect with affection. And Robin, in return, singles him out. When the master outlaw announces his trip to Nottingham, Much the miller's son urges him to go with twelve of his men as a bodyguard; but Robin will take no one with him but John. John, he says, shall carry his bow for him. But this is a subordination too far for John; he refuses the role of bow-carrier, and tells Robin that they shall both carry their own. As they go, he proposes, they shall compete with each other at shooting for penny wagers. But although Robin accepts John's insistence that both of them go armed with bows, he refuses to admit his follower to the kind of equality implied by the terms of the shooting wager. Instead, he says he will bet three pennies for every one of John's. In what seems like an implicit comment on Robin's arrogance, the next stanza describes the shooting match in terms that stress the formal equality in status of the two outlaws: 'Thus shet thei forth, *these yemen too*' (my italics).[1] Though Robin is the master, the two are both of them yemen. And on this occasion, at any rate, Little John is the better archer, and wins as much as five shillings (sixty pennies; so even at a bet of three for one, Robin had been shooting rather badly). Robin refuses to acknowledge that he has lost; he tells John he is a liar and hits him. Now, according to the honour system adhered to by the nobility and gentry, either of these acts would be an intolerable shame to the man who meekly accepted them.[2] Of course, these men are not of gentle blood. Moreover, Robin is John's master. To hit one's servant to correct him was acceptable, even required behaviour.[3] On the other hand, John is plainly in the right on this particular matter. He draws his sword in anger, but then he contents himself with saying that if Robin were not his master, he would certainly have vengeance on him. Commoner though he is, John plainly does believe that he has honour that would normally require vindicating by violent means. But the fact that Robin is his master changes things somewhat. There is a promise between them, whether explicit or simply implied in the relationship of master and subordinate. It is summed up in this quotation from a mid-fifteenth-century indenture of apprenticeship: the apprentice 'shall do his masters no injury nor see injury done to them by others, but prevent the same as far as he can'.[4] John is not Robin's apprentice, but the relationship is closely analogous. To attack one's master is a serious violation. As a measure of how it was seen in medieval England, we might note that if a servant attacked his master and caused his death, he was liable to be found legally guilty not of ordinary murder, but because of his duty of obedience and faith, of a worse offence, petty treason.[5] It was seen as the same order of offence (though lower in gravity) as a treasonous attack on the Crown. John's personal honour as a man, that leads him to refuse to brook insult, is in conflict with his obligations to his master; and although Robin has abused his authority, John cannot fight him without occasioning a breach of his own faith. So instead, he tells Robin to find himself another man somewhere else and walks off into the forest.

When John, safe in Sherwood, hears that Robin has been captured, he sets their quarrel on one side. Now that Robin needs him, John returns to acknowledging him as his 'maister'.[6] Though we need not doubt that his affection for Robin is an important part of his motive, his personal honour is also at issue. One of his responsibilities is to protect his master from his enemies. If he chooses at this point to repudiate Robin's claim on his loyalty, it will seem as if he is a coward – the most dishonourable of conditions.

As we have seen already, John, seconded by Much, eventually wins his master's freedom by his resourcefulness and by putting himself repeatedly at risk. But John, though he proves himself heroically faithful, is not in the least servile. Robin, who refused to honour a debt for five shillings, is now indebted to John for his life; and John has no hesitation in pointing this out. As he says to Robin, 'I have done the a gode turne for an evyll, / Quyte the whan thou may' (or, 'pay off the debt when you can'). Robin can see only one appropriate response: to reverse their positions. 'I make the maister,' he says, 'Off alle my men and me.' But this is not what John wants.

> 'Nay, be my trouth,' seid Litull John,
> 'So shalle hit never be;
> But lat me be a felow,' seid Litull John,
> 'No noder kepe I be.'[7]

'No, by my faith,' said Little John, 'so shall it never be; but let me be a fellow,' said Little John, 'I don't care about being anything else.'

John wants to be a 'fellow': the word is one with a great deal of resonance in the context of relationships in late-medieval England.

In its most general sense, a 'fellow' was simply a companion. However, the word sometimes denoted a servant or an inferior. Generally, when it did, the usage was condescending, or even derogatory. Altogether, such a meaning seems unlikely here; to say the least of it, it would make Little John's request implausibly submissive, considering the drift of the story as a whole. Much more commonly, a 'fellow' was an associate or partner, and in status terms, an equal, both of which senses are far more apt in the context of a reply to Robin's offer.[8] There were other, more specific meanings of 'fellow' that have a bearing on this passage. I shall examine them in detail in connection with *A Gest of Robyn Hode*. For now, it is enough to make the point that these meanings also imply relations of partnership and equality.

The last word in *Robin Hood and the Monk* is given to the King. Furious though he is when he learns how Little John has deceived him, he says of him that there are not in all England three such yeomen as he is; and he clarifies this point in the following line, when he states: 'He is trew to his maister'. The exemplary virtue of Little John, the outstanding yeoman hero, is his absolute fidelity. But this is not the King's final statement on the matter. He continues his reflections with the remark, 'Robyn Hode is ever bond to hym'.[9] There is a double meaning here. The surface sense is plain enough. After John's rescue of him from jail and the gallows, Robin is now bound to him, perpetually obliged to him in gratitude. However, in feudal society, the language of binding was also the language of vassalage and serfdom, and in these contexts to be bound to someone was to be in a relation of owing them service. John has served Robin with a faithfulness that has gone far beyond anything that might reasonably have been expected of him. As a result, Robin, the master, has become 'bound' in an obligation of service to his follower.[10] Robin attempts to dissolve this paradox by offering to give John his place as master outlaw. But John does not choose simply to reverse the order of their existing hierarchical relationship. Instead, he asks to be acknowledged and treated as a 'fellow'.

At least as much as in *Robin Hood and the Potter*, the question centrally at issue in *Robin Hood and the Monk* is the nature of 'good yeomanry'. In *Robin Hood and the Potter*, this is a matter partly of 'courtesy', knowing the proper way to behave to people, and partly of solidarity among men of yeoman status, whether artisan or forest outlaw. In *Robin Hood and the Monk*, the pre-eminent virtue embodied by Little John is loyalty; but his practice of it is not at all slavish. The yeoman demands that he be treated with proper fairness and respect. Moreover, his ideal social relationship is not patterned on the relations of master and servant; it is a partnership between equals.

James Holt dismisses this tale as 'shallow' and sums up the ending as 'a paean for loyal service'.[11] Neither description strikes me as apt. Despite the stress on loyalty, the tale is hardly geared to inculcate such values as might suit the interests of masters. Rather, it speaks to the self-respect of a class of tough henchmen, men who are fully aware of their worth, and who take pride in following their own demanding code of behaviour. These men were their masters' bodyguards and enforcers, as Little John and Much are for Robin Hood in *Robin Hood and the Monk* and *A Gest of Robyn Hode*. In time of war, they went into battle with their masters and fought under their command. Retainers, as the Lawyer points out in *Utopia*, made up the main strength of the army.[12] This had been true since the mid-fourteenth century.[13] More's traveller, Hythlodaeus, is equally correct to point out in reply that such men had a reputation for being all too ready to engage in robbery.[14] It should not surprise us to find them forming an appreciative audience for tales of an outlaw-robber and his companions. Nor is it odd to find that questions of honour are very much at stake in these tales. Living and fighting alongside their masters, yeomen servants absorbed aristocratic ideas on such matters and adapted them to fit their own circumstances. Courage, intolerance of insult, faithfulness to his promise – all these proofs of manly honour are displayed by Little John in *Robin Hood and the Monk*, as he negotiates the tricky labyrinth of principle that arises from being a proud, tough man, with a master who doesn't – at first – treat him with proper respect.

Life in the feudal household will have brought the yeoman servitor into contact with other elements of aristocratic culture besides the honour code; among them, no doubt, the stories and motifs of the outlaw legend as incorporated in romance narratives like *Fouke le Fitz Waryn*. Holt goes so far as to argue that it was only within this milieu that men of yeoman status would ever have come across the tales of outlaw life. He points out that most of the older material is in languages, Latin or French, that imply a knightly audience.[15] This argument will not really stand up. Much outlaw literature has simply not survived, including some important narratives in

English. Vernacular tales and songs about Hereward and his followers certainly existed at one time, and may even have been circulating in oral tradition as late as the fifteenth century.[16] There was also an English version of the romance about Fouke Fitz Waryn.[17] The fact is that we simply don't know how widely within society the outlaw tales were known before the emergence and rise to popularity of the Robin Hood tradition.

However, it is certainly true that, as I noted in Chapter Four, all the early manifestations of the outlaw theme display aristocratic attitudes and values.[18] In one form or another, the narratives that survive concern themselves with the deeds of a man of knightly family or the equivalent whose inheritance is withheld from him unjustly. This theme persists in *The Tale of Gamelyn*, the oldest surviving outlaw narrative in English. However, in this text the status of the hero is highly equivocal – he is a younger son, brought up as a scullion, who nevertheless wins through to a place as a landed gentleman. I have already commented that the story reads very much like a wish-fulfilment fantasy for the younger sons of knights and gentlemen, who, under the custom of primogeniture, were often excluded from inheriting any part of their fathers' estates.[19] Such landless men of gentle birth often took service in feudal households. The Folville brothers were younger sons of very much this type and several of them are known to have been in service as household retainers.[20] In relation to *The Tale of Gamelyn*, I have also noted the role of the hero's pantryman sidekick, Adam, and the latter's glittering prospect of landed wealth.[21] No doubt, considered as a tale of triumphant underdogs, the tale had and has an appeal that is potentially a wide one. But the exploits of Gamelyn and his companion must surely have found their most eager audience among the servants, both gentlemen and commoners, in noble and knightly households.

In the Robin Hood narratives, the endangered inheritance becomes very much a subsidiary theme. It occurs only in *A Gest*, and only in relation to the hero's friend, Sir Richard at the Lee. Robin Hood himself is no landholder. When Sir Richard receives his lands back, Robin, for his part, is given a place in the royal service. This, on the face of it, is appropriate bait to ensure the loyalty and good behaviour of a landless yeoman. But as Dobson and Taylor have pointed out, one of the most striking things about Robin Hood is that he has rejected service; in a society where almost everyone is bound by their ties to a superior, Robin serves no one. And as we have seen, a career of attendance on the King loses its appeal for him very soon. After just fifteen months, he abandons his post at court and runs off again to the greenwood.[22] If, as seems likely, the Robin Hood tales evolved to suit the tastes of yeomen servitors, it is nonetheless true that the values the hero himself embodies are certainly not those of service to a master.

Who, then, is Robin Hood? Alone among the English outlaw heroes, he is a man without personal history. Hereward lost his lands with the Norman occupation; Fouke quarrelled with King John; Gamelyn was outlawed as a result of his brother's plots. The other great yeoman-outlaw tale, *Adam Bell, Clim of the Clough, and William of Cloudesly*, tells how the three heroes of the title 'were outlawed for venyson', for poaching deer.[23] But none of the early tales of Robin Hood supply any hint of a reason as to why he originally took to the greenwood. True, by the first half of the seventeenth century, there were at least three different versions of Robin Hood's outlawing to choose from, but this fact in itself strongly suggests that no tale of the kind had been transmitted as part of the legend's core.[24] For this most famous of the medieval outlaw heroes, his outlawry is not just an episode, but a way of life, and a central part of his identity; outside the greenwood, Robin is nothing and no one, a point driven home during his spell in the King's service. When Robin first comes to court, he brings with him a following of pardoned outlaws and substantial personal wealth. But within the year, he has run through the lot, and since he can no longer pay their 'fe', most of his men have left him. His money has been spent on treating 'knyghtes and . . . squyres' to lavish hospitality with a view to enhancing his prestige.[25] This is, after all, very much the way he had lived when he was an outlaw, spreading a luxurious table and showering largesse on his knightly superiors. But as a yeoman officer of the Crown, it's not a style of living he can sustain.

> Robyn sawe yonge men shote
> Full fayre upon a day;
> 'Alas!' than sayd good Robyn,
> 'My welthe is went away.
>
> 'Somtyme I was an archere good,
> A styffe and eke a stronge;
> I was compted the best archere
> That was in mery Englonde.'[26]

Robin saw young men shooting very well, one day; 'Alas!' then said good Robin, 'My wealth has gone away. Once I was a good archer, resolute, and also strong; I was accounted the best archer that there was in merry England.'

What Robin does not state, but the audience perfectly well knows, is that his former magnificence owed very much less to his marksmanship than to the use to which he had been accustomed to put it: holding up travellers on the highway.

For Robin Hood is, first and foremost, the outlaw hero as robber.

Within the Robin Hood tradition, the theme of robbery, previously a subsidiary element of the outlaw legend, is brought into the foreground. The landless yeoman who refuses to serve has, besides robbery, no other resource; and plunder will keep him in a style far more seductively splendid than ever a master would.

From the beginning of *A Gest of Robyn Hode*, the theory and practice of robbery are central to the story. The narrative starts with Robin's refusing to sit down to dinner until some 'gest' is present who, as he puts it, 'may pay for the best'. In case the listener has missed the point of Robin's desire for a visitor with well-lined pockets, his sidekick, Little John, asks for instructions in terms that make the whole matter absolutely plain. 'Tell us', he says,

> Where we shall take, where we shall leve,
> Where we shall abide behynde,
> Where we shall robbe, where we shal reve,
> Where we shal bete and bynde.

Where we shall take, where we shall leave, where we shall stay behind, where we shall rob, where we shall plunder, where we shall beat and bind.

To this detailed enquiry Robin has an equally detailed answer. 'Loke ye do no husbonde harme', he says – take care that you do no harm to any farmer –

> No more ye shall no gode yeman
> That walketh by grene wode shawe,
> Ne no knyght ne no squyer
> That wol be a gode felawe.
>
> These bisshopes and these archebishoppes,
> Ye shall them bete and bynde;
> The hye sherif of Notyingham,
> Hym holde ye in your mynde.[27]

Nor shall you [harm] any good yeoman who walks among the woodland thickets, nor any knight nor any squire who is prepared to be a good fellow. These bishops and these archbishops, you shall beat and bind them; the high sheriff of Nottingham, keep him in mind.

Robin's dislike of wealthy churchmen has been discussed before; as for the Sheriff of Nottingham, every child knows that for reasons that are now long forgotten, he is Robin's traditional opponent, his steady persecutor and his victim. Should Robin's men meet with any of these, they are to receive rough treatment. However, no injury is to be offered to yeomen, knights and squires – so long as they behave themselves like good fellows.

To a modern reader of *A Gest of Robyn Hode*, this injunction is mildly enigmatic. More than one commentator on the Robin Hood tradition has picked on this term 'good fellow', and on 'fellow' and 'fellowship', as expressing some important values informing the early texts.[28] It's clear to me that they are absolutely right in this, but also that no one hitherto has fathomed more than a part of the implications of these terms in the context of the outlaw tale. In particular, no one has properly explained what it means for the victim of a robbery to show himself to be a 'good fellow'.

As we have seen in connection with *Robin Hood and the Monk*, the word 'fellow' very commonly meant an associate or companion; a 'good fellow', then, was first and foremost a good friend or comrade. However, from the mid-fourteenth century, a 'good fellow' quite often meant a reveller, a boon companion or drinking partner, and this became one of the dominant meanings. We find the preacher John de Bromyard denouncing those 'lechers and gluttons who seek out bad company and taverns, whose feet by night and day run . . . towards wickedness: these,' he complains, 'are called "good fellows"'.*[29] The same theme is taken up in a fifteenth-century sermon in English:

> He that is a ryatour and a grete hawnter of tavernys or of ale howsys, and a grete waster of his goodes, then is he callyd 'a good felaw'.[30]
>
> *He who is a reveller and a great frequenter of taverns or of alehouses and a great waster of his goods, then is he called 'a good fellow'.*

Some commentators have attempted to relate this meaning of 'good fellow' to its appearances in the Robin Hood texts.[31] However, although it sheds some light on the wider associations of good fellowship, and we shall return to it later on, it doesn't really offer much help in clarifying Robin's instructions to his men not to injure those travellers who are prepared to be good fellows.

The expression 'good fellow' also occurs in a rather enigmatic speech in the mid-sixteenth-century playlet that was based on *Robin Hood and the Potter*. When the Potter first meets with Robin Hood, before they begin to fight, he says:

> But if thou be a good felowe,
> I wil sel mi horse, mi harneis, pottes and paniers to,
> Thou shalt have the one halfe, and I wil have the other.
> If thou be not so content,
> Thou shalt have stripes, if thou were my brother.

---

* *boni socii*

> *But if you should be a good fellow, I will sell my horse, my harness, pots and*
> *panniers too; you shall have one half, and I will have the other. If you*
> *should not be content to do this, you shall have a beating, even if you were*
> *my brother.*

Robin pays no attention to this offer, but demands that the Potter pay him
a toll, a demand the Potter resists. Instead, he issues Robin with a
challenge:

> If thou be a good felowe, as men do the call,
> Laye away thy bowe,
> And take thy sword and buckeler in thy hande,
> And se what shall befall.[32]

> *If you should be a good fellow, as men say you are, put away your bow and*
> *take your sword and buckler in your hand and see what will happen.*

Not only does Robin instruct his men, in *A Gest of Robyn Hode*, to do no
harm to 'good fellows', but he himself has a reputation as a 'good fellow' to
which he is expected to live up. It has something to do with fair play in a
fight: a good fellow does not hide behind a distance weapon, but is
prepared, when called upon, to fight hand to hand. It also has something to
do with being prepared to go half shares when this is required of one.

Further light is shed on the expression by a passage in William Caxton's
History of Reynard the Fox, translated from the Dutch in 1481, and roughly
contemporaneous with *A Gest of Robyn Hode*. The Fox is describing how
he and the Wolf, after falling in with each other by chance, agreed to
become 'felaws':

> We promysed eche to other to be trewe and to use good felawship and
> began to wandre to gyder. He stal the grete thynges and I the smalle and
> all was comyn bytwene us.[33]

> *We promised to be faithful to each other and to practise good fellowship and*
> *began to travel about together. He stole the big things and I the small and we*
> *held everything we had in common.*

Here, the expressions 'to become fellows' and 'to promise to use good
fellowship' imply entry into a special kind of relationship. 'Fellows' are
comrades who have promised to be faithful in their dealings with each
other, and who share everything they have. To put it at its most idealistic,
in their treatment of money and property, they resemble secular monks.

However, in *Reynard the Fox*, an intensely satirical text, the presentation
of good fellowship is not in the least idealistic. The Fox claims that as

matters turned out, the Wolf bullied him and kept far more than his half share. Moreover, and this is important, these two, the Wolf and the Fox, are robbers. They are not working men who share what they earn; they are bandits, who have agreed to split their loot. In *Reynard the Fox*, the practice of fellowship in this special sense is located in the context of the subculture of robbers.

In fact, it is clear that it is more or less identical to a practice that flourished, and probably first developed, among soldiers: that of taking a 'sworn brother' or a 'brother in arms'. The institution was recognised by military courts. Men who elected to become 'brothers' swore to support one another in everything and to share equally all the profits of war. Though it had a chivalric colouring, in practice it was commonly a business partnership: your brother in arms was entitled to a half share of your loot, but in return for this, he was expected to help you in your enterprises and to come to your aid if you were in trouble. Sometimes the precise details of the agreement were embodied in a written contract, though this was not invariably the case. The essence of the brotherhood relationship was a bond between equals. It operated at all levels of the military profession, from princes and captains down to ordinary men-at-arms. However, the majority of brothers in arms were of relatively humble rank. It was an institution that particularly suited the needs of adventurers, men embarking on the profession of warfare in the hopes of making their fortunes, who had little to lose by sharing their chances of plunder, and much to gain by pooling their risks. In a high-risk profession, it operated as an insurance.[34]

Neither the *Oxford English Dictionary* nor the *Middle English Dictionary* include 'sworn brother' or 'brother in arms' among the various meanings of 'fellow' or 'good fellow'. However, the evidence of Caxton's *Reynard the Fox* is supported by that of various other texts, dating from the early fourteenth century onwards. For instance, in the romance of *Sir Ferumbras* (*c.* 1380), which belongs to the Charlemagne cycle, Oliver, famous for his comradeship with Roland, says of them both: 'We habbeth be [have been] felawes gode and trewe, in body and eke [also] on herte'. Further examples of this usage are given in the notes.[35]

Though existing studies of the practice of swearing brotherhood have focused on the ways in which it operated in a military context, there is plenty of evidence, albeit from fictional sources, that it had a much wider currency, though perhaps always only within certain specific masculine subcultures. In Chaucer's 'Pardoner's Tale', the three young men who resolve to go as avengers and seek out Death to kill him first swear an oath of brotherhood together, holding up their hands and promising 'To lyve and dyen ech of hem for oother'.[36] These young men are not soldiers but belong to a set of thriftless types who spend their time dancing, gambling and drinking in taverns. They are, in short, 'good fellows' of the kind denounced by Bromyard, though the phrase isn't used in this particular tale. As in *Reynard the Fox*, the treatment of the sworn brotherhood motif is disillusioned and satirical. At the end of the tale, the 'brothers' murder each other out of the purest greed, inspired by the hoard of gold they find which holds out the prospect of a life of endless indulgence.

'The Pardoner's Tale' is, in fact, a sermon, as is appropriate in view of its narrator's professional life as a member of the preaching clergy. The story proper is an anecdote or exemplum which illustrates the main theme, a condemnation of the sin of greed. That the chosen exemplum is also intensely derogatory to the practice of swearing brotherhood is not at all out of keeping. Similar stories occur in actual sermons of Chaucer's time and earlier.[37] The preachers were hostile to the swearing of brotherhood, just as they were discouraging to the outlaw legend.

Despite its chivalric associations, the sort of men who were most likely to swear oaths of brotherhood were rootless adventurers of one kind or another: at best, professional soldiers, and at worst robbers, the human counterparts of Reynard the Fox and his comrade the Wolf. Preachers and satirists were sceptical about the durability of oaths that were sworn by such men. According to the moral theologians, the nature of the robber's sin was greed. When greedy men swear oaths to each other, their commitment is likely to last only so long as their interests are identical. If the Fox and the Wolf should agree to practise good fellowship, the weaker of the two will very soon find that his comrade takes advantage of him. When three self-indulgent and violent young men find a heap of gold lying under a tree, it is entirely plausible that they should plot to kill each other.

However, even when brothers showed themselves true to their oaths, they might well find themselves at odds with the hard requirements of the moralist. To get a sense of how this might happen, it is instructive to look at a text that represents the relationship of sworn brothers from a positive point of view. This is the late thirteenth-century chivalric romance *Amis and Amiloun*, in which the two knightly heroes swear an oath to support each other 'In wele and wo, *in wrong and right*' (my italics).[38] This last turns out to be a condition of some importance in their agreement, since in the course of the story Amiloun is called upon to protect his friend with some very shifty behaviour. This serves to suggest that, idealistic though it might in some ways seem, there was a certain amorality and potential for lawlessness about the whole institution, even (perhaps especially) when it was taken most seriously.[39]

Another narrative in which an oath of brotherhood is treated seriously and positively is the yeoman–outlaw tale of *Adam Bell, Clim of the Clough, and William of Cloudesly*. At the outset of the story, we are told that the three heroes of the title 'swore them brethen', swore to be brothers, at the time they went to the woods as outlaws. Subsequently, Adam and Clym prove their loyalty and faith by risking their lives in a daring rescue of their captured 'brother', William.[40] We know from other fictional texts, as well as from extant written contracts of brotherhood, that one of the most important responsibilities of a man's brother in arms was to do everything possible to have him set free in the event of his being captured. The story of Adam Bell and his companions is a fairly close analogue to *Robin Hood and the Monk*. When he rescues Robin from the Sheriff's jail, Little John is showing himself faithful more in the manner of a sworn brother than of a hired servant. When he asks to be acknowledged as a fellow, it seems fairly certain that an important part of the context for his request, unspoken because taken for granted, is the tradition of swearing brotherhood, with all that this implied by way of equality and partnership.

Adam Bell is not the only outlaw tale in which an oath of brotherhood plays a part. Indeed, there are indications that such oaths of brotherhood or fellowship were reckoned to be a traditional part of the practice of 'going to the wood'. When Gamelyn offers Adam half his land to secure his freedom, he addresses him as 'brother Adam'. Later, before Gamelyn and Adam leave Johan's house for the wood, they take each other by the hand and drink a draught of wine, behaviour that implies the sealing of an agreement.[41] The whole affair is very strongly suggestive of a promise of brotherhood or fellowship. More explicitly, in *A Gest of Robyn Hode*, when Little John and the Sheriff's cook conspire to rob the Sheriff, they first agree to become 'felowes', and then (over a good deal of drink) they pledge themselves formally to go and join Robin in the greenwood.[42]

Among the legendary outlaws of the later Middle Ages, fellowship in the sense of brotherhood was a key institution. It also represented a set of core values, which included, between 'brothers', absolute loyalty, the sharing of resources and a basic equality of status, in addition to a general sense of honourable fair play to all.

These are the outlaws of legend, not of history. However, outlaws, like soldiers, were largely or wholly cut off from the usual networks of kinship; at all times they were highly at risk, and they depended on what they could plunder. As in the case of professional soldiers, the practice of swearing brotherhood would have offered them a kind of insurance, a guarantee of support; it would also have provided elements of social cohesion and stability in lives that otherwise must have had little or none. Altogether, it should hardly surprise us if oaths of brotherhood did indeed flourish among these violent fugitives. Two or three centuries later, the reformed highway robber John Clavell recorded that it was the custom of the seventeenth-century highwaymen, when they 'admitted a Brother' to their 'company', to bind him by an oath to be faithful to them.[43]

What about the highway robbers' victims? This investigation into the meaning of good fellowship took as its starting point a passage near the beginning of *A Gest of Robyn Hode*, in which Robin instructs his men not to harm yeoman, knight or squire 'That wol be a gode felawe'. We shall return to these lines in the next chapter, after we have looked at a very important analogue.

7

Guests at Robin Hood's Table

The story of the three revellers in 'The Pardoner's Tale' is only one of several places in *The Canterbury Tales* where Chaucer uses the motif of an oath of brotherhood. The two heroes of 'The Knight's Tale' have sworn an oath together before the story starts, but as soon as they fall in love with the same woman, all their promises go for nothing.[1] However, the tale with most resonance in relation to the outlaw legend, and especially *A Gest of Robyn Hode*, is 'The Friar's Tale'. This is primarily a satire against summoners, the officials who served summonses to appear before the Church courts. The summoner in 'The Friar's Tale' is a thoroughly corrupt character, who has no compunction at all about using his office to extort money. The story begins when he is riding to summons an elderly widow on a fabricated charge of sexual immorality. On the way, he meets another traveller:

> And happed that he saugh bifore hym ryde
> A gay yeman, under a forest syde.
> A bowe he bar, and arwes brighte and kene;
> He hadde upon a courtepy of grene,
> An hat upon his heed with frenges blake.
> 'Sire,' quod this somnour, 'hayl, and wel atake!'
> 'Welcome,' quod he, 'and every good felawe!
> Wher rydestow, under this grene-wode shawe?'[2]

It happened that he saw, riding ahead of him, a gay yeoman, along by a forest. He carried a bow, and arrows bright and keen; he wore a green jacket and on his head a hat with black fringes.

'Sir,' said this summoner, 'hail, and well overtaken!'

'Welcome,' he said, 'and [the same to] every good fellow! Where are you riding, along by this green-wood thicket?'

77

What are we to make of this yeoman in green, with his bow and arrows, encountered where a road runs alongside a forest? A forest that is also described as a 'grene-wode shawe': the phrase occurs nowhere else in *The Canterbury Tales*, though it is found twice in *A Gest of Robyn Hode*. Its first occurrence is during the passage in which Robin instructs his men how to treat the different classes of traveller; there it rhymes with 'gode felawe', as it does here.[3]

More than one critic has pointed out that the description of the 'gay yeman' is similar to that of the Yeoman, servant to the Knight, who is listed among the Canterbury pilgrims in the 'General Prologue'. Both wear green and carry a bow and arrows.[4] Meanwhile, some commentators have seen in the portrait of the Knight's Yeoman a possible allusion to Robin Hood.[5] So far as I am aware, no one has pointed out the resemblances between the yeoman of 'The Friar's Tale' and the members of Robin Hood's band of outlaws. In this connection, it is perhaps not too trivial to notice that in one very early fragment of rhyme, Robin Hood is described specifically as wearing a hat – though whether it had black fringes is not recorded.[6] More interesting and suggestive, however, is the occurrence of the phrase 'good felawe'. 'Welcome . . . and every good felawe!' So might Little John have hailed a knight, squire or yeoman passing by on the great north road.

The summoner, loath to admit to his despised profession, lies to this new acquaintance and tells him he is a bailiff. Immediately, the yeoman claims to be a bailiff, too. This stamps him as a yeoman officer, whose job is to manage his lord's property, including collecting rents and other due payments. The yeoman then makes a striking proposal. He suggests that as the two of them are both bailiffs, they should swear brotherhood to each other, and mentions that in his own part of the world he has a chest containing gold and silver, from which, if the summoner happens to visit him, he may have whatever he wants. The summoner agrees at once; so they take each other's hands and promise to be sworn brothers until death. As it transpires, the strange yeoman is no more a bailiff than the summoner is. After a while, he admits that he is not really a yeoman at all, but a devil in human form. This fails to warn off the foolish summoner. He is captivated by the thought of obtaining a 'brother's' half share of his new friend's wealth and winnings. When the devil makes a remark which implies that at some point the summoner will abandon him, he is shocked by the suggestion. 'I am a yeman, knowen is ful wyde . . . ' he says, and insists, 'My trouthe wol I holde to my brother, / As I am sworn'.[7] Loosely paraphrased, this means: I am a yeoman, with all that that implies by way of having a reputation to uphold; I won't break my sworn word to my 'brother'. Implicit here is another definition of 'good yeomanry': yeomen, it seems, pride themselves on keeping their promises. In the tales of the

78

Pardoner and the Knight, the oath of brotherhood throws into particularly sharp relief the subsequent betrayals. The irony in 'The Friar's Tale' operates more subtly. As a result of his very insistence on keeping his oath to his 'brother', the summoner is, in due course, carried off to Hell to stay with him for ever.

'The Friar's Tale' is based on a sermon exemplum which exists in various forms in a number of different medieval texts.[8] However, among the elements that Chaucer has added to the tale are the making of the devil into a green-clad yeoman, lurking beside a greenwood shaw, and the formal swearing of brotherhood between the devil and his intended prey. That he intended an allusion to the outlaw tales, I think can hardly be doubted. In the early part of 'The Friar's Tale', a reader or listener well versed in such tales might quite reasonably expect that this will turn out to be another of the same genre. Even when the yeoman describes himself as a bailiff, the claim very much leaves open the possibility that he is really a robber. A bailiff takes other folk's money; for a robber to call himself a bailiff would be a fine joke, and one not without analogues in the literature of robbery.[9] Shortly after this, the yeoman tells the summoner that his home is 'fer in the north contree'. It is often pointed out that this is an important clue to his true identity. Both in biblical tradition and folk cosmography, the north was the region associated with Hell.[10] However, if one had been listening to this tale in Chaucer's London, it would have come at least as naturally to have identified the northern home of this green-clad yeoman with Sherwood, or with places even further to the north: the notorious yeoman outlaw haunts of Barnsdale, Inglewood and Plumpton Park.

What is the point of this extended allusion? Within the tale itself, it operates as a sardonic comment on the Robin Hood legend: the 'gay yeman' in green turns out to be a devil in disguise. The Friar is a member of a preaching order; a general hostility to the outlaw tales would be perfectly in keeping with his professional outlook. In relation to *The Canterbury Tales* as a whole, it is of interest to note that *The Tale of Gamelyn* has only survived because it was widely copied with manuscripts of Chaucer's great poem, sometimes as 'The Cook's Tale of Gamelyn'. The assumption has generally been that it was found among Chaucer's papers at his death, and that he had intended to use it as source material for one of the tales, to be related either by the Cook or the Knight's Yeoman.[11] Taking this in conjunction with the description of the latter in the General Prologue, as well as with 'The Friar's Tale', it is reasonable to speculate that the themes of outlawry and yeomanry, as well as of oaths of brotherhood, played a bigger part in Chaucer's scheme for *The Canterbury Tales* than is apparent from the portions he completed.

'The Friar's Tale' may be roughly dated to the early 1390s. That means that it predates the existing text of *A Gest of Robyn Hode* by at least sixty years or so. It offers a teasing and partial glimpse of the world of the yeoman-outlaw tale at the end of the fourteenth century: a world in which a lone male traveller, passing beside a greenwood shaw, may chance to fall in with a bowman dressed in green, who invites him to take an oath of brotherhood – to become his 'good fellow', in fact.

A man who promises to be your good fellow will share with you everything he has, like a brother. Moreover, he is bound henceforward to promote your interests as if they were his own. He certainly will not take part in any legal case that may be brought against you, since that would be a betrayal of faith. Instead, if you are in trouble, he will know that he is expected to come to your aid.

Did real-life medieval robbers ever extract such promises from their victims? The evidence is very limited. However, according to Henry of Knighton, when Justice Willoughby was captured by the Folville brothers and their associates, he was made to swear a formal oath 'that he would always comply with their instructions'.[12] In the seventeenth century, the highwayman-poet John Clavell stated that highway robbers habitually bullied their victims into swearing that they would neither pursue them nor alert the authorities to the fact that a robbery had been committed.[13]

In the opening stanzas of *A Gest of Robyn Hode*, Robin gives his men their standing orders: bring me a guest who can afford to pay for dinner, but see that you harm no one, yeoman, knight or squire, who shows himself willing to be a 'good fellow' to us. Out of the characters who feature in this tale, who is revealed in the course of the story to be prepared to practise fellowship in good faith?

The first traveller who falls into the hands of Robin Hood's men is the knight with the encumbered estates. Told that he is to dine with Robin Hood, he responds with great courtesy; it is a point worth noting that he addresses Little John, Much and Scarlock in the language of fellowship, as 'My bretherne'. Later, at the end of a magnificent feast, he assures Robin that if he ever comes past that way again, he will repay his hospitality with a meal that is just as good. However, this isn't enough for Robin, who demands that the knight should pay down cash for his dinner. The knight replies that he is too embarrassed to offer Robin the money he has with him, because it isn't enough. Questioned more closely, he claims that all he has is ten shillings. Once Little John has searched his baggage and found that this is the truth, Robin promises to lend the knight £400 so that he can redeem his estates, and Little John counts out the money 'by eight and twenty score', recklessly increasing it to £560. To Robin Hood, the ideal yeoman outlaw, and his men, good fellowship is something more than a mask for naked robbery: it is the ideal by which they live.

At this point Little John demands that the knight should be given cloth for 'a lyveray', and, as the other outlaws enter into the spirit of the thing and call for more gifts to be given him, the knight receives from them two horses, some boots and even a pair of gilt spurs.[14] A livery was a badge or a distinctive item of clothing. Magnates bestowed liveries on the members of their retinues, in order to mark them out. Both Maurice Keen and James Holt associate the references to livery in *A Gest of Robyn Hode*, as well as the green mantles that the outlaws wear, with this context of service to a lord.[15] They view the relationship of the individual outlaws to Robin as that of retainer to master. On this interpretation, by accepting a livery in the greenwood, the knight would be acknowledging himself as personally bound in service to Robin. However, it is not Robin who first proposes to give the knight a livery; the suggestion comes from Little John. Throughout this scene, it is made clear that although Robin is the master outlaw, he does not have the only say: Little John feels fully entitled to increase the sum given to the knight on his own initiative, and all the chief members of the band join in the gift-giving.

Holt describes livery as 'the mark of service', but this was not invariably the case. Liveries could be worn to show membership of certain associations or societies: craft or religious guilds, and also leagues or confraternities of knights.[16] Writing in another context altogether, on the subject of brotherhood in arms, Maurice Keen has drawn attention to the fact that in structure such confraternities resembled an extended brotherhood. The members of a league of knights were equals within the order, whatever their rank outside it. Their heads and other officers were chosen by the members, who swore an oath of loyal service to one another, and not to a lord or superior.[17] If we interpreted Robin's position in his company of outlaws as that of the master or chief in a fellowship of equals, bound together by mutual oaths, it would fit the general tone of the early tales, and it would also make good sense of Little John's assertion, in *Robin Hood and the Monk*, of his right to be treated as a fellow, not as a humble inferior.[18]

It would hardly be surprising if such a pattern of relationships should flourish within the society of outlaws. The seventeenth-century highwayman John Clavell commented on the absence of subordination in the interactions of robbers when he advised innkeepers to be wary of any guests whose servants showed a 'sawcie peremptorinesse' in their bearing towards their masters, for that, he said, was one of the marks of a robber gang.[19] *The English Gusman* (1652), which purports to be a history of the highwayman James Hind, states that when he was first recruited to the band of a robber called Allen, he began by treating his new 'master' with deference. However, when Allen saw this, he had a private word with him, in which he said, '*I would have you be as my companion and friend, and not as a servant, neither do I look for any such respect as you do give me; you shal eat and drink as I do, and if I have money, you shall have part, and want none, and if I want, you must help to get some as well as you can'*. After this, Allen and his companions *'swore him to be true to their Gang*; which being done, they admit him as a *Brother* of their Company'.[20]

When the knight accepts a livery from the outlaws, then, we do not have to interpret this as meaning that he has become Robin's personal retainer; it makes rather better sense as a sign of his affinity with the outlaws as a body. To put it another way: it is a mark of his reception into the outlaw company, or at least of his affiliation with it. Like the Potter in the metrical tale of *Robin Hood and the Potter*, the knight has been given a 'fellowship', the place of a fellow or equal partner with Robin and his men.[21] Later in the story, he shows that he is worthy of this, first when he comes faithfully to repay the loan and brings with him a magnificent gift of bows and arrows, and afterwards when he allows the outlaws to take refuge in his castle and defies the Sheriff of Nottingham on their behalf.

The second of Robin's 'guests' in the greenwood is the Sheriff of Nottingham himself, led into a trap by his erstwhile servant, Little John. He has already been burgled of all his treasure, and no one adds insult to injury by asking him to pay for the dinner he has been made to eat off his own silver plate. After dinner, he is stripped to his breeches and shirt, and forced to sleep in the open, with only a green mantle, like the outlaws have, to wrap himself in. He finds it an uncomfortable night. Next morning, Robin teases him and tells him to cheer up. 'This', he says, 'is our ordre . . . / Under the grene wode tree': it's the order or way of life of the forest outlaw. In reply, the Sheriff puns on 'order', and complains that it is a harder one than that of any friar or hermit. Outlaws pride themselves on their asceticism: another takeover from military values. Medieval soldiers took an explicit pride in enduring rigours far tougher than any religious order required of its members.[22] Though the Sheriff has been given the outlaw livery only in joke, to humble him, he offers of his own accord to become their friend and ally. Robin makes him swear an oath, not only to refrain from doing Robin himself any injury, but also to give any help that he can to any of Robin's men. However, the Sheriff's lack of physical toughness is matched by the frailty of his faith. As we have seen, he quickly goes back on his word, and sets in motion an elaborate plot to lure the outlaws into his power.

The third 'guest' is the high cellarer of St Mary's Abbey, who has featured at an earlier point in the story, when he showed an unattractive eagerness to lay hands on the knight's estates. He is brought to Robin's table unwillingly, behaves discourteously and when he is asked what money he has in his coffers, he lies, and pretends that it is a modest twenty marks (just over £13). Robin tells him (as he did the knight) that if that is really all he has, he will lend him more; but if he finds any more than that, he will take all of it. In the event, Little John finds more than £800 in the monk's baggage, which Robin claims as his repayment from the Virgin for the loan to the knight.

This motif of the robber and the two travellers, the one who tells the truth and keeps his money, and the other, a high-ranking monk, who lies and loses everything, is found in a thirteenth-century French romance, *Witasse li Moine* ('Eustace the Monk'). Introducing the text of *A Gest* in their anthology *Rymes of Robyn Hood*, Dobson and Taylor make the assumption that *Witasse li Moine* must be one of its sources. However, direct borrowing seems unlikely, and it would be better to regard the passages in the French romance as constituting an independent analogue.[23] In *Witasse li Moine*, there are no formal links between the two episodes, and though the moral is stated – the monk loses his money because he has lied – this does not make sense in terms of any scheme of values that is intrinsic to the tale. Witasse (or Eustace) is hardly a Robin Hood figure: he is much more like a human Reynard the Fox, defined by nothing so much as his shiftiness. In *A Gest of Robyn Hode*, the motif is integrated into the pattern of the narrative, through the linked tales of the knight and the monk, and plays a part in illuminating one of the basic values of good fellowship. A good fellow keeps nothing back; he reveals truthfully what he has on him, trusting his comrade to do fairly by him.

Before the reluctant monk is made to sit down to his meal at the outlaws' table, Robin calls for a horn to be blown, 'That felaushyp may us knowe' ('so that we may enjoy fellowship'), and 'Seven score' yeomen arrive at the summons. This is the company for dinner.[24] The feast under the trysting tree, which is such a prominent motif in *A Gest of Robyn Hode*, is a central symbol of fellowship.[25] The intimate links between good fellowship and conviviality are witnessed by the fact that the expression 'good fellow' had such strong connotations of tavern-haunting and gluttony. In 'The Pardoner's Tale', the three young men who swear to be brothers are rioters, heavy-drinking spendthrifts, who swear their oath in a tavern. Little John and the Sheriff's cook seal their agreement to be 'felowes' over a drinking bout; even Gamelyn and Adam, in haste to be away to the woods, find time to drink a draught of wine together. Masculine drinking and masculine bonding are closely associated. The boozy goodwill of the tavern fosters the mutual attachment of those who swear to live and die like brothers. In its ambience, the 'good fellow' who shares with you everything that he gets shades into the popular chap who always stands his round, and who treats his mates to drinks as long as he has any money.

The high cellarer of St Mary's Abbey combines the attitudes of an ecclesiastic and a businessman. He is not equipped to appreciate the culture of good fellowship, nor to recognise any satisfactions in sharing some of his abbey's wealth with a band of outlaws. With ponderous irony, he complains that he could have bought his dinner very much more cheaply in a town along the road. His comment betrays his mentality: he is simply incapable of looking outside the relations of buying and selling, the experiences of acquiring and losing. He cannot understand that for those with the right outlook, the good fellowship of Robin and his men is a treasure beyond price.

The fourth and final 'guest' at the table in the greenwood is the King himself. When Robin and his men first encounter him, he is disguised as an abbot, and travelling with a small retinue of knights disguised as monks. Robin, claiming necessity, asks the 'abbot' for money 'For saynt charyte', for the sake of holy charity. Lest this be mistaken for abject begging, he is backed at the time by a company of outlaws armed with bows. The 'abbot' replies that all he has with him is £40, but that if he had £100, he would bestow the lot on Robin – a very gracious response indeed. Robin takes the £40 and splits it into two halves; half he distributes among his own men *and half he hands back.*[26] A good fellow shares what he has with his friend. Though Robin has the supposed abbot entirely within his power, he shows that he knows what is due to a good fellow by returning him half of his money. In the last chapter, I cited some lines from the May-game playlet of *Robin Hood and the Potter*, in which the Potter challenges Robin to 'be a good felowe', and says that if he agrees, he will share half his property with him. In its confused way, this passage reflects a custom of Robin's that was still remembered in the middle of the sixteenth century: if a traveller agreed to 'be a good fellow', Robin would take only half of his money, and leave him the rest.[27] In George Peele's play *Edward I*, written in the early 1590s, which draws on similar May-games for its sub-plot, the Friar formally announces to some travellers the 'Toule' (toll) demanded by the outlaw chief Lluellen, Prince of Wales, who is masquerading as 'Robin Hood'. The outlaw requires 'the halfe of al such golde, silver, money, and money worth, as the said messenger [traveller] hath then about him, but if he conceal anie part or parcel of the same, then shall he forfaite all that he possesseth at that present'. In response to this, one of the travellers, 'Longshanks' (who is Edward I in disguise) knowingly observes, 'Faith Robin thou seemest to be a good fellow'. He then offers to stake all his money on the outcome of a combat between himself and 'Robin', 'man for man', to which Lluellen joyfully assents: 'Why thou speakest as thou shouldst speak.'[28] A good fellow always fights fairly, and never refuses a challenge.

As for the King in *A Gest of Robyn Hode*, he proves himself a good fellow once again when, after his identity has been acknowledged, he asks Robin to give him and his men the 'mantels of grene' that are the outlaw livery.[29] Even more than in the case of the knight, this only makes sense if the livery is interpreted as the badge of a quasi-military order of which

Robin is the acknowledged head. It wouldn't be at all fitting for the King to adopt a badge that implies a personal service to Robin; but as a soldier – or a good fellow – he might on occasion join an order or fraternity over which another man presided.

Each of the travellers who falls into the hands of Robin Hood and his company of yeomen faces a test of his commitment to the principles of good fellowship.[30] Each of them passes or fails precisely according to whether or not he shows himself to be a good fellow – a man who is willing to trust the outlaws, because he shares the same moral and cultural values. Ecclesiastics are not, as a rule, expected to qualify: 'Ye shall them bete and bynde', says Robin to his men. When, after all, an abbot comes along who shows that he understands what is required of a good fellow, he is very soon revealed as a king in disguise. In *A Gest of Robyn Hode*, the practical application of good fellowship becomes a way of setting the world to rights. In obedience to its requirements, Robin gives money to the honest knight, beggared by buying a pardon to save his spirited son, and takes it from the grasping liar of a monk, who doubtless acquired it through dubious practices and who ought in any case to bestow it in charity. Everyone gets what they deserve.

It's an attractive ideology, communistic, egalitarian. Its chief exponents are yeomen, and there is evidently an overlap between the principles of good fellowship and those of good yeomanry. Nevertheless, there is a place in the fellowship for knights and kings, just so long as they are prepared to embrace the appropriate values. Women are outside the circle. (The fifteenth-century narratives make no mention of Maid Marian.) However, in imitation of the laws of chivalry, it is forbidden to plunder them or show them violence.

There is just one really major problem with it. It is an ideology of robbers and parasites. The open-handedness of the outlaw hero, the ideal good fellow, is founded on his activities as a highwayman. This is something that *A Gest of Robyn Hode*, in its mildly sardonic way, does not omit to acknowledge. When Little John measures out the cloth for the knight's livery, he doles it out in wildly generous quantities. His companion Much is critical, but Scarlock laughs. 'Johnn may gyve hym gode mesure,' he says, 'For it costeth hym but lyght', or, very little.[31] Scarlock means that it is all stolen property. John has the easy come, easy go attitude of the man who lives by plunder. A successful robber can afford to be generous. And no robber is more successful than Robin Hood: a fantasy figure, a bandit so rich and successful that ten shillings, and even twenty marks, does not begin to tempt him, a landless yeoman of the forest who can lend £400 without a blink.

Writing in the introduction to *Rymes of Robyn Hood*, Dobson and Taylor suggest that 'the outlaw leader's famous acts of liberality derive less from any notion of the social redistribution of wealth than from the aristocratic virtues of largesse and display'.[32] There is no doubt that the Robin Hood of *A Gest* is in many ways a quasi-chivalric figure, a yeoman hero who outdoes most knights in his devotion to the forms of religion and his strict adherence to the rules of courtesy. But the controlling values in *A Gest of Robyn Hode* are not precisely those of chivalry, but those of good yeomanry: aristocratic ideals reinterpreted to fit the milieu of the landless yeoman. Largesse and hospitality have been redefined in terms of good fellowship.

However, as soon as Robin leaves the greenwood, the limitations both of largesse and of good fellowship are pretty starkly revealed. When Robin practises good fellowship at court, he simply runs through his money. No reciprocal largesse comes his way from the knights and squires he has unstintingly treated, nor is the King inspired a second time to offer him his purse. For Robin no longer has any bowmen to back him. The contrast between court and greenwood is not laboured; but at this point he chooses to go back to the greenwood for ever.

The story of his departure from the court sheds its own light on the heterodox values that inform his legend. By way of an excuse to leave, he tells the King that he has had a chapel built in his old territory of Barnsdale. This has been dedicated to Mary Magdalene, the most famous of repentant sinners, and he asks leave to travel there on a penitential pilgrimage. It seems as if, like Fouke Fitz Waryn, he is about to repent his crimes and, in Christian terms, consider the health of his soul. However, very soon this turns out to be merely a ruse to escape to the greenwood and return to his life as an outlaw chief. The notion of repentance has been briefly invoked only to be mocked and banished the more firmly. Despite his devotion to the Virgin and his passion for hearing the mass, the mental world of Robin Hood could hardly be more different from that of Langland's remorseful and penitent Robert the Robber.

Robin Hood is the last of the great English outlaw heroes. He is also the first fully fledged incarnation of the heroic robber in English popular literature. What I have called the cult of the robber has deep roots, as we have seen, in very ancient traditions of the outlaw-avenger, and in a certain traditional indulgence towards the crimes of the gentleman robber. In the fifteenth-century Robin Hood tales, it reaches maturity and comes to its first flowering.

The Robin Hood legend did a very great deal to shape the later traditions about highwayman heroes. The stereotype of the 'good' robber, who is courteous and wildly generous, and who shows a proper respect for women, finds its most important original in the tales of Robin Hood, and especially in *A Gest*. Another influential aspect of the legend, as we shall see, was the notion of robbery as essentially a joke or prank, calling for an attitude of light-hearted amusement. The episode in *A Gest* in which Little John takes service with the Sheriff and runs away with the plate from his strong-room is introduced to the listener as 'Goode myrth'.[33] The seventeenth-century clergyman Thomas Fuller, including Robin Hood in the Nottinghamshire section of his *Worthies of England* (1662), excuses him as a '*merry*' robber, whose crimes amounted to little more than 'pranks'.[34]

However courteous he was said to have been, and however merry, Robin Hood's primary claim to heroic status was founded on his exploits as a robber on the highway. His legend, hugely popular as it was, had a powerful effect for centuries on the self-image of the English as a nation. It inspired them to look back with pride on a history that was said to be replete with such valiant robbers. It encouraged them to continue to view with complacency their country's reputation as a famous nursery for highwaymen.

The Rise of the London Underworld

In 1497, a visiting Venetian diplomat wrote a report for his government on the state of affairs in England. Among much else, he gave it as his opinion that 'there is no country in the world where there are so many thieves and robbers'.[1] This was already an old cry; we have heard something like it on the lips of the fourteenth-century preachers Bromyard and Brinton, who thought it was a national disgrace.[2] Sir John Fortescue, lawyer and adviser to kings, took a different view. Writing just over twenty years before the Venetian's visit, he offered it as a proof of the commendable toughness of the English as a breed. I have quoted his remarks on the subject in Chapter One.[3] For at least another three centuries, the propensity of the Englishman for committing robberies would be a regular subject of comment by visitors and natives alike.[4]

However, the robber's environment was changing. Speaking of the consequences of England's crime-ridden state, the Italian observed that 'few venture to go alone in the country, excepting in the middle of the day, and fewer still in the towns at night, and least of all in London'. At the end of the fifteenth century, the risk of meeting a robber in the woods and wild places was perceived to be rather less than those of an encounter with a mugger in urban streets and alleys. The greenwood outlaw was rapidly becoming a figure from the past. The centre of the robber's activities was shifting to the city.

It is not surprising that London was experienced as the most crime-ridden place of all. For London was already very much larger than the largest provincial town or city. Its population in 1500 has been roughly estimated at about 40,000. It was probably about five times larger than the next largest city, Norwich. And it was growing all the time, with a speed that many people found alarming.[5] Moreover, from the point of view of administration, it was a patchwork affair, with the civic authorities having no jurisdiction over the suburbs outside the city limits, nor even over certain enclaves within their own boundaries.[6] Much of the responsibility for day-to-day policing fell on ordinary householders, who were co-opted to fill the office of constable on an annual rota.[7] Meanwhile, there was no shortage of opportunities for the criminal, whether professional or opportunist. London was the country's chief centre of commerce, and its trade, like the city itself, was growing rapidly. Luxury goods and other portable items of value were plentiful. The streets were thronged with people, citizens and visitors, with plump purses hanging from their belts. Wealthy travellers and valuable trade goods regularly surged in and out along the main roads leading to the provinces.[8]

The urban criminal was not a new phenomenon. For centuries, the towns and cities had offered certain kinds of crook their best refuge and prospects. Their greater density of population had provided cutpurses, cheating gamblers and various kinds of confidence trickster with the cover their activities demanded, as well as with greater opportunities for lucrative pickings. Moreover, in many urban centres there had long been people, often alehouse or tavern keepers, who routinely encouraged crooks to use their premises and who undertook to fence stolen property.[9] During the first half of the sixteenth century, as London grew in size and wealth, its communities of professional thieves and con men began to flourish exceedingly.

By this time, even the operations of the highway robber were coming to be quite closely tied to the urban environment. In the populous capital, the robber found a hiding place among the anonymous crowds as good as any woodland thicket, and no doubt much more comfortable. He also found people willing to provide him with services. Some of these were informers, or 'setters' as they were called: inn servants and others, who tipped him off about wealthy travellers and the roads they would be taking. Others were professional mediators between criminals and legitimate society: fences who specialised in disposing of stolen valuables and fixers who knew how to help a man who found himself in trouble with the law. Robin Hood and his men always rob on foot, relying for their escape on their ability to vanish into the difficult terrain of the forest. Their weapons are footmen's weapons, the longbow and the sword and buckler. However, by Elizabeth's reign, at latest, a robber with any reputation was expected to keep a horse, and a good horse too. His usual weapons now were sword and pistols.[10] The mounted robber's chief advantages were mobility over a wide range of territory and a quick getaway after the crime.

The seventeenth-century highwayman John Clavell, writing in 1627, describes how the mounted robbers of his own time habitually robbed on the arterial roads just outside London. Among those he specifically mentions are the Uxbridge (Oxford) Road and the road through Staines to Salisbury and the West Country. Whenever he and his associates had carried out a particularly successful robbery, they would ride at once for the capital, whose size made it easy for them to find a bolt-hole.[11] In his study of crime in Essex between 1620 and 1680, J. A. Sharpe notes that most of the cases of highway robbery took place on the main roads in close proximity to London. Likewise, J. M. Beattie reports that between 1660 and 1800 the majority of robberies in Surrey occurred in the northern parts of the county, on the roads leading to and from the capital.[12]

This picture of highwaymen carrying out regular robberies on all the routes that radiated out from the city comes vividly to life in the record of current events that was kept by Narcissus Luttrell in the years between 1690 and 1700. Luttrell was a keen reader of newsletters, and every few days, he jotted down the latest items to catch his attention. He reports robberies 'near Croydon in Surry', 'on Hounslow heath', 'near Acton', 'on Finchly Common', 'near Barnet', 'in Epping forest' and 'at Shooters Hill', to name only a few of the places mentioned. At a somewhat greater distance from the city, there are robberies 'on Bagshot heath', 'in Maidenhead thicket', 'near Beaconsfeild', 'near St. Albans', 'near Ingerstone [Ingatestone], in Essex', and 'on Gads hill', near Rochester. Some of these spots were notorious. Several times Luttrell records cases of robbers pursued or tracked into the city. When four highwaymen were foiled in an attempt near Ware, their victims, who were armed with pistols, chased after them into London, where three of the robbers were captured in Fetter Lane. On another occasion, three others were 'dogged by a butcher they had robbed near Bagshot', and cornered in 'an alehouse in Shoe lane'.[13] Richard Head was a writer of fiction, but he was plainly commenting on a perceivable effect when he stated in 1674: 'The largeness of the City, and the little cognizance one takes of another therein, is the main reason why so many robberies are committed nigh London, and so few remotely distant from it. . . . twenty or thirty miles about London is the stage on which these highwaymen act their parts'.[14] At such a range, the robber who had a good horse could hope to be back in the city within a few hours.[15] In 1722, the highwayman Ralph Wilson said that he and his associates 'seldom went above five Miles from the Town' in the course of committing their robberies.[16]

Even when mounted robbers were operating further afield, they still travelled to London when they felt the need to lie low for a bit. In September 1695, Luttrell recorded: 'Some highway men were taken in Drury Lane with a considerable summ of money about them, being pursued out of Dorsetshire'.[17] Nearly a hundred years earlier, the highway robber Luke Hutton was hanged at York for robberies committed in Yorkshire, but from the fact that he was originally committed to Newgate, it is clear that he had been arrested in London or Middlesex. When Gamaliel Ratsey and his gang were pursued for a robbery near Bedford, in

1605, they, too, went to ground in London.[18] By the end of the sixteenth century, many, perhaps most of the mounted robbers in England had close ties to the capital.

Long before this, in the early years of the reign of Henry VIII, the world of the London-based robbers had provided material for a couple of dramatic interludes, *Youth*, written for performance in the winter of 1513–14, and *Hyckescorner*, written a few months later, in the summer of 1514.[19] Each of these plays dramatises criminal types in the guise of allegorical personages involved in a typical morality plot about sin and redemption. In *Youth*, the title character is a young gentleman who has just inherited his father's lands. He is led astray by Riot, who in the allegorical scheme represents Youth's thriftlessness and licentious behaviour. At the level of the action, Riot is depicted naturalistically as a wild young tearaway: every moralist's idea of a bad influence. He is Youth's sworn brother, a former jail-bird and an inveterate robber, who doesn't care what he does so long as he can get his hands on some spending money. References to Newgate jail and Tyburn gallows sketchily evoke the contemporary London scene.[20]

The issue was evidently topical. In Sir Thomas More's *Utopia*, published two years later, he mentions as a major cause of robberies what he perceives as a growing tendency to reckless expenditure among many of his fellow-countrymen. Even craftsmen and farmers, he says, are indulging themselves in fine clothing, good food and gambling, and are hanging out in brothels and taverns. These extravagances, he claims, 'soon run through the money of those who have become their devotees, who straightaway go off somewhere with a view to committing robbery'.[21] What More was noticing were probably the effects of a selective rise in living standards. During the second decade of the sixteenth century, there was a marked growth in price inflation, which will have benefited some producers even while it reduced the means of those on fixed incomes.[22] No doubt this was accompanied by an increased consumption of luxuries in certain sections of society. One consequence of this would have been a greater availability of valuable items to tempt the thief and the robber. Perhaps this provoked a few people to compensate for their limited purchasing power by helping themselves to other men's surplus goods. However, it is unlikely that sheer extravagance was the major cause of robbery that More believed it to be. Nevertheless, the notion that many property crimes, especially robberies, were committed by ruined spend-thrifts was becoming part of the received wisdom, and in the allegorical play of *Youth*, we see the beginnings of a new social and literary stereotype: the free-spending young gentleman, addicted to riotous living, who will not stick at robbery to put money in his purse.

Although it was written at almost the same time, and although it stole part of its action from *Youth*, the allegory in *Hyckescorner* has often been seen as muddled and incomplete.[23] Certainly, there are respects in which the play moves towards a much denser realism than anything in *Youth*, setting a trio of street toughs in an early Tudor London viewed from the gutter. The unknown author uses techniques that would later be exploited on the grand scale by the dramatists and pamphleteers of Elizabeth's reign: racy dialogue, spiced with obscenity and slang, and, for greater verisimilitude, a generous sprinkling of references to actual localities in and around London. The names of the principal characters are Free Will, Imagination and Hick Scorner, but for much of the action they might just as well be Will, Tom and Hick (or Dick).

Free Will has no fixed address, and it takes him a moment to remember with which of his whores he has passed the previous night. He thinks he has a noble in his pocket, though when he looks he can't find it and he has probably spent it already. However, he remembers how he came by it: he got it by mugging a friar. Later in the play we learn that he was once imprisoned for a whole year in the notorious criminal jail of Newgate. We also find out that he was born in the stews, the Bankside brothel area. His mother was a whore, his father a cutpurse, who ended his life on the gallows.[24] He represents the small but growing minority of people whose lives, from start to finish, were lived entirely outside the moral and social structures of legitimate society.[25]

Imagination is Free Will's 'fellow', and addresses him as 'my dear brother'. One meaning of 'imagination' was 'scheming' or 'plotting': hence his name. He claims that among his relations, he has 'many a great gentleman'. This is satirical allegory, but it also works on a naturalistic level. It marks him out as belonging to a different class of crook from Free Will. This is the well-born delinquent, surviving on his wits. He boasts of his ability to 'convey clean', to steal without being caught. None of his family has ever been hanged, since all of them are literate men, as befits their superior status. A man who could show that he was able to read his 'neck-verse', a prescribed passage of the Bible, was allowed to claim benefit of clergy, a legal device for escaping the gallows. Imagination's criminal speciality is as a fixer: he knows how and where to drop the right bribe to corrupt a judge or have an arrested man set free from jail. All the same, he himself is a former jail-bird.[26]

When Hick Scorner enters, the mode of the play shifts for a while into satirical fantasy. Hick Scorner arrives in a boat; he is a mariner, a great traveller, with tales to tell of his journeys in a ship full of 'good fellows . . . . Yea, thieves and whores, with other good company'. Hick Scorner himself was the ship's pimp.[27] After this vein has been thoroughly played out, Imagination calls his companions' attention to business:

> Let us keep company all together.
> And I would that we had God's curse,
> If we somewhere do not get a purse.
> Every man bear his dagger naked in his hand,
> And if we meet a true man, make him stand,
> Or else that he bear a stripe.*
> If that he struggle and make any work,
> Lightly† strike him to the heart
> And throw him into Thames quite.

Instead of doing this, they get into a scuffle with each other. When Pity enters in the guise of a magistrate and commands them to keep the peace, the three of them turn on him, bind him and fetter him. Then, once again, Imagination calls on his mates to join him in a robbery:

> Well, fellows, now let us go our way,
> For at Shooters Hill we have a game to play.

We have come across this notorious place before. It was here that the young Henry VIII and his queen met and feasted with 'Robin Hood'. This took place in 1515, a year after the first performance of *Hyckescorner*.[28] By reputation, Shooters Hill was one of the most dangerous places for robberies in all Kent, a county that for centuries was plagued by highway robbers.[29] It was about eight or nine miles away from London, on the Great Dover Road, the main highroad towards Calais and the Continent.

As the play goes on, we hear nothing more about this projected robbery. This is doubtless no oversight. For these young street punks, highway robbery – as opposed to rolling an unarmed friar – is not so much their trade as their aspiration. When Free Will returns to the stage it is with an inglorious story of his having been arrested for the theft of a cup from a tavern. He has been freed from jail after Imagination had come with a bribe to rescue him. Free Will tells the audience how Imagination had raised the cash. First, he had gone skulking after dark through Holborn towards St Giles-in-the-Fields, looking for a victim to mug. Finding no one, he had gone to the Tudor equivalent of the late-night chemist, an apothecary's shop, still open when everywhere else was closed, and had been able to snaffle a large bag of coin, with which he had paid for his lodging at an inn near Newgate. With money in his pocket, 'every man took him for a gentleman', and next day he had had no trouble in arranging for Free Will's release.[30]

---

* receive a blow

† quickly

At this point Free Will realises that there are now other characters on stage: Contemplation and Perseverance, who before his arrival had come and released Pity from his bonds. Free Will jeers at them, but with patient remonstrance they win him round and convert him. In the course of his conversation with them, he reveals more of his history: his birth in the stews and his time spent fettered in Newgate. He also lets slip his dearest dream, which is of the 'three good voyages to Shooters Hill', the three successful highway robberies that would set him up for life. After that, he thinks, he would 'never travel the sea more'; he would be able to afford to turn honest.[31] To Free Will, Shooters Hill is an almost legendary place, the place where with a bit of luck any resolute fellow can seize his share of riches.

By the middle of the sixteenth century, London had developed a complex sector of professionalised illegal activity which had all the features that we associate with an 'underworld'. These are first described clearly in a short book entitled *A manifest detection of the moste vyle and detestable use of Diceplay*, which was published anonymously during or just after 1552.[32] The book's chief purpose is to warn gullible young gentlemen against the crooked practices that were used in certain gaming houses, and to this end it outlines various methods that were used by dice and card sharpers. The author calls these people 'Chetors', or cheaters: it is the first time the word is found with this meaning. The crooked gamblers he describes were not lone operators; they belonged to a loose network of specialist confidence men that functioned in the context of a wider network of interlinked groups of other kinds of illegal practitioner. Apart from the cheaters, the chief groups he identified were three: 'figgers' or pickpurses, whores and their managers, and highway robbers. These groups were distinct, but they were all acquainted with each other, and were prepared, as occasion required, to call on each other's expertise. A victim with well-lined pockets who showed himself reluctant to gamble might have been drawn to the attention of a pickpurse, or, worse, waylaid by a gang of highway robbers, who would have stripped him of everything, even his clothes, and left him tied up or badly beaten.

One important function of the criminal networks was the transmission of skills. The cheating gamblers and the pickpurses required a good deal of training before they could reach a full proficiency in their trades. Another of their functions was putting members in touch with confederates who could provide them with necessary services. The cheaters, and doubtless the other groups also, had connections with certain crooked lawyers, whose usefulness to them may easily be imagined. The author of *A manifest detection* says that the most organised group of criminals were the figgers or fig-boys, who seem, from the sound of it, to have included sneak-thieves as well as pickpurses. An important issue for these particular crooks was the safe disposal of the valuables they filched. The receivers they used were typically pawnbrokers, whose businesses provided them with excellent cover for dealing in stolen jewellery and plate. These receivers, or 'treasurers', as the author calls them, carried out another useful function. A portion of the proceeds of every successful theft was given to them to look after. If any of the thieves were arrested and imprisoned, the money would be used to persuade the victim to drop the case, or else it would be paid out in bribes to keep them from the gallows.[33]

A striking aspect of *A manifest detection* is its reference to the 'queint termes' and 'strange language' that were current among the cheaters and their disorderly associates.[34] 'Cheater' itself is one such term, 'figger' another. The earliest indications that certain marginal and deviant groups were beginning to use forms of language that diverged markedly from standard English speech are found in the 1530s. At that time travelling pedlars were said to be using a special argot, popularly known as 'pedlar's French'. It seems to have been identical with the argot later known as 'canting', which was used by some tramps and beggars.[35] *A manifest detection*, which appeared some twenty years later, is the first document to record extensive samples from the increasingly elaborate special vocabularies used by the thieves and confidence men of London.[36] There is a modest overlap between the terms found in *A manifest detection* and those that are recorded as having been used by criminalised vagrants. 'To strike', meaning 'to get the better of, swindle, steal', is one such term; 'a snap', meaning 'a share', is another.[37] However, in many respects the vocabularies used by vagrants and those used by urban thieves are very different.

This is not surprising; they had different preoccupations. One of the chief functions of a criminal argot, as the astute author of *A manifest detection* correctly notes, is to enable the crooks to discuss the technicalities of their trades.[38] *A manifest detection* includes a long list of the names of the different types of false dice used by the cheaters.[39] The author also comments on the 'mervelus plenty of terms' used by the pickpurses, which, as he observes, were necessitated by the fact that 'Their craft . . . requireth most slyght', or the greatest technical expertise.[40] His comments reveal that he is aware that there was more than one argot in use; each occupational group had its own version, though there was certainly some overlap in vocabulary. In his opinion, the cheaters' use of words that meant nothing to outsiders played a role in helping to hide the real nature of their activities.[41] However, the existence of the argots undoubtedly served a further, much more important function. In any 'underworld' milieu, skilful use of argot, which can only be learned from association with other users, is an important mark of the criminal insider, the professional. It identifies the speaker to other professional criminals as something more than a casual or even a habitual robber, thief or swindler. He or she is immersed in a distinctive subculture, is acquainted with its practices, rules and maxims and shares its attitudes and way of life.[42]

The unknown author of *A manifest detection* was not a member of this subculture. His attitude to it is intensely disapproving. He tells us nothing about the sources of his information, though it is clear that he knows much more about the cheating gamblers than about any of the other groups he mentions. Nevertheless, he is one of the best, as well as the first, of a series of writers who between them invented a new, if minor, genre: the exposé of the practices and subculture of professional crooks. Later writers in this vein included the versatile hack Robert Greene, who published several important pamphlets in the early 1590s, and George Wilkins, an intriguing figure, who combined the profession of writer with that of keeper of an alehouse on the corner of Turnmill Street, a street notorious as the home of thieves and whores.[43] Wilkins's 1607 account of the methods of pickpockets and other thieves, *The discoveries made by Cock Wat*, is one of the most important and neglected works of its kind.

It is, of course, the case that all such purported exposés require careful assessment and interpretation. A few of them are entirely bogus; some others, like Greene's series of 'conny-catching' pamphlets about the London confidence men and pickpockets, contain plagiarisms and elements of obvious invention alongside material that seems to be reasonably authentic. Nevertheless, when all the evidence has been assessed on its merits, there can be no doubt that the underworld subculture that was first described in detail in *A manifest detection* really did flourish in certain milieux in mid-sixteenth-century London, and that it persisted and continued to develop. The techniques that are outlined by this author are unquestionably genuine, and so are many of the swindles and ingenious methods of thieving that are described by later writers like Greene and Wilkins.

A particularly suggestive proof of this is the fact that very similar techniques are detailed in some twentieth-century criminological studies: notably Edwin H. Sutherland's *The Professional Thief* and David W. Maurer's *Whiz Mob* and *The Big Con*. Some of the confidence games described by the author of *A manifest detection* and by other writers, including Greene, are very like some of the 'short con' rackets that were operated by grifters in pre-war America.[44] Indeed, there can be little doubt that somewhere, such games are running still. Similarly, Sutherland's and Maurer's reports of the techniques used by pickpocket teams are strikingly close to some of the descriptions that appear in Greene's pamphlet exposés, and are closer still to the more informative account by Wilkins.[45] Finally, it is an intriguing fact that some of the lexical items of the argots used by American pickpockets and cheating gamblers in the first half of the twentieth century had plainly come down to them from Tudor times. These include 'stall', a pickpocket's team-mate or decoy, a usage noted by Greene in 1591; 'cousin', an easy mark or victim, which, in the sense of dupe, is first found in *A manifest detection*; and 'flat', a die that has been falsified by being made slightly oblong, a term that appears in *A manifest detection*, and which was first recorded a few years earlier, in 1545.[46]

The size of this Tudor underworld and the full extent of its activities are important questions we are unlikely ever to resolve. Modern historians have noted that many of the property crimes that feature in court records were opportunistic thefts, requiring nothing in the way of special techniques, and usually carried out by people who show little sign of belonging to any kind of criminal gang or network.[47] However, we can be sure that crooks with underworld connections will have been heavily under-represented in those cases that came to court. Just like the con men and pickpockets of America in the first half of the twentieth century, early modern criminals knew very well how to buy off a complainant or bribe their way out of a prosecution. The author of *A manifest detection* states that of those thieves who fetched up on the gallows, most were 'unlessoned laddes' – youths who had not had the benefit of a proper underworld training, and who will also have lacked access to the right contacts to have their cases fixed. 'The old theves', he says, 'go thorow with their vsies [read 'vices', 'devices'] wel twenty or thirty yeres together and be seldome taken, or tainted' (he means 'suspected'). Writing in 1955, Maurer estimated that at that time in America the overwhelming bulk of property crime was committed by professionals, while of thieves serving prison sentences, the majority were amateurs, that is, offenders with no underworld affiliations.[48]

According to *A manifest detection*, robbery was known in the subculture as 'high law'. 'Law' is here being used in a sense closely equivalent to 'racket'. The cheaters' practices and body of technical knowledge were known as cheating law, the pickpurses had their figging law and prostitution was called 'sacking law'. The author notes that cheaters took their own name from a legal term: a 'cheat', as he says, was a stray beast or some other thing that fell due to the lord of the manor and was forfeited, or escheated, to his use.[49] He waxes very rhetorical on the cheaters' use of the word 'law', complaining that whereas the true meaning of the term 'signifieth an ordinaunce of good men, established for the common wealth [well-being], to represse all vicius lyving', the cheaters have turned its meaning upside down, 'geving to diverse vile patching [deceitful] shyftes, an honest, and godly titell'. He warms to his theme: 'Bycause by a multitude of hateful rules a multytude of dregges and draffe [rubbish], as it were all good lerning, governe and rule their ydel bodies, to the destruction of the good laboring people. And this is the cause that dyverse crafty sleyghts devised only for guyle, hold up the name of a Lawe, ordayned ye wote to mayntayne playne dealing.'[50] Throughout *A manifest detection* the author is concerned to present his cheaters and their associates as anti-social elements, deceivers, emissaries of Hell, people who made a point of reversing the rightful pattern of things. His insistence that true laws exist for the common good, to enforce honest dealing, suits his theme very nicely. However, he disregards the fact that in mid-sixteenth-century England, there was more than one sort of law, and the laws did not bear equally on all persons. The law of 'cheats', or escheats, for example, was part of manorial law, a law that gave the lord of the manor certain fairly arbitrary rights over the property of his tenants. The use by argot-speakers of words like 'cheat' and 'law' is open to being interpreted not so much as an anti-social inversion of meaning as a sardonic acknowledgement that for many people, much of the time, being under the rule of law was experienced primarily as being subject to continual extortions. A rather similar idea is found about fifty years earlier, in *Robin Hood and the Potter*: Robin and his men joke about charging the Potter 'pavage', road toll, and about taking a 'wed' or fine from him.[51]

The author of *A manifest detection* offers no encouragement to the notion that robbery is a crime that demonstrates the robber's spirit, his readiness to provoke a violent confrontation; a crime whose central act is an open display of courage. Instead, he goes out of his way to make the point that a highway robber can be as much of a sneaky dissembler, a deliberate abuser of his victim's confidence, as any cheating gambler. Concealment, he says, is the first rule of successful cheating, and he develops this point with a simile that has plainly been carefully chosen: the cheater is required 'to be as secret in working, as he that keepeth a man company from London too Maydenhead, and makes good cheere by the way, to the ende in the thycket to turne his pricke [dagger] upward, and cast a weavers knot on both his thumbs behind him'. This is a striking departure from the usual representation of the robber. However, it is very much in keeping with his insistence elsewhere in his book that the basis of all underworld activity is deception: to use his own resonant phrase, 'a counterfeate countenaunce in all things'.[52]

The image of the highway robber as a master of deception is picked up and developed by Robert Greene in the last of his series of criminal exposés, *The Blacke Bookes Messenger. Laying open the Life and Death of Ned Browne* (1592). The Ned Browne of the title is said by Greene to have been an all-purpose confidence man, pimp and thief, before he 'came to the credite of a high Lawyer', or mounted highway robber. He is supposed to have ended by being hanged in France for robbing a church, and the body of the text is presented, most implausibly, as a report of his final words before his execution. In effect, the book is a transparent piece of fiction, and the 'autobiographical' element is little more than an excuse to string together a number of entertaining tales of ingenious thefts and other crimes in a thrillingly sensational framework. Greene undoubtedly had some contacts with professional thieves and con men, but it seems certain that these were fairly limited. By the time he came to write this, his fifth publication of its kind, it is clear that he was running out of authentic material. But *The Blacke Bookes Messenger* is highly innovative in form, and in this respect it was to prove extremely influential. As a collection of 'merry tales' thinly dressed up as the life story of a prankster or similar type, it belongs to an already established genre of popular jest-biography. However, it was the first such 'Life and Death' account of a professional criminal, and as such, it is the forerunner of a number of similar works: most immediately, a pair of early Jacobean pamphlets, *The Life and Death of Gamaliel Ratsey* and its sequel *Ratseis Ghost*, which were published in 1605 to take advantage of the notoriety of an executed highway robber.

The Blacke Bookes Messenger is wildly erratic in tone, but in this it sets a pattern for later works of its kind. The reader is invited by turns to deplore Browne's wickedness, relish his bravado, laugh at the prankish nature of his crimes, be edified by his ultimate penitence and take warning from his fate. His exploits on the highway are confined to a few pages only. Greene strongly emphasises the elements of disguise and trickery in the highwayman's methods; this conforms to the usual approach of the Elizabethan underworld exposés, whose keynote is the claim to reveal otherwise impenetrable frauds. So besides the highway robber's more dashing accoutrements, a sword and a fast horse, Ned Browne goes equipped with a lifelike wig and false beard, a reversible cloak, and even an artificial tail for his horse (which has been docked). Greene has him boast: 'there rests no greater villany than in this practise, for I have robbed a man in the morning, and come to the same Inn and bayted, yea and dyned with him the same day'. Three centuries earlier, in *Fouke le Fitz Waryn*, the mask and false name were made emblematic of the coward, in the episode of Fouke's wicked impersonator, the robber knight Pieres de Brubyle. In *The Blacke Bookes Messenger*, they become the mark of the robber as anti-heroic trickster, a sardonic, self-proclaimed villain, who plumes himself as much on his ingenuity as his boldness.[53]

It would be well over thirty years before the modus operandi of the mounted robber came to be described in detail, in John Clavell's book *A Recantation of an Ill Led Life* (1628). This important work, part exposé, part protestation of penitence, will be discussed later on, in a separate chapter.[54] However, Clavell was not the first highwayman to manifest literary pretensions. The Elizabethan robber Luke Hutton, rumoured to have been the son of the Archbishop of York, published two books, both of which were written while he was in Newgate prison, under investigation.

He was eventually sent to York, where he was executed. The first of Hutton's publications is a lengthy 'repentance' in verse, licensed in November 1595. His second book, *The Black Dog of Newgate*, licensed in January 1596, falls into two parts: a poetic prelude describing the author's experiences in jail and a prose dialogue that invokes the example of Robert Greene in setting out to reveal the ruses – not of robbers and thieves, but of their enemies, the Newgate keepers. According to Hutton, two of these officers regularly misused arrest warrants and employed threats and trumped-up charges to extract money from former jail-birds and from known cutpurses and robbers. What he describes is a version of what twentieth-century American crooks would have recognised as the 'shake', or 'shake-down': officers of the law using their position to extort money from professional thieves. In a culture where the legal process can be bought and sold, the 'shake' is the inevitable accompaniment to the 'fix', though very much less to the comfort of criminals. Hutton expresses a keen indignation at this practice; educated man though he was, his sympathy for the criminals is so overt as to suggest a high degree of identification with the underworld subculture.[55]

In general, most literature about the criminal underworld in the Elizabethan and Jacobean period follows *A manifest detection* in presenting its members as heterodox outsiders, enemies of good order, servants of the Devil. When all the moralising is stripped away, there remains some truth in this perception. The speakers of criminal argots are unquestionably outsiders, set apart in certain ways from the rest of the culture in which they live. Some of the pamphlet exposés, especially those by Greene, achieved an immense popularity. Collectively, they had a great deal of influence on the imagination of the public. From this time on, there is a noticeable split at the heart of the popular image of the robber. The Robin Hood stereotype, the bold and generous hero, unorthodox righter of wrongs, certainly doesn't disappear; but alongside it there emerges a new stereotype, which coexists with it, more or less uncomfortably, often in the same texts. This is the robber as urban criminal, argot-speaker, associate of crooks and whores, haunter of seedy thieves' kitchens; the wearer of masks, 'counterfeit countenances', that are sometimes actual, sometimes symbolic.

9

Gentlemen Thieves in Velvet Coats

In 1596, the Jesuit Robert Parsons, or Persons, looking forward to the death of the elderly Elizabeth I and hoping for a Roman Catholic successor, wrote a detailed memorandum of measures that he urged to the attention of a Catholic administration. One of the matters he concerned himself with was the large number of robbers that infested the English highways, 'more than likely in any other Country of the World'. He noted that these robbers were 'sometimes of no base Condition, or Quality, . . . but rather Gentlemen, or wealthy Men's Sons, moved thereunto not so much of poverty and necessity, as of light estimation of the fault, and hope of Pardon from the Prince'. One of his recommendations was the institution of a police force dedicated to hunting down robbers. In this, he was well ahead of his time. It was not until the mid-eighteenth century that the first steps were taken towards setting up a proper professional police force. The other measure he suggested was making it much harder to obtain a Crown pardon.[1]

When Parsons says that highway robberies were sometimes committed by gentlemen, or by the sons of wealthy families, he is speaking no more than the truth. In his study of crime in England in the reigns of Elizabeth and James I, based on the records of Essex, Sussex and Hertfordshire, J. S. Cockburn notes that gentlemen feature surprisingly often in legal indictments for highway robbery. Frank Aydelotte makes a similar observation about the sixteenth-century records for Middlesex.[2] On the other hand, J. A. Sharpe suggests that most of the robbers who called themselves gentlemen probably had only slender claims to gentility.[3] It is certainly true that many of them seem to have been fairly obscure, the sons of cadet branches or the younger sons of minor landed families. However, there were some notable exceptions. F. G. Emmison reports that in the 1580s, Ludovick Grevill, son-in-law to the statesman and magnate Sir William Petre, had the reputation of being a highway robber.[4] A few decades later, in 1618, Sir George Sandys was hanged 'for taking purses on the highway' in spite of the fact that he was a knight and had good family connections. In 1616, he had been tried for highway robbery and acquitted, and he had also received at least one pardon for similar offences. Gossip had it that his wife took part in his robberies, and even that she continued as a robber on her own account after his execution. In 1626, their son George, on trial for rape, boasted in court of the robberies he had himself committed, for which he had previously escaped detection. He, too, went to the gallows.[5] The author-highwayman John Clavell was the son and heir of a landed gentleman, and heir presumptive to his uncle, a wealthy knight. He was pardoned for highway robbery in 1627.[6]

During the sixteenth century and the early part of the seventeenth, the system of granting pardons, which Parsons thought such an encouragement to robbers, was still very similar to that of which the Folville brothers had taken advantage, more than two and a half centuries earlier.[7] Parsons was not by any means the first person to express concern at the way the system operated. In Chapter Four I cited the comments of the fourteenth-century preacher Thomas Brinton, who was angered that wealthy and well-connected murderers and robbers were regularly 'hanged by the purse' instead of 'by the neck' alongside the poorer felons.[8] In the early 1540s, Henry Brinklow, a former Franciscan friar who became a radical Protestant reformer, had protested that the granting of pardons left robbers free to rob again. In his iconoclastic way, he had even dared to suggest that it amounted to an abuse of the royal authority.[9] This was dangerous ground. The giving of pardons was defended in principle as the means by which the royal justice was tempered by the balancing virtue of mercy.[10] However, in practice, as everybody knew, it was a mechanism by which the monarch and his or her courtiers – who acted as intermediaries, and took payment for doing so – raised useful sums of money from felons and their families.

As a rule, obtaining a pardon required money, legal advice and a friend at court. It was therefore a system that favoured people with good family connections. It also favoured the ambitious and successful criminal over the small fry. Ben Jonson has a sardonic epigram about a man condemned for robbing another of £300. The robber pays over all his loot to a courtier, who negotiates a pardon for him, to the impotent rage of his victim. Drily, Jonson concludes, 'The courtier is become the greater thiefe.'[11] A century later, in George Farquhar's comedy *The Beaux' Stratagem* (1707), the highwayman Gibbet explains that he must always keep a reserve of £200 'to save my life at the sessions'.[12] The practice of granting pardons inevitably encouraged offenders to assume that even if they were arrested and found guilty, they would still be able to escape the gallows. The highway robber James Hind, apprehended in 1651, is reported in a news pamphlet to have said to his father, 'I make no doubt, but that the *State*, will have as much mercy on me, as ever the late King had on *Clavil*'. Hind was referring to the case of John Clavell, who had been pardoned by Charles I. However, Hind's father, an ordinary country saddler, was troubled by his son's over-confidence, and warned him, 'friends that should stir in your business, I have none'. A marginal note points out that 'Clavil . . . *had many friends*': in other words, Clavell was a gentleman, whose relatives could command the attention of some influential men.[13]

The gentleman robber was a recognised social type. The phrase 'a gentleman thief' was current by 1552, when Bernard Gilpin, in a sermon before Edward VI, characterised Barabbas, the robber who had been due for execution at the same time as Christ, but who was released as a Passover concession to the crowd, as 'a notable theef, a gentleman theef, such as rob now a daies in velvet coates'. There is a double image in these words. The velvet-coated robber is representative of the well-born (or well-dressed) highwayman, but he also stands for one of Gilpin's chief targets, the rich landowner who turns his tenants off their farms in order to squeeze more money out of his lands. Both, in their different degrees, exemplify aristocratic rapaciousness, and both are allowed to operate free from legal restraint. Gilpin compares the fate of Barabbas with that of the 'two obscure theeves and nothing famous' who were executed with Christ. 'The rusticall theeves were hanged and Barrabas was delivered: Even so nowe a dayes little theeves are hanged that steale of necessitie, but the great Barrabasses have free liberty to rob and to spoil without al measure'.[14] He is certainly aiming his shafts here partly at the practice of granting pardons to well-off robbers with good connections. The Churches, both Protestant and Catholic, deplored the toleration of the robber, just as the medieval Church had done: for men like Gilpin, Brinklow and Parsons, it represents a serious abuse.

Some twenty years before Gilpin's sermon, in *The Book named The Governor* (1531), Sir Thomas Elyot had bitterly condemned the attitudes that assisted certain kinds of criminal in escaping the rigour of the law:

> A man hearing that his neighbour is slain or robbed, forthwith hateth the offender . . . thinking him worthy to be punished according to the laws; yet when he beholdeth the transgressor, a seemly personage, also to be his servant, acquaintance, or a gentleman born (I omit now to speak of any other corruption), he forthwith changeth his opinion, and preferreth the offender's condition or personage before the example of justice . . . yea and this is not only done by the vulgar or common people, but much rather by them which have authority to them committed concerning the effectual execution of laws.[15]

It is noticeable that the crimes at issue here are violent ones: homicide and robbery. And it is particularly interesting that Elyot, a humanist and friend of Sir Thomas More, makes no bones about the fact that the attitudes he is describing are primarily aristocratic, much more likely to be held by members of noble or gentry families than by ordinary folk. As a result, they were liable to influence the way the laws were applied, since the administration of these was largely in the hands of gentlemen and noblemen. One of the factors that Elyot thinks likely to lead to a man's making excuses for a killer or a robber is if the offender turns out to be one of his own servants. Although the worst excesses of maintenance were beginning to be eliminated, the gentry and nobility still acknowledged obligations of patronage towards servants or acquaintances who were in trouble with the law, and they would often make interventions on their behalf.[16] However, to attract this kind of support, Elyot clearly regards it as important that the criminal should be, to use his words, 'a seemly personage': a well set up, good-looking fellow, and probably well spoken, too.

Another factor that Elyot thinks likely to induce sympathetic feelings is if the killer or robber is 'a gentleman born'.[17] To some extent, this will have been due to a sense of group solidarity on the part of people of similar background and status. There is more to it than this, though, as I have indicated already in Chapter One. Gentle blood was widely considered to confer a positive propensity to commit certain kinds of violent crime, including robbery. Thus, in the earliest extant ballad written for the execution of a highway robber, the 'woefull ballade' supposed to have been composed by Master George Mannington, hanged at Cambridge in 1576, the speaker wishes that he 'had ... / Been bred and borne of meaner estate'. Elsewhere he says, 'I was too bolde', and he calls on 'valiant hearts' to learn from his sad example.[18] An execution ballad from the reign of James I, *The lamentation of Jhon Musgrave*, says of the robber: 'A gentleman he was of courage bould'.[19] Courage was felt to be the pre-eminent mark of gentle blood; and more than a hundred years after Fortescue wrote *The Governance of England*, a preparedness to commit robbery continued to be widely viewed as a sign of spirit, springing from an inbred need to see what Clavell calls 'Action'.[20] As a result, the gentleman robber was regarded with special indulgence, and after his capture, with sympathy and pity.

As we have seen, despite the various loopholes in the legal system, this wasn't always enough to keep him from ending on the gallows. Highway robbery was officially regarded as a serious offence, 'amongst the most hainous felonies', as Sir Edward Coke, the celebrated jurist, described it in the seventeenth century. What made it so heinous was the element of violence: the distinction between the robber and the cutpurse was the fact

104

that the former committed a violent assault, and put his victim in fear.[21] However, this element of open confrontation was, of course, precisely the reason why the highway robber was felt to be a brave man; and there was undoubtedly an undercurrent of opinion that held that the able-bodied male victim of a robber was laughable, a bit of a coward. If he'd had any spirit, he would never have yielded his purse. So to some extent, he deserved what had happened to him.[22]

Such attitudes are nowhere more graphically illustrated than in a minor episode in the history of the Verney family. In 1657, Lady Hobart wrote to her Verney relations about a piece of recent news: Dr William Denton, a well-known physician, with whom they had family connections, had been stopped and robbed while riding with his wife in their coach. The incident, she says, is being gossiped about everywhere she goes, 'and never any man was so lafed at, for ever body macks mearth at it'. She adds that 'if doctor dos intend to dou anything with the country' (she means, report the crime to the authorities, following which he could claim back half his losses), 'he shold have conseled the men though he knew them, for they will surely hang them'. It is clear where her sympathies lie. Meanwhile, another member of the family, Colonel Harry Verney, accused in jest of having been one of the robbers, was said to have enjoyed the imputation.[23] It seems to have been not uncommon for victims of robberies to be reluctant to give evidence against their attackers.[24] Lady Hobart's remarks about the unfortunate Dr Denton suggest something of the social pressures that might come to bear upon such people.

In the matter of highway robbery, official culture, government culture, was at odds with another sort of culture. It would not be strictly accurate to call it a popular culture, a culture of the people, though there is reason to believe that many ordinary folk subscribed to it. There is plenty of evidence to suggest that it was primarily a culture of the gentry, as Elyot indicates; a culture, then, of the governors. Perhaps we might call it an unofficial culture of the governors. As such, it was influential; however, it can hardly be called hegemonic or controlling. It diverged sharply from the thinking behind the criminal law and behind various government drives to suppress robberies. However, it did not promote direct challenges to either, though in practice it certainly had the effect of partly subverting their purposes. It did so both by promoting an image of robbery as a crime for gentlemen and men of courage, and by encouraging leniency towards the perpetrators in precisely those men who were responsible for administering the laws.

Respect and sympathy for robbers ran deep under the skin of many Tudor gentlemen. In 1566, Thomas Harman, a former Justice of the Peace, put together a book out of material he had obtained by questioning

itinerants who came to beg at his house in Kent. *A Caveat for Commen Cursetors* is largely devoted to the activities of thieving tramps and the deceptions practised by beggars. Harman offers it as an aid to law enforcement. A rigid man, he seldom shows any compassion for the stark poverty and desperation that his investigations reveal. He warns his readers against giving alms, since most beggars are not what they seem. When he writes about beggars who claim to be wounded soldiers, he says that most of these have never been near the wars, and even if they have, he implies, they do not deserve charity. 'For . . . the hardist [hardiest] souldiers . . . and [if] they escape all hassardes, and retourne home agayne . . . wyl surely desperatly robbe and steale, . . . for they be so much ashamed and disdayne to beg or aske charity, that rather they wyll as desperatlye fight for to lyve and mayntayne them selves, as manfully and valyantly they ventred [ventured] themselves in the Prynces quarell.'[25] Harman's attitude to such men contrasts powerfully with his contempt for the wandering beggars.

The notion that, for a man who lacks a livelihood, resorting to robbery is far less shameful than begging was a very old one in Harman's time. We encountered it in Chapter Three, in Matthew Paris's account of the post-Conquest outlaws, which dates from the mid-thirteenth century.[26] The pride that Matthew Paris takes for granted in a nobleman or gentleman is for Harman the mark of a soldier, a real soldier, one who is valiant, one who has proved himself by 'manfully' risking his life in battle. In Harman's time, 'manhood' was beginning to be an important theme in the rhetoric of the robber cult. Preachers and moralists had long been troubled by the way men of a swaggering and quarrelsome temper, fighters, casual killers even, were regarded by many folk as 'manly' men, prime exemplars of 'manhood'.[27] From the mid-sixteenth century, words like 'manly', 'manfully' and 'manhood' begin to be used repeatedly in connection with robbers and robbery. In Chapter One I cited Ralph Robinson's 1551 translation of More's *Utopia*, in which he intrudes the words 'manlier' and 'manfully' into More's much more neutral account of the pillaging habits of out-of-work retainers. I also quoted the words of the Elizabethan gentleman soldier Robert Hitchcock, in 1580, to the effect that a man of spirit, by implication a 'real man', will sooner engage in robbery with violence than stoop to beg from people who are his inferiors in courage.[28] Such attitudes were satirised just a few years later by the dramatist Robert Wilson, in his allegorical play *The Three Ladies of London* (1584). Tom Beggar and his companion Wily Will are being sounded out by Fraud, who wants them to join him in a robbery:

And can ye live in this sort, to go up and down the country a-begging?
O base minds! I trow I had rather hack it out by the highway-side.

Tom Beggar's reply shows him well versed in the language and conventions of the robber cult:

> O worthy Captain Fraud, you have won my noble heart:
> You shall see how manfully I can play my part.
> And here's Wily Will, as good a fellow as your heart can wish . . . [29]

In his book *Martin Markall, Beadle of Bridewell*, published in 1610, Samuel Rid divides highway robbers into two classes: 'high lawyers', who 'are called gentlemen robbers', who 'ride on horses well appointed, and go in show like honest men', and 'padders', who 'rob on foot, and have no other help but a pair of light heels and a thick wood'. The first sort, the gentlemen robbers, he says, are chiefly recruited from three sorts of men. First are the younger sons of gentlemen, who are 'brought up in idleness and gaming', and having neither inheritance nor profession, are left without an income when their parents die. Then there are gentlemen who inherit wealth, but being reckless spenders, quickly squander it on 'banqueting with whores, and making late suppers'. All that such men acquire from their robberies they waste in extravagance and debauchery. Finally, there are soldiers, who when they are discharged, or perhaps, desert their colours, 'cannot betake themselves to any honest trade of life, but, loving to live in idleness, betake themselves to robbing and stealing'.[30]

Rid's comments, of course, are purely impressionistic. They are far from being hard evidence as to the true social origins of the majority of mounted robbers in his time. One important category, whose existence is attested in a number of sources, and particularly by Clavell, who was in a good position to know, comprised men of relatively humble birth, who had often spent time in service, but who when they became mounted robbers, affected the dress and manners of the gentry. Rid has nothing to say about 'gentlemen robbers' of this kind. However, his account does provide us with a useful summary of the most important cultural stereotypes of the gentleman robber that were available in Jacobean England. It is noticeable that whereas the well-born outlaw of medieval stories typically took to the woods as a result of some experience of injustice, usually involving the loss of his lands, the well-born robber of the sixteenth and seventeenth centuries is almost invariably portrayed as having been driven to adopt his course of life for economic reasons: his robberies are necessary, it seems, to sustain him in the life of a gentleman, which is otherwise beyond his means.

The most interesting of Rid's three stereotypes is the second: the gentleman who inherits wealth, squanders it all, then takes to the highway for more. It's the beginnings of a tale in itself, a moral tale, and by Rid's time it formed the basis of a stock dramatic type. We have already encountered its earliest incarnation, the figure of Youth in the allegorical play of that title, first performed almost a century before Rid was writing. The spendthrift robber plays a major role in an Elizabethan morality play, *The Contention Between Liberality and Prodigality*. This was performed in front of Elizabeth in 1601, but had probably been written as early as 1568. The extravagant gentleman Prodigality and the churlish countryman Tenacity are rival suitors to Lady Fortune for the custody of Money (a character). Prodigality is successful: but when he spends too much time in the company of Tom Tosse and Dicke Dicer, a pair of gamblers, and their confederate Dandaline the hostess, he finds that Money runs away from him. Money ends up in the care of Tenacity, but when Prodigality learns of this, he and his two gambling companions attack Tenacity on the highway, murder him and take Money back again. The hue and cry is raised, and Prodigality is arrested and brought to court. He pleads guilty and is sentenced to death; but when he expresses his repentance, and begs the Judge to intercede for him, he is told that a petition will be made to the Prince to procure him a pardon. Money, who has become uncomfortably swollen in the keeping of the miserly Tenacity, is given into the care of Liberality, who knows that Money is neither for hoarding nor squandering.[31]

Tenacity is murdered; Prodigality, by contrast, is given the promise of a pardon. Though the prodigal young gentleman is shown to be misguided, he is treated with more sympathy, in this courtly play, than the grasping yeoman farmer. This undoubtedly speaks of the tensions, in Elizabethan England, between the gentry and the social group immediately below them, the yeomanry – at this time identified chiefly with substantial farmers of non-gentle origin.[32] These, taken collectively, were a thriving and confident group. Spared the gentleman's prohibition on manual labour, and also the gentleman's obligations of large-scale hospitality, conspicuous generosity and display, and major office-holding, they were flourishing: so that Sir Thomas Smith, in his *De Republica Anglorum* (written between 1565 and 1577), says of them that 'they . . . daily doe buy the landes of unthriftie gentlemen'. Their sons, he says, often become gentlemen, either because they are educated for one of the professions, or else because they inherit 'sufficient landes whereon they may live without labour'.[33]

In terms of the moral allegory, the disparity in the fates of Prodigality and Tenacity reflect Elizabethan assessments of the relative social damage caused by the two ways of misusing money that they represent. As George Whetstone put it, in 1584, '*Prodigalytie* and *Coveitousnesse*, are two extreame Passions . . . Yet . . . the Coveitous man is the worst of both: for he doth no man (not so much as himself) good with his goods: when the Prodigal, by the undoing of himself, inricheth many.'[34] Wealth is for use; this the majority of Elizabethans believed passionately. The miser's love for his useless money, to us comic and perhaps pathetic, was in those days an obscenity. For all social groups, but especially for the gentleman, the ideal was liberality, both in giving and spending, and the sin of the reckless prodigal was correspondingly felt to be far less socially harmful than that of the skinflint.

Extravagance and a taste for living it up were viewed as especially characteristic of the young. It was thought that as people grew older, they were inclined to go to the other extreme and become careful with money, and greedy.[35] In *The Contention Between Liberality and Prodigality*, Prodigality is characterised as 'yong, wastfull, roysting Prodigality' in contrast to 'old, sparing, covetous niggard, Tenacity'.[36] One conflict represented in the encounter between the two is the battle between youth and age for control of the available resources. Like riotous living, highway robbery was associated with youth; it was sometimes excused as just another expression of youthful high spirits.[37]

The stereotype of the spendthrift gentleman robber was an influential one. By Elizabeth's reign, some authors had begun to reshape no less a hero than Robin Hood to fit the new pattern. In Richard Grafton's *Chronicle at large* (1569), Robin Hood is said to have been an earl, who 'so prodigally exceeded in charges and expences, that he fell into great debt' for which he was outlawed. Another important modification that Grafton makes to the legend is to describe Robin as targeting not only wealthy clerics but also 'the houses of riche Carles' with his robberies.[38] A 'carl' is a farmer; also a man who is not of gentle birth; also a grasping, mean man. William Warner, in *Albions England* (second edition, 1589), copies Grafton in likewise making the hero into a nobleman. In Warner's account, the rich priests and abbots drop out of the picture; Robin's victim-enemies are now 'Churles' (a word cognate to 'carl', and of very similar meanings). As we saw in Chapter Five, it was Warner who took the step, which has proved so influential, of transforming Robin Hood from a wildly generous robber to a man who, moved by ideals of justice, robbed the rich with the express purpose of redistributing their wealth among the poor. Warner's Robin Hood explicitly justifies his robberies by the claim that he returns to circulation the money that 'the Churles abuse or hide' in 'Their Coffers', denying it to the use of the community.[39] Churls, non-aristocrats, disregard the obligations that are recognised by gentlemen to be liberal in giving and spending.

The ruined heir inherits wealth, but squanders it. Some gentlemen had no money to start with. Many of these were 'younger brothers', the first of Rid's three sorts of gentleman robber. The plight of the 'younger brother' has been touched on already in relation to *The Tale of Gamelyn*.[40] During the intervening centuries, it certainly hadn't improved, and by Rid's time it appears to have been becoming noticeably more difficult.[41] Under the

109

custom of primogeniture, to which most aristocratic families adhered, the family lands and the lion's share of the resources went to the eldest son. Younger sons were relatively neglected. The problems that resulted from this practice were chiefly an issue for the gentry. Yeomen families were generally more equitable in their treatment of their children, and noble families could usually find the means to endow their younger sons with enough at least to maintain them in a gentlemanly manner. But the younger son of a gentry family was often placed in an unenviable position, as John Earle's character of 'A Younger Brother' bitingly records:

> His father has done with him as Pharaoh to the children of Israel, that would have them make brick and give them no straw, so he tasks him to be a Gentleman and leaves him nothing to maintain it. The pride of his house has undone him, which the elder's Knighthood must sustain, and his beggary that Knighthood. His birth and bringing up will not suffer him to descend to the means to get wealth: but he stands at the mercy of the world, and, which is worse, of his brother. . . . If his annuity stretch so far, he is sent to the University, and with great heart-burning takes upon him the Ministry, as a profession he is condemned to by his ill fortune. Others take a more crooked path yet, the King's highway, where at length their vizard is plucked off, and they strike fair for Tyburn: but their brother's pride, not love, gets them a pardon. His last refuge is the Low Countries, where rags and lice are no scandal, where he lives a poor Gentleman of a company, and dies without a shirt.[42]

The reference to the Low Countries is to Count Mansfeld's expedition of 1625; his ill-provided soldiers died like flies. In comparison with such a fate as that, the attractions of 'the King's highway' may be easily imagined.

As Earle indicates, careers in the Church were unpopular; the army was highly risky, unpleasant and underpaid. There were few other options. The law brought riches to some, but it was intensely competitive. Some gentlemen found places in noblemen's households, as secretaries, stewards or gentlemen ushers, but from the later years of Elizabeth's reign, the nobility were ceasing to maintain the huge retinues that had been common in earlier generations.[43] A pamphlet of 1598, *A Health to the Gentlemanly profession of Servingmen*, laments a sharp decline in the positions open to gentlemen servants – and says of the discharged servant that since 'he hath not been trayned to any bodyly laboure', he must either resign himself to starving, or else, as the author whimsically puts it, 'make his appearance at Gaddes hill, Shooters hill, Salisburie playne, or Newmarket heath, to sit in Commission, and examine passengers'.[44] It's an old theme adapted to a new situation. The 'younger brother' 's chief remaining choice was apprentice-ship to a trade, and this was a course increasingly followed by gentry

Trade loses gentility

families seeking to provide for their surplus sons. However, it was often said that the gentleman born who went into trade lost thereby his right of birth and blood and could no longer claim gentle status. This, for many, was an agonising prospect.[45] In John Earle's character of 'A High-Spirited Man', written in the mid-1620s, we are told: 'He would sooner accept the gallows than a mean trade, or anything that might disparage the height of man in him'.[46] This hints, again, at the desperate alternative: becoming a highwayman.

In his book *A Mirour for Magestrates of Cyties* (1584), George Whetstone describes how well-dressed robbers could be found mixing with gentlemen of substance in the fashionable London 'ordinaries', or eating houses: 'The brave Companion, who in Apparayle, countenaunce, and bouldnes, wyll cheacke-mate with [behave as the equal of] men of right good worshyp, and lyving, when he . . . in a Greene Thycket getteth a Masked face, a Pystoll, and a Whypcorde, and hath Inheritaunce in the Ile of *Snatch*'.[47] In early modern London, with its seasonal ebb and flow of visiting gentry, a gentleman highwayman might easily be impossible to distinguish from a man with a comfortable income from the rents of his country estates. At gentry level, the boundaries of English society were relatively fluid: 'who can live idly and without manuall labour, and will beare the port, charge and countenaunce of a gentleman, he shall be called master, . . . and shall be taken for a gentleman' – so says Sir Thomas Smith, in his *De Republica Anglorum*.[48] It is easy to see how a man of gentle birth who either lacked means or had run through his inheritance might have found in a career as a robber a way to keep up appearances and therefore maintain his status. Moreover, and this is important, it was a course that many people of his own kind would have condoned, at least in part. In their eyes, anything that smacked of manual labour would irrevocably taint his blood and call into question his claim to be a gentleman. Robbery, on the other hand, might have been a crime, but it was, at least, a gentlemanly crime.

Gentry prefer to stay within genteel callings

The correspondence of the Verney family in the later seventeenth century offers us some insights into the life of just this kind of penniless gentleman robber. Richard Hals was a connection of the Verneys by marriage. Before the Civil Wars, his father had held lands in Cork, but his son seems to have been left with very limited resources. It is quite likely that his father's estates had suffered during the fighting. In 1655, he is nineteen and fatherless. A cryptic remark by his distant cousin, Sir Ralph Verney, suggests that he already has a reputation as a robber. An optimistic aunt does her best to see him settled as a clerk in the office of a lawyer or attorney, but apparently with no success. At some point Hals goes abroad, probably to escape the law, but by 1663 he has returned, and 'a tretcherous frind' has 'betrayed' him 'to the Master Keeper of Newgate' in return for £100. He is in irons, and the same devoted aunt is scraping together money to pay for his pardon. In 1666, he joins the navy to fight against the Dutch, but once back on shore, has trouble extracting his pay. He hopes for a post in the army or navy but can do nothing unless he has money to bribe 'the clarkes att the Navy Office, and . . . my Lord Generall's Secretary'. Three years later, in the course of a sweep against highwaymen, he has a narrow escape from arrest; it is rumoured that he has 'leaped out of a window two storeys high leaving his horse and his cloathes behind'. In 1671, he is imprisoned in Exeter jail, from where he is eventually moved to Newgate. Here, in 1672, he writes to his close friend, Sir Ralph's son, Edmund: 'I have made a hard shift to hould out three or fower yearres in a bad kinde of life, I meane, the highway, for which I am att last condemned to die, justly as to the law, though by the unjustnesse of a falce frende, who fainte-harted, swore against fower of us, to save his owne life.' However, another of Hals's aunts, Lady Hobart (the same who was so entertained by the robbing of Dr Denton) has negotiated a reprieve from the gallows, and later Captain Elliott, his former captain in his engagement at sea, promises to intercede for him. By 1673 he is free; he talks about taking service as a soldier in the Low Countries, but instead he returns to his old way of life. A year later he is in Chelmsford jail, and to save his neck, has turned informer: he has made 'a full discovery of all persones I did or doe knowe that use the pad [highway robbery]'. Pressed to give more detail, he complies. When he learns that even this may not save his life, he is anguished: 'Could they not as well have . . . hanged [me] in my state of inocency, I meane, while I was a pure theife, without blott or blemish, as to make me stincke in the nostrills of my ould assosiates'. But in the end, he escapes the gallows yet again. In 1679, he has found honest if undistinguished employment supervising court bailiffs, but in 1685 he is back in jail. At the age of nearly fifty, he is finally hanged at Tyburn.

Hals's career as a highwayman lasted for more than twenty-five years, on and off. So far as it is possible to tell, this was an unusually long period for a persistent robber to evade the gallows, and suggests how important were his good family connections, and the willingness of some of his relatives to make repeated interventions on his behalf. Although his extended family obviously found him an anxiety, as well as a drain on their purses, it does not appear that they ever refused to receive him or treated him as having passed beyond the limits of acceptable behaviour. Instead, the Verney letters give us glimpses of him as he visits Edmund Verney in his country house, attends the wedding of one of his cousins, and joins another for a round of election visits to Buckinghamshire voters.[49]

The gentleman highwayman, as Robert Parsons shrewdly perceived, was sustained in his predatory course of life by the attitudes and structures of his society. At the start of this chapter, I quoted his observation that men of this kind were encouraged to commit their offences by what he calls the 'light estimation of the fault'. John Clavell puts the matter more strongly; he says that his fellow highwaymen are under the impression that their 'actions . . . are such / As pace with honour'. The ready availability of pardons was experienced by such men as a positive endorsement of their way of life. Clavell says that his fellow robbers believed that they were recognised by the public as 'brave, and valiant', and that because of this efforts would always be made to keep them from the gallows. In his role as moralist, he declares the highwaymen mistaken: he says that 'good and brave men' rightly condemn them as sinful, and pity rather than admire them.[50] The truth, of course, is more complex. During the sixteenth and seventeenth centuries, the cultural messages received by robbers, actual and would-be, were, to say the least of it, decidedly mixed.

Very often, contradictory messages competed for attention from within a single text. *The Life and Death of Gamaliel Ratsey* (1605) offers a case in point. Ratsey is a representative of Rid's third class of gentleman robber: the returned soldier. He is also said to have been a gentleman born. Reading between the lines a little, it appears that he may well have been one of those 'younger sons to younger brothers' that Falstaff found so easy to recruit for his company, and of whom he was so contemptuous.[51] After fighting in Ireland under the Earl of Essex and later Lord Mountjoy, he returned to England in May 1603, and embarked on a brief career as a highway robber. He was executed at Bedford in March 1605.[52]

The Life and Death of Gamaliel Ratsey is supposed to have its source in Ratsey's conversations with some of his friends before his execution. He is said to have wanted the book to be published, 'as well to testifie unto the world his repentance, as to give cawsion to his country-men, to eschew his follie'.[53] At the end of the book there is a long poem entitled '*Ratseys repentance which he wrote* with his owne hand when hee was *in New-gate*'. If Ratsey, as is possible, sold this piece to the publisher as his own work, he was continuing to be true to his thievish profession, since much of it is plagiarised from *Luke Huttons Repentance*, published ten years earlier. On the whole, it is probably more likely that the task of adapting parts of Hutton's poem and composing some extra stanzas was carried out by a professional writer.

The result, in keeping with the genre to which it belongs, is edifying, if rather dull: it expresses anguish at the speaker's situation and remorse for his crimes, warns other robbers to learn from his fate, and concludes with a promise of repentance.[54] However, in *The Life and Death of Gamaliel Ratsey* it is merely the afterpiece to a very different kind of text. The main body of the work is made up almost entirely of amusing or sensational anecdotes about Ratsey and his associates; in fact, it is a jest-biography, like Greene's *The Blacke Bookes Messenger*. The Ratsey of the stories does have very occasional thoughts of repentance, but they never result in his changing his ways. In many respects, he is a traditional robber hero, quick-witted and audacious, capriciously generous, an upholder after his fashion of a rough and ready justice. He robs nine men single-handed, on the strength of his formidable reputation, and intercepts a conjuror out of bravado to prove he is not afraid of him. He introduces himself and his gang to a victim in terms reminiscent of Hitchcock or Harman: 'we are Gentlemen and Souldiours . . . we are in want, and we scorne to crye out our wants in the streets, for we shall not be heard; we will have money if it walke upon the earth'.[55] In one of his wittier moments, he robs two clothiers (middlemen dealing in wool) and insists on knighting them before he will let them go: a satire on James I, whose practice of selling knighthoods to rich men with no claim to gentility was a highly topical scandal at the time. He displays his generosity when he holds up an old countryman and his wife. When he finds that they have, as they protest, rather less than a couple of pounds between them, which they are taking to market to buy a cow to keep them in their declining years, he gives them £2 from his own purse and tells them to buy a second. (However, £2 is small change to Ratsey, who regularly robs his victims of £80 and more at a single time.) On one occasion, he lends a farmer £50 to pay off a creditor, then contrives an opportunity to strip the same creditor of a full £300. This, of course, is a distant variant on the story of Robin Hood, the impoverished knight and the monks of St Mary's.

The Life and Death of Gamaliel Ratsey did well enough to be followed by a sequel, *Ratseis Ghost*. This offers more of the same kind of thing, but certain key themes are stated more explicitly. Ratsey is a prodigal: when he robs a man of an exceptionally large sum, the point is made that he will not use it 'to buy Cattle, or House, or land . . . but to make himselfe merrie with his copesmates [mates, companions]'.[56] His free-spending habits are matched by an impulsive generosity. In one of the new stories, he holds up the daughter of an impoverished parson, but when she begs him not to take her money, his heart is softened. Instead of seizing the couple of pounds her father has given her to buy herself a gown, he gives her another thirty shillings to pay for a petticoat as well. When she tells her brother what has happened, he praises Ratsey as 'the honestest theefe that ever he heard of'.[57]

By contrast, when Ratsey stops a lawyer, and the man pleads with him to show some pity, he responds: 'Faith . . . there is no pittye to be had of thee, nor such as thou art: thou art worse then I, that take it by the highway, for let me meet with a poor man, and take his money, if I perceive him indigent, and needy I give it him again, and somwhat back to boot, but you picke everye poore mannes pocket with your trickes and quillets . . . till you leave them never a penny to blesse themselves'.[58] This

114

is a variant of the conflict between the Spendthrift and the Grasper, a theme with which we have met already in relation to *The Contention Between Liberality and Prodigality* and Warner's *Albions England*. However, this time it is given a new and sharper twist. Ratsey makes the claim that when the highwayman robs the lawyer, the open robber plunders the covert robber, the man who fleeces his victims within the law's protection. This is a motif that often recurs in the later highwayman texts. Much of its power comes from the fact that it draws on standard Christian social teaching. Thus Thomas Becon, in his *Catechism* (1560), intended to assist in the religious education of children, declares that there are many kinds of thief besides specialists in robbery and larceny. Among the numerous examples he lists are people who use crooked dealing in buying or selling, those who seek excessive profit, usurers, lawyers who spin out cases to increase their fees, and even rich men who neglect giving charity to the poor.[59] Of course, it was not Becon's purpose to give encouragement to highwaymen. When Ratsey asserts that lawyers, as a class, are greater and more merciless robbers than he is himself, and especially when he uses this claim, by implication, to legitimate his taking another man's money by force, he is going far beyond anything that is warranted by Becon, or any other orthodox Christian writer. But not beyond the prescriptions of current popular wisdom. 'To deceive a deceiver is no deceit' was a common proverb.[60]

The righteous outlaw of the later Middle Ages, Gamelyn or Robin Hood, chastises corrupt judges and sheriffs, together with hard-hearted monks whose thoughts are set on worldly possessions. In the early modern highwayman tales, the theme persists with a difference. The robber hero is often found plundering those economic sinners who are out of reach of the criminal law: not only misers and unscrupulous lawyers, but usurers and middlemen such as cattle dealers or clothiers, who were widely held to be grasping types, intent on driving hard bargains. Among the targets of Ratsey's robberies are several members of occupations that evoked a measure of social disapproval. Besides the clothiers and the lawyer, his victims include a grazier or cattle dealer, a conjuror, or practitioner of dubious magic, and even a troupe of actors. The financial success of certain actors, including William Shakespeare, and their consequent rise up the social ladder were causing envy and outrage in certain quarters.

Ratsey's relationship with the criminal underworld is a theme that is handled delicately. When he wants to recruit a gang, near the start of *The Life and Death*, he travels to London. Later, when they are on the run after a robbery, he and his comrades make for London again, where they share out their loot at an inn in Southwark, a district of ill repute.[61] Ratsey knows his way around the urban criminal scene. However, great care is taken to distance the generous highwayman from shoplifters, pickpockets and

115

similar underhanded and dishonourable types. *Ratseis Ghost* contains various stories of ingenious thefts. Some of these are downright villainous; in one of them a thief contrives to have an innocent man hanged. All but one of these, a horse-stealing tale, are attributed solely to Ratsey's sidekicks, Snell and Shorthouse, not to the hero himself. Ratsey's underworld connections are never allowed to taint him. Instead, Snell and Shorthouse act as a foil to him, to throw into relief his superior greatness of spirit. His superiority to others of his kind becomes the central issue in one of the tales about his liberality. A group of his fellow robbers take about £3 from a small artisan, enough to beggar him. But when the man encounters Ratsey, the hero, true to his principles, makes good his losses, and gives him another pound as a friendly gesture.

Throughout both these books, the reader is encouraged to find Ratsey's crimes entertaining: the tale of one robbery is entitled 'A pretty prancke', while another is summed up as 'a prettie tricke', and we are told that he and his men regard a horse-stealing episode as 'but a jest of merriment'.[62] In *Ratseis Ghost*, the highwayman plays his role of prankster right until the end. At his execution, seeing a storm of rain coming on, he pretends that he has decided to make a last-minute confession of undisclosed offences. Instead, he rambles irrelevantly, until at last, when the rain has stopped, he tells the Sheriff that he had only been wasting time, 'that he might see them all well washt before he dide'.[63] Only a paragraph earlier, he had expressed his remorse and contrition; but now this turns out to have been the preliminary to setting up a last good belly laugh.

For all the protestation at the start of *The Life and Death*, there is in the end little in either of the Ratsey pamphlets to encourage the reflection that robbing on the highway is a 'follie' to be avoided. If Ratsey is not precisely Robin Hood, he is nevertheless a dashing figure, scourge of economic predators and parasites, trimmer of a little surplus from people who can easily afford it, and who probably obtained it by dubious means in the first place. The overwhelming impression that is left by these stories is that highway robbery is a fine career for a fellow with sound nerves, gentlemanly impulses, a keen sense of humour and an appetite for carousing. And if the end of it is the gallows – well, that, too, is a chance for a man to swagger it and show his quality.

10

Falstaff and the Wild Prince

In Shakespeare's England, the robber's mystique was nourished by tales from popular history. Many people took a certain pride in looking back on a national tradition of bold robber heroes.[1] Prominent among these, second only to Robin Hood himself, was the mighty warrior king, the victor of Agincourt, Henry V. Stories of Henry V's wild youth and his sudden reformation on becoming king had come down to the Elizabethans from his own times. The oldest version of the robbery anecdote recounts how, when his father was alive, the Prince would sometimes disguise himself and together with some of his friends, would lie in wait to rob his own receivers – that is, the officials whose task was to collect the rents and other revenues from his estates. The money, in other words, was his own, and the 'robberies' were more in the nature of larks than crimes. Afterwards, the receivers were compensated for their ordeal, and those who had resisted the 'robbers' most fiercely were given additional rewards.[2]

The legends of the Wild Prince were first treated dramatically in about 1587, in a play called *The Famous Victories of Henry the Fifth*. This is a lively but very rough-and-ready piece of writing. Most of the attention that it has received has been because it provided Shakespeare with one of his sources for the two *Henry IV* plays and *Henry V*. However, considered in the context of the robber cult, it is a fascinating document in its own right.

In the opening scene of *The Famous Victories*, 'the yoong Prince', as he is called, has just waylaid, not his own but his father's receivers. He plainly has some anxiety about this, and demands of his companions, Ned and Tom, 'But tell me sirs, thinke you not that it was a villainous part of me to rob my fathers Receivers?' Here, as very often in Elizabethan English the implications of the word 'villainous' are hovering between the older social meaning (a villain, or 'villein', is a man of unfree birth) and the more familiar moral sense. Ned reassures him: 'Why no my Lord, it was but a tricke of youth.' What might seem rather base or ungentlemanly behaviour, to rob one's father of his revenues, is excused by youth, which must be allowed its licences. Prince Harry makes a habit of robbery: a few lines later he receives some bad news about one of his servants whom he employs 'to spie / Out . . . booties', that is, opportunities for robbery. The man is now on the run, having 'robd a poore Carrier'. Henry responds with instant disgust: 'Now base minded rascal to rob a poore carrier, / Wel it skils not, ile save the base vilaines life'.[3] For Prince Harry, the rights and wrongs of robbery are very much bound up with matters of social status. The robber shows his quality by attacking rich travellers who are able to defend themselves, not poor working men. His servant has proved himself to be a 'villain', or person of the lowest social and moral standing, not by committing a robbery, but by robbing in a cowardly way.

Prince Harry, by contrast, is a gentleman robber. This means, among other things, that he knows what has to be done with the loot. Surveying the bags of money ('a thousand pound') that his companions have taken from the receivers, he declares, heroically, 'as I am true Gentleman, I wil have the halfe / Of this spent to night'. His plans include 'the olde Taverne in Eastcheape' and 'a pretie wench'. He has absorbed the authentic robber ethos, promising his friends, 'We are all fellowes, I tell you sirs, and [if] the King / My father were dead, we would be all Kings'.[4]

In a later scene, the Prince's servant, Cutbert Cutter, is tried by the Lord Chief Justice for his robbery of the carrier. He is insolent, relying on the Prince's influence to save him. When Prince Harry arrives, he tries to excuse the man by claiming that the robbery had been done 'but in jest', invoking the notion that, after all, highway robbery is only a sort of prank. The Lord Chief Justice remains unmoved, and insists on his determination to enforce the law. Harry, in a rage, boxes the judge on the ear, and is sent to the Fleet prison for contempt.

The Wild Prince seems to be about to subvert the legal system altogether. After he has been released from the Fleet, he promises his friend Ned that when he becomes king, he will 'put my Lord chief Justice out of office', and appoint Ned in his place. He is lyrical about the regime that will ensue: 'thou shalt hang none but picke purses and horse stealers, and such base minded villaines, but that fellow that will stand by the high way side couragiously with his sword and buckler and take a purse, that fellow give him commendations; beside that, send him to me and I will give him an anuall pension out of my Exchequer, to maintaine him all the dayes of his life'.[5] The play stops some way short of endorsing this extreme passion for highway robbers. On the death of his father, the Prince reforms, and banishes his old companions from the court. Nevertheless, the robbers are accepted at their own valuation, as brave men who adhere, at least if they are aristocrats, to their own code of honour. Prince Harry's career as a highway robber is even presented as a portent of his military victories to come:

> HENRY 4 Now trust me my Lords, I feare not but my sonne
>   Will be as warlike and victorious a Prince,
>   As ever raigned in England.
> BOTH LORDS His former life shewes no lesse.[6]

The first reference to the Wild Prince in the Shakespearean cycle of English history plays occurs near the end of *Richard II* (*c*. 1596). The usurper Henry IV now rules in place of the imprisoned King Richard, but the behaviour of his son and heir is already causing him grief. The Prince stays away from court, preferring the London taverns, and the company of ruffians:

> Even such, they say, as stand in narrow lanes
> And beat our watch and rob our passengers,
> While he, young wanton, and effeminate boy,
> Takes on the point of honour to support
> So dissolute a crew.[7]

The word 'support' indicates that he uses his position to give protection to his lawless friends; to use the term that was current in the later Middle Ages, he is practising maintenance.[8] This was not yet, in Shakespeare's time, a purely historic problem, even in its more obviously oppressive forms. Lawrence Stone reports that during the 1570s, Giles, Lord Chandos 'protected servants of his who robbed men on the highway near Sudeley Castle, so that the inhabitants dared not arrest the thieves nor the victims prosecute their assailants'.[9] Sudeley Castle is a bare twenty miles from Stratford-upon-Avon.

Shakespeare's Prince arrives on stage, trading banter with Sir John Falstaff, in the second scene of *Henry IV, Part I* (*c*. 1597). The exchanges between the two are a riot of equivocation. One area of ambiguity, as William Empson long ago pointed out in a brilliant reading, is the question of just how deeply Prince Hal has involved himself in Falstaff's robberies.[10] Listening to the interplay between them in the early part of this scene, it is entirely possible to assume that Shakespeare's Wild Prince is as much of a robber, or almost so, as his predecessor in *The Famous Victories*. When Falstaff claims that robbers are 'governed ... by ... the moon', Hal instantly speaks of 'us that are the moon's men' and implies that he, too, knows something of snatching purses. Later, when Falstaff starts to maunder about his intention to reform, Hal puts an end to it by saying, 'Where shall we take a purse tomorrow, Jack?'[11] Yet these speeches occur

119

in the context of a series of exchanges in which Falstaff betrays an evident anxiety that Hal's support for robbers and robbery is less wholehearted than he might wish.

This concern first emerges in a request that, despite Hal's urgings to him to speak 'roundly', strains comprehension with its circumlocutions and rich suggestiveness:

> Marry then sweet wag, when thou art king let not us that are squires of the night's body be called thieves of the day's beauty: let us be Diana's foresters, gentlemen of the shade, minions of the moon; and let men say we be men of good government, being governed as the sea is, by our noble and chaste mistress the moon, under whose countenance we steal.[12]

The thrust of it is clear. Falstaff is concerned with *names*; with the ugly names given to men like himself, who, as he has already acknowledged, 'take purses':[13] names that are accusations in themselves, such as 'thieves', and 'men of bad government' (that is, ill-governed, ill-behaved men). He has some better ones to suggest. Robbers had always had a taste for fancy names: as we saw in Chapter Four, in the early fourteenth century they called themselves 'shaveldours' and 'ryfelours'; later in the same century, they called themselves 'roberdesmen' (Robert's men); and by the 1590s, they were known within the underworld as 'high lawyers'. Other terms that were used for them at that date included 'cutters', 'good fellows' and 'St Nicholas's clerks'.[14] The names proposed by Falstaff are rich in certain kinds of association. A phrase like 'Diana's foresters' invokes potent images of moonlit poaching and outlaw life in the greenwood.[15] Meanwhile, phrases and words like 'squires of the . . . body', 'gentlemen', 'minions' carry insistent suggestions of a world of courtly favourites. Sir John knows very well that what people call you is important: to be called a gentleman is greatly preferable to being called a thief.

A key word in this speech and throughout the *Henry IV* plays is 'countenance'. Your countenance is, of course, your face; in Elizabethan English, it was also, more generally, your appearance. Moreover, by a metaphorical extension, it was your reputation in the eyes of other people, and your standing in the world. Your countenance might be 'lent' to someone else; in such circumstances, it meant something like patronage, favour, protection, even endorsement.[16] In the present passage, the reference to the moon's 'countenance' involves a double metaphor. The moon is being imaged as some great personage, and her countenance is both her 'face', looking down on the robbers as they go about their business, and the favour and protection that she can extend to her followers.

In Chapter Eight we saw that one of the most thoughtful Tudor commentators on professional crime, the author of *A manifest detection of Diceplay*, argues that the basic principle on which all robbers, thieves and swindlers depend is 'a counterfeate countenaunce in all things': that is, the appearance of being honest and reputable, without which they can hardly operate with any success.[17] One of the implications of Falstaff's speech is that he recognises that fancy names, association with popular legend and association with gentle status are all very useful to robbers. Falstaff is asking that when Hal is king, he should give official encouragement to the cult of the robber, to the glorification of robbers. Mystification of that kind is one sort of counterfeit countenance.[18]

There is also the countenance, the reputation or public face, of the individual robber. In the case of a man whose 'cover', to use a modern equivalent, has been 'blown', he may be able to replace this with the metaphorical 'countenance' lent him by some person of standing and influence. This is a matter of crucial personal importance to Falstaff, whose own façade is crumbling; only fifty lines later we hear him complain: 'I would to God thou and I knew where a commodity of good names were to be bought'.[19] Buried in the middle of his ramblings about 'squires of the night's body' and 'minions of the moon' are reminders of Hal's power, when he should become king, not only to sanction misdeeds committed by his 'minions', or recognised favourites, but even to change their names, by giving them office and rank. Once they are servants of the king, men will indeed 'say' that they are 'men of good government': they will hardly dare to say otherwise.

However, for the moment, all that robbers have to rely on are darkness and the moon. And the moon is a changeable mistress; a point that Hal, picking up Falstaff's metaphor, proceeds to stress:

Thou sayest well, and it holds well too, for the fortune of us that are the moon's men doth ebb and flow like the sea, being governed as the sea is, by the moon – as for proof now, a purse of gold most resolutely snatched on Monday night, and most dissolutely spent on Tuesday morning, got with swearing 'Lay by!', and spent with crying 'Bring in!', now in as low an ebb as the foot of the ladder, and by and by in as high a flow as the ridge of the gallows.[20]

In taking to himself the name of a 'moon's man', Hal may be aligning himself with the robbers, but he is also acknowledging that he himself is vulnerable to a change in fortune. He refuses to give Falstaff any comfort; instead, with his ominous gibe about the gallows, he plays on the robber's occupational anxiety. Falstaff's invitation to castle-building is checked by a reminder of life's vicissitudes: Hal is not king yet, and the forces of rebellion that may bring him to his death on the scaffold are already starting to threaten.

But Falstaff, always inclined to push his luck, is not yet prepared to drop the subject; in a few lines more he has returned to the attack: 'I prithee sweet wag, shall there be gallows standing in England when thou art king? and resolution thus fubbed as it is with the rusty curb of old father Antic the law? Do not when thou art king hang a thief.' Once again, the Prince is invited, first, to express his support for robbers in general, and secondly, to commit himself definitely to protecting his present companion after his accession. The Prince replies with a seeming offer of public office, which rapidly resolves into an insult, when he offers Falstaff the post of executioner. In Shakespeare's time, this was invariably reserved for some hardened member of the lowest criminal classes, who was spared from execution on condition he agreed to do the job.[21] Falstaff rallies fast:

> Well, Hal, well; and in some sort it jumps with my humour, as well as waiting in the court, I can tell you.
> PRINCE For obtaining of suits?[22]

Hal's deceptively simple question goes to the heart of what is at stake in this conversation. A 'suit' was a petition. It was an important part of the business of courtiers to petition the monarch, both on their own behalf and on behalf of clients. All sorts of things were the subjects of petitions: offices, trade monopolies, estates, wardships, pardons. It was a lucrative matter; a courtier known to have the royal ear could make a good income out of payments to act as go-betweens for lesser petitioners, as well as from the returns from favours begged on his or her own behalf.[23] A highwayman's prospects of plunder were insignificant, compared to those that were open to a king's favourite. Falstaff turns Hal's question aside with a pun on 'suits', but he suddenly expresses a deep sense of unexplained melancholy. As well he might. He's certainly not getting the sort of assurances he hopes for.

The ambiguity of Hal's relationship with the robbers comes into focus again when Falstaff's confederate Poins enters to give the two of them, not just Falstaff, news of a robbers' 'match' (or meeting), and to offer to supply them with 'vizards'. But when Falstaff asks him if he will join them, Hal turns righteous: 'Who, I rob? I a thief? Not I, by my faith.' Is this another tease, or a sudden statement of principle? Either way, it is important to Falstaff to persuade the Prince to take part in this robbery. He is quite frank about his reason: 'the poor abuses of the time want countenance'.[24] Hal's involvement in robbery can only enhance the dashing, aristocratic image of the highwayman, besides increasing the claim that Falstaff and his confederates have on him for patronage and protection.

The arguments by which Falstaff seeks to persuade him deserve consideration: 'There's neither honesty, manhood, nor good fellowship in thee, nor thou cam'st not of the blood royal, if thou darest not stand for ten shillings.'[25] Falstaff takes the concept of robbery as a crime befitting the courage and hot blood of a gentleman to its logical extreme, by suggesting that only by being prepared to commit it can Hal prove his royal breeding. The joke is a sharp one: as the son of a usurper, Hal's claim to royalty is open to question. A similar idea is glanced at in the word 'honesty', though here, of course, it is complicated with a quibble. In Shakespeare's time, the original meaning of 'honesty', 'honourable position or estate', had not yet been forgotten, though the modern sense, of 'honourable behaviour', truthfulness and fair dealing, was also current.[26] On the surface, Falstaff is saying to Hal, 'If you don't have the courage to commit this robbery, you don't deserve to be regarded as a man of honour, a gentleman.' At the same time, he is making a point of inverting accepted morality; as suits a man who calls for robbers to be known as 'men of good government', and who, as Poins banteringly claims, has sold his soul to the Devil.[27]

As for 'good fellowship', this, as we have seen, is a phrase rich in meaning and in evocation of the robber cult. Falstaff's principal notion of 'good fellowship' would seem to correspond with that of the comic Welshman in an early Tudor jestbook, who when questioned by his parish priest about certain local robberies, freely admitted his involvement. Asked why he had not mentioned them in his confession, he answered, 'he took that for no sin, for it was a custom among them that when any booty came of any rich merchant riding, that it was but a good neighbour's deed one to help another when one called another. And so they took that but for good fellowship and neighbourhood.'[28] As a result of its close association with the subculture of robbers, by the 1580s the phrase 'good fellow' had acquired the additional, slang meaning of 'highwayman'.[29] Its resonances during the late Elizabethan period emerge with particular clarity in *Sir John Oldcastle*, a play by Anthony Munday and others which was written in 1599. This has a highway robber in the character of 'Sir John the Parson of Wrotham', who describes himself as

> an honest theefe,
> One that will take it where it may be sparde,
> And spend it freely in good fellowship.

In one scene, he encounters Henry V in disguise and holds him up. Asked who he is, he says that he is 'A good fellow'; when the King claims to be one too, the robber retorts, 'If thou be a good fellow, play the good fellowes part: deliver thy purse without more adoe.' But the parson of

Wrotham is no Robin Hood; once the King has handed over his money, he keeps it all for himself.[30]

When Falstaff sets 'manhood' at stake in this challenge, he is once again invoking ideas of honour. The first test of a gentleman, according to Sir Thomas Smith, is that he should 'shew . . . a more manly corage . . . than others'. We have glanced in previous chapters at the Tudor notion that a willingness to commit robbery was proof of a man's quality.[31]

Throughout both the *Henry IV* plays, but especially *Part I*, a series of questions hangs in the air. What does it mean to be a man? What does it mean to be a nobleman? What is honour? And for Prince Hal, in particular, there is the crucial question: what is it to be a king? The terms in which Falstaff challenges the Prince to join him in his latest robbery show him sketching out his own reply to these questions. No matter how he masks them with high-sounding ambiguities, Falstaff's definitions of a man, a nobleman, a king are based on a commitment to robbery, to oppressing the weak and taking plunder. Falstaff's conception of nobility is the same as that expressed, more forthrightly, by his confederate Gadshill, when he boasts to his accomplice, the Chamberlain, that his associates are *gentlemen* robbers: 'I am joined with no foot-landrakers, no long-staff sixpenny strikers, . . . but with nobility and tranquillity, . . . such as will strike sooner than speak, and speak sooner than drink, and drink sooner than pray – and yet, 'zounds, I lie, for they pray continually to their saint the commonwealth, or rather not pray to her, but prey on her, for they ride up and down on her, and make her their boots' (that is, their booty, spoil).[32]

When Hal remains unmoved by Falstaff's provocation, Poins takes a hand. He undertakes to persuade the Prince to join them, so long as he can talk to him alone. Falstaff slips a last bid to influence Hal into his reply, tucked slyly into a parenthetical phrase: '(for recreation sake)'.[33] The Prince would only be indulging in a prank, he hints, a jest, a bit of fun. But Hal, on Poins's instigation, turns the joke against Falstaff, when, instead of taking part in the robbery, the two of them, in disguise, lie in wait for Falstaff and the rest, chase them away and appropriate the loot. Hal meets Falstaff's challenge in full, and meets it on his own terms, without stooping to rob honest travellers. In more senses than one, he upholds his honesty.

A great many of the characters in *Part I*, both major and minor, give voice to their own, sometimes quite idiosyncratic, concepts of nobility, honour and courage. For the wine drawers in the Boar's Head tavern, 'a lad of mettle' is a chap who can hold his liquor and excel in their drinking games. This is another test that Hal passes; it is also, of course, a test of his 'good fellowship' in the sense of conviviality. The capacity to carry one's liquor well was widely believed to be one of the marks of a gentleman, as Gadshill's remarks testify. And the last word on drinking and valour is pronounced by Falstaff, whose famous praise of sherris-sack, in *Henry IV, Part II*, elevates pot-valiancy into a heroic convention.[34]

Elsewhere, the fire-eating Hotspur has a telling story of a foppish lord who, he says, had arrived after the battle of Holmedon with messages from the King. This man complained when corpses were carried 'Betwixt the wind and his nobility', apparently taking the view that his birth ought to cushion him from disagreeable experiences. He also held that the nobleman's hereditary obligation to serve his ruler in war had been cancelled by the advent of guns, which killed, he thought, in such a cowardly way.[35] Hotspur himself, famously, is preoccupied with honour, which he pursues obsessively through military exploits. However, he is also keen on booty, in which respect, he is not very different to the highwaymen. His initial rift with the King stems from a quarrel over which of the two of them is to have the ransoming of some prisoners of war. When he rebels, he and his co-conspirators are quarrelling over the division of the country before their campaign has even begun. Falstaff's teasing challenge to the Prince to prove himself 'honest' by robbing on the highway finds an echo in Hotspur's contemptuous dismissal of a lord who refuses to join his rebellion. He calls him 'a shallow cowardly hind'; a hind is a labourer or servant.[36]

King Henry is another character with specific ideas about courage and the way that a nobleman should conduct himself. He tells his son to his face that he thinks it quite likely that Hal will go over to Hotspur's side out of cowardice. His reasoning is that Hal's taste for low company shows 'Base inclination' in him. 'Base' is another of those words in which moral and social meanings come together. In Henry's view, as he makes very plain, Hal's behaviour and his choice of companions are unsuited to his birth and status. This suggests to him that his son is 'degenerate', one in whom the blood of his race does not run true, and therefore, that he is probably a coward. Henry, as he does not disguise, would have preferred to have had Hotspur for a son. When Hal meets Hotspur in combat, he faces the culminating test of his mettle and honour. His triumph puts his courage and prowess beyond further question.

However, it does not provide a complete reply to his father's anxieties. Henry has warned his son against making the same mistake as Richard II. According to Henry, the cause of Richard's downfall was that he was too familiar with his inferiors, and allowed unworthy favourites to abuse his patronage: in Henry's words, he 'gave his countenance against his name'.[37] So, arguably, has Hal. For although Falstaff has failed to establish the claim on the Prince for which he was hoping, a time has already come when Hal has used his position to protect his friend. On the last occasion on which Hal appears on stage prior to his interview with the King, the sheriff comes to the tavern where he and his friends are carousing to arrest

Falstaff for a robbery. Falstaff, on Hal's direction, hides behind the arras, but not before the following exchange has occurred:

PRINCE . . . Now, my masters, for a true face, and good conscience.
FALSTAFF Both which I have had, but their date is out, and therefore I'll hide me.

Without a 'true face' of his own he gratefully accepts the 'countenance' lent him by the Prince, who at this point stands between Falstaff and the gallows. Hal, for his part, sends away the sheriff with a shameless lie; he tells him he has sent Falstaff out on an errand, and though he promises to send him to answer charges next day, his plan, as he reveals at the end of the scene, is to bribe the victims to drop the case ('The money shall be paid back again with advantage').[38]

The pendant to this episode occurs towards the end of *Henry IV, Part II*, when Davy, general factotum to Justice Shallow, requests his master to 'countenance' a friend of his in a legal matter. When Shallow replies that his friend is notorious, and 'an arrant knave', Davy insists: 'God forbid, sir, but a knave should have some countenance at his friend's request. . . . I have served your worship truly, sir, this eight years; and if I cannot once or twice in a quarter bear out a knave against an honest man, I have but a very little credit with your worship'.[39] Shallow is non-committal, but the exchange itself tells us a great deal about his behaviour in office. Soon, however, the Justice will find out from his own experience what happens to the vulnerable when those in positions of authority give countenance to knaves.

Just two scenes later the news comes that Henry IV has died; Prince Hal is now Henry V. Falstaff's reaction is emblematic of his attitudes: 'the laws of England are at my commandment'. His old anxieties have gone, and he is confident of favour. Later, as he and his associates, together with Justice Shallow, stand in the street waiting for the King to return from his coronation, he urges his companions to 'mark the countenance that he will give me'.[40] As so often with Falstaff, the word has more than one meaning. Meanwhile, Shallow has lent him a thousand pounds on his expectations of becoming a power at court. When, instead, the King banishes Falstaff from his presence, the Justice, not surprisingly, wants his money back. Falstaff refuses to let him have it; and whether he ever sees it again is more than we discover.[41]

Shakespeare handles the theme of the Robber Prince with noticeable circumspection. Despite some equivocal talk, the only time we see Prince Hal take part in a robbery on stage is when he holds up Falstaff and his gang. As I said in the previous chapter, proverbial wisdom took the view that 'to deceive a deceiver is no deceit'. However, to set against this, we have Hal's own prior jest to the effect that it is possible to be 'damned for cozening the devil'.[42] Later on in *Part I*, the Prince will pick Falstaff's pocket, though all he finds in it is a tavern bill.[43] Triumphant as he is in everything he undertakes, it is as if something in his blood condemns the Prince to enact meaningless reflections of his father's act in seizing the crown.[44] These type-actions reach a climax in *Part II*, in the scene in which the Prince, believing his father dead, removes the crown from his pillow as he lies asleep.[45]

Shakespeare did not have the final word on the Robber Prince. I have already mentioned the play of *Sir John Oldcastle*. This was written in 1599, the same year as Shakespeare's *Henry V*, very evidently with a view to cashing in on the success of that and the earlier *Henry IV* plays. When King Henry V is waylaid by the robber parson, he tells him, 'The time has beene I would have done as much / For thee'. The play fuses echoes of *The Famous Victories* with direct allusions to *Henry IV, Part I*, as Henry, in an aside, comments that Falstaff is now 'so fat, he cannot get on's horse', and wonders where Poins and Peto, his old confederates, are. The robber reminisces about the time when he himself had been robbed by the Prince and Falstaff, and nostalgically regrets the Prince's reformation: 'It's pittie that ere he should have bin a King; he was so brave a thiefe.'[46] It was this Prince who passed into popular tradition; John Taylor includes him in his list of famous English robbers, and Captain Alexander Smith, the early eighteenth-century 'historian' of the highwaymen, asserts that 'the eldest son of King Henry the Fourth' used to '[rob] on the highway often, with Sir John Falstaff and others'. Smith, characteristically, further embroiders the legend by stating that on 'three or four' occasions the Prince went so far as to hold up his own father.[47]

As for Falstaff: highway robbery, he claims, is his 'vocation'. This makes it the more curious that relatively little attention has been paid to him in the context of the cultural traditions about robbers. Critics have appealed to stereotypes like the braggart soldier and the parasite, and roles like the morality vice, lord of misrule, or the fool, in attempts to clarify his origins and nature. But until now, no one has looked into his relationship to the conventional image – or rather, images – of the highway robber. The 'vocation' joke itself is a good place to start. Shakespeare stole it from Thomas Nashe. Its original context is a description of the bandit chief Schimeon, in a highly coloured account of the Fall of Jerusalem: 'He held it as lawful for hym, (since al labouring in a mans vocation is but getting,) to gette wealth as wel with his sword by the High-way side, as the Laborer with his Spade or Mattocke . . . concluding, as there is no better tytle to a Kingdome then conquest, so there is no better clayme unto wealth, then by the conquest of a strong hand to compasse it.' Nashe is writing satirically.

Despite the exuberant tone, this is not an endorsement of the robber cult, but an account of the ethos of a predatory nobleman whom he makes no bones about calling 'degenerate'.[48]

Falstaff is a more ambiguous figure than this. We are prepared to forgive him a good deal, because of the way he makes us laugh. One source of humour, especially in *Henry IV, Part I*, is the comic discrepancy between the heroic robber he sometimes pretends to be and his actual presence and behaviour. As we have seen, he is very well versed in the language and ideology of the highwayman. Words like 'resolution' and 'manhood' slide glibly off his tongue. Yet when he finds himself offered violence, he runs away.

The language he uses during the robbery is worth some attention. He calls the travellers 'fat chuffs', accuses them of being 'grandjurors', and bellows at them, 'they hate us youth!', and 'young men must live'.[49] A 'chuff' was a countryman; the word is always pejorative, with overtones of 'churl', and it is often used to mean 'miser'. The grand jury, which decided which cases should go forward for trial before the judge, was usually composed mainly of well-off yeomen farmers.[50] The point of this sloganising, of course, is to supply a specious justification for the attack. Falstaff seeks to cast the encounter in what was becoming a conventional pattern: the gentleman versus the yeoman, the spendthrift opposed to the grasper, and the youth in need of some spending money pitting himself against tight-fisted age. In the shout 'young men must live', there is a suggestion of the old doctrine that theft and robbery become morally unobjectionable in cases of serious need. Falstaff, as usual, twists the idea to suit his own purposes, in what the Lord Chief Justice describes in *Part II* as his 'manner of wrenching the true cause the false way'.[51] The spectacle of Falstaff, fat and white-haired, proclaiming himself young, is an excellent joke. It shows him pushing to bizarre extremes his calculated manipulation of language. What Falstaff seeks to claim is the licence given to the young. He wants to have his robberies condoned as youthful wildness: 'a tricke of youth', as Ned declares in *The Famous Victories*.[52]

Falstaff is a gentleman robber, and not merely by courtesy: he is a knight. However, when the sheriff comes to arrest him, he comes with a carrier, one of Falstaff's victims, who has been brought to help identify him. We have no less a word for it than that of Wild Prince Harry, the nation's most aristocratic highwayman, that robbing poor carriers is 'base'. Falstaff flouts the code once again when he borrows money from Shallow and declines to pay it back. His behaviour in that particular episode may be judged in the light of John Clavell's assertion that he himself had turned to robbery in the belief that it was a more honourable means of settling his financial difficulties than borrowing money he knew he could never repay from friends who put their trust in him.[53]

When Falstaff goes to war, he is adhering, after his fashion, to an established tradition. The notion of the robber as a thwarted soldier was a powerful one. John Clavell maintains unconditionally that at the outbreak of war a gentleman robber will join the army, thus demonstrating that his drift into crime was caused as much by 'want of Action' as lack of money. The tougher sorts of criminal, including robbers, were sometimes granted pardons on condition they agreed to be conscripted as soldiers.[54] In Samuel Rowley's early Jacobean history play, *When you see me, You know me*, there is a scene in which King Henry VIII, wandering in disguise through the streets of London by night, encounters the famous highway robber Black Will. Although no coward, Will is by no means a heroic robber – by his own confession, he is both a murderer and a pimp; yet at the end of the episode, his misdeeds are passed over. The King, who 'loves a man', packs him off to the wars with compliments on his 'mettall', a course that Will himself greets with swaggering exultation.[55] Common sense proposes the question: what sort of soldier would such a man really make? When Falstaff becomes an officer, he goes from plundering carriers to preying on wretched conscripts. He deliberately drafts men who he knows will be able and anxious to pay him to set them free. Then he replaces them with a crew of desperate ragamuffins, whom he abandons in the fiercest part of the battle. Here, as he notes with satisfaction, the enemy artillery quickly mows them down. This was a well-known device of unscrupulous captains; the object was to pocket the pay of those who were killed.[56]

There is one aspect of Falstaff that conforms very closely to the usual stereotype of the robber hero. This is his addiction to riotous living. Ageing though he is, he behaves like a prodigal of prodigals. The first thing that we learn about him, from the Prince's opening speech, is that strong drink, rich food and whores occupy most of his waking hours.[57] Young men were expected to run a little wild; there was some suspicion of those who seemed to have no vices. 'Young saint, old devil' was a popular proverb.[58] But Falstaff is old. In him, this kind of excess means something rather different. Not to gloss over it, he is greedy. His 'great belly' is the emblem of a wolfish appetite. From this springs his 'vocation'. As any preacher could have explained, the fundamental sin of the robber was held to be greed: 'covet[ing] . . . other mennes goodes', as the Prayer Book Catechism has it.[59] Complex and slippery though he is, in these respects Falstaff is all of a piece.

When Shakespeare shifted the main responsibility for the robbery episode from the Prince to his companions, he set himself free to examine the cult of the robber critically in a way that was hardly open to the author of *The Famous Victories of Henry the Fifth*. Falstaff is the heroic robber burlesqued: in *Henry IV, Part I*, the young, valiant, open-handed, honourable robber of tradition is translated into an ageing social predator

129

of debauched habits, cowardly instincts and a strictly pragmatic approach to honour. Even Falstaff's occasional gestures towards repentance, parodic as they plainly are, may be understood in terms of an established convention. By the late Elizabethan period, a robber with any claim to virtuous impulses was expected to experience occasional fits of remorse; it was now part of the image, just as much as high living and reckless courage. In 1599, Ben Jonson had his own, very different, satirical crack at the robber cult, in his comedy *Every Man out of his Humour*. Jonson's 'robber', Shift, is a low-grade confidence man who lives mainly by sponging. To impress his patron, the foolish Sogliardo, he pretends that he is a reformed highwayman. When he finally admits the truth, that he has never robbed anyone, 'but only said so, because I would get my selfe a name, and be counted a tall man', Sogliardo cries in outrage: 'By this light, gentlemen, he hath confest to mee the most inexorable companie of robberies, *and damn'd himselfe that he did 'hem*' (my italics).[60] When Falstaff claims that Hal has corrupted him, the humour is once again partly parodic. In George Gascoigne's drama *The Glasse of Government* (1575), a young gentleman is executed for highway robbery after falling under the influence of a rascally servingman; and in the broadside ballad that was written about Luke Hutton, the robber is made to claim that he was 'Inticed' into his career on the highway by bad companions.[61]

Falstaff invokes the rhetoric and conventions of the robber cult strictly to suit his own purposes. The elements of burlesque depend partly on the audience's sense of the discrepancy between his rhetoric and his actions, and partly on his failure (which is often spectacular) to match up to the attributes of the heroic robber. In Shakespeare's hands, the image of the gallant highwayman becomes a self-serving fantasy spun by an elderly waster. Nor does the robber himself believe a word of it. One thing about Falstaff we learn for certain is that he himself is never at the slightest risk of being led astray by the sort of high-sounding language by which he seeks to dazzle and mystify others. 'What is honour?' he asks, and instantly answers, 'A word. What is in that word honour? What is that honour? Air.'[62]

Typically, the early modern highwayman is expected to end on the gallows. However, as we learn in *Henry V*, Falstaff escapes both gunshot and the noose, and dies in his bed. The reports of his death scene are suitably ambiguous. His page prefers to dwell on Falstaff's fears of damnation, and the fact that while he was dying, 'a saw a flea stick upon Bardolph's nose, and a said it was a black soul burning in hell'. A premonitory vision of his destination in the other world? Or a last rococo joke at the expense of Bardolph's drink-ruined features?[63] But the Hostess, who has always been ready to believe the best of Falstaff, has already declared emphatically that 'he's not in hell: he's in Arthur's bosom, if ever man went to Arthur's bosom'. The New Testament story of the Rich Man and Lazarus alludes to a Jewish belief that, after death, the souls of the righteous are 'caryed by the Angels into Abrahams bosome'. In characteristically muddled fashion, the Hostess has confused the Patriarch Abraham with the mythical King Arthur. Who, as everyone knows, never died, but was taken into what Malory calls 'another place' by the fairy Lady of the Lake and a trio of sorcerous queens.[64] The Hostess's words open up a wonderful prospect. In his final moments, Falstaff, the prodigal, the robber, the supreme con man, has once again evaded judgement and has found his way onto the middle road that leads to Avalon or Elfland, there to consort with the heroes of legend.

11

Outlaws in Arcadia

Shakespeare

Falstaff is not Shakespeare's only portrait of a gentleman robber. There is also the outlawed Valentine, in *The Two Gentlemen of Verona*. The date of this play is uncertain. We know that it existed by 1598, but it is generally assumed to be one of Shakespeare's early efforts, written, perhaps, in about 1593. In this lightweight romantic comedy, we are in a completely different world to that of the *Henry IV* plays. It's a far less complex piece altogether, though it does possess a stylised charm of its own. During the course of the action, Valentine, one of the young gentlemen of the title, attempts to elope with Silvia, the daughter and only child of the Duke of Milan. He is betrayed to the Duke and banished. On his way into exile, he is ambushed by members of a band of outlaws, who invite him to become their 'king'. His page, Speed, urges him to accept: 'Master, be one of them: it's an honourable kind of thievery.' Evidently Speed means that highway robbery is honourable. Possibly Shakespeare has a few doubts about this, since in the end Valentine only accepts the role of outlaw chief under duress, the outlaws having threatened to kill him if he declines it. Valentine keeps some dignity, however, as well as displaying his sense of decency, by insisting that under his leadership the outlaws must refrain from doing 'outrages / On silly [helpless] women or poor passengers'. They are shocked at the very idea: 'No, we detest such vile base practices.'[1]

These outlaws, with their 'king', perhaps owe a little to *The Tale of Gamelyn*; they certainly depend a great deal on the Robin Hood tradition. Shakespeare explicitly associates them with it when he makes one of the outlaws swear, picturesquely, 'By the bare scalp of Robin Hood's fat friar'.[2] The prohibition on attacking women and the poor comes from either Grafton's or Stow's chronicle account of Robin Hood.[3] Other elements derive from the traditions of the heroic robber in general. These outlaws are brave: they are prepared, if necessary, to attack a party that outnumbers them. Some of them are gentlemen, under sentence of banishment for

132

various misdeeds, all committed, one of them claims, in a spirit of youthful wildness.[4]

In one passage, when Valentine, alone in the woods, listens to the nightingale and broods over his lost love, the play carries echoes of the outlaw love lyric. In Chapter Two, I mentioned the early fourteenth-century poem 'De Clerico et Puella', in which the lover alludes to his sufferings, hiding in the forest, driven into exile on account of his love for his 'lemman', or sweetheart.[5] The theme is found again, much more elaborately developed, in a love song of the late fifteenth century, 'I muste go walke the woodes so wyld'. In this song, the lover laments that he has been banished, that is, outlawed, as a result of the cunning plots of his enemies, who are probably the relatives of the woman he loves, since the refrain to every woeful stanza runs, 'And all for your Love, my Dere'. Like the Clerk in 'De Clerico et Puella', he experiences the woods as a place of suffering and loneliness: he is continually afraid, and he has nothing to sustain or comfort him but memories and dreams of his beloved. Even the natural beauties around him, the deer, the singing birds, only remind him of what he has lost in losing her. The wild woods of the love song are an image for the lover's state of mind, as the last stanza acknowledges: 'A wofull man such desert lyfe / becumyth best of all'.[6] Valentine similarly finds that 'This shadowy, desert, unfrequented woods' chimes with his lovelorn mood far better than 'peopled towns'.[7]

Nothing in the surviving works of the native tradition of outlaw literature offers a precedent for the way in which Shakespeare uses the outlaws in this play, as a complicating accident, helping to drive the plot, in a tale of romantic lovers. This probably comes, directly or indirectly, from the *Aethiopica*, a late Greek romance by Heliodorus, which was available in Latin and English translations. This was a book that was widely read in Renaissance Europe. Moreover, the Puritan controversialist Stephen Gosson named it in 1582 among the books that, he said, had been 'throughly ransackt' to provide plots for plays for the London playhouses.[8] Its elaborate narrative involves the lovers Theagenes and Chariclea in several encounters with pirates: Thomas Underdowne's English transla-tion, first published in 1587, calls them 'theeves' and 'robbers'.[9] A particularly interesting figure is the bandit captain Thyamis. Thyamis is a nobleman who became a robber after his younger brother had intrigued to have him banished from Memphis, in Egypt, where he was the hereditary high priest. Like all heroic robbers, he is a valiant fighter. He shows his noble breeding in his courteous treatment of his captives, and he prides himself on having never wronged a woman. By the end of the romance, he has been vindicated and restored to his rightful position.[10] In short, the story of this noble robber shares a number of motifs with the medieval English outlaw tales. However, the *Aethiopica*, which was unknown to

133

English authors before the sixteenth century, introduced certain new themes and possibilities. Among these are the fact that Thyamis, the nobleman robber, is credited with being a restraining and civilising influence on his band of wild brigands. Moreover, he is not only honourable in his treatment of women, but he is something of a romantic lover: he is smitten by his captive Chariclea, and forms the intention to marry her.[11] Although outlaw lovers sometimes feature in lyric poems, the surviving medieval outlaw narratives contain very little in the way of love interest. Even when Fouke Fitz Waryn, on the run from King John, seizes a chance to marry a noble lady, the narrative tells us less about her beauty than about her lands and wealth.[12]

To return to *The Two Gentlemen of Verona*: Valentine finds that despite their initial assurance to him, his outlaws are rather given to committing 'outrages' on travellers, and it costs him some effort to keep them under control.[13] In the final scene of the play, he is reunited with Silvia, who has left Milan in search of him. After her, in hot pursuit, comes her father the Duke, together with Thurio, the Duke's preferred suitor for her hand, but as soon as they arrive in Valentine's woodland territory, they are taken captive by his men. Now their fates are in Valentine's power; but he handles the moment, as a good outlaw must, by loyally acknowledging his overlord, in much the same manner as the Robin Hood of *A Gest*. However, he draws the line at handing Silvia over to Thurio, and Thurio shows himself so cowardly that the Duke becomes disgusted. He praises Valentine's 'spirit', declares him a worthy suitor for his daughter, and puts an end to his banishment. In his response, Valentine begs the Duke to extend his pardon to the rest of the outlaws. He assures him, rather unconvincingly, that they are now 'reformed' and 'civil', and in what sounds like a distant echo of *Gamelyn*, he even declares them 'fit for great employment'. The Duke tells him to make whatever arrangements for them he thinks they deserve.[14]

The play thus closes on an interesting prospect: the heiress to the Dukedom of Milan is about to be wed to a former robber chief, who proposes to staff the offices of state with his brigand following. One may imagine Falstaff's envy. Of course, an important difference between Falstaff and Valentine is that Valentine is constructed as innocent of all real wrongdoing. He is modelled very largely on the outlaw heroes of the medieval tradition, where one of the enduring conventions is that the hero is driven into outlawry through no fault of his own: the speaker in *The Outlaw's Song* speaks in representative terms when he says, 'I was not guilty, I am indicted out of malice'. Two centuries later, the outlaw lover in 'I muste go walke the woodes so wyld' similarly declares that he was 'banysshed ... / By craft and fals pretens, / Fawtles, without offens'.[15] *The Two Gentlemen of Verona* updates this old convention of the outlaw's lack of culpability to suit the requirements of a love romance. Only a very hard heart could blame Valentine for the crime of trying to run away with the woman he loves.

The 'good' outlaw, no matter how violent his acts, is always in some sense an innocent man; the 'good' highwayman, no matter how generously he behaves or how socially repellent his victims, is always tainted with the guilt of his crimes. The outlaw, as a rule, returns in triumph, as Valentine does, to reclaim his position in legitimate society. The highwayman's career ends at best on a low key, with his penitence and amendment; at worst, with the drama of the gallows. The outlaw lives in the woods, with all that that implies of a wholesome life lived close to nature; the highwayman makes his base in the city, and spends his time carousing in taverns. Even so, during the early modern period the two remain quite closely associated in the minds of the public. Robin Hood, especially, was widely regarded as the archetypal English highway robber. Moreover, the outlaw tradition bequeathed to the highwayman hero some of his chief attributes: his courtesy and open-handedness, his prankish wit and his penchant for a kind of rough justice, now manifested most often in the plundering of economic sinners such as misers and usurers. At the same time, the differences between, say, Gamelyn and Gamaliel Ratsey are a measure of the extent to which the highwayman and the greenwood outlaw may be seen as constituting distinct cultural and literary types.

It scarcely needs saying that by the time Shakespeare was writing *The Two Gentlemen of Verona* the outlaw had an archaic air. No one in late Elizabethan England expected to find themselves ambushed by forest-dwelling, green-clad archers. A highwayman might ride out and bellow 'Stand!' at you on any steep and wooded stretch of high road round the capital, but an outlaw was a figure from old stories. Even the fashion for amateur Robin Hood role playing was largely dying out.[16] However, even though outlaws didn't exist any more except in the theatre or in narratives and songs, the images of the outlaw and of outlaw life were still going through changes and creative development. In particular, they were becoming more and more idealised.

To a certain extent, this ran with the grain of the tradition. The outlaw of medieval legend had always been an ideal figure. And if the greenwood wasn't always treated as the landscape of a fantasy – some handlings of the outlaw theme focus on its bleakness, especially in winter, and on the rigours of survival in the wild[17] – still, it was very common for tales and songs to praise the pleasures of greenwood life. In the Robin Hood tradition, especially, this is a frequent motif; it is often conveyed, economically, by means of the recurring epithet 'merry'. From the start of the earliest metrical tale, *Robin Hood and the Monk*, we learn that it is 'mery' in the forest in summer, listening to the song of the birds, and watching the deer with a hunter's eye.[18] Robin's men are often 'mery' throughout these tales; Sherwood, we are told, is 'mery'. Well over a century earlier, in *The Outlaw's Song*, the forest of Belregard had been praised for its birdsong and its 'jolyf umbray', its merry or, as we would say, its pleasant shade. And for something more. Belregard is a place where natural justice prevails: it is a haven beyond the reach of oppressors, a place where 'there is no false dealing'.[19] As for the outlaw himself, he is traditionally a righter of wrongs and a protector to those in trouble. We see this principle operating in *The Tale of Gamelyn*, where the outlaw king welcomes the starving Gamelyn and Adam to his table, and, more strikingly, in *A Gest of Robyn Hode*, where Robin lends the knight the money to redeem his lands and Robin's men make him splendid gifts. It forms an important theme in some of the Robin Hood broadside ballads, notably the well-known *Robin Hood and Allen a Dale*, in which the outlaw chief helps a young minstrel snatch his sweetheart at the altar from under the nose of her elderly bridegroom.[20] There is also the ballad of *Robin Hood Rescuing the Widow's Three Sons*, a tale of Robin's disguising himself to save three young poachers from the gallows.[21] The earliest surviving texts of these ballads date from the late seventeenth century, but there is evidence to show that versions of both these tales formed part of the Robin Hood corpus a hundred years earlier and more. The tales themselves are far older: as we saw in Chapter Three, a story of a daring rescue from the gallows was attached to the name of one of the followers of Hereward. Hereward himself, during the part of the *Gesta Herwardi* that deals with his exile from England, is made the hero of a story that already has many of the elements of *Robin Hood and Allen a Dale*, when he comes in disguise to a princess's wedding, takes her by force from her bridegroom and carries her off to marry the man she loves.[22]

Such tales and themes, then, are old, sometimes very old indeed. However, in the Elizabethan period, the idealisation of the outlaw figure took a new twist. From the late 1580s, it became fashionable to write about outlaw life in a way that laid a heavy stress on its traditional pleasures and virtues, at the same time as putting the best gloss on, or even removing from the picture, those typical activities of the outlaw, robbery and the seeking of revenge, that ran counter to conventional morality. I have mentioned Warner's *Albions England* more than once already, as the earliest place in which we hear of Robin Hood's robbing the rich in order to distribute their wealth to the poor. Warner also emphasises the contentment of greenwood life. Robin's men are well fed, and 'lodg'd . . . in pleasant Caves and Bowers', and when Robin contemplates the hard-hearted world beyond the forest, his cry is 'happie we . . . in merrie *Sherwood* that dwell'.[23] Stephen Knight sees 'a touch of pastoralism' in this passage, but it does not seem to me that pastoral writing is an important influence here.[24] Warner's narrator calls Robin Hood a '*Tymon*', after the ancient Athenian who conceived a mistrust of humanity and withdrew to live in the wilderness, and Timon is not usually viewed as a pastoral figure. However, something that is very apparent from Warner's account, especially in his reference to the outlaws' living in 'Bowers', is the influence on the development of the legend of the association between Robin Hood and the pleasures of summertime holidays. As I described in Chapter Five, bowers of branches were often built on greens and in churchyards as a focus for Robin Hood role playing and similar entertainments. Their main function seems to have been as a place for feasting.[25] In the same chapter, I also suggested that the notion that Robin Hood 'took from the rich to give to the poor' crystallised partly as a result of the connections between Robin Hood role playing and the practice of 'gathering' for the parish.[26] Warner's version of the Robin Hood legend takes part of its colouring from images of holiday festivity, and the licensed rule-breaking that was often practised on such occasions.

If Warner took a decisive step in turning Robin Hood into a robber who robbed only from the very highest motives, his contemporary, Thomas Lodge, made something quite unprecedented out of *The Tale of Gamelyn*. In 1588, he whiled away a voyage to the Canary Islands by transforming it into an ornate prose romance. *Rosalynde*, subtitled *Euphues golden legacie*, was written in the fashionable 'Euphuistic' style, replete with elaborate metaphors and other rhetorical devices. The fast-moving action of the original is slowed to a turgid crawl with continual set-piece speeches and internal monologues. The book is best known nowadays for the use that Shakespeare made of it as his principal source for *As You Like It*. However, Lodge's treatment of the outlaw theme was sufficiently original and influential to require some attention on its own account. In *Rosalynde*, Gamelyn becomes Rosader, who, like his counterpart Orlando in *As You Like It*, falls romantically in love with the Rosalynd of the romance's title when he takes part in a wrestling match and sees her among the spectators. Otherwise, the first part of his adventures follows *The Tale of Gamelyn* fairly closely. Driven to flee, like Gamelyn, to the forest, to escape the ill-treatment and injustice of his eldest brother, Rosader encounters there, not a king of outlaws but a real king, the deposed and exiled King Gerismond, surrounded by 'a lustie crue of Outlawes'.[27] From then on, the plot of *The Tale of Gamelyn* is more or less abandoned in favour of a pastoral love romance. Rosalynd and her cousin Alinda (Shakespeare's Celia) have also run away to the forest, where they live among the shepherds and herd sheep. Rosalynd has disguised herself as a boy, Ganimede, and in this shape she once more encounters Rosader. The two of them then pursue an unconventional courtship, much as Orlando and Rosalind do in *As You Like It*.

Considered as an outlaw story, *Rosalynde* is remarkable for two important innovations: first, the prominent and conscious use of the pastoral theme, and secondly the extreme sanitisation of the outlaws, who never commit robbery or any other violent offence. Both these developments are connected. Lodge has chosen to turn the greenwood into a literary territory contiguous to, and in many ways overlapping with, Arcadia: the traditional landscape of pastoral in which idealised shepherds and shepherdesses go about their conventionally stylised business. Arcadia often functions in literary texts as a place of retreat and escape: either from the intrigues and artifice of the court, or from the dishonesty and cheats of the city. It represents the countryside and so the realm of nature: it stands for that which is natural rather than artificial, and for a way of life that is stripped down to essentials rather than over-refined. In contrast to the worlds of court and city, the Arcadians and their society are typically constructed as innocent; in theory, at least, there is no ambition among them, no greed or deceit.[28]

If Arcadia often functions as a retreat, the greenwood of the outlaw legend is always a place of refuge. Hunters go there, and travellers pass through, but no one lives their life in the greenwood unless they are hiding from their enemies. Moreover, the outlaw legend constructs the outlaw as an oppressed innocent, and the world beyond the greenwood as inhabited, or at any rate dominated, by tight-fisted clerics, corrupt legal officers, ungenerous hearts, liars and oath-breakers. By contrast, the greenwood, like Arcadia, is a 'merry' place, where the dominant values are fairness, honesty and open-handedness. Thomas Lodge, then, had some poetic logic on his side when he linked the greenwood with Arcadia and reinterpreted the outlaw theme as a version of pastoral. However, the outlaws of tradition are essentially violent men. They take up weapons to defend themselves and their own and others' rights, to revenge themselves on their enemies, and to persuade travellers to be 'good fellows' and contribute to their subsistence. Shepherds, on the other hand, are peaceable and harmless: pastoral works are inclined to depict them as spending much of their time composing songs and making love to their sweethearts. One of the reasons the shepherd's life has had such a high value set on it is its presumed peacefulness. In this respect, the greenwood is not at all like Arcadia.

Lodge's response to this situation was to limit his use of the word 'outlaw', replacing it for much of the book with the euphemistic term 'forester'.[29] The outlaw thus becomes assimilated to a slightly different stereotype, one that is less warlike and rather less specific. A forester, obviously, is someone who lives in a forest. However, the word was often used to mean 'hunter', particularly in poetry and courtly songs. Lodge may have known, or known of, Sir Philip Sidney's entertainment, *The Lady of May*, which was performed before Queen Elizabeth in the late 1570s, although it didn't appear in print until 1599. In what seems to have been the first introduction of the forester figure into English pastoral, Therion, a forester, and Espilus, a shepherd, compete in a song contest for the hand of the May Lady. Sidney's forester is a poacher, who steals venison to give to his sweetheart. He is wild, sometimes violent, and sets a high value on his freedom. There is a hint in the text that foresters, like outlaws, have a reputation for robbery: an older shepherd, Dorcas, dismisses Therion contemptuously as 'a thievish prowler'.[30] The word 'prowl', in those days, carried strong implications of seizing other people's goods.[31] However, Dorcas may simply be alluding to Therion's propensity for poaching.

Lodge's forester outlaws are remarkably tame and bland. Although they live by hunting the deer, Gerismond and his following cannot even be said to be poachers, since Gerismond is the rightful king. It is impossible to believe that they would dream of engaging in robbery or raiding, and in fact, in one episode, they are sharply distinguished from the band of robbers, 'unbridled villaines', who have made their lair in another part of the forest.[32] *The Tale of Gamelyn* is pre-eminently a story of revenge, but when Lodge's hero Rosader finds Saladyne, his cruel elder brother, sleeping in the forest, he saves his life by killing a lion that is preparing to attack him. After this, the two become reconciled. Gerismond, too, has no thoughts of revenging himself on the usurper Torismond who has driven him out of his kingdom. Instead, we are told that he 'crowneth his thoughts with content, accompting [accounting] it better to govern among poore men in peace, than great men in daunger'.[33] The sentiment is pure pastoral.

Lodge's *Rosalynde* was not the only work with an outlaw theme to show the influence of pastoral. Unfortunately, the text of the 'pastorall plesant Commedie of Robin Hood and Little John', entered in the Stationers' Register in May 1594, has not survived.[34] However, in 1598, Anthony Munday and Henry Chettle plundered the Robin Hood legend for material for a two-part tragic drama, *The Downfall of Robert, Earl of Huntington* and *The Death of Robert, Earl of Huntington*. The original conception seems to have been Munday's; he took the aristocratic Robin Hood who had first begun to evolve in Grafton's *Chronicle* and gave him a title, Earl of Huntington (or Huntingdon), along with a history as an open-handed young nobleman embarrassed by debts and surrounded by unscrupulous enemies. He also turned Maid Marian, until then a fairly shadowy figure, into Robin's equally high-born betrothed, who accompanies him to Sherwood. Both holiday and pastoral influence combine as Robin, seated with Marian in a festive bower, praises the pleasures of life in the forest, like the songbirds and the blossoming trees. He compares them favourably to the artificial attractions of the court, with its musicians and its tapestry hangings.[35]

Pastoral is not the sole, or even the major, influence on the greenwood scenes in these plays. *The Downfall of Robert, Earl of Huntington* incorporates in its action incidents that are clearly based on the Robin Hood ballads and folk plays. In an episode with analogues in the printed broadside ballads, Robin disguises himself as a beggar so that he and his men can rescue two other outlaws, Scarlet and Scathlock, from execution.[36] Another scene ends with a skirmish between the outlaws and a posse led by a wicked priest, Sir Doncaster, and in yet another, Scathlock and Friar Tuck each have a sword and buckler fight with Prince John, who has come to the forest in outlaw disguise. The emphasis is on manly combat and resistance to corrupt authority. However, the other strand in the Robin Hood tradition, represented by the tales of courteous or witty robbery, is largely suppressed. It is true that Munday gestures towards it when he has his outlawed earl, following the example of the Robin Hood of *A Gest*, issue his band with standing orders. All travellers, apart from post-boys, carriers and those taking food to market, must be brought to Robin to feast with him in the greenwood. Naturally, the band are forbidden to harm the poor; on the other hand, Robin commands them never to 'spare a Priest, a usurer, or a clarke'.[37] In Elizabethan England, pre-Reformation priests were thought of in the hostile terms of Protestant propaganda; the anti-clerical attitudes embedded in some of the medieval outlaw tales now fitted in quite tidily with the official outlook of the times.[38] As for usurers, they belong to the category of economic hate figures who were increasingly being treated as fair game in stories about highway robbers.[39] The implication of Robin's injunction not to 'spare' such people is that they are to be stripped of their ill-gotten gains; but it is typical of the play that this is never explicitly stated. Nothing is ever said, either here or elsewhere in the play, about redistributing the wealth of the rich to the poor. Munday's Robin Hood derives from Grafton's *Chronicle* rather than Warner's *Albions England*. However, one of Robin's instructions to his band is the command, modelled on the chivalric code, that they must do everything that is in their power to protect 'Maids, widowes, Orphants, and distressed men'.[40]

The closest we come to a robbery scene in this play is an episode, evidently also modelled on *A Gest*, in which several of Robin's men are lying in wait for 'guests' to bring to their master's table. They intercept an old man who is ostensibly going to market with a basket of eggs. Much the Miller's son wants to let him go, in accordance with Robin's orders; the shrewder Friar recognises the Bishop of Ely, once Robin's enemy, now disgraced and fleeing from Prince John in disguise. True to his principles of helping those in trouble, Robin forgives the Bishop and offers him shelter.[41] Dramatically, the 'robbery' scenario is a handy way to stage the encounter; thematically, the episode simply becomes one of several occasions on which Robin demonstrates his extraordinary magnanimity.

In their treatment of the robbery theme, Munday and Chettle show considerable discomfort with it. They evidently feel that it is too much a part of the Robin Hood legend to be wholly excluded. But it appears that for them, there is a conflict that wasn't visible to the authors of the medieval tales, between Robin's standing as a recognised hero and his profession of robber. Apparently, it isn't even enough to stress that he and his men rob only those people, like usurers and corrupt priests, who truly deserve to be plundered. If Munday and Chettle's version of Robin is to be, as they clearly intend, an admirable, thoroughly chivalric figure, then it seems that he cannot be shown on stage in his role as a robber chief. So thoroughly squeaky clean is this Robin Hood that one of his enemies, the self-consciously villainous Sir Doncaster, says of him, in disgust, 'He does abuse a thieves name and an outlawes, / And is indeede no outlawe, nor no theefe'.[42] Coming from such a quarter, this is presumably meant to be heard by the audience as a back-handed tribute. In fact, it betrays a problem with the whole way the legend is being handled in these plays. An outlaw who is no sort of an outlaw at all, a robber chief whose men are never seen practising robbery, is a contradictory and rather unsatisfying character.

Munday's transformation of Robin and Marian into a pair of fugitive aristocrats had a long-term influence on later literary treatments of the legend. Otherwise, the main interest of his rather wooden tragedy is the way it seems to have sparked Shakespeare into writing an outlaw play of his own. The rivalry between Munday and Shakespeare was commercial as well as professional. Munday was a hired hack who wrote for the impresario Philip Henslowe and the company who played at his Rose theatre, the Admiral's Men. Shakespeare wrote his plays for their main rivals, the Chamberlain's Men, of whom he was himself a full member, with a share in the profits. Munday had made outlaws the latest theatrical fashion; now, with *As You Like It*, dating, probably, from the middle of 1599, Shakespeare made a bid to draw in the audiences that had shown they had a taste for such material. His response to Munday's historical tragedy was to take Lodge's pastoral romance *Rosalynde* and turn it into a romantic comedy.

Shakespeare advertises the play's outlaw interest during the first scene, when Charles the wrestler brings the latest news from court. We learn that 'the old Duke' has been driven out by his younger brother, and that some of his lords have gone with him into exile.

> They say he is already in the Forest of Arden, and a many merry men with him; and there they live like the old Robin Hood of England. They say many young gentlemen flock to him every day, and fleet the time carelessly as they did in the golden world.[43]

Charles begins by invoking the Robin Hood tradition, and the 'merry' life of the greenwood, but when he comes to speak of the 'golden world', the image of the greenwood merges with that of Arcadia. For the golden world was the primal age of innocence, before humankind grew greedy, deceitful and cruel. One of the classic descriptions is by the Roman poet Ovid, in his *Metamorphoses*. He says that in the golden age, no one tilled the ground; the earth produced its fruits freely, and wild honey dripped from the oaks. Everything was held in common. It was a peaceful time, when weapons were unknown. People lived at ease, in a landscape of perpetual spring.[44] This was the classical version of Eden, but instead of a sudden fall from grace, the Greek and Roman poets envisaged a decline that took place in successive stages: typically, from gold to silver to bronze, and finally to the age of iron. The age of iron – the age of land-grabbing, of warfare, treachery and looting – was usually said to be the age in which we are all still living. But from the early sixteenth century, the Renaissance poets liked to imagine that in certain communities, among shepherds, for instance, who do not till the ground, who lead lives of relative leisure, watching over their flocks, and who are simple people, living far from cities, the innocence, peace and happiness that prevailed in the age of gold are still not completely dead. Arcadia is an image, imperfect but still precious, of the life of the age of gold.[45] When he has Charles the wrestler allude to the golden world, Shakespeare is priming the better educated members of his audience to anticipate outlaw pastoral.

Shakespeare's equivalent to Gamelyn and Rosader is Orlando, who fits the usual stereotype of the 'younger brother' more closely than either of his counterparts. Like them, he is a knight's third son, but unlike them, his father has left him only a very modest inheritance of 'a thousand crowns': £250, worth much more than today, of course, but not enough to allow him to live in gentlemanly independence, even if his brother, Oliver, had had any intention of paying it.[46] In fact, Oliver is making plans to kill him, but when Orlando is warned of this by Adam, the elderly household servant, he hasn't the least idea what to do:

> What, wouldst thou have me go and beg my food,
> Or with a base and boist'rous sword enforce
> A thievish living on the common road?[47]

Orlando knows what is expected of him, as the younger son of a gentleman with no resources besides his sword and his courage. However, in stigmatising highway robbery as 'base', or ungentlemanly, he rejects the cult of the robber, and, in particular, the mystique that surrounds the gentleman highwayman. He also repudiates the rapacious values of the age of iron, which at this point his devious and homicidal brother exemplifies so completely. Indeed, antagonism between brothers is precisely one of the evils that was held to be characteristic of the iron age.[48]

Like their counterparts before them, Orlando and Adam run away to the woods, where they soon begin to starve. Here, Orlando, searching for food, encounters a company of men, dressed, as the stage direction has it, 'like outlaws', eating a meal among the trees. Faced with this scene, he does not think of the courteous outlaws of English legend, still less of the conventions of pastoral. What he expects to meet, in this wild and distant spot, are wild or 'savage' men, bandits or little better, whom only violence can possibly impress.[49] Forgetting his earlier conviction that robbery is base, or else regarding it as justifiable in a case of life and death, he approaches them with his sword drawn and tries to threaten them into giving him some food. He behaves, altogether, as if he assumes he is confronting the bandits of romance: rough fellows, who can nonetheless usually be relied on to respond satisfactorily to firm handling from a gentleman of spirit.[50] However, these are not ordinary outlaws, and despite the fact that he is a younger brother, Orlando is not destined to rob on the highway. Instead, as the audience is already aware, he has wandered into the court of the exiled Duke, and the realm of outlaw pastoral.

The keynote of the outlaw scenes has been established earlier, on the Duke's first entry. He hails the forest as a place of safe retreat: the court is full of envious plotters, but in the woodland nothing bites but the winter wind. With this powerful image, Shakespeare straightaway sets a distance between his version of outlaw pastoral and that of his theatrical rival. When Munday's outlawed earl praises the greenwood, he dwells on the delights of birdsong and blossom. He and his Marian court one another in a landscape marked by the signs of early summer. By contrast, in Shakespeare's play, in the scenes set at Duke Senior's exiled court, images of winter, wind and ice are a recurrent motif.[51] The expectations of life in Arden that have been set up by Charles the wrestler – who, after all, is only repeating hearsay – begin to be drastically modified. These are not holiday outlaws, acting out a perpetual Whitsun festival. Nor is the Forest of Arden a golden world of unchanging spring. If it provides a refuge from the iron life outside it, it does so at a cost in chilled flesh. Moreover, the Duke and his men are by no means primeval innocents, living on fruits and wild honey. In case we should miss this point, the Duke himself expresses his regret that their subsistence in the forest depends on their killing those 'poor dappled fools', its 'native burghers', the deer; and the sardonic moralist Jaques reportedly goes beyond this in arguing that when they hunt, the exiles themselves become 'usurpers' and 'tyrants'.[52]

In the pastoral tradition, the shepherd's life is often viewed as the life of contemplation, as opposed to one of activity.[53] The Duke is a would-be contemplative, who looks for moral lessons in the world of nature, and who claims that the secluded life of the forest permits them to see 'good in everything' around them.[54] But Jaques's contemplations – and 'contemplation' is the precise word that is used of his reflections[55] – are not so shallow and self-serving. He sees that the Duke and his men have retreated from conflict in their own sphere, only to invade the forest and turn it into an iron world of mass slaughter. The violence has simply been displaced. If there really is an innocent way to live, it cannot be this one. Later in the play, in a hunting scene, it is Jaques who says of the successful huntsman, 'Let's present him to the Duke like a Roman conqueror'. Taken in the context of his earlier remarks, together with the pastoral setting, this is by no means so commendatory as it might sound. For from an anti-heroic, pastoral viewpoint, conquerors are a manifestation of the iron age and the fallen world. Indeed, St Augustine, in a famous passage, compares them scathingly to robbers.[56] Here and earlier, Jaques calls into question the rationale of forester pastoral.

There is a fundamental incongruity between the pastoral genre, which has its roots in descriptive poetry and lyric, and which presents an image of the life of contemplation, and the English outlaw tale, which, as I have said before, is essentially an action genre. The principal motive for the action in these narratives is revenge: whether it is Hereward's ferocious vengeance on the Normans who have killed his brother, or Robin Hood's light-hearted tricking and robbery of his enemy the Sheriff in *Robin Hood and the Potter*. Indeed, even when the outlaw theme manifests in the lyric tradition, the speaker is inclined to brood on vengeance. We see this in *The Outlaw's Song*, and, more incongruously, in 'I muste go walke the woodes so wyld'. The final stanza of this courtly love song has an oddly threatening ring, as the outlawed lover wishes 'wo' to those 'That ar the causers of this stryfe'.[57]

In *The Tale of Gamelyn*, revenge is the mainspring: Gamelyn's personal vengeance on his wicked brother, and also his role as the scourge of men in holy orders, whom he targets exclusively with his robberies. However, once Lodge adapts the story as a pastoral romance, revenge is excluded from the picture. Even warfare in a just cause is not really compatible with the pastoral ideal. Both Lodge's King Gerismond and Duke Senior, his counterpart in *As You Like It*, are curiously passive figures, who merely wait for events to turn in their favour. As for robbery, that too, of course, is a manifestation of the iron age, when, according to Ovid, 'people lived by what they could seize'.[58] Accordingly, there is no voice raised in *As You Like It* to excuse it as 'an honourable kind of thievery'. Quite the opposite: the play's hero dismisses it, succinctly, as 'base'.

Once the greenwood has been reinvented as an adjunct of Arcadia, the outlaw becomes an entirely factitious construction, divorced from cultural tradition as from any kind of lived existence, present or past. One obvious shortcoming of outlaw pastoral, at any rate from a theatrical perspective, is that there is very little for such outlaws to do. Shakespeare's outlaws hunt, feast, sing and make sententious speeches. Nothing more. As the green-wood in *As You Like It* is defined as a male enclave, they cannot even court their loves, that favourite activity of pastoral folk, without crossing over into Arcadian territory. In the last three acts of the play, outlaw pastoral becomes a very minor note, as Orlando spends most of his time among the shepherds, learning to woo his Rosalind.

After *As You Like It*, the history of representations of the outlaw is more or less the same as the later history of the Robin Hood legend. And the legend has most often been interpreted through Elizabethan lenses. Warner's notion that Robin Hood and his men stole from the rich to give to the poor passed very quickly into oral tradition and is now an inseparable part of the story. Grafton and Munday's aristocratic Robin Hood has probably found a wider currency in later plays and novels than the yeoman hero of *A Gest*. *The Downfall of Robert, Earl of Huntington*, mediocre though it is, has cast a particularly long shadow, partly because of the way it integrates Marian into the story, and with her the theme of romantic love. The play also offers a model for the many representations of Robin Hood that combine elements of forester pastoral with an emphasis on the hero's chivalry and his high-minded approach to the business of robbery.[59] Strict Robin Hood pastoral is rare: though we do find it in Ben Jonson's unfinished comedy, *The Sad Shepherd*, which was found among his papers after his death in 1637. From an outlawed robber and poacher, Jonson transforms Robin into a 'Wood-man', Marian into his 'Lady', a huntress, and their men into 'Wood-men' and 'Huntsmen'. It is, perhaps, needless to say that they live on excellent terms with the neighbouring community of shepherds.[60]

After Jonson, there is only one major thematic innovation in the legend, and that comes much later: the radicalisation of Robin Hood, his portrayal as a freedom fighter and primitive socialist. This springs principally from Joseph Ritson's influential introduction to his anthology of Robin Hood materials, which appeared in 1795, at a time of great radical ferment.[61] But to pursue that topic further would be to diverge too far from the central thread of this book.

Once outlaws have been made suitable for residence on the borders of Arcadia, they are no longer very much at all like 'the old Robin Hood of England'. However, the memory of an earlier Robin Hood, prankster, daring robber, patron and friend of manly men, continued to live on in printed street ballads, many of which are directly in the tradition and spirit of the medieval tales.[62] In this chapter, I have emphasised the differences between the image of the outlaw and that of the early modern highwayman. Nevertheless, during the seventeenth century, many, perhaps most people saw no sharp disjunction between the greenwood robber of legend and the highwayman of their own times. In a letter of 1626, the then Lord Chief Justice describes the activities of 'one Duckett', who had 'committed a number of robberies in all the countries [counties] about London'. He says that Duckett and his men had 'robbed up and down, eight or nine in a company, with pistols, *like Robin Hood and his men*' (my italics).[63] As for the highwaymen themselves: John Clavell depicts his fellow robbers, with a wit that must have given them great pleasure, using the whistling of the tune of '*Robin Hood*' as the signal to mount an attack.[64] Finally, as we saw with the books about Gamaliel Ratsey, the adventures of Robin Hood remained a model for many of the tales that were told about the highwaymen in popular biographies. And when a ballad-writer came to concoct his piece on the apocryphal exploits of James Hind, the Cavalier robber who became a popular hero, he wrote it to be sung to the tune, which he obviously thought most appropriate, of '*Robin Hood revived*'.[65]

12

The Robber Repentant: Clavell's *Recantation*

We have already met with John Clavell a number of times in this book. His verse pamphlet, *A Recantation of an Ill Led Life*, subtitled *A Discoverie of the High-way Law*, is an exceptionally informative account by a one-time highwayman of the mounted robber's way of life, attitudes and modus operandi. As its title implies, it is something of a hybrid: in part a convicted criminal's 'repentance', which helps to explain why Clavell chose to write it in verse, and in part an exposé of the highwayman's methods, together with advice on precautionary measures. Clavell wrote it in jail. Convicted of various robberies early in 1626, he was reprieved from execution and promised a pardon, but was then kept waiting for many months while his pardon remained unsigned. No doubt the intention was to punish him. His pardon was finally signed by the King in November 1627. By that time, Clavell had been in prison, under the threat of the gallows, for the best part of two years, and it was in these circumstances that he wrote his *Recantation*. One of his chief aims in writing it seems to have been to convince the authorities that he truly was a reformed character, who deserved a second chance. It was published in 1628; a second edition was called for within the year.

After his release from jail and the success of his first book, he seems to have had some hopes of making his living as a writer. In 1629, or thereabouts, but certainly before August 1631, his play, *The Soddered Citizen*, was performed in London by a leading company of actors, the King's Men. As its title suggests, it is a satirical city comedy, in imitation of the work of dramatists like Thomas Middleton and Philip Massinger. However, despite one or two mildly interesting cameo parts, it is not a very good play. The company probably commissioned it to cash in on Clavell's standing as a minor celebrity, following his conviction for the glamorous crime of robbery on the highway. It survives in a single playhouse script which bears signs of having returned quite quickly to the possession of the

147

author. This suggests that the play failed in performance. Certainly, from this point on, Clavell abandoned his attempts to make money through writing.

The Soddered Citizen and *A Recantation* both contain references to events in their author's life. However, most of what we know about Clavell is the result of the extensive archival researches of J. H. P. Pafford, his editor and biographer. In his book, *John Clavell, 1601–43: Highwayman, Author, Lawyer, Doctor*, Pafford documents his chequered career and, for the first time since 1634, reprints the full text of *A Recantation*.[1]

Clavell was born in 1601, into an undistinguished but ancient family of Dorset gentry. In 1619, he was admitted to Brasenose College, Oxford. Two years later, he broke into the college strong-room and stole some items of plate. His crime was found out, though not until after he had disposed of his haul. Fortunately for him, his family had enough influence to arrange a pardon. The terms on which it was granted, in April 1621, imply that at that point he was completely friendless, since he was excused from finding sureties to go bail for his future good behaviour. In 1623, his father died, leaving Clavell, his only son, with little beside debts and a modest country estate whose disposition was restricted by an entail.

By this time he was living mainly in London, and was already running up ruinous debts of his own. One of his chief creditors was a money-lender named William Banks. In 1629, Clavell brought a lawsuit against him, detailing the shady methods that he claimed Banks had used to get control of his assets. Whatever was the truth of the relations between the two, it is clear that he came to hate Banks and blame him for most of his problems.[2] In *The Soddered Citizen*, he satirised him under the name of Mountain, a devious financial shark and the play's principal villain. In one scene, a character condemns Mountain to his face as

> the man that crush'd the hopefull youth,
> That Infamy nowe boasts of, for those ills
> Hee did soe gloriously; him didst thou force
> By th' Cheate of his first fortunes, to fly out,
> And pillage on the Roade, for livelyhood.

The identification of 'the hopeful youth' with Clavell himself is clinched in the lines that follow, when we are told that the erstwhile highwayman has now become a poet, and is planning to write a play that will expose 'Mountain''s infamous practices.[3]

It's a neat little tale, and belongs in the world of the city comedy: the young heir to a country estate who turns to crime when he is stripped of his resources by the machinations of a conscienceless money-lender.[4] As an account of what happened to Clavell, it may well contain some truth.

However, we should bear in mind that this was not the only self-justifying story that he told about his reasons for becoming a highwayman. Earlier, in his *Recantation*, he had claimed that he had turned to robbery on the highway because he thought it 'more legitimate' than borrowing from his friends in the knowledge that he could not repay them. His reasoning, he said, was that the man who borrows what he knows he cannot pay back is betraying a trust, while a robber is quite straightforward about his intentions. *A Recantation of an Ill Led Life*, as I have said, was written while he was still in jail, desperate to have his pardon signed and to obtain his release. At that point, he was very concerned to stress his reformation; and he also wished to present his crimes in the best possible light, as the misguided behaviour of a well-intentioned young man who had been led astray by false notions of honour. However, the excuse that he had committed his robberies so as to avoid borrowing money is distinctly disingenuous. By the time of his first recorded highway robbery, in November 1624, he had already stretched his credit as far as it would go, and not only with the loan-sharks, either. A lawsuit brought in 1625 regarding some transactions of his in the previous year claims that at that time he was surviving mainly by sponging off other young gentlemen.[5]

Another of Clavell's statements in his *Recantation* offers a much more persuasive insight into the spirit in which he commenced his career as a highwayman. He says that in his youthful naivety, he had been foolish enough to be impressed by the highway robber's mystique and to long to embark on such a life himself:

> I whose easie youth, with fond admire
> Was drawne at first this ill course to desire,
> Hugg'd it in dreames, and in my waking fitts
> Doted upon't, to my worse losse of witts;
> Whilst I esteem'd none brave or good but this . . .[6]

Here and elsewhere in *A Recantation*, he condemns such thinking as mistaken; but although he never returned to robbery after his release from jail, it is clear that he relished the prestige that accompanied his fame as a highwayman. *The Soddered Citizen* opens with a prologue which advertises its author's former exploits on the roads, with evocative references to the historic robber haunts of Shooters Hill, Gadshill and Salisbury plain.[7] Moreover, the speech that I quoted earlier shows signs of a powerful ambivalence. Clavell may concede that his alter ego, 'the hopefull youth', has given himself over to 'Infamy', but this does not deter him, with striking self-admiration, from describing his offences as having conferred much glory on him.

*

If Clavell's career as a highwayman gave him something to boast about, this seems to have been all that he gained from it. In terms of financial rewards, he found it deeply disappointing. He complains in *A Recantation* that despite his best care, his expenses always swallowed up his booty. Although he tried not to spend money too lavishly, knowing that this might arouse suspicions, he was never able to save. He says that at the time he was sentenced to death, he didn't have enough money left to buy a coffin and pay for his burial. The people who did well at the expense of Clavell and his victims were the keepers of some of the inns and taverns that he and his men frequented, who knew that they were highwaymen and padded their bills accordingly. They were confident that the robbers, as hunted fugitives, would never dare to challenge them for fear of being betrayed.[8]

Clavell's complaint reminds us of one of the attributes of the 'good fellow', namely, that he can always be relied on to buy his friends a drink. None of the medieval texts underline what is fairly certainly the truth, that on some of those occasions when a 'good fellow' foots the bill, it is because unless he pays up smilingly, his jovial drinking mates might choose to turn him in. Ben Jonson, that shrewd observer of manners, depicts precisely that kind of drinking relationship in *Bartholomew Fair* (1614), though there the man under covert threat is a cutpurse, not a robber. When Daniel Knockem, the drunken horse dealer, says to Ezekiel Edgworth, the cutpurse, with mock naivety, 'thou hast money i' thy purse still; and store! How dost thou come by it?', Edgworth knows how a good fellow must reply: 'Half I have, Master Dan. Knockem, is always at your service.' And Knockem makes him count it out, too, and calls for Edgworth's cup to be filled so he can drink Knockem's health.[9]

By this date, the practice of swearing brotherhood had almost entirely lost any aristocratic and chivalric associations. When Shakespeare and John Fletcher adapted Chaucer's 'Knight's Tale' for the stage as the tragi-comedy *The Two Noble Kinsmen* (late in 1613 or early in 1614), the theme of sworn brotherhood was edited out, and replaced by a typically Renaissance preoccupation with the ideal of manly friendship.[10] During the early modern period, there are only a handful of references to the swearing of brotherhood, and most of these associate it with the rougher kinds of male society.[11] In his verse collection *More Knaves yet?* (1613), the satirist Samuel Rowlands has a story of two robbers who swear to be true to one another and divide equally everything they gain on the highway. The arrangement breaks down when one of them falls ill. Later, when he has recovered, he demands his share of the loot that the other has won single-handed. The second robber takes out both a bag of money and his naked sword, promising his 'sworne brother' that he can have his half of the plunder, so long as he also agrees to let him inflict on him half of the

[handwritten marginalia: "in the swearing of oaths HW Mystique"]

[handwritten marginalia: "HWM Oath"]

wounds that he himself has been given while robbing alone. The first robber abandons his claim. This is a hoary old tale. A slightly different version, about a couple of knights who agreed to share their tournament winnings, had been circulating three centuries earlier.[12] What Rowlands's satire tells us is that part of the mystique of the highwaymen, as of the outlaws before them, involved the swearing of oaths of brotherhood; and that moralists still viewed such oaths with a sceptical eye.

Clavell speaks of the highwaymen's oath from personal experience. It was administered whenever a new member was 'admitted a Brother of the company'. One article laid down what he must do if he were arrested. He must not betray his associates, nor must he reveal how he himself had come to be recruited into the robber's life. If pressed hard, he should invent details of imaginary confederates. Clavell says that following his capture, he had done this himself, since it had been made clear to him that his prospects of a pardon depended on his making a good show of co-operating with the authorities. Clavell is vaguer about the other articles in the oath. He calls it 'hellish', and says that those who took it feared that if they broke it they would damn themselves; so it would appear that they were made to swear upon their own soul's salvation. He also says that it bound them to sin, so that in effect, they were damned either way, whether they kept the oath or broke it. This statement is elucidated by a passage further on, where he says that all highwaymen were 'sworne to use these courses still': that is, never to abandon the robber's way of life.[13]

The text of quite an elaborate oath, supposed to have been administered by a gang of mounted robbers who were active in the first decade after the Restoration, is given by the eighteenth-century writer Captain Alexander Smith in his *Complete History of the Highwaymen*. Smith is not a reliable source; on the other hand, he is at least as much of a compiler as an original author, and he undoubtedly plagiarised a great deal of earlier material, much of which is lost. He probably found this oath in some late seventeenth-century pamphlet. As he gives it, it would have bound the new recruit to obey his captain and to be faithful to his companions 'in all their designs and attempts'. He was made to swear that he would always attend at the agreed rendezvous, that he would respond if called upon at any time, day or night, and that he would die fighting rather than flee 'from an equal number of opposers'. He also promised never to desert his companions, nor leave them, wounded or dead, in the hands of the enemy, to help them if they were captured, imprisoned, sick or otherwise in trouble, and to confess nothing if arrested. 'And this oath, when I break in the least tittle may the greatest plagues and Damnation seize me here and hereafter.'[14]

According to Clavell, the highwaymen had many accomplices among people who were outwardly respectable. Some of these were innkeepers. It was usual for guests who stayed at an inn overnight to leave their money and valuables in the care of the host. If it were the kind of place where highway robbers were encouraged, he would tip off his robber customers as to which of the day's travellers were going to be worth their while to ambush on the road. After all, he would make much more money from the highwaymen than out of any ordinary guest; highwaymen, Clavell says, spend 'full thrice as much in wine and beere' as anyone else is likely to spend on their whole board and lodging. At other inns, highwaymen often got information from the chamber servants: these people knew which travellers had well-lined purses, or cloak-bags that, by their unexpected weight, showed signs of containing gold. Sometimes the highwaymen took the trouble to place an accomplice in such a post; otherwise, they relied on tempting existing servants with bribes. The inn servant who was a confederate of a gang of robbers was a well-recognised security problem; forty years earlier, William Harrison had declared in his *Description of England* that few highway robberies took place in which the robbers had not first received a tip-off from a servant at some inn, whether chamberlain, tapster or ostler. He says that these people would draw the guests into conversation to find out which road they were taking.

Clavell tells us that the highwaymen's accomplices also included some of the professional security guards who were engaged to see travellers safely to their destination. These men would conduct their employers to some lonely spot where the robbers were lying in wait. They would pretend to put up a fight, but it would all be for show. Afterwards, they would muddle the pursuit, telling lies about the direction in which the robbers had made off. Clavell's basic message to travellers is, Trust no one. He warns them not even to tell their close relatives how much money they would be carrying, nor when they were setting off. He says that for the sake of a share of the proceeds, he had known sons scheme with robbers to have their fathers waylaid, brothers take part in plots against their brothers, and friends betray their friends. In the pamphlet life of the gentleman robber Charles Courtney, who was executed in 1612, Courtney says (or is made to say) that his own success as a highway robber had been down to the fact that he had never committed any casual robberies. He had always known in advance how much his victims had with them and where they were going.[15]

Clavell gives travellers much advice on how to avoid being robbed. He tells them to take the minor roads, since highwaymen kept to the highways, where they could pick out the likeliest victims from among the passers-by. He warns them strongly against bunching up close together when passing through dangerous places, since in practice this made it easier for the robbers to surround the whole party. Travellers who spread out would be left unmolested, for fear lest any should escape the ambush and raise the alarm. Clavell also advises them to be very careful with whom they associated while they were on the road. They should be wary of men who muffled themselves in their cloaks, or wore a handkerchief round their necks, ready for them to pull up over their mouths and noses; also men who, when stared at, were quick to turn their faces aside, or whose bushy beards didn't seem to look quite right. Other disguises Clavell mentions include the wearing of hoods, wigs, eye-patches, masks, and even imitation facial warts or similar blemishes.

He describes in detail a trick that was sometimes used when the robbers were targeting a traveller who they knew would be carrying a large sum. Since someone in that position could be expected to be very much on his guard, one of the gang would disguise himself as a country labourer,

> Cloathed in russet, or a leatherne slop,
> Which roules of rotten hay shall underprop,
> Meeting his hobnaild shoes halfe way the legg;
> His wastcote buckled with a hathorne pegg;
> His steeple felt, with greasie brims, inch broad,
> Shall totter on his noddle . . .

Sitting on a wad of straw in place of a saddle, this seemingly harmless fellow would insinuate himself into the traveller's company. He, taking a snobbish enjoyment in his companion's dialect speech and ignorant chatter, would abandon all suspicion. When the supposed yokel began to whistle '*Robin Hood*', the traveller would think nothing of it: but it would be a signal to the gang, and next moment, the man would rush him, and hold him till his confederates could reach them.[16]

In his chosen role as the exposer of the highwaymen's pretensions, Clavell taunts the robbers for their dependence on disguises and their fear of showing their true faces. At another point in his poem, he suggests that the notion that robbing on the highway is an honourable and valiant way of life, a notion that the highwaymen themselves believe and put about and that is shared by some members of the public, is another, metaphorical disguise: it covers over the real truth, that the robber's life is worthless, and shows no proofs of genuine courage. Buried in his comments is the thought that there is a contradiction between the highwaymen's image of themselves as very bold men and the fact that they rely so heavily on subterfuge and disguises: on a counterfeit countenance, in fact, though Clavell doesn't use the phrase.[17]

One of Clavell's recommendations to travellers is rather unexpected. He advises them that if they are carrying large sums of money, they should

travel by night, for then, he says, the mounted robbers wouldn't be abroad. The reasons he gives make sense. He says that the highwaymen assumed that no one who was worth robbing would be travelling after nightfall; that at night, the robbers couldn't see what they were doing, nor whether their intended victims were carrying pistols; and finally, that in order to avoid suspicion and maintain their cover as law-abiding members of the community, it was necessary for highwaymen to 'Keepe lawfull howers', as he puts it.[18] At this date, legal curfews were still in force, and you could be arrested for being out after curfew time without a very good reason.

Clavell's statements on this point contradict the stereotype completely. In the popular imagination, it is by night-time and moonlight that the highwayman chiefly rides out. Nor is this a modern belief. Thirty years before Clavell was writing, Shakespeare had made Falstaff request of Hal that robbers should be known as 'minions of the moon . . . under whose countenance we steal'.[19] In fact, although Clavell and his gang may have preferred to operate by day, some mounted robbers found it both possible and profitable to rob during the hours of darkness. In 1722, one Ralph Wilson, who like Clavell was a reformed highwayman, wrote an account of the robberies in which he had participated as a member of a well-known London gang. He says that during the evenings, he and his companions, John Hawkins and George Sympson, would go out robbing private coaches in the city suburbs. The very first robbery in which he took part was of this kind, and the robbers had mounted up at 'about ten a-clock'. However, they also committed numerous robberies by day, or at any rate, early in the morning, stopping the scheduled stage-coaches on their way out of London to the provinces.[20]

Though Clavell recommends the night as the safest time to travel, he admits that people who followed this advice might be risking an attack by footpads. As a mounted robber, a 'knight of the road', Clavell felt far superior to ordinary muggers of that kind. He dismisses them as 'Base Padding Rascalls' and disdainfully denies all knowledge of their modus operandi, which he refers to as the '*kill calfe* law'. The name itself tells us something about the ways in which they worked: 'kill-calf' was a slang term for a butcher, and one might well guess that kill-calf methods of robbery were brutal and violent. We know from other sources that padders, or footpads, often carried long staves, with which they were fully prepared to take on men on horseback.[21] An eighteenth-century robber of this kind, who was hanged in 1722, commented that such robberies could not be carried out without considerable cruelty, as it was impossible for a footpad to escape 'unless he either maimed the man, or wounded his horse'.[22] The usual approach of such robbers was to attack without warning and strike down or overpower the victim, who was given no chance to reach for weapons or take evasive action. Like modern muggers, they often

Modern perception ot 154 HWM
being better than normal robbers

worked after dusk. Considering their modus operandi, it is easy to appreciate that darkness would have provided them with useful cover.[23]

All the same, when two such robbers attacked the diarist John Evelyn in 1652, it was at the height of a hot June day. Evelyn, who had sent his servant ahead, was travelling between Tunbridge Wells and Bromley. He made the mistake of riding at the edge of the road, under the shade of the trees. Two 'Cutt-throates' came out at him, struck at his horse with their 'long staves' and catching the reins, dragged him down. Although he was armed with a sword, he could make no resistance and they easily took it away from him. After they had manhandled him 'into a deepe Thickett, some quarter of a mile from the high-way', they relieved him of money, rings and a pair of jewelled buckles. They pulled off his boots, tied him hand and foot, propped him against an oak and left him, 'with most bloudy threatnings to cutt my throat, if I offerd to crie out'. It took him nearly two hours to free himself, and during this time he suffered very much from 'the flies, the ants, and the sunn', as well as anxiety as to how he should get free in such a lonely spot.[24]

In contrast to the footpads, the mounted robbers were generally reluctant to risk injuring or, worse, killing their victims. Clavell says that most travellers were far too easily intimidated. He urges them to put up more of a fight. He says that however violent the highwaymen's threats, they were unlikely to carry them out, partly out of conscience, and partly because they knew that any robber who caused the death of a victim would be strenuously hunted down. Moreover, once captured, he would be made to pay dearly for his offence. Clavell himself was rumoured to have pleaded in mitigation at his trial that he had never struck or wounded anyone he had robbed, nor had he done them any actual violence.[25] Similarly, Charles Courtney, in his pamphlet life, states that during his career as a robber, he 'never . . . shed any blood, but still my care was how to prevent that stayne to my soule'.[26] In 1617, the Scots traveller Fynes Moryson noted as a peculiarity of highway robbers in England that although they were more common there than in any other country he had visited, they 'seldome or never' killed those they robbed. His statement that the highwaymen avoided fatal force is borne out by J. A. Sharpe, whose study of crime in Essex between 1620 and 1680 turned up only a single case of a murder that occurred during a highway robbery. Like Clavell, Moryson urged the traveller to fight back, saying of the highwaymen, 'The true man, having strength, armes, and courage, may cheerefully resist them'.[27]

Times had changed a good deal; there is a world of difference between the mentalities revealed in these early seventeenth-century texts and the brisk attitude to murder found in *Robin Hood and the Monk*: let alone Chief Justice Fortescue's bracketing of robbery with homicide in his comments on the superior courage of the English. For Fortescue, the chief point

155

about robbery was precisely that its perpetrators displayed a willingness to commit open violence.[28] However, from the seventeenth century onwards we find a growing tendency for the English to congratulate themselves on the *lack* of genuine violence displayed by their robbers. Philip Massinger's comedy *The Guardian* was licensed for performance in 1633, five years after the appearance of Clavell's *Recantation*. The play, which is set in Naples, has a sub-plot founded on the story of an exiled nobleman, who has become the leader of a crew of banditti. Under his leadership, we are informed, these robbers have behaved quite differently to the usual run of Italian banditti; they imitate 'The courteous English Theeves', and have not committed a single murder.[29] English pride that most of their robbers refrained from brutality, or were thought to do so, is vividly communicated by Henry Fielding's hero Tom Jones, in the novel of that name, published in 1749. Expressing his sympathy for highwaymen who are driven to rob out of need, Tom makes the point that he only means those 'whose highest Guilt extends no farther than to Robbery, and who are never guilty of Cruelty nor Insult to any Person, which is a Circumstance that, I must say, to the Honour of our Country, distinguishes the Robbers of *England* from those of all other Nations; for Murder is, amongst those, almost inseparably incident to Robbery'.[30] For a sceptical voice, we might listen to the Abbé Le Blanc, only a few years earlier; referring to the English highwaymen, he comments, 'notwithstanding their boasted humanity, the lives of those who endeavour to get away are not always safe. They are very strict and severe in levying their impost, and if a man has not wherewithal to pay them, he may run the chance of getting himself knock'd on the head for his poverty'.[31] Half a century earlier, between 1690 and 1700, Narcissus Luttrell noted in his diary brief details of five murders that were perpetrated by mounted robbers.[32] However, it is fair to state that he also recorded a great many such robberies at which no murders or even brutalities seem to have been committed. All the same, though most highwaymen probably were quite loath to risk fatally harming their victims, there is no doubt that once they felt themselves cornered, they could be extremely dangerous. Luttrell reports quite a number of murders committed by highwaymen who were resisting arrest.[33] No doubt this reflects the desperation of men who knew they faced trial on a capital charge, but there is also some evidence that killings of this kind were regarded by the public as rather more excusable. A broadside ballad of 1674 gives an account of a current news item, the arrest and conviction of several highwaymen after a violent stand in which two of their pursuers were killed. In this first-person ballad, the robbers are made to express their remorse for the deaths. However, they explain that, once surrounded, they decided to make their 'couragious retreat' because they regard it as 'a nobler thing, / To fall by the Sword then to peep through a string'. When

Moll's highwayman husband arrives in Newgate, in Daniel Defoe's *Moll Flanders* (1722), the first she hears of it is that three highwaymen, 'brave topping Gentlemen', have been brought to the jail 'after a gallant Resistance, in which I know not how many of the Country People were wounded, and some kill'd'.[34]

The belief that there was a distinctively English way to rob was still alive at the end of the eighteenth century. In 1794, we find the radical writer Mary Wollstonecraft, of all people, first sneering at the French for, according to her, preferring to pilfer rather than rob, and then suggesting that when they do commit robbery, they are cruel and murderous out of fear; 'whilst in England, where the spirit of liberty has prevailed, it is useful for an highwayman, demanding your money, not only to avoid barbarity, but to behave with humanity, and even complaisance'.[35] The English highway robber's vaunted forbearance is thus, rather oddly, made into a mark of his and his victims' indifference to fear. The thing that hasn't changed, in more than three centuries, is the sense that the behaviour of English robbers somehow proves the superiority of the English over the French.

To go back to Clavell's time: why did the attitude to violence change? One factor was certainly the lessening prestige of the purely martial virtues, and the high value that was now placed on order and internal peace. This is amusingly illustrated by some of the concluding stanzas to a version of the Robin Hood story which was published in 1632, in which the author, Martin Parker, a well-known ballad-writer of the period, takes a prudent man's view of the hero's exploits:

> A thing impossible to us
> This story seemes to be;
> None dares be now so venturous;
> But times are chang'd, we see.
>
> We that live in these latter dayes
> Of civill government,
> If neede be, have a hundred wayes
> Such outlawes to prevent.
>
> In those dayes men more barbarous were,
> And lived lesse in awe;
> Now, God be thanked! people feare
> More to offend the law.
>
> . . .
>
> Let us be thankefull for these times
> Of plenty, truth and peace,

And leave out great and horrid crimes,
Least they cause this to cease.[36]

One thing that is clear is that by Clavell's time, the highway robber is in a deeply contradictory position. He is proud of what he feels to be his courage, and he believes, not without some reason, that many people admire him for it. Nevertheless, the limited toleration he is accorded by the authorities and the public is now largely conditional on his restricting himself to purely token violence. He fears very much to find himself with blood on his hands; and those chiefly at risk from him are the weak, the severely outnumbered and the cowardly.

A successful robbery, especially if it is to be bloodless, requires that the robbers maintain dominance over their victims. Clavell and his associates had a sound grasp of how to seize and keep control of the situation. They would lie in wait 'In some odde corner', and when they saw a likely party of travellers, they would ride out towards them. Then, on a given word, something ordinary that would not arouse suspicion – Clavell gives '*what's a clocke*' as an example – the strongest robbers would seize the travellers' bridles, while the rest of the gang, shouting the highwayman's cry of 'Stand and deliver!', would menace them from a short distance with pistols and swords. These would set out to terrify the victims, while those holding the bridles would speak soothingly and try to persuade them not to resist. Clavell was intrigued by the often unpredictable reactions shown by the people whom he robbed. Some who were big strong men would 'cry like Children at the word *Deliver*', while others who were much smaller sometimes put up a spirited resistance.

As soon as the travellers had been overpowered, they would be taken off the road into a place of concealment, where they would be thoroughly rifled. Clavell says that if the robbers found that their victims had sewn their gold into their clothing to hide it, they would call them villains and accuse them of trying to cheat them. In the manner of Robin Hood, they behaved as if they had a right to the money they stole. But unlike Robin Hood, these were not generous robbers. If a traveller begged them to spare him, and said that what they were taking was all he had, they would pay no attention.[37] The Ratsey books, as we have seen, had contained several stories of the highwayman's reputed magnanimity, either in returning some or all of what he found, or even, Robin Hood fashion, lending money to those in trouble. Such tales became a staple part of the popular lore about robber heroes.[38] Clavell offers nothing to substantiate the notion that real highwaymen might sometimes have engaged in such behaviour; though perhaps we should keep in mind that in his *Recantation*, it was hardly to his purpose to be seen to show robbers in a favourable light.

He says that he himself had soothed his conscience with the thought that anyone whom he robbed would be repaid at what he calls 'the Countries cost'.[39] He means that they could legally claim their money back from the people of the hundred, or county division, in which the robbery had taken place. This is not, in fact, the strict truth. As the law then stood, unless they were able to capture the robber and hand him over to justice, the inhabitants of the hundred were bound to pay out half of the value of the goods or money stolen.[40] Clavell seems to have assumed that victims would routinely pad their claims. Indeed, elsewhere he says in so many words that they often doubled the size of the sum they said they had lost. Altogether, his experiences as a highwayman seem to have given him a low opinion of the travelling public. In addition to inflating their losses, the victims of robberies often exaggerated the numbers of their assailants, and they would invent stories about their brave resistance when the truth was that they had given in without a fight. Sometimes, when a robbery was already in progress, a new party of travellers would arrive at the scene. Rather to his disgust, Clavell found he could often persuade them to ride past and abandon the victims to the robbers, even though they might easily have rescued them.[41]

Once in the highwaymen's hands, Clavell advises victims to be very polite to them. Blatant hypocrisy, like saying they wished they had more money for them, would go down well, he says. Handing over some of their money before they were searched might, if they were lucky, enable them to escape a thorough rifling, since the robbers would be in a hurry to finish the business. Clavell warns them against keeping their hands over the place where their money is hidden, since by doing this they give themselves away. Once they had finished their search, and exchanged any horses that were better than their own beasts, the highwaymen would make their victims swear not to follow them, nor to raise the hue and cry: that is, to notify the nearest constable, so that he could organise an official pursuit. It is doubtful how far the highwaymen would really have expected them to keep this last promise, since raising the hue and cry would have been a necessary first step towards obtaining partial restitution of their losses from the hundred.

In a vivid passage, Clavell describes the anxieties that beset the fleeing highwaymen after a robbery. They are afraid of every movement in the bushes, for fear that it is a sign that they are under attack. Clavell recalls an occasion when a gang of fleeing robbers were startled into greater speed at the sound of an owl hooting by daylight, which they took for the whooping cries of the pursuit.[42] Nevertheless, Clavell had a low opinion of the ordinary law enforcement officers, the constables and watchmen. He says that the constables, many of whom were uneducated men of relatively low social standing, often arrested the innocent, and that sometimes such unfortunates ended by being hanged for other men's crimes. Charles

159

Courtney says that he himself had become very disturbed in conscience after a pair of innocent men were executed for one of his robberies.[43] As for the companies of watchmen who were sometimes set to watch the roads after a robbery had been committed, Clavell regards these as worse than useless. All they achieved was to make the travellers feel safer, and, as a result, grow careless. The watchmen themselves he dismisses as 'Poore, silly, old, decrepid men', and he points out that though footmen armed with halberds might be effective against footpads, they could hardly be a match for robbers on horseback. He even claims that on one occasion, he and his gang had robbed several passengers while a dozen of these old fellows stood by and watched them, much too afraid to intervene.[44]

After a robbery, the highwaymen generally made for an inn. For choice, they frequented high-class establishments with landlords of impeccable reputation, since they believed that such places were less likely to be searched by the constables. Clavell has some advice for honest innkeepers on how they should recognise such guests. One sign of the highwayman was his particularity over the care of his horse. He would insist that the animal was groomed with extra attention, and fed on special mashes and fodder; even on 'Christians Bread', or food fit for humans. If the ostler expressed surprise at this, he might find the guest responding cryptically that the horse deserved it, and that the cost would be more than repaid by the beast's good service. Another mark of the highwayman was his inquisitiveness; he would be forever asking questions about the other guests, wanting to know where they were travelling and when they were setting off. Should an innkeeper grow suspicious about a particular party of travellers, he ought to speak separately to each member of it and ask him the names of his companions, and then set his servants to ask the same questions. If the men were robbers, he would soon catch them slipping and muddling one another's aliases.

Once concealed in their room at the inn, the robbers would share out the loot. This they always did at the first opportunity, since none of them trusted their confederates. Clavell states that he himself had sometimes caught associates of his trying to keep back more than their share. Reynard the Fox had just the same problem with his 'fellow', the Wolf. Just like the Wolf, such double-dealing robbers are violating their oath to their brother robbers; as Clavell savagely comments, by actions of this kind, they forswear themselves and damn their souls to Hell.[45]

Though Clavell had sworn never to abandon the highwayman's way of life, he came to the conclusion that as the oath itself was unlawful, it could not be strictly binding. His reformation undoubtedly had a great deal to do with the shock of being arrested and sentenced to death, and the months he spent after his trial cooling his heels in prison. It may well have been assisted by the fact that in the course of this period, all his old associates had themselves been captured. A highwayman's career was usually a short one. Just over a year separated Clavell's first recorded highway robbery from his arrest.[46] How far his revulsion against his life of crime was motivated by the reflection that robbery had by no means been the rewarding source of income he had hoped is something we cannot know.

In his *Recantation*, Clavell says several times that when he is set free, he will join one of the armies sent to fight in the King's wars overseas. This, he maintains, is the only honourable course for a gentleman robber in time of war. By serving as a soldier, he will demonstrate that his crimes were committed as much from 'want of Action' as desire for money.[47] However, this stirring idealism had not impelled him to join the force that was raised in 1624 to fight in the Palatinate; nor had he volunteered for the expedition to Cadiz, in 1625. Since both of these overseas adventures had ended in disaster, this was probably just as well, from his point of view, but it rather undermines his martial rhetoric. After he was released from jail, instead of taking the next chance to fight in the wars, by joining the fleet that sailed for La Rochelle in 1628, he tried his luck, as we have seen, at writing a play for the London stage: the last resort of desperate poverty, as he himself jokes in the text.[48] In 1629, Clavell was still an undischarged bankrupt. Eventually, his uncle, Sir William Clavell, whose putative heir he was, took him in hand. Sir William sent him to Ireland, to represent him in a property dispute: in effect, he became a sort of seventeenth-century remittance man. In this new, colonial setting, he prospered; despite a lack of qualifications, he began to practise both as a lawyer and a physician, and in 1635, he married the only daughter and heiress of a wealthy Dublin vintner called Markham.[49] An exploitative arrangement, no doubt. At the time of the wedding, his wife was a child of nine. However, before we mistake Clavell for a sexual pervert, or misunderstand the society in which he lived, we should note that in those instances (which were rare) in which girls were married off at a very young age, it was usual to delay consummation until they were considerably older.[50] It is clear from a letter that Clavell wrote shortly after the marriage that the child was still living in her parents' household, where he himself had also taken up residence. He speaks of her with affection, as 'the center of all our happiness', and notes with satisfaction that 'she improves in growth of body': something on which, one might argue, he would have been rather unlikely to comment with pleasure, if he had been really a man who was sexually drawn to pre-pubertal girls.[51]

In this businesslike marriage, a union between bankrupt old blood and commercial riches, Clavell's life again takes on a flavour of city comedy. The wild young gallant has restored his fortunes by marrying a wealthy heiress. Whether he ever took possession of the Markham inheritance, we do not know. However, it is certain that he never inherited his uncle

William's estates. Instead, he predeceased him, dying of pleurisy in 1643, at the age of forty-one.[52]

13

Knights of the Road

On 3 September 1651, Oliver Cromwell defeated Charles II at the battle of Worcester. A few weeks later, on 9 November, a fugitive from the King's army, a trooper called James Hind, was betrayed by a former comrade and arrested in London. Hind was not an ordinary Royalist soldier. He had already been the subject of a pseudo-biography, *Hind's Ramble*, which made him out to be something of a legend: a highwayman who was rumoured to have engineered Charles's escape after the fight at Worcester, and even to have been the Scoutmaster General to the royal army. However, after his arrest, Hind declared quite truthfully that he had played no part in helping the fugitive King. He did not, though, deny that he had once been a robber.[1]

Over the next few months, Hind remained in jail. He was tried for high treason at the Old Bailey on 12 December, but his trial was adjourned. A news pamphlet says that it was adjourned to Oxford, but the next time we hear of him in court, he has been tried at Reading for murder, early in March 1652. It appears that he had once got into a fight over a gambling debt with a friend of his named Poole: they had bet each other that they could leap their horses over a particular gate. Poole had lost, but had refused to pay up, and in the violent quarrel that followed, Hind had killed him. Hind was found guilty of manslaughter, but since this was his first conviction, he was allowed to plead his 'clergy', that is, prove himself a literate man, as a means to escape the gallows. To his great dismay, he found himself unable, after all, to decipher the passage from the Psalms that he was supposed to read aloud. Whatever rudimentary learning he might have once possessed had deserted him. However, Parliament had recently passed an Act of General Pardon and Oblivion, with the aim of promoting national reconciliation. On the day after his trial, Hind was granted a pardon under the terms of this act. Unfortunately for him, someone with influence wanted him dead. There was still an outstanding indictment against him for treason. He was taken to Worcester, where on 24 September he was hanged, drawn and quartered.[2]

During the first few weeks after his arrest, while he was still in London, imprisoned in Newgate jail, Hind was treated by the press as a popular hero. A series of news pamphlets described his arrest, his committal to Newgate and his trial at the Old Bailey. At the same time, a string of pseudo-biographies celebrated him as a cherishable robber who carried out his robberies '*with a Grace*', or as we might say, with style, and who showed admirable courage, presence of mind, ingenuity and, above all, a prankish wit.[3] One news pamphlet reports that when a curious visitor to Newgate showed him copies of the two earliest of these biographies, *Hind's Ramble* and a follow-up book, *Hind's Exploits*, and asked if he had seen them, Hind 'answered, yes: And said upon the word of a Christian, they were fictions'. However, he added: 'But some merry Pranks and Revels I have plaid, that I deny not'.[4] While denying the literal truth of the stories in these books, Hind was nevertheless keen to present himself as if he were indeed the hero of exactly that kind of narrative: a 'merry' highwayman, an essentially harmless prankster. Towards the end of *Hind's Ramble*, the fictional Hind is summed up as one who was 'charitable to the poor; and . . . a man that never murdered any on the Road; and always gave men a jest for their money'.[5] The real Hind was more than happy to play up to such a flattering image, and even to improve on it. On his arrival at Newgate, he is reported in a news pamphlet to have made a statement defending his activities as a robber. 'I owe a debt to God, and a debt I must pay; blessed be his Name that he hath kept me from shedding of bloud unjustly, which is now a comfort to me: Neither did I ever wrong any poor man of the worth of a penny: but I must confess, I have (when I have been necessitated thereto) made bold with a rich Bompkin, or a lying Lawyer, whose full-fed fees from the rich Farmer, doth too too much impoverish the poor cottage-keeper'.[6] And in a 'Declaration' published a few days later, evidently with Hind's authorisation, he repeats his claim that he had never shed a single drop of blood, and continues: 'Neither did I ever take the worth of a peny from a poor man; but at what time soever I met with any such a person, it was my constant custom, to ask, *Who he was for?* if he reply'd, *For the King*, I gave him 20 shillings: but if he answer'd, *For the Parliament*, I left him, as I found him.'[7] These statements indicate that Hind, with the co-operation and perhaps the active suggestion of the journalist who took them down for him, was intent on positioning himself as a 'good' robber. He has never killed or injured any of his victims. He has robbed only when he was in need, and only from men who have arguably deserved it: wealthy farmers, or the crooked lawyers who, he asserts, make good money helping the farmers find ways to undermine the traditional rights of the rural labourers. He insists that he has never robbed the poor;

instead, he claims to have been consistently generous towards any poor traveller who was prepared to proclaim himself a Royalist.

Altogether, it is clear that Hind wanted to be recognised as following in the tradition of Ratsey and the more genial incarnations of Robin Hood, as a robber who had been accustomed to give liberally to the poor, and who had practised a rough, but not brutal, justice in a manner that was calculated to make people laugh. To some extent he may have been trying to sway public opinion in advance of his trial. But it is unlikely that this was his only or even his chief concern. In any case, as one of the visitors who came to view his arrival at Newgate pointed out, Hind was not facing charges of robbery, but of treason. To this, Hind instantly replied, 'I value it not a three pence, to lose my life in so good a cause; and if it was to do again, I should do the like'.[8] These are not the words of a man bent on conciliation at all costs. For Hind, it was necessary to show himself a loyal supporter of King Charles II, even when he was in the hands of that King's enemies and facing trial on a capital charge. In much the same way, it was important to him that the public should think of him as a particular kind of highwayman, the merry and generous kind, a robber who had some right on his side. It is likely that that is how he needed to think of himself.

Several of the pseudo-biographies make a special point of stressing Hind's devotion to the Royalist cause. A popular story, first found in *Hind's Ramble*, describes how Hind is supposed to have robbed a committee man, a member of one of the county committees appointed by Parliament to manage local government. So far as the Royalists were concerned, committee men were hate figures, since one of their functions was arranging the sequestration of the lands and property of those who supported the King. They also organised the regular taxation that financed the Parliamentary army. The committee man in the Hind story has to make a journey to London, so in order to escape the attention of robbers he provides himself with a worn-out old coat and an elderly horse kitted out with the cheapest gear. When he encounters Hind, the highwayman takes him at face value, as the poor broken-down old fellow he appears to be, and gives him a gold piece. The committee man pretends to be overjoyed; he promises he will spend the evening drinking Hind's health. However, once he has arrived at the inn where he is staying, he is stupid enough to boast of his escape, and curses Hind for a rogue. The inn is one where Hind himself often puts up; when he arrives there that evening, after the committee man has gone to bed, he is told what the old man has said about him. The next day, Hind stops the committee man on the road and robs him of £50.[9] One of the morals of the story is that you can't trust a committee man, and it is implied that they all have their hands in the public coffers. Another of the morals, of course, is the old one, that compared to some of the grasping types who operate with the backing of law, the highwayman is an honest fellow, who may even be said to make good some of the harm that they do, when he takes their ill-gotten gains and redistributes them.

One highly intriguing story, very much out of the common run of English highwayman tales, is first found in *The English Gusman*, published in January 1652. It tells of an encounter between Hind and an old woman who begs an alms from him as he is riding through Hatfield. Hind's horse immediately stops dead and refuses to go on. Hind, who doesn't like the look of the woman, gives her five shillings and tells her that he is in a hurry, but she insists that she has something important to say to him. It transpires that she wants to give him a special charm which will protect him from danger '*for the space of Three Years*'. It takes the form of 'a *little box*', which contains a dial with a movable needle, at one end of which is a star. She tells him that whenever he is in trouble, he should open the box and ride in whichever direction he sees the star pointing. Then she strikes him 'with a *white Rod* that was in her hand' and switches his horse on its hindquarters; the beast gallops off so furiously that Hind is unable to thank her, which he guesses is her intention.[10]

It would be interesting to know the source of this story. No earlier version survives; in extant English tradition it is told only of Hind, and yet it bears several marks of being a traditional tale. The identity of the old woman is not altogether clear. In the title to the story, she is described as a 'cunning woman', or white witch. However, in early modern folk tradition, it was fairies who typically carried white rods; it was, in fact, the form taken by the original fairy wand.[11] And the taboo on giving thanks belongs to fairy belief; it was fairies, not witches, who should never be thanked for any good turn they might choose to do you.[12] Nor was it by any means unknown for a helpful fairy to appear in the guise of an old woman.[13] It seems quite likely that an older version of the tale was one in which a beneficent fairy placed a spell of protection on a famous robber.

In his book *Bandits*, Eric Hobsbawm says that the possession of magical protective charms is a common attribute of traditional robber heroes in places as far apart as southern Italy and Indonesia. He suggests that one of the functions of such stories is to express a sense of what he calls the noble robber's 'spiritual legitimacy'.[14] This theory would certainly fit Hind's case. In *Hind's Ramble* and *The English Gusman*, as well as in the various later biographies that plagiarise these books, the reader is clearly invited to sympathise with Hind's Royalist convictions, and to see him, moreover, as something of a Robin Hood figure: he steals from the supporters of Parliament and gives generously to the poor and to people in trouble. In this context, his charmed invulnerability from capture during the three years of his career as a highwayman may be understood as a special grace that marks him out as no ordinary robber. Hind and, by implication, the cause to which he adheres are backed by hidden but powerful forces of magic and luck.

Nothing is known for certain about Hind's real activities during his life as a robber. However, we do know just a little about his origins. At his trial, he told the court that he had been born in 'the merry town of Chipping-Norton in Oxfordshire'.[15] *The English Gusman* adds to this the further detail that Hind was the son of a saddler who was 'in good Reputation and Credit'. The parish registers of Chipping Norton duly confirm that James, 'son of Edward Hinde, saddler', was baptised there on 15 July 1616. Surviving records also show that Hind's father had been three times appointed churchwarden, which suggests that he was indeed a man of some standing and substance. In one record, that of the burial of his daughter Anne, in 1624, he is called 'Edward Hinde, Gent.', which implies that he belonged to the category of wealthy yeomen and artisans who, while not strictly entitled to be regarded as gentlemen, were nevertheless very highly respected within their own localities.[16] *The English Gusman* says that Hind's father sent his son to school to learn 'to read *English*, and to *Write*', but that James was a poor pupil. This receives some support from his later history. We have seen that after his conviction at Reading (which took place some weeks after *The English Gusman* had appeared in print), he made an attempt to read his 'neck-verse', evidently assuming that he ought to be able to do this, but discovered that he couldn't make any sense of it. According to *The English Gusman*, once his father realised that James wasn't willing to study, he took him out of school and tried to teach him his own trade of saddler, without success; finally, he apprenticed the boy to a butcher in Chipping Norton. The fact that 'Captain' Hind, the famous highwayman, had started in life as a butcher seems to have been part of the general gossip about him, since it is mentioned in other sources. Whether *The English Gusman* is correct that he broke his indentures, running away from his master after only one year's service, is something we cannot be sure of; it may be merely a plausible fiction.[17]

One thing that emerges with clarity is that Hind, the saddler's son, the former butcher, was not a gentleman robber, or at any rate, not in the sense that John Clavell was one, or even Gamaliel Ratsey. He was not a man of old family, looking for a way to maintain himself without resorting to labour and giving up his blood-right as a gentleman. He belongs instead to what was undoubtedly a much larger social group: robbers with no claim to gentle birth who came from a background in service, farmwork or trade. What did such men expect to achieve by turning to robbery on the highway? The easy answer is a quick path to money, and certainly a successful robbery could make them rich far beyond any prospects that their former careers might have offered. But the life of a highwayman also held more and subtler attractions. John Clavell indicates this when he says that the reason low-born highwaymen were reluctant to leave the life was because it brought them 'A kinde of state, ne're knowne to [their] beginning': a dignity, a prestige, of which they could hardly have dreamed had they remained in their original places near the bottom of the social hierarchy.[18] *The English Gusman* makes a similar point in one of its stories. When the young James Hind, recently arrived in London, meets Allen, the leader of a gang of highwaymen, Allen promises him that if Hind will serve him, he will 'learn him such an *Art*, as would for ever make him a *Gentleman*'.[19] The art that makes a man a gentleman is, of course, robbery on the highway. Just as impoverished gentlemen sometimes turned to highway robbery in the hopes of preserving their status, so some men of humbler background cherished the notion that in becoming highway robbers, and especially mounted robbers, they had found a way to make themselves into gentlemen.

Becoming a gentleman: what might this have meant to someone like a runaway butcher's apprentice in the middle years of the seventeenth century? Certainly, it would have involved having plenty of money in his pocket. But also, and this is a point we may miss, nowadays, it meant spending money freely, and even giving money away. Among the marks of a gentleman was generosity, in liberal tipping of servants, giving to beggars, making benefactions to those in need. The open-handed highwayman of the Hind legend, who doles out gold pieces to the poor, is conforming to an important aspect of the aristocratic code, albeit in something of an exaggerated fashion; he is behaving, perhaps, like a poor man's fantasy of a gentleman. Another of the marks of a gentleman was, of course, that he should look and act the part. It was expected of him that he live expensively and dress well. In the words of an Elizabethan treatise on English political and social institutions: 'As for their outward shew, a gentleman (if he wil be so accompted [accounted]) must go like a gentleman'.[20] The 'gentleman robber' had no problem complying with this. In Chapter Nine, I cited George Whetstone's complaint, made in 1584, about highway robbers who in clothes and behaviour could not be distinguished from the wealthy gentlemen with whom they consorted in high-class London eating houses.[21]

The English Gusman claims that Hind's 'master' Allen and his gang used to go out robbing in the guise of 'Noblemen and their servants'. In one story, the inn where they are staying is searched by the local constable, who has been notified to look out for them, but the splendour of Allen's clothes and the number and dress of his 'servants' combine with the lordly affability of his manner to deceive the man completely. In early modern England, personal attendants were an important indicator of status. Later in the book, Hind, who by now has acquired the courtesy title of 'Captain', and who is reported to be mixing with gentlemen on equal terms, acquires a 'servant' of his own who acts as his accomplice in a hold-up.[22] This kind of relationship between a 'gentleman robber' and his sidekick or confederates was not at all unusual. Indeed, Clavell advises innkeepers that one way to spot a robber gang is to take careful note of parties of travellers where the 'servants' don't seem to be showing the proper degree of deference to their 'masters'.[23] As for robbers going magnificently dressed: on 15 November 1692, Narcissus Luttrell recorded in his diary that 'a noted highwayman' had been arrested in the genteel neighbourhood of Covent Garden, wearing 'a scarlet cloak and coat laced with gold'.[24]

One of the qualities that was held to adorn a gentleman was an affinity with horses. A mid-seventeenth-century description of 'The true Gentleman' states, '*He delights to see himself, and his servants well mounted*: therefore he loveth good Horsemanship.'[25] For a highwayman, a fast horse was, of course, one of the necessities of his trade. But possession of a horse was also the attribute that lifted him above the ordinary run of robbers; that entitled him, indeed, to the name of a 'gentleman' robber. This becomes explicit in Samuel Rid's Jacobean account, cited in Chapter Nine, of the two different sorts of robber: 'gentleman robbers' and 'padders' or footpads.[26] However, the notion is already lurking in Gadshill's boast to the Chamberlain in *Henry IV, Part I*: 'I am joined with no foot-landrakers, no long-staff sixpenny strikers, . . . but with nobility and tranquillity . . . such as . . . ride up and down' in their quest for booty.[27] Gadshill himself, whom the Chamberlain addresses respectfully as 'master', but who is clearly far outclassed by the aristocratic company in which he robs, is evidently, like Allen and Hind, a 'gentleman' solely by virtue of his profession of mounted robber.

When Ben Jonson satirised the cult of the robber in the character of the impostor, Shift, in *Every Man out of his Humour*, he didn't neglect the contribution to the highwaymen's mystique that was made by their reputation as riders of fine horses. Sogliardo, Shift's deluded patron, boasts on behalf of his supposedly glamorous friend that 'he has had his mares and his geldings, he, ha' been worth fortie, threescore, a hundred pound a horse, would ha' sprung you over hedge, and ditch, like your grey-hound'.[28] In *The English Gusman*, Hind begins his career as a robber by shrewdly selecting 'the very best' horse out of Allen's stable. A marginal note in the next chapter says that he fed his horse 'with flesh', presumably with the idea of giving it more strength and stamina. Later in the book, he becomes the master of another splendid beast, which he steals from a horse-courser, or dealer in second-hand horses. The narrative lavishes no sympathy on the unfortunate horse-courser; rather like second-hand car dealers nowadays, such men had an unsavoury reputation for fraud, passing off broken-down beasts as sound. When Hind's friends, impressed by his new horse, ask him how much it cost, the highwayman quotes the old tag: '*to deceive the deceiver is no deceit*'.[29] The report of the real Hind's trial at Reading shows that he and his associates certainly did take a reckless pleasure in feats of horsemanship; his quarrel with the man he killed began with a wager the two of them had as to whether they could put their horses over an unusually high gate.[30]

A gentleman's lavish spending on clothes, luxuries and horses was normally supported from the rents of an estate in land; as Sir Thomas More remarked in *Utopia*, 'gentlemen ... live idle ... lyke dorres [drones], of that whiche other have laboured for: their tenauntes I meane' (Robinson's translation, 1551).[31] An important mark of the gentleman was that he never worked with his hands; indeed, many gentlemen did no work at all. In his *Anatomy of Melancholy* (1621), Robert Burton declared, 'amongst us the badge of gentry is idlenesse: to be of no calling, not to labour, for thats derogatory to their birth, to be a meere spectator, a drone, ... to have no necessary employment to busie himselfe about in Church and commonwealth (some few governers exempted)'.[32] Henry Peacham, in *The Compleat Gentleman* (1622), is sourer: 'to be drunke, sweare, wench, follow the fashion, and to do just nothing, are the attributes and marks now adaies of a great part of our Gentry'.[33] Idleness was a sin and a social evil – whenever it was practised by the poor. For the gentry and nobility, the rules were different. The radical writer Gerrard Winstanley protested in 1650 that the clergy, lawyers and justices were continually 'checking the Labourers for idleness, and protecting the Gentry that never work at all'.[34]

The high-status life, then, was the life of maximum leisure – so long as it was accompanied by the appropriate signs of affluence. Moreover, such was the looseness of English definitions of gentility that all that was strictly required to become a gentleman was to maintain a gentlemanly appearance: good clothes, good horses, personal servants, a lavish way of life and, of course, freedom from the need to engage in any demeaning occupation. As Sir Thomas Smith slyly observes, in his *De Republica Anglorum*, written in Elizabeth's reign, 'gentlemen ... be made good cheape in England', and he explains that in the final resort, any man who dressed and behaved like a gentleman and was able to 'live idly and without manuall labour' would be 'called master, ... and ... be taken for a gentleman'.[35] The Jacobean dramatist George Chapman is more succinct. In his comedy *May–Day* (1602), a swaggering soldier confidently assures a rich young citizen, 'there's no prescription for gentility but good clothes and impudence'.[36]

In Smith's opinion, the ease with which it was sometimes possible for a man who was not born of old family to slide into the role of gentleman was in no way harmful to society. He argued that the only risk was to the parvenu himself, 'who hereby perchance will beare a bigger saile [put on a more extravagant display] than he is able to maintaine'.[37] However, the existence of an elite whose chief distinguishing mark, especially when they were away from their own neighbourhoods, was the possession of wealth without visible occupation, and which was, at least to some degree, open to anyone who was able to meet this qualification, undoubtedly had socially damaging effects that Smith omits to consider. By no means all self-made gentlemen were rich yeomen farmers, or merchants turned landed proprietors, whose wealth had been obtained by methods within the law. There were also a number of men with pretensions to be 'taken for' gentlemen who were involved in various kinds of crime. We have seen something of this already, in the cases of those men of good family, like John Clavell and Sir George Sandys, who turned to highway robbery and sometimes to housebreaking. But the phenomenon extended much more widely than this. In 1592, Robert Greene, who undoubtedly moved, on occasion, in some very shady circles, spoke of the presence in London of men who '[lived] gentlemen-like of themselves, having neythere money nor Lande, nor any lawfull meanes to maintain them'.[38] When he describes them further, it transpires that some of the men he is thinking of were cheating gamblers, while others practised various kinds of confidence trick. The great city was a magnet to gentlemen from all over England. A plausible confidence man, living on the proceeds of successful fraud, might be almost impossible to distinguish from a landed man with an income from the rents of his estate. Cheats and con tricks were far safer than robbery, since they were not punishable by death. They were, however, reckoned to be intrinsically dishonourable and ungentlemanly.

Highway robbery was another matter. Some verses published in 1643 which are put into the mouth of a discharged soldier make the point quite clearly:

> To beg is base, as base as pick a purse;
> To cheat, more base; of all theft that is worse.
> Nor beg nor cheat will I – I scorn the same;
> But while I live, maintain a soldier's name.
> I'll purse it, I, – the highway is my hope;
> His heart's not great that fears a little rope.[39]

Activities such as cheating and picking purses were regarded as 'base', that is, low, dishonourable, because they are committed in underhanded ways. By contrast, the robber confronted his chosen targets face to face and was ready to fight it out. The confidence trickster often masqueraded as a gentleman, but since his profession was a disgraceful one, this could not be anything more than a pretence. The highway robber was in a different position. Many low-born highwaymen undoubtedly believed that as a result of their violent exploits they had won the right to be regarded as men of honour.[40] Not for nothing did highwaymen commonly assume military titles like 'Captain'.[41] It seems that they saw their position as analogous to that of a soldier whose tested courage results in his winning a commission, and with it the formal status of a gentleman. Their pride in their profession was expressed in what Clavell tells us was their preferred name for themselves, the quasi-aristocratic title of *'Knights of the Roades'* (later, and more usually, 'knights of the road').[42] To sum up: when highway robbery is represented in *The English Gusman* as 'an *Art*' that could make a man into a gentleman, it is partly because it enabled the robber to live without manual labour, and to live the high life, too; partly because, with the proceeds, he could purchase the trappings of a gentleman, and enjoy the marks of deference that these enforced from ordinary folk; but most of all, because it was a way of life that required, or was believed to require, the fighting courage that was still very widely felt to be the gentleman's defining quality.

At the time most of the Hind pamphlets appeared, in the early 1650s, the poor man turned 'gentleman robber' was certainly not a new social type. What was new, and marked a definite cultural shift, was the focusing of intense public attention on a highwayman of this kind. Ever since the Elizabethan period, virtually all the robbers who had achieved a degree of fame through being featured in the press, in books or broadside ballads, had been men with at least some pretensions to coming of gentle stock. This is true, among others, of Mannington, Luke Hutton, Ratsey, Charles Courtney and, of course, Clavell. As we have seen, even the legendary Robin Hood, a yeoman in the earliest narratives, had been transmuted into a nobleman.[43] But now James Hind, the saddler's son, emerges as the first of a new breed of highwayman hero, whose origins lie in the lower ranks of society. Instead of being spendthrift heirs or penniless younger brothers, these men are typically reported to have begun their careers as household servants or runaway apprentices. Famous highwaymen of this sort included Claude Du Vall, who had once been a servant to a nobleman and who was executed in 1670, and James Whitney, the Jacobite robber, hanged in 1693, who had been a butcher, like Hind.[44]

It is noticeable that the appearance of the low-born robber hero took place against a background of voices declaring ever more loudly that robbery was not, after all, in any way, a suitable activity for a gentleman deserving of the name. In Thomas Fuller's collection of character studies, *The Holy State and the Profane State*, published in 1642, death on the gallows for highway robbery is one of the miserable fates foretold for 'The Degenerous Gentleman'. Twenty-five years later, Samuel Butler wrote a character of 'An Highwayman' in which he remarks, contemptuously, that despite the common notion that the highway robber was 'the most heroical' of thieves, 'he is really one of the basest, that never ventures but upon surprizal, and where he is sure of the advantage'.[45] It was now becoming quite unusual for a man of old family to embark on a career as a highwayman. In 1683, the author of a handbook for attorneys on the laws relating to robbery on the highway, noting that highwaymen 'glory in their invention of the most *Gentile* [gentlemanly] Trade of Ruining Mankind', indignantly dismissed the lot of them as mere imitation gentlemen ('fellows by their own Heraldry intitling themselves *Gentlemen of the Road* '). He concluded: 'if you look into their *Pedigree*, you will find them so far from men of Honour or Vertue, that nothing can be made of them but a pack of idle dissolute Rascals, the best of them but *Cadets*, most commonly the spawn of broken Tradesmen and worst of *Debauchees*'.[46] The arrival of the low-born 'gentleman robber' as a hero of popular narrative occurred as the robber of gentle birth was disappearing, and also at a time when the highwayman's claim to be a man of honour and courage was being more and more insistently debunked. We shall pick up this thread again in the next chapter.

To return to James Hind: one of the most interesting statements that is made by the historical Hind is his claim that he had selected his victims carefully, according to a clear set of principles.[47] We may reasonably take this assertion with a generous pinch of salt. However, in seeking to justify his robberies in this kind of way, Hind is following some long-standing precedents. In *The Life of Charles Courtney* (1612), Courtney, a well-born highwayman and burglar, declares that he 'never tooke from the needy, . . . but all my aime either at house or highway, were at such Curmugions, who care not who starves so themselves bee Corne fed' – misers, in other words: rich men who disregard the imperative to be charitable and hospitable.[48] Hind's claim is more specific than this. He states that all the victims of his robberies had been either well-off 'bumpkins' or else lawyers. The latter, he explains, are handsomely paid by the wealthy farmers to provide them with the sort of legal advice that results in the impoverishment of already poor cottagers. It is likely that Hind is referring to the enclosure of common land, and to moves by freeholders to restrict the rights of the labourers to share in such common-land resources as grazing or fuel. Despite the fact that Hind was a Royalist, it sounds as though he may have caught some echoes of the radical ideas of the time. Certain political groups, notably the True Levellers, or Diggers, were very outspoken on the subject of common-land rights. Nevertheless, if Hind's declaration has a radical tinge, his challenge to the status quo is quite carefully restricted. Gerrard Winstanley, the leading pamphleteer among the Diggers, never shrinks from pointing a finger at the aristocracy. In a typical passage, he denounces the fact that 'the government we have gives freedom and livelihood to the gentry to have abundance, and to lock up treasures of the earth from the poor'.[49] Hind, though, confines his attention solely to the activities of 'bumpkins'. This term of abuse for countrymen with crude, rustic manners is strictly status-bound: a bumpkin, by definition, is not a gentleman.[50] Substantial freeholders of yeoman status did exist, and were often keen enclosers. However, between them, the nobility and gentry owned much the largest share of the land; nor were they generally backward in seeking ways of increasing their incomes by restricting the customary rights of the poor.

Hind's claim to have directed his campaign of robberies principally against rich countrymen of non-gentle status offers us an enlightening glimpse of his mentality. The wealthy farmers to whom he refers are people of quite similar social standing to his own father, the well-off country saddler. However, Hind is intent on recasting himself in the mould of the gentleman robber. He has set aside any loyalties to or identification with the social stratum which he himself might have ordinarily aspired to join, the group just below the lower ranks of the gentry, made up of prosperous tradesmen and substantial yeoman farmers. Instead, as a 'gentleman robber', he takes such men for his traditional prey. In Elizabethan times, as we have seen, the gentleman robber's frequent opposite, enemy and victim was 'old Tenacity', the grasping miserly yeoman farmer.[51] Considered in this context, Hind's enclosing bumpkins reveal themselves as a topical variant on an old stereotype. Altogether, it seems highly probable that, like Allen, the mentor who instructs his fictional alter ego in *The English Gusman*, Hind did indeed understand his life as a robber as having made him into a gentleman. His passionate Royalism may well spring from similar roots. Those who adhered to the King's side during the Civil Wars included nearly all the nobility, together with a great number of the gentry. The Royalist forces were led almost exclusively by members of these two groups. The Parliament side, on the other hand, though steered by gentry and backed by a handful of peers, drew much of its support from the yeomen and well-off tradesmen. Many of the party's rank and file harboured powerful feelings of mistrust and hostility towards the aristocracy.[52] The aspirations and social pretensions of a 'gentleman robber' would have made little sense in such company.

Nearly two years before James Hind was captured and jailed in Newgate, a man whose political sympathies were very different from his had also invoked the notion of the highway robber who strips the rich of their ill-gotten wealth. Abiezer Coppe was a preacher and writer, a prominent member of the group of Commonwealth radicals known to its enemies as the Ranters. He published his most famous book, *A Fiery Flying Roll*, at the start of 1650, and was almost immediately arrested as a blasphemer. *A*

174

Fiery Flying Roll is a work in the tradition of the biblical prophetic books; its title page calls it 'A Word from the Lord' and a 'warning piece'. It reveals Coppe as a mystic, battling to communicate his visionary sense of God and of proper human relations. Coppe stresses that in the eyes of God, the poorest of the poor, even the most despised and morally degraded, were 'every whit as good' as the 'great ones' and 'Rulers' whom he admonishes in his book.[53] He calls on the rich to give away their possessions. Everything should be held in common. Yet Coppe did not believe in direct political action. Though his emphasis on equality is reminiscent of the Levellers and his communism has parallels in the manifestos published by the Diggers, he expressly rejected both 'sword-levelling' and 'digging-levelling'. Instead, he relied on the power of his divinely inspired words, backed by his prophetic certainty that if he were ignored, God himself would send plagues and disasters on the recalcitrant.

In one of his most striking passages, Coppe elaborates on a theme he takes from a biblical text (a composite text, in fact): 'behold now I come as a thief in the night'. For Coppe, these words are a cue for an elaborate metaphor in which he imagines 'the Lord' coming back to the world in the guise of a highwayman: 'Thou hast many baggs of money, and behold now I come as a thief in the night, with my sword drawn in my hand, and like a thief as I am, – I say deliver your purse, deliver sirrah! deliver or I'l cut thy throat!' Coppe's Lord God is coming to recover everything that the rich believe they own, which in reality belongs to him, and to him alone. They are ordered to deliver their wealth to the poor, and not only to the respectable poor, either: 'deliver, deliver, my money which thou hast to . . . poor creeples, lazars, yea to rogues, thieves, whores and cut-purses, who are flesh of thy flesh, and every whit as good as thy self in mine eye . . . . *Come! give all to the poore and follow me, and you shall have treasure in heaven.*'[54] It is impossible to imagine that Coppe would have developed the image of the Lord coming 'as a thief' in quite this direction if he hadn't had the Robin Hood legend in his thoughts, in the influential form it had acquired during the Elizabethan period, of the highway robber whose ethos and practice was redistribution from the rich to the poor.

This conception of the 'good' highwayman is far more radical than anything in the early Hind material, either the pseudo-biographies or his own self-justifying statements. The most that Hind ever claims is that he had been in the habit of handing out magnificent tips to peasants who said they supported the King. However, the legend of the righteous robber who stole from the rich in order to give to the poor was a very potent one. In time it co-opted Hind's memory. In a poem first published in 1734, but said to have been written in the previous century, we read:

175

some point dunlop

Hind made our Wealth one common Store;
He robb'd the Rich to feed the Poor.[55]

Just like Robin Hood. The belief that some highwaymen were, or had been, engaged in active redistribution to the poor of the wealth that they took from the propertied was now becoming part of the national folklore.

In Captain Alexander Smith's *Complete History of the Highwaymen* (1719), there are a couple of stories of highway robbers who justify themselves with exactly this argument. In the better of these tales, a highway robber called 'Captain Dudley', said to have flourished in the reign of Charles II, holds up the Earl of Rochester and his retinue. When his lordship's chaplain challenges his behaviour on religious grounds, Dudley responds, '*I don't think I commit any sin in robbing a person of quality, because I keep generally pretty close to the text "Feed the hungry and send the rich empty away".*' Smith editorialises: 'Which was true in the main, for whenever he had got any considerable booty from great people, he would very generously extend his charity to such whom he really knew to be poor.'[56] It is likely that this story, like many others in Smith's book, was taken from some late seventeenth-century pamphlet. The 'text' that Dudley cites in support of his activities is based on a verse from the Magnificat, the Virgin Mary's song of praise made after she has been told that she will bear the Messiah. But Dudley's version has been heavily adapted, and in the process it has been twisted out of its original meaning. In the Bible, the verse runs: 'Hee hath filled the hungry with good things, and the rich hee hath sent emptie away.'[57] The words are spoken of God in a figure of speech; they certainly are not, as Dudley makes out, an injunction to the Christian to expropriate the goods of the rich.

However, the robber's version evidently had some currency. A close echo of it is found in a broadside ballad of 1695, in which a highwayman called Biss is made to defend himself in court by the claim that he had showed a true Christian charity to those in need:

> He said, The Scriptures I fulfill'd,
> though I this Life did lead,
> For when the Naked I beheld,
> I clothed them with speed:
> Sometimes in Cloth and Winter-frize,
> sometimes in Russet-gray;
> The Poor I fed, the Rich likewise
> I empty sent away.[58]

The judge, we are told, condemned him regardless. Biss was quickly forgotten, but his ballad survived, and decades later was slightly rewritten to accommodate a new hero: 'bold Turpen'.[59] The real Dick Turpin was a

176

vicious thug, and there is no evidence that he ever gave a penny to anyone, but the legend absorbed him just the same. It was what the public wanted to be told: stories of open-hearted highwaymen who cut the rich and heartless down to size and befriended people in need. The appetite for such tales is at least as ancient as *A Gest of Robyn Hode*. However, towards the end of the seventeenth century, we start to hear at times a sharper note, an emphasis on giving not just to the unfortunate but specifically, and systematically, to the very poor, the destitute and starving, as in the lines just quoted. Christopher Hill, the great historian of seventeenth-century radical thought, has suggested that this may have been inspired by the social teachings of some of the mid-century communists, like Coppe and Winstanley.[60] There may be truth in this. Certainly it was the case that the highwayman cult was being largely abandoned by the gentry. From the mid-seventeenth century onwards, most of the highwaymen who featured in ballads and popular narratives were drawn from the ranks of relatively humble folk: footmen, apprentices and struggling tradesmen. If we make the reasonable assumption that many of the readers of these works belonged to these and similar social groups, it is not hard to see why some of them should have been strongly attracted by reports of robbers who humbled the rich and handed out money to the poor.[61] Another and rather different factor that is likely to have been operating was the need, at a time of changing social values, to make the highwayman hero more acceptable. The mere practice of violent confrontation was no longer always felt to be enough to justify the robber's claim to possess heroic qualities. One answer to this problem was to depict him as acting from the best-intentioned of motives.

Were there ever any robbers who made a point of distributing their booty to people in need? It is sad, but hardly surprising, that in England, at least, there are no authenticated instances of this. All the stories of outstandingly generous deeds supposed to have been performed by various robber heroes are at best unsupported. Sometimes they can be shown to be fabrications. A case in point is that of Benjamin Childe, hanged in 1722 for robbing the Bristol Mail. In his book, *Crime and Punishment in Eighteenth-century England*, Frank McLynn cites as fact the story that Childe once freed the debtors in Salisbury jail by using his loot to pay off their debts.[62] Childe's legend has grown with retelling. It originates in a pamphlet published in the year of his execution, which claims that when he was imprisoned in Salisbury jail, he spent part of his haul on securing the discharge of several of his fellow prisoners who had been committed for debt. A generous highwayman, indeed! However, it is plain from its jaunty style that this particular pamphlet life, *The Whole Life and History of Benjamin Child*, is the work of some hack writer. In fact, near the start of the book, the author even tips the wink to the reader not to mistake his piece of pulp fiction for a reliable report of what happened.[63] As it happens, *The Whole Life and History* was preceded by, and partly draws upon, a much more sober account of the robber, *A Narrative of the Life of Mr. Benjamin Childe*. The publisher of this earlier pamphlet introduces the major part of the text as a statement written by Childe himself in support of his attempt to secure a pardon. Since Childe had at various times been a clerk and a schoolmaster, there is no reason to doubt his capacity to produce such a document, and its rather bleak reporting of his blighted career and his activities as a highwayman readily carries conviction. Nothing is said about any benefactions to the debtors of Salisbury jail.[64]

In his book *The London Hanged*, Peter Linebaugh briefly cites the case of an obscure eighteenth-century robber, Thomas Easter, who is reported to have once declared that he robbed the rich to give to the poor. As Linebaugh observes, 'It is the classic defence of the highwayman'. However, Linebaugh gives only limited information as to the circumstances under which Easter made this striking claim. It is recorded in a statement made by one of Easter's friends and confederates, a robber called Jesse Walden, who was hanged in 1742. A few days before he died, Walden dictated an account of his life to the Ordinary, or chaplain, of Newgate jail. Many of his robberies had been committed in partnership with Easter, who had himself been executed some time before. Walden describes in detail an episode that took place in Suffolk, on the road between Elvedon and Barton Mills. He had accosted a gentleman who, not realising that the two were confederates, fled from him to ask the help of Easter, who was at a little distance. When Easter, too, presented a pistol and asked for his money, the horrified traveller exclaimed, '*I took you for an honest Man!*' The robber's answer came pat. '*So I am* (said *Easter*) *because I rob the Rich to give to the Poor*.' The context suggests that this response was at least as much of a joke as a manifesto. Walden had already described how, some days or weeks earlier, he and Easter had stopped a blacksmith, but when he told them 'he was a poor Man, and had a large Family' they gave him back the four shillings that was all the money he had on him, and tipped him 'another Shilling to drink our Healths'.[65] Gentlemanly of them, but hardly magnificent. If there were other episodes of a similar kind, Walden does not mention them. It tickled Easter's fancy to claim the moral authority of a Robin Hood, but though he and his friend were not the most hard-hearted of robbers, there is nothing in Walden's account to suggest that they ever engaged in any serious practice of redistribution from the rich to the poor.

Against this anecdote we may set another, somewhat earlier episode, in which a low-born robber showed much more magnanimity towards members of the gentry than towards ordinary folk who were trying to make a living. Lewis Deval (or Louis Duval, as he was also, and more correctly, called) was almost certainly the brother of a much more famous highway robber, Claude Du Vall. Before he took to the roads, he had been in service with an English aristocrat. One story that was published early in 1670, not long after he had been hanged, tells how 'Deval' and his gang robbed a dozen or so 'Market-Men and Women' on their way home from London. These would have been farmers and farm servants who had travelled to one of the city's markets to sell produce. No pity was shown to any of the country people; they 'had their Money taken away one by one'. In the middle of the robbery, a couple of gentlemen arrived on the scene. Deval and one of his companions rode up and stopped the gentlemen's servants, taking all the money they had in their pockets. After this, *they let the gentlemen themselves pass without being searched*, having returned the only thing that had been taken away from either of them, a sword and sword-belt. This story is not one of the standard highwayman tales; indeed, it is so untypical it seems quite likely that it represents an actual incident. The point of the robbers' behaviour on this occasion seems to have been that it satisfied some desire that they had to deal with the gentlemen on terms of social equality. They even told them their own names. Deval, in particular, had quite a conversation with one of the two, telling him, 'how he was armed, what number of Pistols he had ready charged, and that he was resolved never to be taken alive'.[66]

I believe that we should be wary of idealising the highwaymen, or imagining them as social radicals. The early chapters of *The English Gusman* depict the young James Hind, first as a lazy schoolboy, always ready to hear reports of robberies, and later as a disgruntled youth, trying to persuade his fellow apprentice '*That it was better to rob on the high way*' than to lead the '*Slavish* life' of a butcher's boy. This is fiction, of course, but many a lad in Stuart or Georgian England must have felt the power of that particular dream. But it was an individualist, not a Utopian or a collective dream. It was a fantasy of rising, as if by magic, above the drudgery of everyday life and the constraints imposed by low status. It was the hope that by becoming a robber on the highway, a poor man might be transformed by 'such an *Art*, as would for ever make him a *Gentleman*'.[67]

179

14

'The profession is grown scandalous'

In one of the various compendiums of criminal 'lives' that appeared in the course of the eighteenth century, there is a report of the conversation that took place one night at an alehouse in Moorfields, in the middle of 1726. This was an establishment much frequented by underworld types, who used to make arrangements to meet there before they went out to rob, swindle or thieve. One of the characters of the place was a man named Barnham, who had been involved in crime for almost twenty years, and who would often entertain a fascinated audience with the stories of criminal exploits that were recorded in his memory. One evening, as the report states, he 'took it in his head' to lecture his listeners on the declining prestige of the highwayman.

Barnham quote

In former days, said he, knights of the road were a kind of military order into which none but decayed gentlemen presumed to intrude themselves. If a younger brother ran out of his allowance, or if a young heir spent his estate before he had bought a tolerable understanding, if an under-courtier lived above his income, or a subaltern officer laid out twice his pay in rich suits and fine laces, this was the way they took to recruit; and if they had but money enough left to procure a good horse and a case of pistols, there was no fear of their keeping up their figure a year or two, till their faces were known. And then, upon a discovery, they generally had friends good enough to prevent their swinging, and who, ten to one, provided handsomely for them afterwards, for fear of their meeting with a second mischance, and thereby bringing a stain upon their family. But now-a-days a petty alehouse-keeper, if he gives too much credit, a cheesemonger whose credit grows rotten, or a mechanic that is weary of living by his fingers-ends, makes no more ado, when he finds his circumstances uneasy, but whips into a saddle and

Men of lowly profession became involved int

thinks to get all things retrieved by the magic of those two formidable words, *Stand and Deliver.* Hence the profession is grown scandalous . . .

Barnham's discourse on the lost golden age of the highwaymen was the prelude to an evening in which the other drinkers present freely exchanged anecdotes they had heard about the robbers and thieves of the past. The whole occasion made such an impression on a young man called Edward Reynolds that on the very next night he took his first step into crime by robbing an acquaintance of a coat and a shilling. For this amateurish piece of thuggery, he was soon arrested and hanged. Before he died, however, he confided in someone the story of his visit to the alehouse and Barnham's elegiac tribute to the gentlemen robbers.[1]

Even allowing for the fact that it has been filtered at least twice – first through Edward Reynolds and then through whoever interviewed him and wrote his story up for the press – Barnham's alehouse oration is a fascinating witness to a piece of eighteenth-century folk history. Like all folk history, it is impressionistic. The time when all mounted robbers were gentlemen is a time that never was. However, as we have seen, there had been a period, not so very long before, when the gentleman whose spending outran his income had certainly constituted the dominant stereotype of the mounted robber. But now, in 1726, this time is past. In the popular perception, the typical highwayman is the ruined tradesman or the alienated workman. And the reputation of the 'knights of the road' has gone down in the world.

Barnham was certainly right that attitudes were changing. One striking manifestation of this is the near disappearance of the highway robber with aristocratic connections. Indeed, robbers with even vague claims to be regarded as gentlemen had now become very rare. The extensive printed collections of eighteenth-century criminal biographies contain details of only a handful of such men. One of these, Thomas Butler, was the son of a Jacobite army officer who had followed James II into exile. The proceeds of his robberies enabled him to live well and dress fashionably, and on appropriate occasions, his accomplice, Jack, attended him in livery as a footman. Butler was sent to the gallows in 1720. Later gentlemen robbers included William Parsons, cast-off son of a baronet, who was hanged in 1751, and Paul Lewis, a clergyman's son, hanged in 1763. Lewis had served as a naval lieutenant and had taken part in a number of engagements. He is reported to have made a speech at the gallows in which he said that his situation wounded him the deeper in that he had been 'bred up among gentlemen', adding, 'to whom much is given, of him the more is required'.[2] A gentleman was now expected to know better than to take part in criminal activities. We are a long way from the notion that a little purse-taking is only to be expected of a cash-poor gentleman who has been trained to arms.

Some of the older attitudes to robbery continued to retain a certain currency. It is reported that when Joseph Picken, who had formerly been an innkeeper at Windsor, lost his livelihood and could find no work, he said to his wife, '*I am now quite at my wits' end. I have no way left to get anything to support us; what shall I do? Do,* answered she, *why, what should a man do that wants money and has any courage, but go upon the highway.*' Picken took her advice, and went to see a friend of his who had previously suggested the same plan. This fellow was delighted that Picken was now prepared to go along with his proposal that the two of them rob in partnership. 'He told him that for his part he always thought danger rather to be chosen than want, and that while soldiers hazarded their lives in war for sixpence a day, he thought it was cowardice to make a man starve, where he had a chance of getting so much more than those who hazarded as much as they did.' Picken and his companion (who is never named) were caught within a week of embarking on their new careers as highwaymen. Once Picken was in custody, his wife never came near him. He was hanged in February 1725.[3]

James Wright, a maker of perukes, turned highwayman to support his extravagant lifestyle. He had absorbed enough of the traditions of the heroic robber to pride himself on the fact that he had never robbed a poor man, 'but always singled out those who from their equipage were likeliest to yield him a good booty, and at the same time not be much the worse for it themselves'. He believed that 'as the rich could better spare it than the poor, there was less crime in taking it from them'. After his fashion, he was an honourable man. The first time he was arrested, he refused to do what many criminals would have done: betray his accomplices in the hopes of doing a deal with the magistrate. As it happened, the jury acquitted him. But his luck ran out a short while later, when one of those same accomplices was arrested himself, and having fewer scruples than Wright, saved his own neck by grassing him up. Wright was executed in 1721.[4]

Many poor men still treasured the notion that robbing on the highway was a way to become a gentleman. When John Levee 'fell into some company at an ale-house in Holborn', at some point in the early 1720s, he heard it said 'that any brisk young fellow might easily make his fortune, and live like a gentleman, by going upon the high-way'.[5] The street ballad of *The Flying Highwayman*, which probably dates from about 1780, exploits the same durable fantasy. It begins 'Come all ye bold and swaggering Blades', and it invites its hearers to contemplate the history of a robber named Morgan:

Young MORGAN was a flashy blade

'The English padder'. Frontispiece to *The English Rogue*, 1665.
A gang of mounted robbers stop travellers on the highway.

The Extravagant Prentices with their Lasses at a Taverne Frollick.

'The Extravagant Prentices with their Lasses at a Taverne Frollick.' Illustration from *The English Rogue*, Part II, 1671. Highwaymen traditionally took to the road to fund a taste for riotous living.

John Clavell at the age of 25. Frontispiece to the third edition of *A Recantation of an Ill Led Life*, 1634. The engraving, or at least the drawing on which it was based, must have been made in 1626 or 1627.

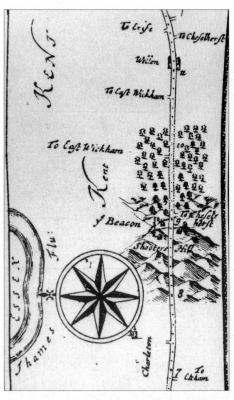

Shooters Hill in Kent, from John Ogilby's map of the Great Dover Road, 1675. For at least six centuries, Shooters Hill was one of the most notorious spots for highway robbery in England.

'Whitney Robbing an old Userer tyeing his hands behind him with his face to the horses tail'. Illustration from *A General History of the Lives and Adventures of the Most Famous Highwaymen* by 'Captain Charles Johnson', 1734.

Dick Turpin in his cave in Epping Forest. Engraving of 1739.

'Newgate's Lamentation, or the Ladies' Last Farewell of Maclaine', 1750.
The print shows the highwayman James Maclaine (centre, in irons), surrounded
by fashionable visitors, most of whom are women.

Woodcut of a hanging, from a seventeenth-century broadside ballad.

Stephen Gardiner, dressed in his shroud, makes his 'last dying speech' from the cart at Tyburn. Illustration from *The Newgate Calendar; or, Malefactors Bloody Register*, 1773.

'The Hornsey Gate'. Illustration by George Cruikshank to the fourth edition of *Rookwood*, by W. Harrison Ainsworth, 1836. Dick Turpin, mounted on Black Bess, leaps a turnpike gate near the start of his ride to York.

'Dick Turpin': figure from a Victorian toy theatre.

Illustration by 'Phiz' (Hablot K. Browne) to *Barnaby Rudge*, by Charles Dickens, 1841. The public room of the Maypole Inn, scene of Chapter One. The highwayman is the haggard figure in the centre, slouched over the table.

> No youth had better courage,
> Much gold he got on the highway,
> That made him daily flourish.
> Grand Bagnios* was his lodging then,
> Among the flashy Lasses;
> Soon he became a Gentleman,
> And left off driving Asses.

It's a pity about the asses, which have all too obviously been dragged in for the sake of an easy rhyme. But no doubt the ballad's intended readers were inclined to forgive such crudities, contented with the bright dreams inspired by the story of a young highwayman who tells us frankly:

> I robb'd for gold and silver bright,
> For to maintain my Misses,

and who goes to his trial resplendent in a 'beaver hat and surtout coat'. He is, of course, convicted, and taken through the city to be hanged at Tyburn, but as soon as all the pathos possible has been milked from his impending death, the ballad changes direction, and in a final twist, the King takes pity on him and spares him.[6] Just what any would-be 'swaggering blade' could wish to hear.

During the eighteenth century, the English remained quite liable to brag that their native robbers were a special breed – either for their exceptional spirit[7] or else on account of their considerate treatment of their victims. Thus, in *Colonel Jack* (1722), a novel by Daniel Defoe, we find a reference to a highwayman gang who followed what Defoe calls 'the *English* way of Robbing generously . . . without Murthering or Wounding, or Ill using those they robb'd'.[8] It wasn't only the English who thought that the nation's highwaymen showed remarkable restraint. A series of visitors from overseas recorded in their letters and memoirs that robbers in England, especially the mounted robbers, were far less brutal and, in particular, less likely to murder their victims than was usually the case on the Continent.[9] It is arguable that by behaving like this the highwaymen were acting against their own best interests. Of course, all highway robbers hoped, when their turn for arrest came, that they would receive a pardon. By this date, such favours were now granted mainly to those who informed on their accomplices. A robber who had committed murder was very unlikely to be selected for the role of witness for the Crown.[10] All the same, the robber who systematically killed his victims might well have been safer

---

* brothels

from arrest in the first place. In a journal article of 1723, there is an anecdote about a highwayman who complained that he was going to the gallows, not for robbery, but for sparing his victim's life. If his victim had had the same compassion on him, and had declined to appear as a witness, he would not have been convicted. 'The Gentlemen of the *Highway* in *England*,' this robber is reported to have said, 'are generally put to Death for their Humanity and generous Usage of those they Rob.'[11] It was a reasonable point to make, and it raises quite sharply the question of why the English highway robbers behaved in this way.

The folklorist Graham Seal has suggested that there is, or was, a specific tradition, which he calls 'the outlaw hero tradition', that in certain circumstances became available to violent outsiders of the highwayman sort as a 'cultural script', or guide to attitudes and conduct. According to Seal, one element in 'the outlaw hero tradition' was the refusal to perpetrate murder or excessive brutality. I have one or two problems with the way Seal conceives of 'the outlaw hero tradition'; chiefly, with the way he presents it as what he calls a 'cultural constant', unvarying over time and place. As this book has shown, the English traditions about the outlaw and robber exhibit many changes over time, corresponding broadly with changes in the nature of English society. In Chapter Twelve, for instance, we saw that the notion that the 'good' robber will do his utmost to avoid the shedding of blood and the related idea that English robbers were much less bloodthirsty than those on the Continent only began to find expression in the early seventeenth century. This criticism made, however, it seems to me that Seal's theory of the 'cultural script' is interesting and suggestive.[12] By the 1720s, the English had been congratulating themselves on the lack of brutality shown by their robbers for close to a hundred years; perhaps longer. The sense that 'the generous Usage' of victims was a proud national tradition fairly certainly did have an influence on the behaviour of individual highwaymen. Adherence to an accepted code of conduct will have confirmed for them that they were not complete outcasts, but maintained a place of their own in the social order. In Seal's terms, the traditions of English robbery provided them with a 'script', or core set of attitudes and practices, around which to improvise their interactions with those they robbed.

We can glimpse such cultural influences at work in an episode in 1749, when two highwaymen, James Maclaine and William Plunket, held up Horace Walpole, the writer and society gossip. Maclaine's hand slipped on the trigger and he narrowly missed blowing Walpole's head off. Two days later, the robbers wrote a letter to Walpole, partly to try to arrange to sell back to him his watch, seals and sword, but also to urgently assure him that the shooting had been an accident: 'for tho' we Are Reduced by the misfortunes of the world and obliged to have Recourse to this method of

Seals outlaw Hero tradition

getting money Yet we have Humanity Enough not to take any bodys life where there is Not a Nessecety for it'.[13]

Closely related to the idea of the 'humane' robber is that of the 'courteous' robber.[14] The 'courteous' robber is a much older figure, of course. The most famous example is the eponymous hero of *A Gest of Robyn Hode*, who is tagged right at the start of that poem as the most 'curteyse' outlaw who ever lived. However, the tradition goes back earlier still; we find traces of it in *The Tale of Gamelyn*, and in one of the stories about Fouke Fitz Waryn.[15] Robin Hood shows himself 'curteyse' partly by his considerate treatment of his 'guests', but also when he demonstrates his grasp of courtly etiquette, as he does when he and Little John serve dinner to the monk of St Mary's Abbey with a strict observance of ceremony.[16] During the Middle Ages, this was a very common use of 'courtesy', to mean the rules concerning protocol and formal behaviour that were in use in courts and great households, with particular attention to the rules relating to service at table. By the eighteenth century, elite culture was fostering some rather different conceptions of mannerly behaviour, which crystallised round a new term with a widening currency: 'politeness'. Exaggerated formality was now felt to be rather old-fashioned and awkward. More than anything else, the polite person aimed to put people at their ease by treating them with respect and consideration. To be considered truly polite, it was necessary that a person should display polished manners and an accomplished (but never domineering) conversational style. Though politeness was primarily an ideal for gentlefolk, people in a lower station of life could still aspire to practise it. It emerged at a time when status barriers were relaxing, even if only a little, and it undoubtedly functioned partly as a mechanism for furthering frictionless social intercourse: this, in an urban environment in which people were continually encountering persons whose precise background and standing were not at all clear. In such a context, it made sense for a gentleman to show his superiority, not by haughty behaviour and a demand for deference, but by the high gloss on his manners. One more thing about polite culture: it encouraged males to socialise with women, who were regarded as a civilising influence.[17]

If the medieval outlaws of legend had been renowned for their courtesy, eighteenth-century highwaymen were sometimes quite astonishingly polite. This seems to go thoroughly against the grain of their profession. To rob with some ceremony, like Robin Hood, is one thing; to rob in a way that is unassuming and aims to put people at their ease is another matter entirely. Nevertheless, some highwaymen certainly attempted it. A Swiss visitor to England, César de Saussure, described in 1726 how a highwayman would accost a coach full of passengers: 'With one hand he will present a pistol, with the other his hat, asking the unfortunate

185

passengers most politely for their purses or their lives.' Smooth-spoken such robbers might be, but no one usually dared to risk enraging a man with a gun in his hand, so every traveller would toss a share of his or her money into the outstretched hat. A few sentences later, de Saussure adds: 'I have been told that some highwaymen are quite polite and generous, begging to be excused for being forced to rob, and leaving passengers the wherewithal to continue their journey.'[18] De Saussure (who was probably reporting what he had heard) gives the impression that all English highwaymen were respectful and well-mannered. It is clear from other sources that this was far from true; there were plenty of truculent, menacing and even brutal robbers.[19] The stories that de Saussure was told had achieved a particular prominence precisely because they were somewhat surprising. They also, no doubt, suited the notions of his hosts as to how a superior English robber ought properly to conduct himself. At the same time, de Saussure is not alone in reporting the existence of respectful and even apologetic highwaymen. Such men certainly existed.[20] Once again, we come back to the question of why on earth they behaved like this.

Politeness, like courtesy, was to some extent a status marker. In eighteenth-century England, polite manners were promoted by influential commentators as a sign of true gentility – and were practised by many of the nobility and gentry, and also, assiduously, by that section of society that, possessing no claim to gentle birth, still aspired to be thought genteel. Robin Hood's ostentatious courtesy is one of the proofs that he possesses the qualities expected of an aristocrat – though he often expresses them in forms that were specifically appropriate to a yeoman. It is noticeable, for instance, that rather than sitting down to eat with the monk, he serves him at table; he preserves the distinctions of rank between the two of them, even while he is engaged in a robbery. (The monk, not surprisingly, is unimpressed. He thinks Robin would be showing a more genuine courtesy if he would refrain from taking all his money.)[21] Centuries later, the eighteenth-century mounted robber expresses himself politely, partly because, in Seal's terms, this is in his script: courtesy is what tradition requires of him, and proper courtesy now demands that he demonstrate polite manners. But this is further reinforced by the fact that in line with a more recent tradition, he thinks of himself as a 'gentleman of the road' – a man of a certain standing, which requires that he conduct himself in a gentlemanlike fashion. This is well illustrated by an account of the life of a highwayman who was so punctiliously polite, he was nicknamed 'Civil John'. His real name was John Turner, and he was executed at Tyburn in 1727. Like James Wright a few years earlier, Turner was a maker of perukes. His trade brought him into frequent contact with members of the gentry, and he began to dream of leading the same sort of life as the fashionable 'beaux' and 'gallants' who came into his master's shop. The easy and obvious route was to become a highwayman, which he eventually did, quickly gaining a reputation as a 'genteel' robber with impeccable manners. Like the highwaymen described by de Saussure, he would stop coaches, hold out his hat and take whatever money the travellers chose to give him; he would also return some of it, 'if the dress or aspect of the person gave him room to suspect that their wants were as great as his'. He spent the proceeds of his robberies on fine clothes, dancing and carrying on his numerous relationships with women. However, his career as a pseudo-beau lasted a mere six weeks. As the narrative of his life points out, his painstakingly polite behaviour only made him the more conspicuous, and therefore the easier to track down and arrest.[22]

The courteous, chivalrous Robin Hood would never rob a woman, or even a company of travellers in which a woman was present. Later robbers, even in works of fiction, seldom or never show themselves quite so scrupulous. However, the 'polite' highwayman is sometimes reported as showing a special gallantry towards his women victims. The earliest and best such story is told of the highwayman Claude Du Vall in a pamphlet published in 1670, the year he was hanged. He and his gang are supposed to have waylaid a coach in which, as they knew in advance, a knight and his lady were travelling with £400 in money.

> The Lady, to shew she was not afraid, takes a Flageolet out of her pocket and plays; *Du Vall* takes the hint, plays also . . . upon a Flageolet of his own, and in this posture he rides up to the Coach side. Sir, sayes he to the person in the Coach, your Lady playes excellently, and I doubt not but that she Dances as well, will you please to walk out of the Coach, and let me have the honour to Dance one Corant with her upon the Heath? Sir, said the person in the Coach, I dare not deny any thing to one of your quality and good *Mine* [mien]; you seem a Gentleman, and your request is very reasonable: Which said, the Lacquey opens the Boot, out comes the Knight, *Du Vall* leaps lightly off his Horse, and hands the Lady out of the Coach. They Danc'd, and here it was that *Du Vall* performed marvels; the best Master in *London* . . . not being able to shew such *footing* as he did in his great riding *French* Boots. The Dancing being over, he waits on the Lady to her Coach; as the Knight was going in, says *Du Vall* to him, Sir, You have forgot to pay the Musick: [for, (as I should have told you before,) there being no Violins, *Du Vall* sung the Corant himself.] No I have not, replies the Knight, and putting his hand under the seat of the Coach, puls out a Hundred pounds in a bag, and delivers it to him: Which *Du Vall* took with a very good grace, and courteously answered, Sir, You are liberal, and shall have no cause to repent your being so: this liberality of yours shall excuse you the other Three Hundred Pounds . . .[23]

187

Dancing, of course, was very much a polite accomplishment.

The contradictions implicit in the notion of robbing 'politely' are exposed by George Farquhar in his comedy *The Beaux' Stratagem* (1707), along with the new importance for the genteel highwayman's image of knowing how to behave towards the ladies. At the outset of a burglary, Captain Gibbet the highwayman confides to one of his accomplices, 'there's a great deal of address and good manners in robbing a lady. I am the most a gentleman that way that ever traveled the road.' Shortly afterwards, we get a chance to see what he means:

> GIBBET Ay, ay, this is the chamber, and the lady alone.
> MRS SULLEN Who are you, sir? What would you have? D'ye come to rob me?
> GIBBET Rob you! Alack a day, madam, I'm only a younger brother, madam, and so, madam, if you make a noise I'll shoot you through the head. But don't be afraid, madam.[24]

The rise of the 'polite' robber coincided with the highwayman's development into a conspicuous object of female desire. The breathless response of some young women to the robber's ambiguous charms was mocked in 1709 in a spoof advertisement in the *Female Tatler*:

> Whereas several sprightly young fellows that keep horses and ride out every day to Hampstead Heath, Epping Forest, etc. are, thro' their idleness and extravagance, suspected by some malicious people to salute coaches in the dusk o' the evening. Mrs Mary Fanciful, having heard a world of stories about highwaymen, has a curiosity to see one. She sets out for the bath,* on Monday next, with ten guineas (not hid in the privat'st part of her coach) therefore, if any of these gentlemen please to clap an uncharg'd pistol to her breast, only that she may know how it is to be robb'd, they shall receive the ten guineas with a sincere promise never to be prosecuted for the same. Her sister, Mrs Sarah Fanciful, wants mightily to see a ghost.[25]

At this date, the prefix 'Mrs' was not used only for married women. Mary Fanciful, whose surname is the same as her sister's, is evidently an unmarried girl. What she naively longs for is a symbolic deflowering: the vaginal purse to be yielded up on sight of the phallic (but not too imperative) pistol. The robber's sexiness is partly to do with his aura of dangerousness, a dangerousness that is kept under control by the 'cultural script' that requires him to behave 'humanely' and 'civilly'. It is also partly

---

* Bath

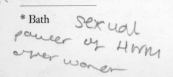

to do with his supposed courage; as a seventeenth-century essayist has it, 'nothing drawes a woman like to [valour], for valor towards men, is an Embleme of an abilitie towards women'.[26] The braver the man, the more potent the lover, apparently.

Nevertheless, the highwayman was never quite so sexy as when he was tamed: arrested, imprisoned, condemned to death. It was reported of Claude Du Vall that after his capture he was visited in jail by a great many ladies, some of them from aristocratic families. These women so lost their hearts to him that they tried to arrange a pardon; when this failed, they accompanied him on his final journey to the gallows.[27] Some of the stories about Claude Du Vall provided inspiration for a late seventeenth-century broadside ballad called *The Life and Death of George of Oxford*. This tells the tale of a handsome highwayman who won the love of a 'Lady *Gray*'. His high-born sweetheart intercedes for him with the judge, kneeling and weeping, and even offers 'Gold' and 'Lands' to save him, but with no success. 'Georgy' must hang. In the second half of the broadside, George himself delivers his 'Confession', though it is more of a self-advertisement: no male, however so bold, has been able to resist his prowess, while the 'Ladies' were always 'delighted' at the opportunity 'To take a dance upon the Green' with him. And why not, for he himself assures us that he is 'a proper handsome fellow'. The poem ends with the robber's procession to execution, followed by a huge crowd, and his being hanged, in a very genteel fashion, in a 'silken string'. Death in a silken halter was reserved for criminals of gentle birth, in cases where they had especially petitioned for the privilege.[28]

George of Oxford is an invented figure; the legend of Claude Du Vall was certainly touched up a little after he was dead; but there was one captured highwayman whose magnetic appeal for the ladies is well documented. This was James Maclaine, mentioned earlier for the letter that he wrote to Horace Walpole after he had held him up. Maclaine acquired the handle of 'the Gentleman Highwayman', though his claims to coming of gentle family were rather obscurely founded. He turned to highway robbery after failing first as a grocer and then in his attempts to restore his fortunes by dazzling some heiress into marrying him. However, before his arrest in 1750, he had moved in elegant society; Walpole describes him in a letter as 'a fashionable highwayman'. While Maclaine was in jail, fashionable London flocked to see him, but as Walpole notes, with pleasant malice, his most devoted visitors were a couple of society women, Lady Caroline Petersham and a certain Miss Ashe. Lady Caroline, who had known him before his arrest, even appeared for him as a character witness; however, she did not succeed in preventing his execution. The women's fascination with the jailed robber was so notorious as to have resulted in the issue of a print that showed him in his Newgate cell surrounded by a crowd that was largely made up of modishly dressed ladies.[29]

The 'Gentleman Thief' and the nature of true gentility are the themes of an episode in Defoe's novel *Colonel Jack*, which was published in 1722. The book's narrator and protagonist, Jack, is a bastard of unknown family, whose care has been farmed out to a foster-mother. After she dies, he has nowhere to go but the streets. Here, he learns to pick pockets, and becomes the accomplice of a boy named Will, who is six years older than himself. Once Will grows up, he largely drops Jack's company, and Jack continues thieving on his own. But eventually, Will seeks him out and makes an offer to introduce him into what he describes as 'a brave Gang . . . where you shall see we shall be all Gentlemen'. Will explains that he and his new associates spend their evenings in footpad robberies and their nights in burgling houses.[30]

The prospect of becoming a gentleman is powerfully alluring for Jack. His foster-mother has told him that his mother was a 'Gentlewoman' and his father a 'Man of Quality'. She has also passed on the chief instruction given her by his father: that 'she should always take care to bid me *remember, that I was a Gentleman*'. It was his father's opinion, she told him, 'that sometime or other the very hint would inspire me with Thoughts suitable to my Birth, and that I would certainly act like a Gentleman, if I believed myself to be so'. Whatever the word 'gentleman' meant to Jack's father, it is plain, at least, that he felt it to be a transparent term, its meaning and value self-evident. However, his son, abandoned to poverty and the life of the streets, is driven to clutch hopefully at any definitions he is offered. Fired by the bare word, he agrees to spend a night robbing with Will and his gang.

In financial terms, the expedition is very successful, and Will is delighted. His dream, as he explains to Jack, is for the two of them to acquire enough cash to 'buy a Couple of good Horses' and 'take the Highway like Gentlemen.' Then, he says, they will 'get a great deal of Money' and will 'live like Gentlemen'. However, Jack cannot forget an incident that had happened when they were robbing passers-by in Gray's Inn Fields. He had held up a couple of women who were walking together; from one of the two, an elderly woman, he had taken 22 shillings. By the standards of the footpad's trade, Jack has behaved in an exemplary fashion, addressing them civilly, speaking to them reassuringly, and threatening them only in the most restrained manner, but he cannot hide from himself the nature of what he has done. The old woman he robbed is constantly on his mind; she had cried desperately at parting with her money, which was, she said, 'all she had left in the World'.[31]

To Will, the street boy turned footpad, a gentleman is a robber on a horse. However, Jack has already come in contact with another, quite different conception of what it might mean to live like a gentleman. He illustrates this with a story of an incident he had observed while sleeping rough at a glass factory, where he and other down-and-outs gathered in the warmth of the kilns. A well-dressed gentleman in a coach arrived to buy some goods. However, in bargaining with the proprietor, he swore so often that in the end the man reproved him for it, saying that this was not the kind of behaviour that was 'like a Gentleman'. This made a considerable impression on Jack, who gave up swearing immediately.[32]

This episode has many resonances. Swearing was one of a cluster of practices, which included drinking deep and fighting, that had been considered for centuries to be among the marks of a gentleman. Indeed, 'to swear like a lord' and 'to swear like a gentleman' were both proverbial sayings.[33] In opposition to such notions, Defoe invokes a conception of a civilised gentility which in its essentials was not particularly new, but which was currently acquiring a greater prestige and influence by association with the elite ideal of politeness. According to this, a gentleman showed his quality, not by his toughness and lordly contempt for rules, but by his avoidance of vices, such as swearing (which was not only irreligious but also against the law), and his adherence to principles of civility and considerate behaviour.[34]

It is significant that in *Colonel Jack* the mouthpiece of this view of how a gentleman should behave is not a man of old family but a successful businessman. In reproaching his well-bred but foul-mouthed customer, Defoe's glasshouse proprietor expresses his views on gentlemanly manners with a striking confidence, commensurate with the growing confidence of the trading and manufacturing class of which he is a representative. This was the group to which Defoe himself belonged, by family background and much of his life experience: the people in what he called 'the middle Station of Life', whose achievements he took pleasure in celebrating.[35] It is not hard to see why the values, explicit and implicit, that Defoe is promoting in this interchange might have been particularly likely to commend themselves to members of this class. They have, after all, an obvious usefulness to people who seek to achieve their purposes by negotiating and bargaining, rather than by brow-beating or force; people for whom civility and a smooth public presentation of the self are the oil that eases their dealings with each other.

In Jack's narrative, this episode rather symbolises than explains his access to a model of gentlemanly conduct that is very different to that which is implied in Will's dream of becoming a 'Gentleman Thief'. Conforming to this model has not only kept him from swearing, but also from indulging in drink, and from what he vaguely calls 'Vice'. It has not kept him from stealing, but it has meant that he has often been troubled by a feeling that he was 'going wrong'. From time to time, he tells us, he would stop to ask himself, 'if this was the Life of a Gentleman?' Now, following the robbery, as he remembers his treatment of the old woman, he feels disgust at his own cruelty, and it comes to him 'that certainly this was not the Life of a Gentleman!' He resolves never again to go out robbing with Will and his gang. The rightness of this decision is underlined by the fate of the unfortunate Will. Arrested shortly afterwards for a burglary, Will says to Jack, who visits him in prison: 'I was far out . . . when I told you to be a notorious Thief, was to live like a Gentleman'.[36] He is tried, convicted and ends on the gallows.

Later in the book, when Jack is at last on the path to settled respectability, he comes to the conclusion 'that to be a Gentleman, was to be an *Honest Man*, that without Honesty, Human Nature was Sunk and Degenerated, the Gentleman lost all the Dignity of his Birth, and plac'd himself, even below an Honest Beggar'. Interestingly, he associates these reflections with the words of the glass manufacturer, although they do not appear in his original account of that episode. The connection is symbolic: in Defoe's mind, they belong with the same set of values, the same kind of conception as to what a gentleman is or should be. They also offer a challenge to the notion, now a very ancient one, that robbery was a less shameful means of subsistence than begging.[37]

The old thief Barnham believed that highwaymen were no longer respected as much as they had been; also that the highwayman of the 1720s was much more likely to have a background in trade than to belong to an old gentry family. He was right on both counts, though doubtless he was wrong when he inferred that the main reason the profession had become disreputable was because of the 'intrusion' of shopkeepers and other such vulgar persons. Daniel Defoe, himself a failed businessman, promoted his own culture hero, the upright, fair-spoken 'gentleman-tradesman',[38] at the expense of two older versions of the gentleman: the man of gentle status who assumes that his position entitles him to disregard the ordinary moral and social rules, and the man who aspires to become a gentleman of sorts through a career in robbery. We are witnessing signs of a new era in English society.

'The rising greatness of the *British* nation', said Defoe in 1726, 'is not owing to war and conquests, . . . but it is all owing to trade, to the encrease of our commerce at home, and the extending it abroad'. England was now pre-eminently a trading country – 'the greatest trading country in the world', Defoe exulted[39] – and along with the new importance of commerce had come some changes of outlook. By the 1720s, only the most old-fashioned people would insist that the man of old family who went into trade lost for ever his right to be regarded as a gentleman. Meanwhile, people of ordinary stock who made a success of their business enterprises could hope in due course to establish themselves among the gentry; or, at any rate, to gentrify their children. Snobbery towards those in trade was by no means dead, of course, nor even moribund. Nevertheless, the status of the merchant and even the shopkeeper had risen considerably.[40]

As the businessman's prestige increased, the highwayman's declined. The stereotype of the heroic robber was now little more than an archaic survival. In a culture in which commerce was officially valued over warfare, it no longer made complete sense. Moreover, the activities of highwaymen disrupted travel and the transport of mail and goods: they were grit in the machine of British trade. Thus, we find the anonymous author of *Hanging Not Punishment Enough* complaining in 1701 of 'a frequent interruption given to Trade and Business, by Robbing of Packets, and intercepting Letters of Correspondence and Advice; to say nothing of the insecurity of sending *Exchequer* and *Bank-Bills* by the Publick Conveyances'.[41] His suggestion: that convicted highwaymen, along with housebreakers and murderers, should be executed by means of some form of slow torture, both as a special deterrent, and to mark the gravity of the offence. Poor boys might dream of the life of a 'gentleman highwayman', and many of the poorer sort of people certainly relished a robber who showed daring and ingenuity and successfully thumbed his nose at the authorities,[42] but to the sober businessman, the highway robber was little more than vermin. As for the gentry, though older attitudes lingered – I cited in Chapter One of this book the story of the gentleman who was robbed by Dick Turpin and later had a bet with him at the races – they were less inclined to indulge the robbers than had once been the case.[43] For one thing, such men were no longer even remotely likely to be their cousins or younger brothers. As in previous centuries, many highwaymen were soldiers, and others were former household servants. Many more were losers under the new economic order: tradesmen on the edge of going bankrupt, and workmen with no more enticing prospects than a grinding routine of poverty and labour.

One of the signs that public attitudes were hardening had been the introduction of new policing methods. The ancient system of 'raising the hue and cry', which was still legally in force, had originated during the Middle Ages. It required that all thefts, robberies and other felonies be reported by the victims to the constable of the place where the crime was committed. In theory, the constable then 'raised the parish': called on the able-bodied men to accompany him in the search for whoever was responsible. If the perpetrator, or perpetrators, could not be found, the constable went to the next parish, notified the constable there, and the procedure was repeated. The idea was that offenders should be pursued from parish to parish until they were captured. The strength and weakness of the system was the reliance on community participation. Even the constable was not a professional policeman; he was elected or co-opted to the post, usually for the period of a year, and received nothing more than his out-of-pocket expenses. For him and the other men of the parish, taking part in the hue and cry meant setting aside their own concerns and giving up their working time in order to conduct house-to-house searches and scour through woodland in a hunt for potentially dangerous criminals. Not surprisingly, there was a tendency to look for soft options. In 1587, William Harrison reported that sometimes constables would flatly refuse to carry out their responsibilities under this procedure, on the grounds that they had better things to do. By the early seventeenth century, the whole process was tending to become formalised. Constables were inclined to cover themselves by simply sending a written notification of the crime and the suspects to the constable in the next parish. As one might imagine, it was not an effective approach.[44]

The newer methods were sneakier; one might even call them dishonourable; but in some ways they probably worked better. After the Restoration, a series of royal proclamations offered rewards of £10 a time to anyone who arrested a highwayman or burglar, and also offered a pardon to any offender who gave evidence against his or her accomplices.[45] In 1692, the reward system was put on a statutory basis: any person, or group of persons, who captured a street or highway robber and successfully prosecuted him was now to receive the substantial reward of £40, plus the offender's horse, arms and money, provided that these had not been stolen.[46] It should be noted that during the early modern period, prosecutions for crimes like robbery were effectively brought as what we would now call private prosecutions; it was the responsibility of an individual, usually the victim, to pursue the case at his or her own expense.[47] Furthermore, as we have just seen, it was entirely usual for ordinary male citizens to take part in arrests. As Sir Thomas Smith explained in the sixteenth century, describing the procedure in the hue and cry, 'everie Englishman is a sergiant to take the theefe'.[48] The 'vigilantes' and 'have a go heroes' who are nowadays officially discouraged were an essential part of the policing system. The £40 reward was intended to provide an incentive to such behaviour, and also, one may guess, to overcome the reluctance that some prosecutors and witnesses certainly felt in giving evidence that would be liable to send a defendant to the gallows.[49]

The act of 1692 contained a further provision. From now on, any highway robber still at large who chose to give evidence against his accomplices, and who by doing so brought about the conviction of two or more, was entitled to a pardon for all the robberies that he had previously committed. Besides this statutory right, there was also a customary practice that related to prisoners who had already been arrested. Magistrates often encouraged them to betray their confederates by the promise of what was usually called a 'pardon'. In some cases, such witnesses were indeed formally tried, reprieved and pardoned. However, during the eighteenth century it seems to have been much more common for criminals who impeached, or gave evidence against, their accomplices, to be released without a trial once they had played their part in court.[50]

Arranging for criminals to be betrayed by their associates has always been one of the most effective weapons available to the policeman. Robert Carey, Earl of Monmouth, records in his memoirs that in 1598, when he was Warden of the Middle March, the Border country was troubled by 'two gentlemen thieves, that robbed and took purses from travellers in the highways'. Carey, an old hand at keeping order, dealt with them briskly: 'I got them betrayed, took them, and sent them to Newcastle gaol, and there they were hanged.'[51] Betrayal into the hands of the authorities was so common it might almost be said to be the robber's typical fate. Hind was captured after an intimate friend, who had been his comrade in the King's army, gave information as to his whereabouts, and even 'went along with the Guard that were appointed to secure him'.[52] Nearly fifty years earlier, Ratsey is said to have been apprehended after his confederate Snell, arrested for stealing a horse, gave away details of the other man's bolt-hole in return for a promise of 'favour'. It did him no good; he and Ratsey were hanged on the same day.[53] The thing that was different after 1692 was that betrayal in return for a pardon or a reward had now become an institution, and formed, in fact, a leading feature of the English system of law enforcement.

The practice of offering inducements to criminals to give evidence against one another was certainly effective in breaking up highwayman gangs. Not surprisingly, it bred suspicion between fellow robbers. Writing in 1722, Ralph Wilson describes how after his first robbery, his old friend Jack Hawkins, who had persuaded him to take part in it, 'was now become my Tyrant: he gave himself a great deal of trouble to let me know, that I was as liable to be hang'd as he, and in all his Actions express'd a Satisfaction that he had me under a hank', or as we would say, he had a hold on him. Wilson continues: 'I have great reason to believe that this Pleasure of his did arise from his having one more added to his Number, to make use of when his Occasions required.'[54] Another member of the gang meant one more person available for Hawkins to betray, if this became necessary to save his own neck. One of the drawbacks of the policy under which criminals received immunity in return for impeaching their accomplices was that the more experienced and unscrupulous crooks could often continue in their predatory careers for quite a considerable period, while a series of relatively harmless dupes were sent to the gallows on their evidence.[55]

In the dog-eat-dog world of the eighteenth-century highwayman, which emerges so vividly, and so unattractively, from the pages of Wilson's little pamphlet, it would not have been surprising if Hawkins had indeed harboured the intention to buy his own life with Wilson's if this should become expedient. However, it should be noted that Wilson was far from being a disinterested witness to the character of his former confederate. In fact, he had plenty of reason to have a bad conscience about the man, and making him sound as villainous as possible served a purpose in helping him to exculpate himself. For in the end it was he who had impeached Hawkins. According to Wilson, he had taken part with Hawkins and George Sympson, another member of the gang, in robbing the Bristol Mail twice within a week. A few days later, he was picked up on suspicion and questioned by the officials of the Post Office. Wilson claims that he had remained staunch until one of the officials showed him an anonymous letter in the handwriting of his accomplice, Sympson. Sympson, who was still at large, was evidently hoping to take advantage of the 1692 Act; he was offering to 'secure' his two confederates in return for the reward and a pardon. Wilson responded by instantly turning evidence, and in due course, both his companions, Hawkins and Sympson, were arrested, convicted and hanged. He justifies himself on the grounds that Sympson's scheme to betray him put an end to what he calls their 'League of Friendship'. He also stresses, a little too emphatically, that he and his companions had never sworn oaths of loyalty to each other, and argues that even if they had, 'no Oath is binding, the keeping whereof is a greater Sin than the breaking of it'.[56] Wilson had found himself in a terrible position; on the other hand, his decision to impeach Hawkins could hardly be justified by the fact that their fellow gang member, Sympson, had been planning to betray them both. However, by the time matters had arrived at that stage, securing Hawkins's conviction had become indispensable to Wilson's survival, as he very well understood. The records of eighteenth-century crime are full of similar episodes.

The English were strongly resistant to the idea of a professional, paid police force. They associated that kind of thing with despotic regimes like that of France. They recognised that if any such force were put at the disposal of government, it would inevitably come to be used for political ends.[57] One effect of the reward system was to encourage the activities of professional 'thief-takers', who operated as independent agents. These undertook to track down criminals and secure evidence against them in return for the blood money payable when a conviction had been secured. In the case of a highwayman, this would be all or part of the £40 and the other inducements offered under the statute.[58] If the man had taken part in robbing the mails, there would be an additional reward put up by the Post Office.[59] A few thief-takers may have been reasonably honest. Many of them were corrupt.[60] The most famous was Jonathan Wild, who was executed in 1725 for his involvement in a shoplifting case, and who for a dozen years before this had pursued a double career.

Wild's public face was that of a thief-taker, in which capacity he was conspicuously industrious and successful. Indeed, after a while he took to calling himself 'Thief-Taker General of Great Britain and Ireland'. As a thief-taker, he did not scruple to make use of perjured witnesses to swear away the lives of those who were hauled into court on his information. Sometimes his intention was to protect himself from people who might give evidence of his own criminal activities, and sometimes he simply had his eye on the reward. In addition to catching thieves and robbers, he would also undertake the retrieval of stolen goods. The legal owner of the property paid a fee for its return, no questions asked and no prosecution to be mounted. This service was popular with the public, though it was scarcely legal, since it amounted to an agreement to 'compound a felony', or cover up a serious offence. Wild was able to carry on this business because of his complex web of connections within London's criminal subculture; he could often find out easily, or even guess from the circumstances, who it was who had committed a particular theft or robbery. Some property crimes, perhaps a great many, were carried out at his direct instigation. When he was unable to arrange the return of goods to the owner, or he did not choose to do this, he had methods for profitably fencing the swag. Finally, the terror he wielded as a thief-taker enabled him to bring pressure to bear on recalcitrant crooks to fall in with his system and dispose of their loot as he told them. Wild's was a lucrative and almost seamless enterprise, but his corruptions became too blatant. In the end, he was sentenced to death at the end of a trial that was as relentlessly rigged as any he had orchestrated himself.[61]

After the public exposure of his methods that accompanied his trial, Wild's name became legendary for evil. Around the time of his execution, there were numerous pamphlet 'lives' and similar publications. One of the best of these productions is sometimes ascribed to Daniel Defoe.[62] Later in the century, his reputation as a criminal mastermind was turned to account by Henry Fielding in his *Life of Jonathan Wild the Great* (1743). This was a spoof biography of Wild that was designed as a satire on the former Prime Minister, Sir Robert Walpole. Walpole, then recently driven from office, had been renowned, among other things, for his rapacious management of the nation's affairs.[63] Almost a hundred years after this, in 1839, the novelist Harrison Ainsworth made Wild a prominent character in his underworld tale *Jack Sheppard*.[64] The book was a huge success and ensured that Wild had a long subsequent history as a villain on the Victorian stage. But the most interesting use of the Wild figure is found in John Gay's *The Beggar's Opera*, which was first staged in 1728, less than three years after the thief-taker's execution. The reports on Wild and his underworld empire were Gay's chief source for the character of Peachum, consummate double-crosser and dealer in human blood. *The Beggar's Opera*, though, must have a chapter to itself.

15

'Why are the Laws levell'd at us?'

John Gay's musical play *The Beggar's Opera* was easily the biggest theatrical hit of the eighteenth century. Opening on 29 January 1728, it ran for sixty-two performances. No play before it had ever had anything like such a long first run. Nor was its success short term. There were revivals of it in every year throughout the rest of the century. It continued to be popular until well into the reign of Queen Victoria.[1] What were the reasons for its vast appeal? When it first appeared, it gained some of its applause as a skilful parody of the Italian operas that had dominated the London stage for almost two decades.[2] Gay invented a new form, the ballad opera. Instead of Italianate arias, his characters sang verses set to popular airs of the time: dances, drinking songs and tunes from street ballads. He threw out sung recitative and replaced it with spoken dialogue, creating a new kind of musical drama. The public loved both the parody and the eminently singable songs.

The subject matter of opera seria is sentimental and heroic, its tone lofty, its plots concern the affairs (the love affairs, mostly) of rulers or military leaders. It was patronised by the fashionable and rich. Gay opens his burlesque opera with a framing dialogue between a Beggar and a Player. This introduces the piece as the work of the former, an impoverished poet, who says that he wrote it originally to entertain an audience of beggars. High society is replaced by the very lowest, a trope that is carried through in the play's main action. Staple elements in the opera plots are the pair of lovers whose progress towards eventual union is troubled by the intrigues of those around them. Accordingly, in *The Beggar's Opera*, Gay gives us the relationship between a highwayman, Captain Macheath, and Polly Peachum, the daughter of a thief-taker. At the end of the typical opera of the time, it is usual for the way to be finally clear for the lovers to wed. At the outset of Gay's mock opera, in a neat reversal, Macheath and Polly have already married, secretly – and find that

199

their problems are only beginning. Polly's parents are appalled at the match. Her crooked father, Peachum, who combines profiting from blood money with dealing in stolen goods, is afraid that Macheath will now arrange for him and his wife to be hanged. Macheath will have the motive to do so; as Polly's husband, he has the prospect of inheriting their ill-gotten wealth. In addition, as a result of Polly's knowledge of her parents' secrets, he will have access to the necessary evidence of their illegal activities. Peachum and his wife join in trying to persuade their daughter to impeach Macheath. When she refuses, they resolve to do so themselves.

Macheath is no constant lover, any more than he is a nobleman or a prince. He and Polly promise each other their undying love; then he leaves her arms for a tavern and the company of a bevy of 'free-hearted Ladies'.[3] But two of these have conspired, for a bribe, to tip off Peachum, who arrives with an escort of constables and takes Macheath to Newgate. The principal source of the complications in Macheath and Polly's relationship is Peachum's determination to see Macheath hanged. However, once Macheath is banged up in jail, a further threat appears, in the shape of Lucy Lockit, whose father is the keeper of Newgate. Lucy is another of Macheath's mistresses; indeed, she is pregnant by him. In opera seria, the dominant emotions are love, jealousy and rage. Lucy's part encompasses displays of each of these, with a special emphasis on the two last. Nevertheless, Macheath is able to use Lucy's love for him to convince her to help him escape from prison. In doing so, he has to pretend to reject Polly, who, however, is not so easily driven away. Macheath's chagrin, caught between two besotted, demanding women, is a recurrent source of humour in the second half of the play. Lucy does help Macheath to escape, but he is soon rearrested (in the arms of yet another woman) and taken back to Newgate.

If the plot of *The Beggar's Opera* conformed to the standard conventions, it would end with Macheath and Polly reunited, and the removal of the obstacles to their union. But this will hardly do, since, for one thing, they are married already. Instead, Macheath, who is now in the condemned cell, is visited, not only by Lucy and Polly, both of them tenaciously loving to the last, but by no fewer than four of his previous mistresses, each of them bringing a child. Sometimes lovers' reunions can be a bit too much of a good thing. The moment echoes, sardonically, the earlier scene in the tavern, in which the tom-catting highwayman relaxes pleasantly among the 'Women of the Town'. But to take his pick from among a roomful of women is one thing; to find himself in a cell crowded with women and children, each of whom is staking some sort of claim on him, is another matter entirely. Macheath summons the sheriff's officers to conduct him to his only way out – the gallows. But the hero cannot be hanged. The Player who appeared in the Introduction steps forward to object, out of the

Heartthrob/womaniser

wisdom of his theatrical experience. Such an ending would go against convention: 'an Opera must end happily'. Worse than that, it would go against 'the Taste of the Town'.[4] The Beggar reluctantly agrees, and orders the actors to call a last-minute reprieve. Macheath is brought back, and the play concludes with a country dance, in which Macheath is paired with Polly, and other partners are found for Lucy and the four unnamed women who have just turned up.

Traditionally, the formal dance was a symbol of union and harmony.[5] But this dance of Macheath among his 'Wives' stirs up echoes of an earlier scene, in which he dances in the tavern among the 'Women of the Town'. And his final song teases with its hints that Macheath is incapable of sticking to one woman for longer than a single night:

> Thus I stand like the *Turk*, with his Doxies around;
> From all Sides their Glances his Passion confound;
> For black, brown, and fair, his Inconstancy burns,
> And the different Beauties subdue him by turns:
> Each calls forth her Charms, to provoke his Desires:
> Though willing to all; with but one he retires.[6]

If the words, as seems likely, reflect the figures of the dance, the final image of the play is of Macheath weaving his way from partner to partner, until he finds himself back again – but for how long? – with Polly. The dance then becomes a fine stylised visual image of the play's recurrent motif.[7]

If *The Beggar's Opera* had been nothing more than an amusing skit on Italianate opera, its vogue would have been short. However, the play also operates as a wicked satire on the social and political life of the time, and this is certainly what helped to give it the powerful charge that kept it so long in the theatrical repertoire. In the self-presentation of Gay's characters, the subculture of thieves, fences and whores becomes a microcosm of respectable society. So Peachum, poring over his 'Book of Accounts', noting down the anticipated returns on betraying various members of his gang to the authorities, is a grotesque parody of a tradesman in his counting-house. Unlike most tradesmen, Peachum makes nothing, he invests in nothing: instead, he traffics in stolen goods and human lives. And yet he claims that his is 'an honest Employment': just as honest, he argues, as that of a lawyer, who also 'acts . . . both against Rogues and for 'em'.[8]

Throughout the play, Peachum speaks almost entirely in the language of profit and trade, and he is most often seen in the company of an account book. So far as he is concerned, selling his friends and acquaintances for blood money is simply a matter of 'Business'; as he explains to Polly, 'there is no Malice in the Case'. Given such a cold-blooded attitude to the lives of his friends, it is not surprising that, in his opinion, the demands of 'Business' are fully sufficient to justify the occasional murder, should it happen in the course of a robbery. He has no regard for the highwayman's pact with the public, his traditional code of honourable behaviour. Peachum has a partner in his trade, in the shape of Lockit, the keeper of Newgate. But Lockit does not trust Peachum; he expects him to try and cheat him, and plots to cheat him back. He, too, claims to see no distinction between his and Peachum's professional ethos and that prevailing in legitimate business circles. At one point, he compares the two of them to 'honest Tradesmen', competing to find out which will succeed in managing to swindle the other.[9]

If Peachum and Lockit see themselves as tradesmen, and represent the underworld equivalent of a profit-oriented, complacent middle class, Macheath, the hero, inevitably represents the gentry. Here, the stereotype of the 'gentleman robber' comes patly to Gay's use. Macheath, like Captain Hind before him, considers himself to be 'a Gentleman by his Profession'.[10] As a mounted highwayman, he is an aristocrat among thieves.[11] Even Peachum admires him and regrets the need to bring about his betrayal. Where the commercially minded Peachum speaks mainly of business and profit, Macheath is inclined to talk about 'Honour', the gentleman's supreme attribute. He believes that as highwaymen, he and the other members of his gang are entitled to consider themselves 'Men of Honour'; in other words, as gentlemen.[12] A passage added to the 1723 edition of Bernard Mandeville's satire *The Fable of the Bees* was surely one of Gay's inspirations for Macheath and his gang of robbers. 'Rogues have the same Passions to gratify as other Men, and value themselves on their Honour and Faithfulness to one another, their Courage, Intrepidity, and other manly Virtues, as well as People of better Professions; and in daring Enterprizes, the Resolution of a Robber may be as much supported by his Pride, as that of an honest Soldier, who fights for his Country.'[13] Macheath's courage is something we have to take on trust. However, Peachum bears witness to it, and so does Matt of the Mint, a member of Macheath's robber gang.[14] As to Macheath's faithfulness to his associates, we shall hear more about that in a moment.

Macheath does not only mix with criminals. Like earlier 'gentlemen of the road', he aspires to live the life of a man of wealth and fashion.[15] He is addicted to gaming houses, where he rubs shoulders with the gentry, and loses most of his money to them.[16] As Peachum drily remarks, 'The Man that proposes to get Money by Play should have the education of a fine Gentleman, and be train'd up to it from his Youth.'[17] As a gentleman, Macheath can't quite cut it, and Gay has a neat visual correlative for this. In a stage direction to a scene in which the highwayman is preparing for an

[handwritten margin note: Gentlemanly]

evening's gambling, it is specified that he enters 'in a fine tarnish'd Coat'.[18] The coat, evidently, has been a good one, but it is either badly faded or (more probably) stained.

Macheath's underworld associates have no sympathy with his passion for gambling. Peachum thinks it is folly; no profit in it. The whore Jenny Diver thinks it is a blot on his cherished honour, or so she says: 'Cards and Dice are only fit for cowardly Cheats, who prey upon their Friends.' As she herself is just about to betray him to Peachum for a reward, there is considerable irony in this remark. However, Macheath's two closest companions, Ben Budge and Matt of the Mint, also despise gamblers. Ben regrets that his captain should pass his time in 'such ill Company', and Matt dismisses them as 'Mechanics', or craftsmen. The only reason, Matt states, that such people are admitted into polite society is because so many of them are 'of the Quality'. Thus, in a splendidly ironic inversion, he makes it clear that he sees Macheath as a decent highwayman corrupted by high company. In the world of the play, robbers and their friends regard gamesters as a conscienceless, predatory lot: as Mrs Peachum says of Macheath, 'What business hath he to keep Company with Lords and Gentlemen? he should leave them to prey upon one another.'[19] The highwaymen, by contrast, make a point of presenting themselves as a band of faithful comrades. 'Who is there here that would not dye for his Friend?' one of them cries rhetorically.[20] Macheath feels no loyalty to his gambling associates; on the contrary, he arranges with Ben Budge to point out a particular man who has won a lot of money from him, so that Ben can lie in wait for him on his way home. But when Matt proposes to rob another of the gamblers, Macheath demurs, explaining, 'He's a good honest kind of a Fellow, and one of us' – in other words, a highwayman.[21] Macheath is true to his own kind. Earlier in the same scene, he has demonstrated his honour as a highway robber in a very traditional fashion: when his fellow gang members, Ben and Matt, have had an unsuccessful stint on the road, he shares his own money with them. However, little in this play takes place without a satirical glance at one or another group in middle or high society. Here it is courtiers: Macheath expressly prides himself on being more than 'a meer Court Friend, who professes every thing and will do nothing'. After a song to emphasise the point, he concludes, 'But we, Gentlemen, still have Honour enough to break through the Corruptions of the World.'[22]

Highwaymen who claim to be more honourable than courtiers. Thief-takers doing nicely on blood money and the proceeds of fencing who maintain that they are no more dishonest than tradesmen or lawyers. The social satire is sharp and it is also pretty wide-ranging. At the same time, it is cleverly undercut. These are ruffians and scoundrels speaking. Gay encourages his audience to play with the highly subversive possibility that legitimate society may be just as crooked as the underworld, if not rather more so. But because he puts these sentiments into the mouths of robbers and fences, we are at liberty to decide quite how seriously we want to take them. It's a question of moral authority. The wit can cut in more than one direction: against the pretensions of the highwaymen as well as against the reputed corruptions of courtiers and well-born gamblers. As Bernard Mandeville remarks, in another passage in *The Fable of the Bees*, 'Every one loves to hear the Thing well spoke of, that he has a Share in, . . . nay, Thieves and House-breakers have a greater Regard to those of their Fraternity than they have for Honest People'.[23]

Much of the satirical comment that runs through the play is pointedly political. So Peachum, in the song with which he opens the play's main action, sardonically reflects upon '*the Statesman*', who, as he says, '*because he's so great, / Thinks his Trade as honest as mine*'.[24] In Peachum's view, the statesman is misled into regarding himself as a decent man, when in fact his profession involves him in rather more devious behaviour even than Peachum's does. Being 'great' doesn't make him respectable; it merely puts him above the reach of the law. The play's original public appreciated this kind of crack. They applied it to the government of the day, and found that it fitted.

The head of that administration, Sir Robert Walpole, was one of the most brilliant political managers England has ever known. He effectively created the office of prime minister, and he sustained himself in it for over twenty years, gaining in the process a shocking reputation for his methods of political control. He made a ruthless use of the extensive patronage at his disposal to encourage his supporters and increase his power base. Whenever his political tools were caught engaging in corrupt behaviour, he did his best to protect them. Somewhere along the way, he lined his own pockets very well; though it must be said that when he finally lost his grip on Parliament and his opponents tried to charge him with corruption, they failed to find any evidence against him. But at the time *The Beggar's Opera* was first produced, Walpole's downfall was still many years in the future.[25]

There are coded allusions to Walpole and his Whig associates scattered throughout the play.[26] Some of these are jibes of a snidely personal kind, and lost their impact as soon as they ceased to be topical; long, long before *The Beggar's Opera* slipped out of the standard theatrical repertoire. But Gay has other, and more interesting, ways of making his satirical points. For one thing, as we have seen, characters like Peachum and Macheath are rather given to drawing comparisons between their own behaviour and that of 'statesmen' and 'courtiers'. Such comments, biting in themselves, contribute towards Gay's further strategy. As an opposition newspaper pointed out at the time, Gay invites his audience to see an analogy between the Whig administration led by Walpole and the robber gang captained by

Macheath. To this, one might add that Walpole's management of state affairs is also glanced at in the guise of the complex criminal enterprise directed by Peachum (a point the eighteenth-century journalist partly acknowledges).[27] Also, that behind Walpole and his friends stands a bigger and less time-bound target: Gay is attacking crooked statesmen in general, as much as the individual specimens of the class who infested public life in the 1720s.

The comparison between the politician and the highway robber draws its logic from a very old moral theme, one we have met before: that the dishonest person who operates in ways that the legal system cannot or will not control is at least as much of a robber as the out-and-out highwayman.[28] In the Elizabethan and early Stuart periods, it had mainly been used to snipe at relatively powerless groups and professions, such as misers, usurers and lawyers. However, by Gay's time, its application to rapacious statesmen had become a satirical commonplace. In the late 1660s, Samuel Butler attributed to his 'Modern Politician' the belief that 'there is no Way of thriving so easy and certain as to grow rich by defrauding the Public: for public Thieveries are more safe and less prosecuted than private'.[29] In a letter of 1723, more than four years before he was to write *The Beggar's Opera*, Gay himself had observed sardonically, 'I cannot indeed wonder that the Talents requisite for a great Statesman are so scarce in the world since so many of those who possess them are every month cut off in the prime of their Age at the Old-Baily. How envious are Statesmen! and how jealous are they of rivals!'[30] This is where the image of the statesman robber finds its sharpest bite: at the point where the great social predators control the system of laws by which they arrange for the small-time crook to be judged and condemned to death. As the preacher Thomas Wimbledon had proclaimed, more than 340 years earlier, it is often the case that those whose crimes are more deserving of death pass condemnation on people whose crimes deserve it less.[31] Towards the end of *The Beggar's Opera*, the Beggar explains why, in his opinion, the play should have ended with Macheath's execution: ''Twould have shown that the lower Sort of People have their Vices in a degree as well as the Rich: And that they are punish'd for them.'[32]

In 1761, a young highwayman was hanged at Oxford. His name was Isaac Darkin; his father had been a London tradesman, a cork-cutter, and he himself was a midshipman in the navy. A pamphlet life of Darkin which appeared just after his execution reports that 'during his Imprisonment . . . he diverted himself one Evening . . . by reading the *Beggar's Opera*, when he appeared to enter thoroughly into the Spirit of *Mackheath's Part*, and seemed greatly to enjoy the Character'. Some years later, *The Malefactor's Register* (1779), a compendium of condensed biographies of criminals, reported Darkin's enjoyment of the play and went on to remark: 'We cannot conceive but that this play, however witty, and however applauded, has tended, beyond any piece of writing, to increase the number of thieves. Young fellows have thought it right to copy Mackheath, because Mackheath is represented as a *gentleman* highwayman.'[33] This accusation was by no means a new one. *The Beggar's Opera* had first been accused of glorifying robbers and encouraging crime only a few weeks after its opening night. Argument on the subject raged for the rest of the century and well into the next.[34] More interesting than the debate itself is what the anxieties about the play suggest: that despite its burlesque form, it was experienced by many of its audience primarily as a sympathetic portrayal of the life of robbers and thieves. In Augustan England, it would have been inconceivable for a serious play to have a hero who was a highwayman and a female lead who was the daughter of a fence. It would have been felt by the critics to be an artistic outrage. Such a piece could only have been composed, as *The Beggar's Opera* was, in a mock-heroic, parodic mode. And yet, conspicuous though the elements of burlesque and satire are in the play, they cannot overwhelm a powerful illusion of the vivid life of the characters. In some, that life aroused disgust. In others, attraction and self-identification. There is something very touching about the image of the doomed young robber cheering himself by reading about Macheath. At the time he was hanged, Darkin was not yet twenty-one.[35]

He was certainly not alone in having a close imaginative relationship with the hero of *The Beggar's Opera*. A couple of years later, a young man of much higher social standing, a Scottish aristocrat, James Boswell, entered in his journal some details of what happened one evening when 'two very pretty little girls' accosted him in the street. He warned them that he could not afford to pay them for sex, but they were willing, just the same, to come with him to a tavern. For the price of a bottle of sherry, Boswell had an exquisite time: 'I toyed with them and drank about and sung *Youth's the Season* and thought myself Captain Macheath; and then I solaced my existence with them, one after the other, according to their seniority. I was quite *raised*, as the phrase is'. 'Youth's the Season' is the song Macheath sings in the tavern scene, with the 'Women of the Town' as chorus. It is clear that Boswell's exhilaration with this episode (his 'blood still thrilled with pleasure' when he recalled it the following day) depended crucially on the glamour shed on it by his sense that for a while he was living the life of Macheath, irresistible to women, melodious in his cups, and an outlaw to morality and convention.[36]

It is not surprising that it was one of Macheath's songs, specifically, that helped to trigger Boswell's state of exaltation. For if we take only the action into account, the play is extraordinarily bleak. Its central themes are cheating and betrayal. Over and over again, the characters plot against each other, or they betray one another casually, or they collude in the treachery of others. The single exception is Polly. For all his talk of honour, Macheath is faithless in love, alternately sweet-talking and betraying both Polly and Lucy. But the pervasive presence of the music brings a powerful emotional counter-current into the play. The songs, and especially the melodies, are the vehicle for some very different themes. Even where the words are sardonic, the tunes are often lively or romantic. And some of the most memorable tunes carry messages of hedonism, love or hope: '*I would love you all the Day*', '*Fill ev'ry Glass*', '*Youth's the Season made for Joys*', and (the final line of all) '*The Wretch of To day, may be happy To-morrow*'. The preface to a volume of sermons that was published in 1763 says that 'several Thieves and Street-robbers confessed in *Newgate*, that they raised their Courage at the Playhouse, by the Songs of their Hero *Macheath*, before they sallied forth on their desperate nocturnal Exploits'.[37]

Much later in his life, Boswell was still very fond of *The Beggar's Opera*, though leaning towards the side of those people who believed in its power to corrupt. As he observed, 'the gaiety and heroism of a highwayman [are] very captivating to a youthful imagination'.[38] Concerns about the play's potential to lead its viewers astray always centred around the figure of Macheath; and understandably so. We hear of no one who fantasised living out the life of the double-crossing Peachum – even for a single evening. One very interesting aspect of Boswell's comment is the fact that he does not mention Macheath by name, but shifts into the generic: 'a highway-man'. Macheath is something more than a character; he is an evocation of a powerful tradition. Behind him looms the figure of the heroic robber. All Gay has to do is to strike certain notes and legend supplies the rest. 'Sure there is not a finer Gentleman upon the Road than the Captain!' says Mrs Peachum. With equal admiration, Peachum speaks of 'his Personal Bravery, his fine Stratagem'.[39] Speeches like these resonate with buried allusions, so that, with just a few words spoken, Macheath acquires the debonair manners of Claude Du Vall, the ingenuity and courage of Captain Hind. This is part of what makes him so alluring: he is invested with all the mystique of the 'gentleman thief'. Nor is this heavily undercut by satire. True, his attempts at playing the gentleman are less than completely successful; true, his courage in the condemned cell comes, as he himself acknowledges, out of a bottle; but in both instances, we can find his behaviour touching as much as ridiculous. The highwayman's swagger, his sexual magnetism, his generosity and loyalty to his friends are all left largely unmocked.

But not his and his fellow robbers' belief in the moral superiority of their own subculture, their faith that the gang is an enduring repository of virtues that are no longer found in the wider society. Macheath is disillusioned when he finds that the principal witness against him at his

207

trial is his comrade Jemmy Twitcher: "'Tis a plain Proof that the World is all alike, and that even our Gang can no more trust one another than other People.'[40] The truth is that for all their pride and vaunted honour, the highwaymen cannot claim to live by their own separate system of values. They are far too dependent on Peachum. When the quick-tempered Matt wants to shoot Peachum to protect the gang, Macheath forbids him, explaining, 'Business cannot go on without him. He is a Man who knows the World, and is a necessary Agent to us.' Peachum knows how to dispose of stolen valuables like watches, and also how to arrange to cash banknotes safely. Eighteenth-century banknotes worked rather differently from modern 'paper money'. They were receipts for actual cash deposited. Because they were made payable to the bearer, it was possible for thieves to present them and demand the money, but they were traceable, and it was easy to put a stop on payment for them. Without the expertise of the criminal entrepreneur and the services with which he provides them, the gentlemen of the road would go short of funds.[41]

In *The Beggar's Opera*, the highway robber is presented as thoroughly involved in the social and economic networks of a criminal subculture. This is something fairly unusual. In the Ratsey pamphlets, for example, the robber hero is carefully kept at distance from any of the more sordid manifestations of the early seventeenth-century underworld.[42] Likewise, none of the numerous stories about Captain Hind purport to tell us very much at all about his business connections or arrangements. Even the author highwayman John Clavell, who tells us so much, only gives us half a story in this respect. He describes his relations with conniving innkeepers, but not how he fenced his loot. He must have used a fence. The record of his robberies, summarised in his pardon, show that among the things he stole were a watch, a gold ring and some very fancy articles of clothing.[43]

Gay's main source for Peachum and his complex criminal enterprise was undoubtedly the sensational case of Jonathan Wild, as this was mediated through some of the many, many pages of reportage that appeared at the time of his downfall. However, some interesting parallels to the relations between Peachum and the highway robbers are found in a pamphlet of 1722, *A Narrative of the Life of Mr. Benjamin Childe*. The author, a convicted highwayman, gives a sober and persuasive account of how he was drawn into the robber's life by a fence called William Wade. Wade, a thorough-going entrepreneur of crime, suggested suitable targets to Childe, supplied him with horse and pistols and made two attempts to fix him up with confederates. He also arranged the conversion into money of looted banknotes. As in the case of Peachum and his wife, Wade's house was a social as well as a business centre for the robbers who depended on his agency. Childe says that when he went there, he often ran into other highwaymen. Each of these men, he discovered, had a mistress. An intriguing point of connection between this text and *The Beggar's Opera* is Childe's account of the behaviour of the women in this circle. He says that whenever they knew that one of the robbers had made a successful haul, they would threaten 'to make a Discovery' of him to the authorities unless he lashed out some money on them. Childe thought they were very dangerous and tried to have as little as possible to do with them.[44] Macheath shows less sense of self-preservation.

In this play about criminals, no crime takes place on stage. This is partly dictated by the mock-operatic form. In opera seria, action is generally attenuated in favour of emotion, expressed in sung interludes, and the principal theme is usually love. *The Beggar's Opera* gives us its hero as a lover, and only secondarily as a robber. A womanising highwayman was nothing new. After all, such behaviour goes with the general reputation for profligacy. A song sung by a highwayman in a Jacobean play paints a picture of the warm sexual welcome he receives when he comes back after his evening's robberies to the inn where he makes his headquarters:

> if my whore be not in case,*
> My hostess' daughter has her place:
> The maids sit up and watch their turns . . . [45]

Macheath, though, preening himself in the middle of eight of his women, takes this tendency to heroic extremes; which is unquestionably the point. The hero, after all, must be larger than life, and more valiant than other men.

Though we never see the highwaymen in action, Gay does give us the scenes in which they are drinking in the tavern, working up their nerve before spending an evening holding up travellers on Hounslow Heath. The various members of the gang give one another encouragement, each of them coming out with justifications for the robber's way of life. Jemmy Twitcher is the first to begin: 'Why are the Laws levell'd at us? are we more dishonest than the rest of Mankind?' If the laws against highway robbery are unfair, and robbers are no more dishonest than anyone else, then it follows that everybody must be engaged in grabbing whatever they can. Twitcher continues: 'What we win, Gentlemen, is our own by the Law of Arms, and the Right of Conquest.' By invoking the law of arms, Twitcher suggests that highwaymen are in the same position as soldiers in warfare. Strictly speaking, the taking of booty was only permissible under the law of arms once a war had been defined as a 'just' war. Twitcher doesn't trouble to establish this point, nor does he say who he thinks is the

---

* in the house

enemy. But then, if everyone is more or less equally dishonest, the question of who has right on their side is one that hardly has meaning. Buried in Twitcher's speech is the implication that everyone in the world is at war with everyone else. This is, after all, what the philosopher Thomas Hobbes believed was 'the Naturall Condition of Mankind'. Hobbes argued that in this situation, there is no such thing as law.[46] Twitcher is less straightforward; but in his mouth, the phrase 'Law of Arms' becomes nothing more than a high-sounding screen for the resolve of the strong to take whatever they can from whoever they find at a disadvantage. Towards the end of the play, Jemmy Twitcher is named as the member of the gang who has betrayed Macheath and appeared in evidence against him at his trial. His slippery but ultimately uncompromising statement of his right to dedicate himself to his own self-interest gives warning that he of all the robbers is the one least to be trusted.

Some of the other members of the gang seek to justify robbery by praising what they maintain are their own professional virtues: indifference to death, courage, loyalty, even what one of them terms their 'indefatigable Industry'. Like Falstaff, they labour in their vocation. The most radical declaration comes from Ben Budge. Hinting at the agenda of the mid-seventeenth-century political visionaries like Coppe and Winstanley, he proclaims that the highwaymen are communists: 'We are for a just Partition of the World, for every Man hath a Right to enjoy Life.'[47] But this is just one man's notion. Logically considered, it is far from being compatible with the equally ringing pronouncements of Jemmy Twitcher. The gang have no shared coherent manifesto or programme.

The last word on the subject of robbery is given to Matt of the Mint. Highwaymen, he says, 'retrench the Superfluities of Mankind'. They take what people don't really need. The implication is that Macheath's band of robbers, like that of Robin Hood, only plunders the rich. And as in the case of William Warner's Elizabethan Robin Hood, their victims come, or so Matt likes to pretend, from a particular section of the rich: the 'covetous' people who pile up money by dishonest means and don't know how to spend it. 'These are the Robbers of Mankind', Matt says, using an argument that is at least as old as the story of Ratsey and the lawyer. 'Money was made for the Free-hearted and Generous'.[48] The claim that robbers know how to spend money is visually counterpointed, of course, by the spectacle of the gang at their tavern table, smoking, and knocking back the wine and brandy.

At the end of their drinking bout, the highwaymen march off to the sound of one of the best tunes in the play. Gay appropriated it from Handel, who wrote it for his opera *Rinaldo*, in which it accompanies the traverse across the stage of an army of crusaders. The words Gay wrote to it are sung by the fiery robber Matt of the Mint:

210

Let us take the Road.
>Hark! I hear the sound of Coaches!
>The hour of Attack approaches,
To your Arms, brave Boys, and load.
>See the Ball I hold!
>Let the Chymists toil like asses,
>Our Fire their Fire surpasses,
>And turns all our Lead to Gold.[49]

The 'Chymists', of course, are alchemists, obsessed with finding the formula that will transmute lead into gold. The highwaymen have their own formula, symbolised by the leaden pistol ball and the reference to gun-fire. In just a few lines, Gay catches and articulates the dream that motivates the robber: a dream of the transformational power of violence. Just by reaching out to take it, the robber can have whatever he wants; or so it appears. With the application of violence, he dissolves the social structures that constitute property. He does away with the need for hard work or careful calculations. He has the power to overturn rank and hierarchy. In short, he finds himself, temporarily, in a state that is deceptively similar to the innocent existence of the golden world. Robbery puts gold in his pocket; it gives him the purchasing power he lacks, or has never had. It transmutes the man himself into refined metal: a 'gentleman thief', a 'man of honour'.

16

The Shadow of Tyburn

'In no place shal you see malefactors go more constantly, more assuredly, and with lesse lamentation to their death than in England': so claims Sir Thomas Smith, writing in Elizabeth's reign, and he adds: 'The nature of our nation is free, stout, haultie [haughty], prodigall of life and bloud'.[1] If the robber on the highway was for many an icon of English courage, so, likewise, was the condemned man or woman who could travel the road to the gallows with an undaunted air. A similar attitude persisted, at any rate among ordinary folk, until well into the eighteenth century: so, in the late 1730s, the Frenchman Jean Bernard Le Blanc observes, disapprovingly: 'an English mob is delighted to see such persons go thro' their last scenes with resolution, and applauds those that are insensible enough to die as they had lived, braving the justice of God and men'. Such displays of nerve were, he says, 'esteem'd an honour to the nation.' Le Blanc thought they were solely due to drink.[2]

Under English law, robbery was a capital offence, and this was the case regardless of the value of the property taken from the victim. Something had to be taken, otherwise the assault was not technically a robbery, but if violence or threats were used to extract money or goods of even the smallest value, then the offender was guilty of robbery, and if convicted in court, was liable to be hanged on the gallows.[3] This was the theory; in practice, there were various escape routes. During the Middle Ages, a man in clerical orders might not be hanged by the secular authorities, whatever his offence had been. He had to be handed over to his ecclesiastical superiors, who had their own procedures. In the later Middle Ages, this privilege, called 'benefit of clergy', was extended to any literate male offender. All that was required was that he demonstrate his literacy by reading a verse from the Psalms: the 'neck-verse', as it came to be called.[4] However, offenders convicted of certain serious crimes such as murder, highway robbery, and also housebreaking, in cases where the inhabitants of

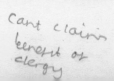

Cant claim
benefit of
clergy

the house had been put in fear, lost the right to claim benefit of clergy in 1547.[5] Sometimes sympathetic judges continued to allow clergy in cases where it was not legally available, but this was strictly discretionary, and appears to have become less common as time went on.[6]

Women were not allowed to claim benefit of clergy until a very much later date. However, for many centuries a woman who was convicted on a capital offence was allowed to 'plead her belly', that is, claim pregnancy. If her claim was allowed, she would be reprieved until the birth of the child, in order to preserve the innocent life within her. After that, she might be sent to the gallows, but during the early modern period, at any rate, it was common for women who successfully pleaded pregnancy to use the period of respite to obtain a pardon.[7] In 1613, in a rare case in which a woman was charged with committing a violent robbery, Cecily Mann, a spinster of Ingatestone, Essex, was convicted of assaulting a man on the highway and taking away his purse. She claimed to be pregnant, so, following the procedure in such cases, she was examined by a 'jury of matrons'. They concluded that this was not true, so she was marked in the records of the court to be sent for execution.[8]

The other way of avoiding the gallows was to procure a pardon, as discussed in Chapter Nine. A pardon might be absolute or conditional. Until the later seventeenth century, most pardons were absolute, but some were granted upon conditions, most commonly that the recipient should agree to serve in the army. The policy of transporting convicted prisoners to England's overseas colonies, where they were usually put to work as labourers, originated in 1615. From 1654, a custom grew up of offering such prisoners a pardon, conditional on their agreeing to be transported. The numbers being sent overseas, usually to plantations in North America and the West Indies, began to increase considerably. From this time on, it became less common for pardons to be granted without a condition attached. In *Polly* (1728), his sequel to *The Beggar's Opera*, Gay follows the fortunes of Polly Peachum in the West Indies, where she has gone in search of Macheath, who has been transported there after his last-minute reprieve from hanging.[9]

In spite of these somewhat haphazard devices for limiting the effects of the capital laws, England for a long time had the reputation of a country where executions were exceptionally common. Sir John Fortescue, writing in the early 1470s, seems to have been the first writer to touch on this theme; as we have seen, he regarded the numbers who were hanged for crimes of violence as an index of superior English courage. In 1596, the Jesuit Robert Parsons claimed that more people were put to death in England for robbing on the highway 'than in many other Nations together'. Parsons did not share Fortescue's complacency; he deplored the frequency of robberies and he was disturbed by the very large numbers who were sent to execution. All the same, in cases of robbery, he would have applied the death penalty more rigorously, not less, in order to discourage would-be robbers. However, he argued that it ought to be removed in certain cases of theft, where all that had been taken was a small sum of money or articles of low value.[10] At that date, theft of anything worth a shilling or more was a capital offence. Even at Elizabethan prices, that was still a relatively modest sum; it was typically a day's wage for a skilled craftsman.

In 1599, Thomas Platter, a visitor from Switzerland, wrote in his diary: 'Rarely does a law day in London . . . pass without some twenty to thirty persons – both men and women – being gibbetted.'[11] However, the number of days on which criminal trials were held in London varied from year to year, so, vividly suggestive though this is, it is of limited help in establishing an overall figure. For this, the closest we have is a rough estimate supplied by some informant to a German tourist, Paul Hentzner, on his own trip to England the previous year. Summing up the English national character as 'cunning, treacherous, and thievish', Hentzner noted that 'above three hundred are said to be hanged annually at London'.[12] High though this figure is, it may well be roughly accurate, as long as we assume, as is likely, that it includes the totals executed for crimes in Middlesex and Surrey. Like the executions for London, those for Middlesex normally took place at Tyburn, which was well outside the Tudor city, near the end of what is now Oxford Street. The usual place of execution for Surrey was at a spot called St Thomas a Watering, two miles from the city along the Old Kent Road.[13] Surviving records show that just a few years later, in James's reign, the numbers hanged by the Middlesex justices fluctuated from just over fifty to just under a hundred a year, averaging out over ten years at about seventy a year. The equivalent records for London are lost; but since the population was higher, it is reasonable to assume that the number of those who were hanged was at least as great.[14] The figure given by Hentzner thus turns out to be quite plausible, so long as we assume that in 1598, and especially in the years that immediately preceded it, the number of executions per annum had been hovering somewhere at the top of the usual range. And indeed, such sketchy evidence as there is suggests that this was indeed the case. It is likely that years of bad harvests in the mid-1590s, with the resulting economic stresses, had resulted in a surge in the crime rate.[15]

More than a hundred years later, César de Saussure, like Platter, a visitor from Switzerland, wrote in a letter to his family: 'Executions are frequent in London; they take place every six weeks, and five, ten, or fifteen criminals are hanged on these occasions.'[16] Once again, we are dealing with an impression, rather than hard statistics. However, it is noticeable that although de Saussure thought that this was a lot of executions – and it is, of course – the numbers of people being hanged were now far lower than had been the case in the late 1590s. The first substantial drop in the execution rate had taken place during the 1630s. It continued to decline, partly, no doubt, because of the availability of the alternative penalty of transportation, until about 1751, after which it again began to rise.[17]

A high proportion of the prisoners who choked out their lives as they swung from the gallows were robbers of one sort or another. Analysing the records of hangings in Surrey between 1722 and 1748, J. M. Beattie found that well over half of those who were sent for execution had been convicted of street or highway robberies. Many of the others were burglars. Surrey, contiguous to London, and with a fringe of urban parishes by the Thames, was a county much infested by highwaymen and footpads. The same could equally be said of Middlesex and, of course, the capital itself. Statistics published by John Howard, the eighteenth-century prison reformer, for the period between 1749 and 1771 show that out of 678 offenders executed during those years in Middlesex and London, 251, that is, rather more than a third, had been found guilty of robbery on the highway, while a further 118 had been convicted of housebreaking. Howard's figures also show that highway robbery, in particular, was one of the offences for which the penalty was least likely to be commuted to a lesser punishment, such as transportation.[18]

The gallows cast a shadow of fear on the minds of the people, and especially on those whose routine activities put them within reach of its noose. It left its marks on their speech, as they struggled to find ways of repressing that fear. Proverbially, hanging was said 'to go by destiny', to be purely a matter of fate. This saying goes back at least as far as the fourteenth century, since the preaching friar Bromyard cites the case of 'the robber who is led out to be hanged', who says, 'this has been preordained for me', an outlook that Bromyard condemns.[19] We are told that robbers and thieves encouraged one another to adopt an attitude of bravado. Thus Sir Thomas More, in 1534: 'a man may heare theves* not let [hesitate] to say, that he hath a fainte stomake, that will stycke for halfe an howres hanging, to lyve seven yeres in plesure'. The satirist Bernard Mandeville, writing in 1725, gives a shorter and blunter catchphrase, that he says was current among 'Profligates' in his own day: '*there is nothing in being hang'd, but a wry Neck, and a wet pair of Breeches*'. In 1607, George Wilkins imagined a condemned thief in Newgate jail comforting himself with a series of such sayings: 'tis but halfe an houres hanging, twill save mee half a yeeres drinking; twoe turnes, the knot under the eare, and a wry

---

* *latrones*, robbers, in More's Latin original.

mouth, will doe it; . . . tis but the way which many a good fellow has gone before'.[20] Wilkins, who kept an alehouse in the middle of one of London's most notorious criminal neighbourhoods, must have heard such street philosophy many times.

Some robbers encouraged themselves with crude travesties of Christian doctrine. John Clavell says that his fellow highwaymen laughed at the thought of being hanged, and called it being 'pull'd to heaven in a string'. They pointed out that a man who was sentenced to be executed was given the attentions of a clergyman and time to repent of his sins. He was, they claimed, less likely to go to Hell than someone who was struck down suddenly by an illness.[21] Almost a hundred years later, in *Moll Flanders* (1722), Daniel Defoe makes his gentleman highwayman explain that the reason why he would rather be hanged than transported is because 'at the Place of Execution there was at least an End of all the Miseries of the present State, and as for what was to follow, a Man was in his Opinion, as likely to Repent sincerely in the last Fortnight of his Life under the Pressures and Agonies of a Jayl, and the condemn'd Hole, as he would ever be in the Woods and Wildernesses of *America*'; moreover, 'that Servitude and hard Labour were things Gentlemen could never stoop to'.[22] Better the gallows.

Clavell says that the highwaymen he knew took comfort from the thought that if they were sentenced to be hanged, they would not die alone, but with 'a great audience of the people by, / For whose faire warning th'are content to die'.[23] A hanging was a public spectacle, and the condemned prisoner was the centre of attention. Often, as we shall see, prisoners interacted with members of the crowd as they passed on their way to the place of execution. Some of the condemned made speeches at the foot of the gallows; the spectators were their 'audience' in a literal sense, while, in words of earnest penitence, they hammered home the 'warning' that their fate was intended to provide. One of the implications of Clavell's remark is that the highwaymen assumed that the crowd that attended their execution would be felt by them to be a supportive presence. In the light of V. A. C. Gatrell's work on the execution crowds of a later age, this is extremely interesting. Gatrell demonstrates that in the late eighteenth and nineteenth centuries, the crowd's behaviour was highly variable, depending on the circumstances under which the execution took place: the crime committed by the condemned person, and other factors. He argues that to read the crowd's engagement with these killings as a matter of pure ghoulishness is a serious oversimplification.[24]

The earliest detailed description I have found of a routine English hanging was written in 1618 by Horatio Busino, the chaplain of the Venetian

Ambassador in England. As it is clear and informative and not nearly so well known as many of the later accounts, I shall give it here in full:

> They take them [the condemned prisoners] five and twenty at a time, every month, besides sudden and extraordinary executions in the course of the week, on a large cart like a high scaffold. They go along quite jollily, holding their sprigs of rosemary and singing songs, accompanied by their friends and a multitude of people. On reaching the gallows one of the party acts as spokesman, saying fifty words or so. Then the music, which they had learnt at their leisure in the prisons, being repeated, the executioner hastens the business, and beginning at one end, fastens each man's halter to the gibbet. They are so closely packed that they touch each other, with their hands tied in front of them, wrist to wrist, so as to leave them the option of taking off their hats and saluting the bystanders. One careless fellow availed himself of this facility to shield his face from the sun. Finally, the executioner, having come down from the scaffold, has the whip applied to the cart horses, and thus the culprits remain dangling in the air precisely like a bunch of fat thrushes. They are hard to die of themselves and unless their own relations or friends pulled their feet or pelted them with brickbats in the breast as they do, it would fare badly with them. The proceeding is really barbarous and strikes those who witness it with horror.[25]

They died slowly because, in most cases, they were slowly strangled; there wasn't enough of a drop to make sure they would break their necks. That was why those who cared about them pulled on their feet, to put a speedier end to their suffering. This detail is mentioned by Thomas Platter, and by many later witnesses.[26]

At some places of execution, the condemned prisoner was made to climb a ladder, from which he or she was then 'turned off' by the executioner. Thomas Nashe describes the procedure graphically in his proto-novel *The Unfortunate Traveller* (1594). His hero, Jack Wilton, has been condemned for a murder he has not committed and is standing on the ladder: 'I had the knot under my eare, there was faire plaie, the hangman had one halter, another about my necke was fastned to the gallowes, the riding device [slip knot] was almost thrust home, and his foote on my shoulder to presse me downe'.[27] Use of a ladder meant that the drop was longer, and the operation more likely to result in the easier death of a broken neck; more likely still if the prisoner summoned the nerve to throw him or herself bodily off the ladder. Those people who found the resolution to do this were accorded a special place of esteem in the legendary history of crime and hanging. The burglar Richard Hannam died like this, in Smithfield, London, in 1656, and so did the famous highwayman Dick Turpin, hanged at York for horse-stealing in 1739.[28] To make sure that the condemned were thoroughly dead, it was usual for the bodies to be left hanging for half an hour;[29] even so, there are a few reports of executed prisoners who revived after being cut down.[30]

The 'music' that Busino mentions, which he says that the convicts had learned while in jail, will have been the singing of a metrical psalm or similar devotional piece. In George Whetstone's play *Promos and Cassandra*, published in 1578, there is a procession to the gallows of six prisoners, who sing a penitential hymn as they enter and leave the stage.[31] De Saussure, writing in 1726, describes how when the cart has arrived at the gallows, 'The chaplain who accompanies the condemned men . . . makes them pray and sing a few verses of the Psalms.'[32] As for the sprigs of rosemary, these, as Busino notes, were customarily carried by mourners at funerals.[33] The condemned person going to be hanged was effectively taking part in his or her own funeral procession.[34]

Officialdom had firm ideas as to how condemned prisoners ought to behave. The chaplain mentioned by de Saussure was the Ordinary of Newgate, who attended all the executions of prisoners from the jail. It was his business to see that the condemned were properly instructed in what was expected of them. He was a powerful figure in his way, with the right to deny the sacrament to those prisoners who he thought were not sufficiently penitent. One of his jobs was to extract confessions, which were used by the authorities to implicate other criminals. To this end, he told the condemned that unless they confessed to him all their crimes in detail, along with the names of their accomplices, they would not be showing themselves truly repentant, and could not expect to be received into Heaven. The confessions he noted down were of very considerable benefit to the Ordinary himself. Beginning in 1684, the holders of the office supplemented their incomes with the proceeds from a serial publication, the Ordinary of Newgate's *Account*, which appeared just after each hanging day. In it, the Ordinary used his privileged access to the condemned to offer the public a report on their lives of crime, together with their behaviour in their final days and hours, and any disclosures they might have made.[35] These 'Accounts' were extremely popular with the public. Writing in 1694, yet another Swiss visitor, Béat Louis de Muralt, states that they were 'in the Opinion of many People one of the most diverting Things a Man can read in *London*'.[36] Evidently de Muralt and his friends were not reading them in the chastened and reflective spirit that the Ordinary might have preferred.

The Ordinary attended the condemned at the gallows; in the seventeenth century, though not, apparently, in the eighteenth, he sometimes travelled with them in the cart.[37] He was supposed to offer them spiritual admonitions and consolation. He it was, as we have seen, who led them in singing a final psalm, shortly before they were hanged. Some convicts entered very fully into the role of pious penitent. Stephen Gardiner, hanged for housebreaking in 1724, chose to go to his execution wearing nothing but his shroud. It was February at the time, so this really was an additional, wholly self-chosen, torment.[38] Others probably went through the motions of public penitence because they knew it was the part they were expected to play. In 1607, George Wilkins imagined his condemned thief discussing with his woman how he intends to dress on the day of his hanging: 'let me sweete hart . . . have a white sheete tyed about mee, and my black wrought Cap on my head, my nosegay in my hand'.[39] The white sheet was the traditional garb of a penitent.[40] However, as we saw above, there is nothing of either repentance or religion in the street sayings that Wilkins represents his thief as repeating to himself for consolation. The nosegay is a reference to the symbolic sprig of rosemary 'for remembrance', in this case made up into a small bouquet with seasonal flowers. As for the 'black wrought Cap', this will have been a cap of the nightcap variety, a deep-crowned dome-shaped cap normally worn indoors to protect the head from draughts. Such caps were standard wear for the condemned. Just before the hanging, the hangman would pull the cap right down so that it covered most of his victim's face. This was so that the spectators could not see the condemned person's features as they distorted in the throes of strangulation.

Though Busino does not give us the substance of the 'fifty words or so' that he reports as having been addressed to the crowd by one of the condemned men, it was fairly certainly a confession of guilt and penitence, together with a call to the onlookers to take warning from his fate. In 1618, it was already a very old custom for the condemned to make a speech at the gallows. As a slang euphemism for being hanged, the expression 'to preach at Tyburn' is first found more than a hundred years earlier.[41] The phrase is indicative of the kind of tone that the condemned person was expected to adopt. In the gallows-foot scene of Whetstone's play *Promos and Cassandra*, several of the prisoners are represented making such 'sermons'. One 'hackster' (armed thug), who speaks longest, instructs the audience to search their consciences and repent of their faults. He tells them to view the fates of the condemned as an example of what might happen to them. Speaking of his own downward career, he warns them against dicing, and against 'wanton Dames'; these, he says, 'suckt my welth', with the result that he fell into bad company, and 'was intic'd by lawles men on theevish spoyles to feede'. Gentleman prodigal that he is, we are probably supposed to take him for a robber. After his speech, some of the other condemned add their own words of advice to the crowd. One of these is a woman.[42]

The speeches are highly stylised, but so too, undoubtedly, were many of their counterparts in real life. At a later date, many such speeches were printed, some from papers left by the condemned person and some of them as they were noted down by reporters. These range from quite lengthy addresses, which really do amount to miniature sermons,[43] to statements that are as brief as the 'fifty words' mentioned by Busino.[44] Typically, they include an admission that the prisoner is guilty of the offence for which he is being hanged, sometimes a short account of his other crimes, a request to the onlookers to pray for him, an exhortation to avoid following his example, and an account of the sins that he says have brought about his downfall. It was fairly common for robbers to make speeches blaming their career of crime on 'bad women'. In a dialogue between a thief and a whore, written in 1592 by Robert Greene, Nan, the whore, declares, 'I pray you Lawrence when any of you come to your confession at Tyborne, what is your last sermon that you make? That you were brought to that wicked and shamefull ende by following of harlots'.[45] An example of just such a 'sermon', one of many couched in similar terms, is the speech reported to have been delivered by John Dyer, a specialist in footpad robberies, at his execution in 1729. This begins, 'Good People, I desire all young men to take warning by my ignominious death, and to forsake evil company, especially lewd women, who have been the chief cause of my unhappy fate.'[46] Some robbers acknowledged an addiction to drink and gambling. James Turner, a London solicitor and businessman, hanged in 1664 for the burglary (with violence) of one of his business associates, declared that his own descent into crime had begun with his habit of swearing.[47] Turner's execution speech was unusually long; Samuel Pepys, who was present, records in his diary that Turner went on for over an hour, 'delaying the time by long discourses and prayers one after another, in hopes of a reprieve; but none came'. Pepys all this while was standing 'upon the wheel of a Cart, in great pain', in order to get a better view; a privilege for which he had handed over a shilling.[48] Turner, who had deeper pockets than many condemned prisoners, probably paid the executioner to allow him extra time. Usually, the time allocated for speeches, and for saying last farewells to friends and relatives, was about a quarter of an hour.[49] It was not at all unknown for reprieves to arrive at the last minute, or even after it. One person who passed into the folklore of Tyburn was 'half-hanged Smith', sentenced for burglary. Luttrell says that his reprieve came 'after he had hung about 7 minutes, . . . so he was cutt down, and immediately let blood and put into a warm bed, which, with other applications, brought him to himself again with much adoe'. This was in 1705.[50]

Some, perhaps many, of the published gallows-foot speeches were fakes, or at any rate were extensively doctored, either by the Ordinary or a journalist. In Jonathan Swift's satirical poem, 'Clever *Tom Clinch* going to be hanged' (1726), his anti-hero, hearing 'his last Speech' being offered for sale in printed copies by hawkers in the street, 'swore from his Cart, it was all a damn'd Lye'. When the burglar Richard Hannam was executed on 17 June 1656, three quite distinct versions of his execution speech were swiftly brought out by different publishers. The only thing they all have in common is a statement clearing his former landlord and landlady from knowledge of his crimes. It seems as if this detail had been noted down by reporters, or perhaps had become part of the city gossip, while the journalists simply felt free to make the rest up, chiefly out of standard pieties and platitudes. 'Last speeches' sold well enough for it to be worth faking them; and everyone knew the sort of thing they ought to contain.[51]

Nevertheless, many of the extant speeches include the kind of material that suggests at least some input from the condemned person: a desire to exonerate relatives or associates, or to make it quite clear that although he was fully prepared to admit that he had been a robber, and that he had been led astray by 'bad women', he would not want the public to think that he had also been a drunkard or a gambler. Even the most stereotyped speeches may still represent fairly closely the actual words spoken by the dying offender. A satirical description of a 'typical' hanging day, written in 1708, portrays 'a poor shivering Malefactor' delivering his 'last Dying Speech' only after he has been 'admonished' to do so, evidently by the Ordinary. Meanwhile, the 'Spectators' are so familiar with the expected content of such speeches that many of them are able to chant almost in unison with the wretched man as he delivers his ritual self-denunciation: 'I confess I have been a very wicked Offender, and have been guilty of many heinous Sins, especially Whoring, Drunkenness, Sabbath-breaking, and all the rest, which has brought me to this shameful End; therefore pray take Example by me, that you may mend your Lives'.[52] It is hardly surprising that many of the condemned chose at this moment to interpret their personal histories in the terms that they were offered by orthodox Protestant discourse. They had, after all, been taught to believe that their chances of going to Heaven depended upon their doing precisely that. In the execution scene of Whetstone's *Promos and Cassandra*, one of the figures in the background is the Preacher, who, at the end, as the condemned move on, to trudge to the gallows just off stage, is 'whispering some one or other of the Prisoners styll in the eare'.[53]

The verse repentances, mentioned in earlier chapters, bear an obvious relationship to the convention of the 'last dying speech', and so, too, do those humbler productions, the execution ballads. These were hawked by street singers on the occasion of every important execution.[54] The earliest dates from 1576, when a gentleman highway robber called George Mannington was hanged at Cambridge; its publisher entered it in the

Stationers' Register as 'A woefull ballade made by master George Mannyngton an houre before he suffered at Cambridge castell'.[55] The claim that the condemned man had written it himself is found in some later examples; so that in 1598 the title of *Luke Huttons lamentation* continues '*which he wrote the day before his death*', and nearly a hundred years later, *The Penitent Robber* is subtitled 'The Woeful Lamentation of Captain James Whitney, On the Morning of his Execution'.[56] By the date of Whitney's execution, in 1693, the pretence that the ballad was a direct statement from the mouth of the condemned man had long been one of the recognised conventions of the genre. A character study of a ballad-maker, published in 1626, noting the importance of the execution ballad to the cut-price rhymester's economy, comments on how it was expected of him that he should 'make that recantation as if himselfe were the Theame he writes on'.[57] However, there remains the intriguing and apparently unanswerable question: were any of the early pieces really the work of the condemned prisoner who is named in the title?

In Nashe's *The Unfortunate Traveller*, his hero, Jack Wilton, imprisoned and condemned for a murder he has not committed, tells us that before he was taken out to the gallows, he 'had made a Ballad for my Farewell in a readines called *Wiltons wantonnes*'. Similarly, in the comedy *Eastward Ho* (1605), written by Ben Jonson, George Chapman and John Marston, there is a prison scene in which the dishonest apprentice, Quicksilver, awaiting trial on charges of stealing his master's goods, sings the 'Repentance' he has made, 'in imitation of Mannington's, he that was hanged at Cambridge'. It is a knowing parody of the genre, culminating in a final stanza of exhortation: 'Farewell, dear fellow prentices all, / And be you warnèd by my fall'.[58] But Wilton and Quicksilver are invented characters.

I have already mentioned the execution ballad that purports to have been written by Luke Hutton. Hutton, a gentleman robber in Elizabeth's reign, published a verse 'repentance' and *The Black Dog of Newgate*, a poem about his experiences in jail.[59] Both are written in heroic verse, rhyming in sestets, and are replete with mythological references. The impression they leave is of a man who had had a classical education (Hutton had studied at Cambridge) and who deliberately chose a poetic idiom that had some social prestige. The broadside ballad called *Luke Huttons lamentation* is a much more rough and ready piece. In many ways, it is more attractive than *The Black Dog of Newgate*. It has a fine dramatic opening, 'I am a poore prisoner condemned to dye', and part of the refrain depends for effect on an apt use of metonymy: 'Be warned yong wantons, hemp passeth green holly.' Switches made from flexible holly suckers were used to beat children; hemp, of course, is a reference to the noose. Some stanzas are suffused with sardonic humour; so 'Hutton', on his way to be tried in York, recalls:

With clubs and staves I was garded then,
ah woe is me woe is me for my great folly,
I never before had such waiting men
be warned yong wantons, hemp passeth green holly.
If they had ridden before amaine,*
Beshrew me† if I had cald them againe.[60]

But this kind of thing is very different to Hutton's authentic work. The virtues of *Luke Huttons lamentation* are those of good popular poetry. It cannot be doubted that the real author was a professional maker of ballads.

If any of the extant execution ballads were truly written by the condemned person, the most likely is the earliest, the 'repentance' ascribed to Mannington. This begins: 'I Waile in wo, I plunge in pain, / with sorowing sobs, I do complain', and continues in a similar fashion for a further seventy-eight lines. Its uncertain grasp of metre suggests an amateur, while the heavy alliteration, the many deliberate pleonasms and the occasional use of antithesis indicates that the author had probably received a basic education in rhetoric. If it were not, in fact, composed by a youthful gentleman robber in an agony of fear and regret, it is a remarkably good imitation of what such a man might have written. Unlike most later pieces of this kind, it tells us very little about either Mannington or his crimes, preferring to concentrate, in the manner of a 'last dying speech', on expressions of penitence and moral exhortations to the hearers. One of the more interesting stanzas begins with an address to the students of Cambridge, who are imagined as attending the execution in some numbers (as, when the event took place, they probably did). The condemned man speaks of this, or is made to speak of this, as their 'profered curtesie'.[61] Like Clavell's statement that his fellow robbers were 'content' with the knowledge that their deaths would be attended by 'a great audience', it indicates that the presence of onlookers was felt to matter to the dying person; that their attendance at the execution was a generous gesture, and something from which the condemned might draw a certain strength.

---

* *as hard as they could*
† *Curse me*

17

'Dying like a Heroe'

What an English crowd liked to see at an execution were people who faced their deaths steadfastly and with unbroken spirit. In 1587, William Harrison, the Essex parson, claimed that the English 'are found alway to be such as despise death . . . . And this is one cause wherefore our condemned persons do go so cheerfully to their deaths'.[1] The kind of behaviour that was expected is represented in a stanza in *Luke Huttons lamentation*, describing the robber's behaviour after he has been told he must stand trial at York:

> When no intreaty might prevaile,
> . . .
> I calde for beere, for wine and ale,
> . . .
> And when my heart was in wofull case,
> I drunke to my friends with a smiling face.[2]

In a later age, cynics would dismiss all such displays of prison and gallows-foot courage as sustained entirely by heroic quantities of booze. So Gay gives us Macheath, in the condemned hold, knocking back wine and brandy, until he feels able to declare: '*And now I can stand the Test. / And my Comrades shall see, that I die as brave as the Best.*' Soon after, when the liquor is all gone, he turns up the empty bottle and pot to the refrain, '*See, my Courage is out.*' Bernard Mandeville, who felt that English executions were conducted in altogether the wrong sort of atmosphere, noted that along the road to Tyburn, 'the Cart stops . . . three or four, and sometimes half a dozen Times, or more' to allow the prisoners a chance to top up their already considerable alcoholic load. He sneered that otherwise they might sober up, and lose their courage. But the Swiss traveller de Muralt, who had less of a satirical axe to grind, noting the

224

apparently unmoved demeanour of many of the condemned as they stood in the cart, thought that there was more behind it than simple drunkenness. 'The Brandy which they swallow before their setting out, helps to stun them; but all this would have no Effect on any other People, so that the *English* must be influenced by some stronger Reasons to be deduced from their Constitutions.' His conclusion that the English must be made of unusually tough stuff would have met with an eager agreement from his hosts. More interesting, though, is one of his other comments: 'I have been sometimes considering what might be the Source of this Insensibility, which appears to me very extraordinary . . . . I believe, indeed, that the frequent Executions, the great Numbers that suffer together, and the Applauses of the Crowd, may contribute something to it.'[3]

In Augustan England, the condemned were sometimes virtually lionised, as Mandeville describes:

> The whole March [journey to the gallows], with every Incident of it, seems to be contrived on Purpose, to take off and divert the Thoughts of the Condemned from the only Thing that should employ them [that is, thoughts of death and the afterlife]. Thousands are pressing to mind the Looks of them. Their *quondam* Companions, more eager than others, break through all Obstacles to take Leave: And here you may see young Villains, that are proud of being so, (if they knew any of the Malefactors,) tear the Cloaths off their Backs, by squeezing and creeping thro' the Legs of Men and Horses, to shake hands with him; and not to lose, before so much Company, the Reputation there is in having had such a valuable Acquaintance.[4]

As an unnamed hack writer put it, in *Memoirs Of the Right Villanous J[ohn] H[all]* (1708), 'there is a great deal of Glory in dying like a Heroe, and making a Decent Figure in the Cart'.[5] The prisoners well understood the part they had to play to win the crowd's approval. In 1697, a French observer, Henri Misson, reported that 'He that is to be hang'd . . . first takes Care to get himself shav'd, and handsomely drest, either in Mourning or in the Dress of a Bridegroom'.[6] To dress well was, first and foremost, to show pride and an uncrushed spirit. As we see, the heroes of the death cart in the late seventeenth century were offered a choice of acceptable styles: mourner or bridegroom.

There is a certain grim appropriateness in a condemned prisoner's going to his hanging dressed like a mourner. A documented example is found in 1656, when a well-known burglar, Richard Hannam, went to his execution in the kind of clothes that a comfortably-off man of the middling sort would have worn to attend a funeral: 'a stuffe suit laced in the seames with a small silver lace, a most pure rough Hat, a black Cloak with things sutable thereto; all which upon the Ladder he bequeathed to the Hangman'.[7] That last bit was Hannam's little joke; the clothes which prisoners wore to their executions had long been recognised as the hangman's perquisites.[8] Hannam carried the necessary cap in his pocket, and gave it to the hangman to pull over his head at the very last moment; the hangman tied it on with the mourning band that he took from Hannam's hat.[9]

Weddings and funerals are often thought of as symbolic opposites; for a man to dress himself for execution as if he were going to his wedding appears to involve a deliberate incongruity. However, Misson is not the only witness to this custom. The author of *Memoirs Of the Right Villanous J[ohn] H[all]*, describing the usual appearance of the condemned men, comments, 'one would take 'em for Bridegrooms going to Espouse their Old Mrs. *Tyburn*, being as Spruce as a Powder'd Wig, a *Holland* Shirt, clean Gloves, and a Nosegay, can make 'em'. In 1728, Defoe wrote: 'the Criminals go to Execution as neat and trim, as if they were going to a Wedding'. Condemned women (of whom there were far fewer) were also known to dress up for the occasion; Misson says, 'Sometimes the Girls dress in White, with great Silk Scarves, and carry Baskets full of Flowers and Oranges, scattering these Favours all the Way they go'.[10]

In Shakespeare's *Measure for Measure* (1604), Claudio, in the condemned cell, trying to 'fetch' sufficient 'resolution' to face his execution boldly, cries out,

> If I must die,
> I will encounter darkness as a bride
> And hug it in mine arms.[11]

His sister Isabella praises him for an utterance that is worthy of his father's son; of a gentleman, that is. When a condemned man dressed as a bridegroom he dramatised Claudio's metaphor. The symbolism has something in it of Stoic and Christian disregard for life, but more of Christian mystical ecstasy at the prospect of a union after death, either of the soul with God, or of the soul with the redeemed and perfected body.[12] On a mundane level, it indicates a determination by the powerless to retrieve some power by behaving as though inevitable death is a matter of choice and celebration.

From the late seventeenth century onwards, there are many references to condemned persons going to their executions dressed in white, or wearing something white about them. Sometimes this was meant to signify innocence;[13] but the custom is often mentioned in contexts where this interpretation doesn't make sense. Jonathan Swift's impenitent thief, 'Tom

Clinch', goes to his hanging resplendent in a white waistcoat, breeches and stockings. Peter Linebaugh, who has documented a number of such references, associates the wearing of white with wedding garments, and it is true that white was a bridal colour, for men as well as women. Linebaugh also connects the practice with the eighteenth-century tradition of wearing white to the funeral of a young virgin or childless married woman.[14] Though he does not say so, the same custom was sometimes observed at the funerals of young unmarried men.[15] Moreover, the condemned girls who, as Misson tells us, scattered flowers as they went were likewise following a custom that was used both at weddings and at virgin burials.[16] On this interpretation, the condemned feature, once again, as the mourners at their own funerals, funerals marked with a special sign of pity at a death which had come untimely. But white was a colour with many symbolic meanings. It was the colour in which the dead were buried, and the convict on his or her way to execution was already one of the living dead.[17] White is also the colour repeatedly mentioned in the Book of Revelation as worn in Heaven by the redeemed servants of the Lamb – and by his Bride, the Church.[18] However, it strains belief to imagine that this kind of symbolic and religious thinking really meant much to the average early modern robber or burglar. In the end, it was the current fashion that counted most, and the importance of making the best possible show. As Misson, speaking of a typical condemned man, drily observes: 'When his Suit of Cloaths, or Night-gown, his Gloves, Hat, Perriwig, Nosegay, Coffin, Flannel-Dress for his Corps, and all those things are bought and prepar'd, the main Point is taken care of, his Mind is at Peace, and then he thinks of his Conscience.'[19]

Those of the condemned who were able to endure execution with an outward appearance of coolness were commended for their courage by the people who watched or who heard about it afterwards.[20] In 1666, one Fred Turville, a gentleman of sorts, and like Richard Hals a family connection of the Verneys, was hanged for burglary at Hertford. One of his cousins wrote to assure Sir Ralph Verney that at least Turville had made a decent end: 'he died as we are informed a very good christian, with a most undanted corage showd nothing of conserne at all, but told all thouse persons that where with hime at the place, which where divers gentlemen of great quallity, that he did not fear to die'.[21] De Muralt, writing in the mid-1690s, observed: 'Those that die merrily, or that don't at least shew any great Fear of Death, are said to die like Gentlemen'.[22] A hundred years earlier, Falstaff, posturing for effect, exclaims, 'If I become not a cart as well as another man, a plague on my bringing up!'[23] The gallows is the final test of the gentleman robber's courage, and he proves his quality by his resolute bearing in the cart. Those who, without his breeding, still face their deaths with boldness are given the ultimate accolade: they have behaved like gentlemen.

De Muralt, as we have seen, decided that it was this kind of tribute from the crowd that helped to inspire such men to their remarkable displays of indifference. Mandeville stressed the effects of alcohol, but he also thought that a powerful influence was the fear of being mocked by the crowd as a coward. He drew attention, also, to the effects of example; a point that was made incisively by Henry Fielding in 1751: 'The Thief who is hanged to Day hath learnt his Intrepidity from the Example of his hanged Predecessors, as others are now taught to despise Death, and to bear it hereafter with Boldness from what they see to Day.'[24] It is likely that all these factors were operative to some degree, but Mandeville probably exaggerates the importance of alcohol, which, after all, might just as easily have resulted in a maudlin penitence as in the kind of bravado that Mandeville finds so deplorable. The hardened tough on his way to execution had usually seen many others of his kind travel the same journey. Unless his offence was a loathsome one, he is likely to have experienced a sense that the crowd was on his side, willing him to conduct himself bravely: to prove himself gentleman-like, a superior being, and to uphold the honour of the English in front of foreign travellers.

A too impassive demeanour was not entirely approved of, at least by respectable, God-fearing people. When Sir John Reresby attended the execution of Captain Vratz for murder, in 1682, he observed: 'The captain died without any the least symptom of fear . . . and seeing me in my coach as he passed by in the cart, he made a bow to me with the most steady countenance, as he did to several of the spectators he knew, before he was turned off; in short, his whole carriage . . . savoured much of gallantry, but not at all of religion.'[25] Vratz, of course, was not an Englishman. At Fred Turville's execution, his 'undanted corage' was not felt to be blemished, but rather enhanced by a public display of his religious faith. Turville told the onlookers 'that he would not troble them with a formal speech only desired there prayers, and after he hade read some prayers which he hade in wrighting he weept, and made noe confession there, he told them he hade don that to God'.[26]

Sometimes the condemned engaged in behaviour that respectable people deplored as unseemly. In 1598, John Chamberlain, man about town and assiduous correspondent, reported, in a tone that falls somewhere between amusement and scandal, that 'certain mad knaves . . . tooke Tabacco all the way to Tiborn as they went to hanging'.[27] When Samuel Richardson set out to describe a typical execution, in 1741, he wrote that two of the prisoners wore expressions of 'Horror and Despair', but three others behaved in ways that he holds up for disapproval: 'They swore, laugh'd, and talk'd obscenely', and wished good luck to their thievish friends, who had come to watch them hang, 'with as much Assurance as if their Employment had been the most lawful'.[28] Earlier in the same century, Jonathan Swift satirised such conduct in his poem about 'clever *Tom Clinch*', who 'hung like a Hero'. Swift's robber makes jokes, kicks the hangman, refuses to pray or sing a psalm, and instead of a last confession, makes a speech of encouragement to his thievish associates.[29] Luttrell records a case of similar behaviour that was reported as a news item in 1694: a prisoner 'kickt the ordinary out of the cart at Tyburn, and pulled off his shoes, sayeing, hee'd contradict the old proverb, and not dye in them'. Evidently this was meant for a joke; 'to die in one's shoes' was to be hanged.[30]

Gallows humour had a long history, and not an entirely disreputable one. Sir Thomas More had made several quips at his execution for treason in 1535; though it is true that the chronicler Edward Hall took these as an occasion to sneer at him as not sufficiently serious-minded.[31] In William Cavendish's *Pleasante and merrye Humor off a Roge*, a series of dramatic scenes written in the later 1650s, the Rogue is represented exchanging jokes and insults with the crowd as he passes on his way to the gallows, and even as he is standing on the ladder. The piece is, of course, a comedy, but it is clear from other sources that the Rogue's behaviour is not untypical.[32] De Muralt refers to condemned men who 'die like . . . Fools, for having no other View than to divert the Crowd'. He tells a story that was circulating in 1690s London:

One of these Wretches, being come to the Place of Execution, desir'd to speak to some of his Neighbours that he happen'd to see in the Throng. They came to him, and then he told them, that he was unwilling to die without asking their Forgiveness for a great Injury he had done them. They answer'd, that they forgave him heartily, but that they could not imagine what it could be. The Thief seem'd to be in much haste to tell it, and at last own'd that he had to do with their Wives, which had troubled him very much.[33]

The thief's malicious disclosure – or lie, most likely – will have gained in destructive power from the presumption that a confession at the gallows must be a true one, since a person who was facing immediate death was almost bound to speak the truth for the sake of his or her soul.

By comparison with this story, the final prank attributed to Gamaliel Ratsey seems pretty harmless. I described in Chapter Nine how he is reported to have made the sheriff and the onlookers hang about in the rain while he pretended that he was about to confess to some hitherto undisclosed crimes. If anything like this really happened, it is likely that Ratsey was trying to prolong his life in the hopes of a last-minute reprieve.

There is no condemnation of his clownish behaviour in the pamphlet that describes it, *Ratseis Ghost*, which given the nature of that publication is not particularly surprising. Instead, the author comments that Ratsey died as he had lived, 'carelesse, and resolv'd, yet verie patient for his sinnes'.[34] Carefree, even to the point of cracking jokes; bearing himself resolutely; and at the same time showing due penitence. This was how the gentleman robber was supposed to face the gallows.

How did it feel to stand in the crowd at a hanging? When Pepys watched James Turner die, he noted in his diary, 'A comely-looked man he was, and kept his countenance to the end – I was sorry to see him.' Pepys had known Turner personally, and disliked him; after Turner's arrest he wrote that he was 'a mad, swearing, confident fellow', and 'a known rogue'.[35] However, to see him hanged was a different matter. It would hardly be surprising if Pepys, an ambitious social climber from a background in trade, felt a certain sympathy, even an identification with the flashy London merchant whose own ambitions had brought him to such a desperate end. What he expresses, though, is something slightly different: respect for Turner's exemplary calmness – he 'kept his countenance' – pity for his fate, and mixed up with all this, a sense that the victim was a handsome man, which somehow added to the pity. In 1676, Henry Savile, in a letter to his friend, the Earl of Rochester, commented sarcastically on how an acquaintance of theirs, 'being dead is pittyed as a man of parts, I suppose as *all who are hanged are called proper men*' (my italics).[36] The saying was proverbial, though perhaps no less true for being so. In 1613, the satirist George Wither sneered that for a robber or pirate to be hanged at Tyburn was not the disgrace that it ought to be: 'No, 'tis their credit, for the people then, / Wil say, *'tis pitty, they were proper men.*' And a couple of years later, another satirist scornfully observed, 'every fellow with an entire doublet is called *propper man* when hee rides to Tiburne'.[37] A proper man is a 'real' man; also, a handsome, well-made man. Centuries before Wither's time, onlookers at hangings were being credited with much the same sentiments. The Dominican preacher John de Bromyard, writing in the late 1320s, observes: 'Those who see a handsome man being led to be hanged feel pity for him, and say, "Alas, that a person so handsome must die in this way." '[38] Bromyard has no more respect for this easy sympathy than Wither has. Taken in context, what becomes most noticeable about Pepys's response to Turner's hanging is how utterly commonplace it was, how much it appears like a conventional effect of the situation and the feelings that were culturally attached to it.

Two of the most extraordinary passages of *The Beggar's Opera* are those in which Gay, with his satirist's eye, exposes to view the element of voyeuristic lust that is lurking here not far below the surface. First, Mrs Peachum:

> If any Wench *Venus*'s Girdle wear,
> Though she be never so ugly;
> Lillys and Roses will quickly appear,
> And her Face look wond'rous smuggly.
> Beneath the left Ear so fit but a Cord,
> (A Rope so charming a Zone is!)
> The Youth in his Cart hath the Air of a Lord,
> And we cry, There dies an *Adonis!*

This is desire deliciously complicated by the fact that the body of the desired is both completely inaccessible and completely vulnerable, at the mercy of the executioner, and so, by proxy, of the watching crowd. Mrs Peachum ascribes such responses to women: it is women, she says, who 'think every Man handsome who is going to the Camp or the Gallows'.[39] In Cavendish's *Pleasante and merrye Humor off a Roge*, it is a woman who, while the Rogue is on his way to execution, says, 'mee-thinkes nowe, hee Is a verye Proper man' and a man who replies contemptuously, 'Whye so theye are all thatt are Hangde'.[40] And when Swift's Tom Clinch passed by in his finery, it was the servant maids who said, 'lack-a-day! he's a proper young Man'.[41] These instances are all from works of the imagination. It is possible that they simply bear witness to the agreement of male authors to project exclusively on to women the emotions and behaviour that they find disturbing. Certainly, there were plenty of men in the execution crowds of the seventeenth and eighteenth centuries, and Pepys is a witness to the fact that men, too, could feel a complicated mixture of pity, admiration and sharp physical awareness when they viewed a condemned man in his final moments. On the other hand, there may be a certain amount of truth in the notion that women were particularly likely to find themselves stirred by the execution of a vital-looking male. Writing in the *London Magazine* in 1783, James Boswell, who attended many executions, claimed that it was observable on such occasions that 'the greatest proportion of the spectators is composed of women'.[42]

More complex than the emotions expressed by Mrs Peachum are those of Polly immediately after she has overheard her parents plotting Macheath's betrayal. Polly is distressed, of course; but she slides very quickly into a pleasantly painful daydream in which she witnesses her lover's journey to Tyburn gallows:

> Methinks I see him already in the Cart, sweeter and more lovely than the Nosegay in his Hand! – I hear the Crowd extolling his Resolution

and Intrepidity! – What Vollies of Sighs are sent from the Windows of *Holborn*, that so comely a Youth should be brought to disgrace! – I see him at the Tree! The whole Circle are in Tears! – even Butchers weep! – *Jack Ketch** himself hesitates to perform his Duty, and would be glad to lose his Fee, by a Reprieve.[43]

Macheath in the cart is a sex object made more desirable by the fact that he is the object of the frustrated desire of others, the watchers 'from the Windows of *Holborn*'; and the imagined tears of the crowd propel Polly towards a titillating emotional release.

It is easy enough, nowadays, to recognise the elements of perverse sexuality in the responses of many of those who were drawn to attend executions. What may be harder to appreciate is the way in which a spectacle that seems to us to be merely one of cruelty was redeemed for many people by the fact that it was also, ideally, an exemplary display of courage. There are close parallels with the brutal sports of the early modern period, bear-baiting, bull-baiting and above all cock-fighting. Where we see cruelty, their aficionados saw, first and foremost, an admirable courage: the resolution of the dog that will not let go its grip and the unquenchable fighting spirit of the cock that refuses to turn and flee. A man, they thought, could learn to be valiant from regularly watching such scenes.

A fighting cock was a 'cock of the game', as opposed to a 'dunghill cock', a cowardly cock, so called in contempt as only fit for barnyards. Cock fanciers deliberately bred game-cocks for ferocity and persistence, what in the eighteenth century they called 'hardness'.[44] The same language might be used of the condemned prisoner who died without showing fear. 'God Damn, says one Rogue to another, *Jack* Such-a-one made a clever Figure when he went to *Tyburn* the other Day, and died bravely, hard, like a Cock': so reports Defoe in 1728.[45] Later in the century the expression 'to die game' is recorded, meaning 'to suffer at the gallows without shewing any signs of fear or repentance'. Its opposite was 'to die dunghill'.[46] Attitudes had changed since the Restoration period, when, as in Fred Turville's case, a show of public penitence was certainly not felt to call in question the quality of the condemned man's courage. What has not changed is the sense that a man's execution is the ultimate test of his resolve, nor that the way in which he faces it is an index of the breed he springs from: whether he comes from an old family (as very few robbers did by then), or is simply proud to call himself an Englishman.

*

---

* the hangman

Summing up the English attitude to execution, the Frenchman Misson observed: 'The *English* are People that laugh at the Delicacy of other Nations, who make it such a mighty Matter to be hang'd; their extraordinary Courage looks upon it as a Trifle, and they also make a Jest of the pretended Dishonour that, in the Opinion of others, falls upon their Kindred.' Misson was not alone among visitors from abroad in coming to the conclusion that among the English, to die a criminal's death was no dishonour. De Muralt says that executions were 'scarcely look'd upon to be infamous', and de Saussure expresses a similar view, though he attributes such attitudes specifically to the lower classes.[47] De Saussure may, perhaps, be right in what he says, though it depends what section of society he had in mind. But educated English people, at any rate, are never found voicing the opinion that death on the gallows was no disgrace; rather the contrary. In *The History of Tom Jones* (1749), Fielding's hero expresses his pity for highwaymen who are driven 'by unavoidable Distress' to what he calls 'such illegal Courses, as generally bring them to a shameful Death'.[48] Sir Ralph Verney's relative, Fred Turville, while professing himself unafraid to die, acknowledged that 'the manner of his death trobled hime'. In this, as in other things that he said, he sounds remarkably like Gamaliel Ratsey, who is reported as saying at the gallows, 'I sorrow not to dye, but I grieve at the manner of my death.' Ratsey, like Turville, goes on to express his penitence for his crimes.[49] Clearly, this little script, from beginning to end, was all part of the gallows-foot etiquette. But that doesn't detract from the point at issue.

In his *Recantation*, John Clavell reminds his former comrades that hanging is a death that not only brings 'shame' on the sufferer, but 'scandall' to his innocent family.[50] He is thinking not only of public opinion, but of the fact that a gentleman who was found guilty of a serious offence such as robbery incurred what the lawyers called 'corruption of blood': not only he but his children lost their gentle status, and also any rights of inheritance. A pardon might put things partly right, though any children living at the time of his conviction would still remain under certain legal disabilities. If he were hanged, of course, the 'corruption of blood' would continue. However much he faced his death 'like a gentleman', in the eyes of the law he would no longer be one.[51] For a man of old family, this was a serious matter.

To conclude: for most people in early modern England, death on the gallows always carried some stigma. But the men who faced hanging with boldness, and even managed to cut something of a dash, were commonly regarded with admiration, and although their disgrace was acknowledged, so, too, was their exemplary pride and courage.

18

'Give me a highwayman': the Age of Nostalgia

The last highwayman to achieve popular notoriety was Jerry Abershaw. He operated chiefly on Putney Heath and Wimbledon Common, and was hanged in 1795, after shooting a police officer in the course of his arrest.[1] By that point, the incidence of robbery on the highway was already in sharp decline. Twenty years later, the mounted robber had almost completely vanished from the roads around the capital. Various theories have been put forward to explain his disappearance. The policing of London was gradually becoming professionalised, and in 1805 a mounted body of police was established for night-time patrolling in the districts around the city. Meanwhile, an increased use of banknotes, more traceable than gold coins, was making it harder for the robber to profit from his loot. However, the historical criminologist J. J. Tobias believes that the biggest problem for the mounted robber was the extension of the system of turnpikes, or gated toll-roads, which made it more difficult for him to move around unnoticed. Even when the turnpike-men were open to bribery (and it was widely believed that many were), every payment of this kind reduced the highwayman's takings, without necessarily making him safe from betrayal. J. M. Beattie takes note of another factor: changes in the London environment. After 1780, the population of London rose steeply, and the great open spaces near the heart of the city began to be heavily built up. Many of the highwayman's favourite haunts began to shrink very fast, buried under acres of mortar and brick.[2]

The last mounted highway robbery is said to have taken place in 1831.[3] By that time, highwaymen were so little feared by the public that they were becoming objects of nostalgia. Already, in 1830, Edward Lytton Bulwer had published his novel *Paul Clifford*, whose eponymous hero is characterised as 'one of those accomplished and elegant highwaymen of whom we yet read wonders, and by whom it would have been delightful to have been robbed'.[4] Elsewhere, Bulwer refers to 'the fascination of that

234

lawless life' – the life of the 'gentlemen highwaymen'.[5] It is plain that he himself felt that fascination strongly.

Paul Clifford is the epitome of the heroic highwayman: handsome, generous, brave and highly skilled at managing a horse. He conforms to more or less every trait that idealism ever ascribed to the noble robber. He refuses to commit violence, much less to kill, and more than once intervenes to keep his associates from such brutalities. He despises all crimes of stealth and deception. His companions sometimes swindle, pick pockets or break into houses: not so Paul. The 'gallant' and 'heroic' crimes of the robber on the highway are the only ones he will commit.[6] Like Robin Hood, he robs only the rich; like Ratsey and Hind, he is fond of a joke, and the reader is assured that his robberies were always far more prankish than alarming. Like the dashing Claude Du Vall, he is adored by all the ladies.[7] He has an underground hideout, modelled on one that was used by Dick Turpin, though Paul's is much bigger and better, and plainly owes more than a little to the cave of the Forty Thieves in the *Arabian Nights' Entertainments*.[8]

Bulwer's novel is supposed to be set in the 1780s, but the historical colouring is very slight. Even the criminal argot spoken by Paul and his associates is, anachronistically, mainly that which was current when Bulwer was writing. In *Paul Clifford*, the highwayman has become a figment of romantic fantasy, floating free of historical period or specific social environment. The liveliest writing in the book occurs when Bulwer sets his highwaymen in action. The various hold-ups are well done; more stirring still is the incident in the cave where the robbers are betrayed to the Bow Street Runners, and the subsequent episode, where Paul engineers the rescue of his friends at the cost of his own capture. If he had been so content, Bulwer might have been a capable exponent of the adventure story. He might have combined such a tale with a serviceable love romance. When Paul attempts to leave the robber's life by a long-traditional route, seeking to make his fortune by winning the hand of an heiress, he finds himself falling in love with the beautiful and sweet-natured Lucy Brandon. As a result, his heart, never a very hard one, is softened, and he starts to experience a moral reformation. In the best traditions of the heroic robber, he makes plans to enlist as a soldier, in a foreign army, where he hopes, by proving his courage, to restore his honour. However, he is shot down and arrested before he can put this into practice.

Regrettably, Bulwer was not content to stick to writing light fiction. He fancied himself as a satirist and critic of society. Taking a hint from Gay and Fielding, he introduces an element of burlesque, and attempts to satirise the leading politicians of his own time under the guise of members of a robber gang. But his satire is clumsy and forced; it distracts from his narrative and soon becomes tedious.[9]

Another means by which he attempts to load his book with some intellectual weight is by offering Paul's career as a model of the way in which the penal system of his own time was, as he saw it, supremely calculated to corrupt the poor and powerless folk who found themselves trapped in its machinery. This is how Paul himself represents his life, in the speech he makes at his trial.[10] He claims that what turned him to a criminal career was an incident that happened when as a youth he was sent to the house of correction for a crime he did not commit. Unfortunately for the logic of the book as a whole, this is mostly humbug, though neither Paul nor Bulwer ever notice. Granted, Paul has grown up as a nameless orphan, but Bulwer has given him an indulgent foster-mother, the landlady of a public house, who has even paid for him to have a classical education. It is pride that sends him away from her, and pride that keeps him from asking her help after he has escaped from the house of correction. The truth is that Paul from his earliest years is just as fascinated as Bulwer with the idealised highwayman of tradition. As a boy, we are shown him avidly devouring a chapbook account of Dick Turpin, '*the great* highwayman', as he emphatically calls him.[11] Before he is sent to the house of correction, he has already been drawn to the company of the 'gentlemen highwaymen', with their free-spending ways and swaggering panache. No doubt Bulwer's outrage at injustice was genuinely felt. However, if his heart is in it, his thoughts are somewhere else: cantering over a moonlit common, with pistols and a mask.

All the same, he makes Paul the mouthpiece for some splendid rhetoric. In the speech he makes at his trial, and earlier, in conversation with his friend and fellow robber Tomlinson, Paul denounces the injustice of a society in which laws are invoked relentlessly against the poor, punish the robber, but protect the frauds and hypocrisy of tradesmen and lawyers, who are allowed to prey upon the public with impunity. These themes, of course, are old; what is relatively new here, and sharply political, is the conviction with which Paul declares himself to 'acknowledge no allegiance to society' and its laws. Instead, he declares himself its enemy: 'Between us are the conditions of war.'[12] He is echoing quite closely the words of another fictional robber, the generous and humane Mr Raymond, who features in an episode of the novel *Caleb Williams* (1794), by the radical thinker William Godwin. Raymond proclaims: 'We, who are thieves without a licence, are at open war with another set of men, who are thieves according to law.' Though Godwin's hero, Caleb, soon rejects the robbers' way of life as destructive of those who follow it, as well as 'incompatible with the general welfare', the robbers, and especially the articulate idealist Raymond, are viewed with considerable sympathy.[13] Raymond's declaration resonates in a novel in which the image of an unjust, hostile and punitive society is always before the reader. However, in Bulwer's *Paul Clifford* the social vision is far less clearly focused.

Paul and his closest associates are 'gentlemen highwaymen'; this is agreed by all, from the ostler of the London inn where they keep their horses to the self-regarding peer Lord Mauleverer. As a mounted robber, the orphan brought up in a sleazy public house is transformed into a figure of authority and style, able to hold his own in fashionable society as confidently as he does in the underworld. Bulwer is vague about how this unlikely metamorphosis takes place. He relies on evoking the conventional mystique of the 'gentlemen of the road', and the equally conventional, and far older, mystique of gentle birth. For nameless Paul is the legitimate son of a man of ancient family, and the 'inborn air of gentility' that his friend Tomlinson detects in him reflects his true, lost identity.[14]

The flaw in society that ruins the life of Caleb Williams is the ability of the gentry to exercise an arbitrary power over others. By contrast, for all Bulwer's rhetoric about injustice, he shows little sense of it as an effect of specific power relations. As for his take on gentility, this is shallow and romantic. Paul's gentle blood is the secret grace that permits him to transcend his surroundings. Moreover, in the end, it is gentry privilege and wealth that rescue him from the consequences of his actions. The judge who tries him for robbery, Sir William Brandon, discovers after the trial that Paul is his son by a secret marriage. Feeling that the relationship disgraces him, he declines to acknowledge it, but he uses his position to recommend Paul for mercy, for transportation rather than the gallows. Sir William is also Lucy's uncle, and when he dies, of shattered pride, she inherits his considerable fortune. Meanwhile, Paul, transported to Australia, quickly escapes. The end of the novel sees him in America, making his way through honest effort and married to the faithful Lucy. Just as his father's influence has saved him from execution, so his money, Paul's rightful inheritance, put at his disposal by his marriage to Lucy, allows him to retrieve his honour by making restitution to his victims.

Paul Clifford was an immediate success with the public.[15] The vein of highwayman romance that it opened up was speedily exploited by William Harrison Ainsworth in *Rookwood* (1834). Ainsworth's avowed intention in this book was to imitate the Gothic novels of Ann Radcliffe, while transferring the setting from Italy to England: 'substituting,' as Ainsworth explains, 'an old English squire, an old English manorial residence, and an old English highwayman, for the Italian marchese, the castle, and the brigand of the great mistress of Romance'.[16] The 'old English highwayman' he chose to suit his purpose was the famous Dick Turpin, the object of Paul Clifford's boyish admiration. At the time *Rookwood* was published,

Turpin had been dead for nearly a hundred years; but he had remained a potent hero of oral tradition, as well as of popular ballads and chapbooks.

When Turpin first features in Ainsworth's novel, he is disguised as the hard-riding, convivial Jack Palmer, who mixes unquestioned with the Yorkshire gentry on the strength of his prowess at hunting. However, Ainsworth soon nudges the reader's attention by giving the supposed Jack Palmer a jocular speech, in which he sets out to 'prove' to his drinking companions the proposition 'that a highwayman is a gentleman'. 'A real highwayman', he says, 'would consider himself disgraced, if he did not conduct himself in every way like a gentleman'. He develops his point by claiming that, like the 'fine gentleman', the highwayman is a man of the world. He does what he likes; everyone has heard of him; he has money at command; and all the women adore him. Highwaymen of this kind are unique to England, and the country ought to be proud of them. The encomium culminates in a fervent hope – another wink from Ainsworth to the reader – that 'The day will never come' when the mounted robber has disappeared and only the footpad remains.[17]

Despite his eloquent praise of the gentlemanly qualities of the highwayman, Ainsworth's robber is more coarse-grained than Bulwer's Paul Clifford. In the best traditions of the ideal knight of the road, he is loath to hurt or kill anyone – but he reserves the right to do so in self-defence, and in the course of the book he kills twice, shooting one of his associates by accident, in the heat of an arrest, and another when the man has turned traitor. He prides himself on his civility, but his manners are hearty rather than polished. Unlike Paul Clifford, he sees no shame in a little swindling, and even carries a set of false dice. Nor does he shrink from burglary. Altogether, considered as a professional criminal, he is a rather more convincing creation than Bulwer's hero.

Nevertheless, Dick shows many of the heroic robber's traditional virtues. He is extremely generous, keeps his word and gives fair play to his enemies. Ainsworth tells us that he is chivalrous to women, though this does not keep him from trying to force a kiss from an unwilling girl in a hold-up. However, his courage and horsemanship are beyond all criticism, and even his enemy, Major Mowbray, publicly acknowledges his admiration for him.

Even more than Bulwer, Ainsworth stresses his highwayman's abilities as a horseman. Horsemanship is important in both these books as the quality that distinguishes the highwayman from the footpad – and marks out the romantic robber of the past from the mugger in the night-time streets. Once, the robber had been accorded prestige primarily because his crimes were felt to show courage. But during the later eighteenth century, attitudes had changed a great deal. The public had become far less tolerant of private violence. The perspectives of the later Middle Ages were coming to feel very alien.[18]

What survived for literary exploitation was a vague sense that with the disappearance of the mounted robber, something had been lost that was very special, in some way admirable – a specialness that had a lot to do with reckless gallops on superb horseflesh. In *Rookwood*, Dick Turpin's horse, Black Bess, is a character in her own right, and the only convincing love scene in the book is the very brief interlude where the mare responds affectionately to the highwayman's approach and caresses. Black Bess is Dick's special bit of grace, his magical talisman. Riding Black Bess, no one can catch him, and so swiftly does he move from place to place that she even provides her master with apparent alibis for his robberies.[19]

But *Rookwood* is a Gothic romance. Its dominant strain is melodrama and its groundnote is the gruesome. The plot is a matter of ancient curses and old and new betrayals. Its machinery proceeds by way of poisoned locks of hair and booby-trapped sepulchres, and the incidental action includes death omens and a fatal thunderbolt. In such a milieu, the highwayman, fond of a drink and a rousing song, often seems out of place. However, in the end, even he cannot escape the prevailing impulse towards doom. His love for his horse ends in tragedy, when he rides her to death in an epic chase from London to York. The legend of Dick Turpin's ride to York was already in circulation when Ainsworth took it up. There is no truth in it. It was foisted on Turpin in a chapbook, as late as 1808: one of the recurring motifs of the highwaymen tales, like the marvellously fast horse.[20] Ainsworth added to it the name of the horse, which afterwards passed into tradition, Dick's sentimental affection for her, and the sad ending, when Bess founders and dies on the outskirts of York.[21] (In earlier versions of the tale, the horse survives the journey.) In case we should miss the parallel, Dick himself points out that he is treating his beloved horse, his surrogate sweetheart, just as Luke Rookwood, the novel's erratic anti-hero, has behaved to his gypsy mistress, whom he has driven to take poison.[22] Once Bess is dead, Dick has lost his luck, and we are not surprised in the last chapter to read of his execution. Ainsworth gives us, though briefly, the scaffold scene that Bulwer had evaded. Dick, we are told, dies well, confronting the ultimate test of a highwayman's nerve with firmness and resolution, living up to his own pronouncement, expressed at an earlier point in the book, that 'the gallows .... never yet alarmed a brave man'.[23]

Although he is supposedly a subordinate character, the supporter and occasional henchman of the equivocal Luke Rookwood, Turpin runs away with Ainsworth's novel. He dominates nearly all the scenes in which he features, and his adventures are given much more space than their relevance to the plot would warrant. Ainsworth was aware of this. In his final paragraph, he half apologises for it, half justifies it, observing frankly: 'We have had a singular delight in recounting his feats, and hair-breadth escapes; and if the reader derives only half so much pleasure from the perusal of his adventures as we have had in narrating them, our satisfaction will be complete.' In the same passage, he anticipates another criticism: that he has portrayed his highway robber from 'too favourable a point of view'. Ainsworth more than half expects to be accused of glorifying crime; and he has very little to offer by way of defence. Instead, he effectively repeats himself, falling back on a hope, expressed somewhat obliquely, that 'the benevolent reader' will content himself with appreciating his author's efforts to entertain.[24]

Ainsworth's anxieties were not immediately justified. *Rookwood* became a best-seller and its author a celebrity.[25] At the same time, the popular image of Dick Turpin was immensely enhanced. It ought to be noted that the only qualities that the historical Turpin can be shown to have shared with Ainsworth's character were his defiant bearing at the gallows and his ability to evade arrest for a relatively long time. The contemporaneous records of his crimes in newspapers and trial transcripts reveal him as a particularly vicious bully, a member of a gang who specialised in forcing their way into houses and putting their victims in fear in their own homes. He only turned to robbery on the highway after most of his associates had been captured.[26] But since the publication of *Rookwood*, he has become far and away the most famous of all the English highwaymen, remembered, much as he is depicted by Ainsworth, for his daring, his generosity, and his swift black horse.[27] It was not through sales of *Rookwood* alone that Ainsworth's conception of Turpin spread and took hold. There were dramatised versions of the novel; there was even at least one text for toy theatre; and from the 1840s until the early years of the twentieth century there were many penny serials, that, inspired by *Rookwood*, took Turpin for their hero.[28] Black Bess and the ride to York were the subject of at least two Victorian street ballads;[29] and for many years visitors to York racecourse were shown the exact spot where Turpin's mare was supposed to have collapsed and died.[30]

An early imitator of *Paul Clifford* and *Rookwood* was the historical romance writer G. P. R. James. In 1838, he published *The Robber*, set (very loosely) in the Restoration period. James's sole claim to originality was to supply his robber chief with a temperament modelled on the heroes of Byron's poetry: he is rebellious, moody and violent, quite lacking in Paul Clifford's good-natured sociability or Turpin's conviviality. In other respects, he fits the stereotype well enough: he dresses very stylishly, is generous, honourable, and demonstrates the obligatory feats of horseman-ship.[31]

Five years after *Rookwood*, in 1839, Ainsworth returned to the robber theme with *Jack Sheppard*. The hero of the book is the eighteenth-century housebreaker of that name, whose fame rests mainly on his daring and skilful escapes from various London jails. In 1724, over a period of about eight months, he successfully escaped four times. Two of his escapes were made from Newgate, the capital's chief criminal prison; on the second of these occasions, he broke his way out in spite of the fact that he was not only loaded with irons but had been chained to the floor of his cell. His exploits made him a popular hero; however, his ingenuity as an escaper was not equalled by any equivalent skill at evading capture. After his final break-out, on 15 October, he was at liberty for just over a fortnight. On the last day of the month, he was found in a London gin shop, helplessly drunk, and returned to Newgate. Once back in custody, he was massively fettered and carefully watched. He was hanged for burglary on 16 November, in front of a vast crowd of spectators.[32]

Jack Sheppard is a more satisfactory book than *Rookwood*. Ainsworth abandons the lugubrious trappings of Gothic romance, and he sticks a good deal closer to the documented facts of his robber's career. The great set-piece action episode, equivalent to Turpin's ride to York, is provided by Sheppard's second escape from Newgate, which Ainsworth describes with a wealth of detail drawn from accounts that were published at the time. *Jack Sheppard* was an enormous success, bigger even than *Rookwood*. It was serialised in *Bentley's Miscellany*, alongside *Oliver Twist*, and published in three-volume form in October 1839, while the serial still had several months to run. At once, there were adaptations for theatre, seven of them opening in the month of publication. In December, a pantomime version opened at Drury Lane. Opportunities for merchandising were not neglected. In one theatre 'Shepherd-bags', containing a basic housebreaking kit – several picklocks, a screwdriver and a crowbar – were hawked to the audience in the lobbies. Under the copyright laws of the time, Ainsworth himself made nothing from these bags, nor from most of the dramatisations, though he did receive a modest fee for giving one production his personal endorsement. However, sales of the novel were outstanding.[33]

Popular though the book and its theme were proving to be with the public, the reviewers were mostly hostile. They thought it was melodramatic and sensationalised, which it certainly is; and they feared its impact on the morals of the young.[34] The *Athenaeum* complained that Ainsworth had attempted 'to invest Sheppard with good qualities, which are incompatible with his character and position'.[35] Ainsworth's Sheppard, even more than his Turpin, is a gentlemanly robber. He prides himself on keeping his word, and he refrains from violence. He is a youth of some sensibility. He becomes a robber out of despair at failing to win the girl he loves, and later he claims that memories of her have kept him from committing any really wicked offences. After his great escape, he is finally recaptured, not in a gin shop, like the historical Sheppard, but weeping at the side of his mother's coffin. Like Paul Clifford, he has planned to restore his honour by service in a foreign army. It comes as small surprise to the reader when it is eventually revealed that Jack, brought up in poverty, is the grandson of a knight. His gentlemanly instincts are hereditary. To complete the portrait of a gentleman robber, he spends the proceeds of his robberies on dressing in the height of fashion.[36]

In a bravura passage of *Rookwood*, Ainsworth demands to know, mock-plaintively, what has become of the 'Knights of the Road', and why, 'with so many half-pay captains; so many poor curates; so many lieutenants, of both services, without hopes of promotion; so many penny-a-liners, and fashionable novelists; . . . so many detrimental brothers, and younger sons', no 'new race of highwaymen' should have appeared in late Hanoverian England. 'Why do not some of these choice spirits,' he enquires, 'quit the *salons* of Pall-Mall, and take to the road; the air of the heath is more bracing and wholesome, we should conceive, than that of any "hell" whatever, and the chances of success incomparably greater.' This 'hint', as he teasingly calls it, seems to have stirred very little disquiet among his bourgeois readership.[37] *Jack Sheppard* contains no comparable passage, recommending the prospects for burglars. Yet it, not *Rookwood*, provoked the protests.

In 1842, Ainsworth's friend Laman Blanchard looked back over the *Jack Sheppard* controversy in a fiercely partisan article. Not unreasonably, he points to the contradictions in the position of those who condemned the book:

Critics, who had always had a passion for heroes in fetters before, now found out that housebreakers are disreputable characters. They were in raptures with the old-established brigand still, and the freebooter of foreign extraction; they could hug *Robin Hood* as fondly as ever, and dwell with unhurt morals on the little peccadilloes of *Rob Roy*; nay, they had no objection to ride behind *Turpin* to York any day, and would never feel ashamed of their company; but they shook their heads at *Sheppard*, because low people began to run after him at the theatres; he was a housebreaker![38]

Highwaymen are delightful; but burglars are irredeemably low. Moreover, though Blanchard disregards this, Ainsworth had said this once himself. In the same passage in *Rookwood* in which he extols the life of the highwayman, he asserts: 'All that we regret is, that we are now degenerated from the grand tobyman to the cracksman and the sneak, about whom there are no redeeming features.' By a 'grand' (usually 'high') 'tobyman' Ainsworth meant a mounted robber – the term was a 'flash' one that had entered the criminal argot in the first decade of the nineteenth century – while a 'cracksman' was a housebreaker, and a 'sneak' was a pilferer who entered houses through doors that had been left open.[39]

In thus heavily disparaging the housebreaker, Ainsworth was probably taking his cue from *Paul Clifford*, where the activities of the cracksman are more than once stigmatised as vulgar and ungentlemanly.[40] This attitude had very little by way of tradition behind it. In the days when many gentlemen and others had regarded robbery as an acceptable, even an honourable course of life, precisely because it was a crime that took some courage, there had been no sound reason to stigmatise the man who broke into houses, risking or even courting a confrontation. If the housebreaker lacked something of the glamour that attached to a 'knight of the road', he was still granted a share of the prestige that was accorded the daring robber.[41]

By the 1830s, the glaring difference between the highwayman and the housebreaker was, of course, the fact that the one sort of robber was extinct, while the other continued to operate much as he always had. Accordingly, it was perfectly safe to relish the exploits of highwaymen, since no one any longer expected to lose their purse to such a robber, let alone their life. But the figure of the housebreaker was still associated with a sense of real anxiety. In writing a romance in which a leading character was a young, bold, stylish *burglar*, Ainsworth had brought on himself the charge he had once feared that the earlier book might attract: that of glorifying crime and the criminal.

One commentator with a deeply personal interest in the whole controversy was Charles Dickens, at that time a rising young journalist and novelist. *Oliver Twist*, his second novel, had begun to appear as a serial in 1837; it was published in book form in November 1838. In 1841, when it reached its third edition, Dickens added a preface, in which he hit back at various critics of his own.[42] The mildest charge that had been laid against him was that in portraying scenes and characters from the criminal underworld, he was drawing to the attention of the public matters that should have been left in a decent obscurity, and of which the young, in particular, ought to be spared an awareness.[43] He was accused, too, of encouraging a taste for fictions about criminals and their associates. Finally, it was said by some that he was an imitator of Ainsworth, and that *Oliver Twist*, along with *Jack Sheppard*, invested thieves and ruffians with a spurious attraction.[44]

In his preface to *Oliver Twist*, Dickens defends himself with vigour. Describing his reflections at the point when he was devising his characters, he observes:

I had read of thieves by scores – seductive fellows (amiable for the most part), faultless in dress, plump in pocket, choice in horseflesh, bold in bearing, fortunate in gallantry, great at a song, a bottle, a pack of cards or dice-box, and fit companions for the bravest. But I had never met (except in HOGARTH) with the miserable reality. It appeared to me that to draw a knot of such associates in crime as really do exist; to paint them in all their deformity, in all their wretchedness, in all the squalid poverty of their lives; to show them as they really are, forever skulking uneasily through the dirtiest paths of life, with the great, black, ghastly gallows closing up their prospect, turn them where they may; it appeared to me that to do this, would be to attempt a something which was greatly needed, and which would be a service to society.

This is not solely a hit at *Rookwood* and *Paul Clifford*, but a wholesale attack on their sources as well. Dickens comprehensively rejects the whole literary and popular convention of the heroic robber, as it had come down by way of chapbooks, street ballads and the various eighteenth-century compilations of criminal biographies. He continues:

In every book I know, where such characters are treated of at all, certain allurements and fascinations are thrown around them. Even in the Beggar's Opera, the thieves are represented as leading a life which is rather to be envied than otherwise .... Johnson's question, whether any man will turn thief because Macheath is reprieved, seems to me beside the matter. I ask myself, whether any man will be deterred from turning thief because of his being sentenced to death, and because of the existence of Peachum and Lockit; and remembering the captain's roaring life, great appearance, vast success, and strong advantages, I feel assured that nobody having a bent that way will take any warning from him, or will see anything in the play but a very flowery and pleasant road, conducting an honourable ambition in course of time, to Tyburn tree.[45]

Despite these comments, he excuses Gay's ballad opera from the full force of his criticism, because of its satirical aims; and on the same grounds, he excepts *Paul Clifford* from his strictures. It is likely that he hoped to avoid upsetting Bulwer, with whom he was on good terms. However, his next paragraph contains an unmistakable allusion to Bulwer's novel. Defending *Oliver Twist* from the charge that it was a dangerous book for the young, Dickens demands, rhetorically,

What manner of life is that which is described in these pages, as the everyday existence of a Thief? What charms has it for the young and ill-disposed, what allurements for the most jolter-headed of juveniles? Here are no canterings upon moonlit heaths, no merry-makings in the snuggest of all possible caverns, none of the attractions of dress, no embroidery, no lace, no jack-boots, no crimson coats and ruffles, none of the dash and freedom with which 'the road' has been, time out of mind, invested.[46]

The remark about 'the snuggest of all possible caverns' only makes sense as a dig at *Paul Clifford*; in which, moreover, much is made of the charms of the moonlit canter.[47]

Out of the material supplied by the traditional cult of the robber, Bulwer and Ainsworth between them had developed a new literary type: the Romantic Highwayman. The romantic highwayman sometimes carouses in London taverns, but his true affinities are with the wild places. Paul hides out, not in some city dive, but in a woodland cave near Maidenhead. It is almost inevitable that Bulwer should compare the surrounding landscape to Sherwood. When Dick Turpin first appears in *Rookwood*, it is in the guise of a dedicated rider to hounds – and an apologist for poaching.[48] The highwayman is being partly reconstructed on the pattern of that much older figure, the greenwood outlaw. Meanwhile, in the age of the ever-encroaching city, nostalgia for the mounted robber becomes an aspect of the yearning for the countryside. An important sign of the romantic highwayman's identification with the world of nature is his outstanding talent as a horseman and his close bond with his horse. The early 1830s saw the beginnings of mass machine travel, with the arrival of the steam passenger locomotive: already more than three times as fast as the fastest horse, and, when it was working properly, with far more staying power. As Turpin gallops frantically to York, nostalgia for the figure of the highwayman merges into regret for the time, the very recent time, when the swiftest form of travel was the skilled horseman on a fast mount.[49] The romantic highwayman and his horse are very much creatures of the moonlit night; a Shakespearean note which Bulwer and his successors struck with relentless enthusiasm. As gas street lighting spread and spread, moonlight became less ordinary, at least for city dwellers. It became more strongly associated with the wild countryside, its glamour of otherness newly enhanced.

Dickens's preface to *Oliver Twist* sums up the attractions of the romantic highwayman shrewdly and comprehensively. His reaction against the conventions of robber romance, and his absolute determination to avoid any trace of what he calls its 'allurements', have left some odd marks on his own underworld novel. His principal robber, the burglar, Bill Sikes, is badly dressed, ill-tempered and uncivil; his brutal nature impels him in the end to the murder of the young prostitute, Nancy. All this is doubtless a good deal closer to life than Paul Clifford's innate good taste in clothes and his ludicrous shrinking from violence. Sikes is also assigned a rather more arbitrary attribute: he can't sing. Instead, when he gets drunk, he is heard 'yelling forth ... most unmusical snatches of tune'.[50] Bulwer's and Ainsworth's highwaymen are accomplished singers to a man, following the example of Macheath. It is seldom that they pass up a chance to entertain the reader with a song. The lyrics are invariably given in full, and are about the joys of being a robber and similar subjects. In place of the highwayman's horse, Sikes has a dog, which he treats with extreme savagery, in sharp distinction to the sentimental attachment of the romantic highwaymen to their horses. In the end, it is his dog that betrays him, by drawing attention to his hideout when he is on the run. The contrast with Black Bess, who dies to keep her master safe from pursuit, seems a little too pat to be purely coincidental. While Sikes is made the opposite of the gentleman robber in every way that enters Dickens's head, his associate, 'flash Toby Crackit', the 'heavy swell', with his cheap finery, his excessive pride in his top-boots, and his reputation for impressing maidservants, is an obvious travesty.[51]

At the time Dickens's preface to *Oliver Twist* was published, he was working on his fifth novel, *Barnaby Rudge*. It is set in 1780, at the time of the Gordon Riots – roughly the point at which Bulwer's Paul Clifford is supposed to have been embarking on his seven-year career as a highwayman. There is a highwayman in *Barnaby Rudge*, but as in *Oliver Twist*, Dickens sternly rejects the romantic stereotype. His highwayman, a relatively minor character, enters the story in Chapter One, as a stranger under the curious gaze of the regulars at the Maypole Inn. But this is no convivial companion; instead, he is grim and uncommunicative. He is not a young man, either, but a battered-looking, seedy figure of about sixty. When one of the local men, Tom Cobb, reacting to the stranger's air of menace, whispers to his friend, Phil Parkes, 'A highwayman!', Parkes pours scorn on the idea. 'Do you suppose highwaymen don't dress handsomer than that? ... It's a better business than you think for, Tom, and highwaymen don't need or use to be shabby, take my word for it.' But it is Tom who turns out to be right; the stranger is a robber; and after he leaves the Maypole he commits a cowardly attack on a man on foot, riding him down with his horse and stabbing him for the sake of his purse.[52]

In *Barnaby Rudge*, the dashing highwayman of romance features only in the fancies of the ignorant, like the countryman Parkes, or, later in the book, the ridiculous prentice Simon Tappertit, who wishes he had been born 'a corsair or a pirate, a brigand, gen-teel highwayman or patriot – and they're the same thing'.[53] In *Rookwood*, Ainsworth had invoked the notion, by this time extremely ancient, that the special qualities of the English highway robber gave grounds for national pride. Simon Tappertit, as jolter-headed a youth as might well be imagined, has embraced this doctrine wholesale. But in place of a 'genteel highwayman', Dickens has given his readers a stick-at-nothing ruffian, who, later in the book, turns out to be a murderer, who has killed and robbed his own master. This desperate, treacherous, blood-stained figure is Dickens's bleak comment on the countryman's naivety and the apprentice's juvenile fantasies.

Across the pages of other authors, the romantic highwayman went on cantering in an eternal moonshine. Thomas De Quincey was old enough to remember a world in which an encounter with a mounted robber was a real if occasional hazard of travel.[54] However, in an essay he wrote in the early 1850s, he looks back on the eighteenth-century highwaymen with all the nostalgia of a man who lives in a settled society for the days when men were bold and life exciting, and with the enthusiasm of someone who is quite sure that he will never have to meet one.

> As to the profession of robber in those days exercised on the roads of England, it was a liberal profession, which required more accomplishments than either the bar or the pulpit; from the beginning it presumed a most bountiful endowment of heroic qualifications – strength, health, agility, and exquisite horsemanship, intrepidity of the first order, presence of mind, courtesy, and a general ambidexterity of powers for facing all accidents .... The mounted robber on the highways of England, in an age when all gentlemen travelled with firearms, lived in an element of danger and adventurous gallantry; which, even from those who could least allow him any portion of their esteem, extorted sometimes a good deal of their unwilling admiration. By the necessities of the case, he brought into his perilous profession some brilliant qualities – intrepidity, address, promptitude of decision; and if to these he added courtesy, and a spirit (native or adopted) of forbearing generosity, he seemed almost a man that merited public encouragement ...[55]

Robert Louis Stevenson, looking back in 1887 on his boyhood reading in the 1850s and 1860s, joyously recalled:

> Give me a highwayman and I was full to the brim; a Jacobite would do, but the highwayman was my favourite dish. I can still hear that merry clatter of the hoofs along the moonlit lane; night and the coming of day are still related in my mind with the doings of John Rann or Jerry Abershaw; and the words 'post-chaise,' the 'great North Road,' 'ostler,' and 'nag' still sound in my ears like poetry.[56]

Stevenson's own highwayman romance, *The Great North Road*, begun in 1884, was never finished. Interestingly, he broke off writing it at the point where his gentleman highwayman, incognito, seeks out and tries to comfort the mailcoach guard he has shot and seriously wounded, perhaps to death.[57] It is a painful scene, and it is not hard to understand why Stevenson might have found problems in continuing with the book. In the face of truthfully represented violence and its consequences for the innocent, the notion that armed robbery is nothing but a glorious adventure, and one, moreover, in which the mortal risks are reserved for the robber alone, is exposed as a hollow mystification.

No similar spirit of realism had been allowed to infect the portrayal of the highwayman Tom Faggus, a secondary but important character in R. D. Blackmore's hugely popular *Lorna Doone* (1869). Blackmore based his account of Faggus on folk legends current around Exmoor, and it seems likely that it was from this source that he took some of Faggus's exploits, as well as his quasi-magical horse, the 'strawberry mare', Winny, who far outshines even Black Bess in beauty, intelligence and devotion to her master.[58] It may have been folk legend, too, that provided Faggus with a traditional justification for his outlaw career. He is supposed to have been a farmer and blacksmith who only turned to highway robbery after oppressive legal machinations had deprived him of his land and livelihood.[59] However, when Faggus, looking back on his life as a robber, nostalgically cries out, 'Those were days worth living in. . . . How fine it was by moonlight!' he betrays his close affinity to the now hackneyed stereotype of the romantic highwayman.[60]

Moonlight and high wind set the scene at the start of Alfred Noyes's much-anthologised narrative poem 'The Highwayman'. Ever since its publication in 1906, the popular image of the highwayman has been greatly influenced by this famous recitation piece.[61] Noyes assembles his poem out of some very familiar properties, both in the setting – the moon, the road, the old inn – and the highwayman's costume – lace, red coat, high boots. 'The attractions of dress', to use Dickens's phrase, here become fetishised: the 'doe-skin' breeches that fit 'with never a wrinkle', the boots that go 'up to the thigh'.[62] This is the sexiest literary highwayman since Macheath, and an ancestor to those dangerously charming highwaymen who dazzle women in ephemeral love romances.

Much of the power of Noyes's narrative lies in its manipulation of tension. In the first part, this is sexual tension, as the highwayman arrives by night at the inn, and the landlord's daughter opens the window at his whistle. He himself is little more than a lay figure in some very enticing clothes. His sweetheart is described chiefly through her physical attributes: she is 'red-lipped', 'black-eyed' and has 'long black hair'.[63] In case the reader should be in any doubt, her dark beauty underlines the fact that, highwayman's mistress as she is, she is Not a Good Girl. Her red lips promise sensuality; but the highwayman, with robbery on his mind, cannot stay, and the door to the inn remains symbolically closed. The unbroken sexual tension is heightened further by the fact that the highwayman cannot even reach to kiss his sweetheart's lips; he can only touch her hands and kiss her hair.

In the second part of the poem, the sexual tension is absorbed into the tension of imminent danger, as the lovers are betrayed, and the highwayman ambushed by soldiers. The soldiers go where the highwayman did not go, into the inn, into the girl's bedroom; they even, in mockery, kiss her lips. Somewhat implausibly, they leave her tied up with a musket by her side; after much struggling, she frees herself sufficiently to be able to reach the trigger. When the highwayman is heard approaching the inn, she fires the gun, warning her lover and killing herself with the shot. The tension is released in a quasi-sexual climax, with a violent death that is also a submission and a sacrifice. It now remains only for the highwayman to discover what has happened, and to gallop back 'like a madman' to his own brutal death from the soldiers' bullets. He is compelled to his doom by love, and by his own promise the previous night to return to his sweetheart 'though hell should bar the way'.[64]

At the end of the poem, we are taken back to its beginning, as the lovers return to the inn as phantoms and play out their parts in a continually repeated pattern. Noyes leaves the highwayman where he found him, and as he has been ever since: a seductive ghost, haunting the roads and the rustic inns of the popular imagination.

19

The Turpin Legend

Of all the outlaw heroes of the Middle Ages, the only ones who retain a place in English popular culture are Robin Hood and the members of his band: Little John, Will Scarlet and the rest. As for the traditions associated with the highwaymen, most of those that have not been forgotten have been rolled into a single package and attached to the name of Dick Turpin. This is curious, for the historical Turpin was a most unpromising candidate for the role of legendary hero.

The records of Turpin's criminal career have been thoroughly investigated by Derek Barlow. His earliest reported crimes were committed in association with a large gang of poachers turned housebreakers, led or at any rate dominated by a man named Samuel Gregory. Beginning on 29 October 1734, Gregory and his confederates committed a series of robberies in the counties bordering London. Their modus operandi required little finesse. They usually targeted isolated farmhouses and similar dwellings. They would wait till dusk, then force their way into the building, overpowering the occupants, threatening them with violence and stripping the place of all the valuables they could easily carry away. Sometimes the violence went beyond threats. In one robbery at which Turpin was present, an old man was beaten and pistol-whipped and a maidservant was raped. The rapist was Gregory, but it was Turpin who began the brutal maltreatment of her elderly master.[1] Turpin and his friends were not in any sense honourable or courteous robbers. In fact, they were fairly average examples of the 'bad' robber or thug. But after all, without the shadow cast by the 'bad' robber, the courteous robber cannot operate. His interchanges with his victims depend on the implicit threat that unless they conform to his demands, he will change his manners for the worse. For the encounter to go his way, it is crucial that they should believe that any resistance on their part will be met with a violent response.

In effect, it is the 'bad' robber who does the 'good' robber's dirty work for him.

Turpin's career as a highwayman did not begin until some time in 1735, after the gang had been split up and most of its members arrested. Then, for a while, he robbed on the highway in company with one of the other survivors, Thomas Rowden. Like other highwaymen of the time, they robbed mainly on roads that passed through some of the tracts of wild countryside around the capital: Barnes Common, Hounslow Heath, Blackheath and Putney Heath. After only a few months, they separated, and then began a long period in which Turpin lay very low. For a while, rumours placed him in Holland. Early in 1737, he became active again as a highwayman, this time in association with a couple of new confederates, Matthew King and Stephen Potter. They committed a few robberies in Leicestershire, before coming south and commencing to rob in the neighbourhood of Epping Forest. However, they made a serious mistake when they stole a racehorse called Whitestockings. The beast was not only valuable but highly distinctive. They stabled it temporarily at an inn in Whitechapel, but it was quickly traced, and an ambush was set up. When the robbers came to retrieve it, early in the morning of 2 May, King was mortally shot. Turpin rode off; King was captured and, dying slowly in jail, gave evidence against his accomplices. Potter was arrested at his lodgings, but Turpin was more fortunate; warned that men had come to arrest him, he jumped out of bed and escaped across the roofs of the houses. He took refuge in Epping Forest, in what sounds like a ready-prepared bolt-hole, a cave concealed in a thicket. However, he was spotted by a gamekeeper's assistant, who tried to capture him, doubtless with an eye to the reward. Turpin, though, shot the man dead and once again made off. This was on 5 May 1737.[2]

At this point, Turpin, now hunted for murder, wisely went to ground. Nothing certain was reported of him until 1739. It was in this vacancy that the Turpin legend first began to develop. Turpin had survived the break-up of two gangs and two recent attempts at arrest. He had established that he was formidable and very hard to catch. And as with James Hind, more than eighty-five years earlier, or the Folville brothers, over four centuries earlier, his exceptional luck could even be read as a kind of vindication: a proof that powerful forces were working on his side.[3] Moreover, although he had become a murderer, it was the kind of murder, committed in the course of an attempted arrest, that the early modern public found easiest to condone in a highwayman.[4] As a street ballad of 1739 puts it,

> At Epping they said they would kill
> Turpin that had never done them Ill,
> But he, more nimbler than they,
> Shot his Carbine, and Dead was he.[5]

For a while after the shooting, there were continual reports in the newspapers of highway robberies that were supposed to have been committed by Turpin acting alone. This is Turpin as he is generally imagined today: the solitary horseman, single-handedly carrying out daring hold-ups, always one step ahead of the pursuit. In reality, few if any of the robberies that were ascribed to him at this time were actually committed by Turpin himself. However, the legend gained credit from the fact that more than one highwayman saw certain advantages in taking on Turpin's identity.[6] There can be little doubt that such masquerades contributed to another enduring element in the Turpin myth: the impression of his marvellous ubiquity.

The less than glamorous truth is that following the break-up of his second gang, Turpin changed profession. He may have committed the odd robbery to finance his getaway. But about a month after the Epping Forest incident, he arrived in Brough, in the East Riding of Yorkshire, where he set himself up as a horse-dealer. Instead of buying horses, though, he was stealing them; a sneaky sort of crime, with none of the prestige that attached to the life of the mounted robber.[7] But, of course, it is more than likely that Turpin was not very interested in his reputation as a highwayman. He was merely a common criminal on the run, surviving as best he could. Until he made a bad mistake: on 2 October 1738, he came back from a shooting expedition and in a moment of destructiveness, shot a domestic cock. When he was reproached for this by a man who had witnessed the incident, he threatened to shoot him, too. From this point on, his new identity gradually fell apart. First, he was arrested and taken to Beverley house of correction. Following this, he was investigated by some of the local JPs, who found that there were grounds to suspect him of stealing horses. They moved him to York Castle and committed him for trial at the assizes. He might quite easily have been hanged as an obscure horse-thief, under his Yorkshire alias of John Palmer. However, in February 1739, he sent a letter to his brother-in-law at the village of his birth, Hempstead in Essex. His handwriting was recognised, witnesses were sent north to identify him, and he was duly tried and executed under his own name of Richard Turpin. He showed some courage at his death; in this, at least, conforming to the stereotype of the valiant robber.[8]

By the time of his execution, the Turpin legend had already taken on a largely separate life. The first pamphlet and ballad about him had appeared in 1737, in late June or early July, during the time when he was still hot news. The pamphlet declares, erroneously, that he had fled to Ireland. It is a curious mixture of extracts from newspapers, mangled gossip about the capture of King, and one or two comic stories of Turpin's reputed exploits. The ballad is tagged on to the end of the pamphlet. However, it also existed independently, and was still in print, in modified form, some eighty years later. In it, the brutal housebreaker who did not stick at beating up a helpless old man is reinvented wholesale as an eighteenth-century Robin Hood:

> He only taketh from the rich
> what they well can spare;
> And after he hath served himself,
> he gives the poor a share.[9]

The ballad tells a tale that was told of Gamaliel Ratsey, and later of Hind: about a debtor in desperate circumstances and the robber who lends him the money to pay his debt and who afterwards robs it back again from the creditor.[10] In this variant, the debtor is a poor tenant, whose ruthless landlord plans to seize his goods. Turpin lends him the £50 he needs and lies in wait for the landlord after he has been to collect it. The story is, of course, a very much simplified version of the medieval tale of Robin Hood, the debtor knight and the greedy monks. This image of Turpin as a Robin Hood figure was sustained in several later ballads and became part of the popular traditions about him.[11]

One of the stories in the 1737 pamphlet casts Turpin in the long-established role of the highwayman joker:

Turpin lately saluted a gentleman in the following manner; *Good-morrow Sir, do not you hear talk of one Turpin a robber? O Lord Sir, I heard an account of him in the public newspapers.* Turpin replied, *Sir I have a small matter of money at me, and am very much afraid of being robbed, but for security I have put it in my boot tops, Sir,* says the Gentleman, *that is a very good Place! well Sir, my money is all carried in the cape of my coat.* Riding about two miles further, *Sir,* says Turpin, *Pray Sir, what might be your business or calling? Sir,* says the gentleman, *I am a lawyer.* Then says Turpin, *if you are a lawyer, I am a cutter, and must cut the cape of that coat of yours before we go any further.*[12]

The punchline turns on a pun: a 'cutter' was a slang term for a highwayman. By Turpin's time the expression was distinctly archaic, and in fact, the story is almost identical to one that had previously been told of James Hind.[13] In March or early April 1739, while Turpin, now identified and back in the news, was waiting at York for his execution, the tale was reworked, this time as a street ballad, under the title of *Turpin's Rant*. The author jettisoned the cutter joke, which was musty with age, and sharpened up one of the story's other points: the fact that, as a lawyer, the highwayman's victim belongs to a profession that was generally held to be peopled by crooks. Accordingly, his losses get scant sympathy:

> [Turpin] rob'd the Lawyer of all his Store,
> But he knows how to Lie for more.[14]

In a somewhat later version, published as *Turpin's Valour*, the wording is slightly but significantly altered:

> Turpin robb'd him of his store,
> Because he knew he'd lie for more.[15]

Now we have Turpin plundering the lawyer precisely because he regards him as a professional liar. Moreover, in *Turpin's Valour*, which is three times the length of *Turpin's Rant*, the robbery of the lawyer is only the first of a series of episodes in which the highwayman goes on to rob, in succession, members of several other not very popular professions: an exciseman, a judge and a usurer. In this ballad, Turpin has been transformed into a version of the righteous robber who goes outside the law in order to punish anti-social elements who cannot otherwise be touched.

This is one of the most enduring themes of the English robber tradition. We can trace its origins as far back as the fourteenth century, to the time of the 'Folvilles' laws', when Eustace Folville and his brothers murdered the oppressive baron, Bellers, and plundered Willoughby, the unjust judge, and in doing such things, gave their name to a catchphrase. The Folville brothers, to some degree, lived in accordance with a code that set out how a man was supposed to act when he found that the laws had been twisted and used against him and against his family and affiliates. Even so, the evidence indicates that their motivations were not all that pure, their lives and actions, to say the least of it, chequered. As I suggested at the end of Chapter Two, they did not become a legend so much as they were co-opted by one.[16] The same is far more true of Turpin, whose life offers no warrant whatsoever for the uses to which his name was put by jobbing ballad-writers. But in the 1730s, the tradition of the righteous robber, though growing old and threadbare, still retained enough power to co-opt this lucky highwayman, with his exceptional talent for evading capture. Moreover, Turpin's very nullity, his failure, in his career as a robber, to demonstrate even any flashes of wit or style, let alone any sort of principle, made it more or less necessary for the street poets who attempted to cash in on his notoriety to fill the gap with whatever came to hand: which consisted of ancient motifs embedded in often repeated tales. So Turpin fell heir to a whole corpus of stories about righteous and generous robbers, and his name survived into later generations as that of a pattern highwayman.

However, the most interesting and revealing stanza of *Turpin's Valour* is the penultimate one:

> He ventur'd bold at young and old,
> And fairly fought them for their gold;
> Of no man he was e'er afraid . . .[17]

The ballad-maker, perhaps without noticing, has strayed away from the main argument of his ballad, which attempts to vindicate the robber hero by pitting him against a selection of devious or dislikable figures. Now, suddenly, Turpin is described as a man who was prepared to rob anyone, 'young and old'. His robberies are justified, it seems, simply because they are 'fair', in other words, confrontational, and because they require boldness of the perpetrator. This is the sort of outlook that is implicit in Fortescue's comments on the English propensity for robbery, as well as in innumerable other passages and anecdotes.[18] The crime is considered to be redeemed, at least in part, by the robber's courage, and it is regarded as fair on the grounds that the victim can always fight back. It is on such attitudes and assumptions that the robber's prestige has always crucially depended. However, if we look coolly at this view of robbery, we can see just how much is being suppressed or distorted. Samuel Butler, the Restoration satirist, cuts through the mystifications as crisply as anyone: the highwayman, he says, 'never ventures but upon surprizal, and where he is sure of the advantage'.[19]

It is not altogether clear at what point Turpin's name began to be attached to the legendary exploits of other, less famous robber heroes. The process was already well under way in the early nineteenth century, during the boyhood of Harrison Ainsworth, who was born in 1805. Ainsworth spent much of his childhood in Cheshire, and in his preface to *Rookwood* he refers to the existence of local traditions about Turpin that he had heard about from his father.[20] He embeds one of these stories in the novel. In a ballad sung by Turpin himself, the highwayman describes how, once, after he had been recognised in the course of a hold-up, he had established an alibi by galloping across country to the Cheshire village of Hough* Green. There he joined the bowls players on the green, having casually drawn their attention to the time. When the victim of the robbery arrived

---

* pronounced Hoo

to accuse him, Turpin had a number of witnesses ready to swear that he could not possibly have been the perpetrator.[21] This is a version of a well-known traditional tale that had previously been told of other mounted robbers.[22] At least one other form of this tale, one with which Ainsworth was certainly familiar, since it became the basis of an episode in *Rookwood*, also has Turpin for its hero. In this, the highwayman provides an alibi for himself by a more impressive feat: riding between London and York in the course of a day, and without changing his horse.[23] However, there is no reason to doubt that the Hough Green story genuinely existed as a local variant. In *Traditions and Customs of Cheshire*, published in 1937, the folklorist Christina Hole records a more savage version, in which the victim of the robbery is a lawyer, whom Turpin leaves dead on the road. In this account, Turpin goes straight to the inn at Hough Green, where he slashes an ostler with his whip before he demands the time. The ostler, his memory branded by the blow, provides Turpin with an unshakable witness to exonerate him of the murder.[24]

This story, in its differing forms, is only the most dramatic of a whole cluster of Cheshire traditions about Turpin: that he robbed the coaches on a certain road, drank at a certain inn, hid in a secret hiding place in a certain thatched cottage. It is likely that behind them lie memories of a real robber, or perhaps of several.[25] One thing that is certain is that whatever stimulated the emergence of these legends, it was not any activity by the historical Turpin. There is no evidence that Richard Turpin even so much as visited Cheshire. Instead, his name has become attached to traditions that must once have existed independently. The same must be true of the scraps of 'Turpin' folklore that have been collected in Warwickshire and Wiltshire, since, once again, there is no documentary evidence to link Turpin with either of these counties.[26] As Charles G. Harper explained, in 1908, 'so widespread in rural districts had his fame early grown, that "Turpin" became almost a generic name for local highwaymen . . . . It was a name to conjure with: and this no doubt goes some way to explain the infinitely many alleged "Turpin's haunts" in widely separated districts: places Turpin could not have found time to haunt, unless he had been a syndicate.'[27]

The most important development of the Turpin legend after the eighteenth century was Harrison Ainsworth's invention, in his novel *Rookwood*, of Dick's famous mare, Black Bess. The alibi stories that were told about Turpin clearly presupposed his possession of a preternaturally fast horse. Moreover, the ascription to him of numerous robberies in widely separated localities could also be rationalised, in part, by assuming, again, that he must have been very well mounted.[28] Ainsworth's inspiration was to supply Turpin's horse with a name and a distinct identity. Black Bess is a thoroughbred racer, beautiful and very, very fast. More than this, she is intelligent, great-hearted and totally in tune with her master.[29] I described in the last chapter how the appearance of *Rookwood*, in 1834, had a massive influence on the growth of the Turpin legend.[30] It was *Rookwood*'s runaway success with the public that established Dick Turpin as the highwayman hero par excellence, and led to the almost total neglect of the memories of earlier famous robbers, like Hind and Claude Du Vall. Nowadays, *Rookwood* itself is neglected, not without reason; it is read, if at all, only as a period piece. As a result, it is largely forgotten that the earliest narrative of Turpin and Black Bess is brought to a cruel end when the highwayman rides his faithful horse to death.

Something that has made a much deeper mark on the popular imagination is the way Ainsworth portrays Turpin and his mare as existing in a relation of mutual attachment. This is what all modern English people 'know' about Dick Turpin: that he was inseparable from a horse called Black Bess. In a country in which close relationships between humans and their animals, particularly dogs or horses, are regarded as a highly sympathetic trait and assigned great cultural and moral value, this element has been hugely important for the continued popularity of the Turpin legend. Turpin's possession of Bess famously allows him to thumb his nose at all authority.[31] Mounted on his black thoroughbred, he is never less than a stride or two ahead of the pursuit. And that, of course, is always quite enough. Together, the highwayman and his horse form a potent emblem of escape and freedom.

20

Conclusion

'No body will be so mad as to expose himself upon the highway, when he can make better bread in an honest and industrious manner.' These are the (reported) words of the Scots philosopher Adam Smith, in a lecture on 'police' (or public order) that was delivered in about 1764.[1] Some of the phrasing sounds a little unfortunate to a modern ear, but the sentiment pretty well sums up one of the commonest assumptions that is made about any kind of property crime: that its principal, even its only cause is poverty, or, at any rate, serious economic disadvantage. It's a common-sense view of the matter: it presumes that when people take, by force or stealth, the goods of others, it must be because they are in need of them. However, criminal motivation is nearly always a much more complex business.

Smith's dictum about robbery appears in the context of a suggestion that the best way of maintaining good order is 'The establishment of commerce and manufactures'. As he explains, 'The common people have better wages in this way than in any other, and in consequence of this a general probity of manners takes place thro' the whole country.'[2] In Smith's view, property crimes, including robbery, are virtually always perpetrated by members of the working classes, the 'common people'. This assumption, too, is very familiar. Ever since Smith's time, the conventional wisdom about crime has been that the kind of people who take part in it are normally members of the lowest stratum of society.[3]

As an initial disproof of Smith's dictum, let us consider a minor case from history: that of the seventeenth-century highwayman Richard Hals, whose career as a robber I summarised in Chapter Nine. Hals was born a gentleman. He received a good education. He also had influential relatives, in the shape of the Verneys and the Hobarts, who certainly did not lack concern for him. When he was young, attempts were made by his extended family to establish him, quite respectably, as a clerk to a lawyer or attorney, but these came to nothing. As Sir Ralph Verney warned young Hals's aunt, 'the Humour of the man' was not at all suited to life in a lawyer's gown. Nearly twenty-five years later, after a long career in crime, Hals obtained a position as a court bailiff, and seemed to be about to settle down. Yet even after this, at an age when most violent criminals have long grown tired of the life, he returned to robbing on the highway.[4] We have no direct insight into his motivation, but it defies reason to believe that the pressures that drove him were purely or even primarily to do with making a living.

In modern times, the former armed robber John McVicar has described how he himself first came to embark on the life of a professional criminal. He explains that as a teenager during the 1950s, growing up in a respectable lower-middle-class household, what drew him into crime was only secondarily the prospect of acquiring money. Far more important was the attraction for him of the criminal code of behaviour, which, as he represents it, was based on such appealing values as gameness, courage, loyalty and staunchness. 'Staunch', by the way, is an interesting term in this context; it was already part of the criminal lexicon as early as 1750, and it implies not only personal dependability but also solidarity with criminals and their culture. McVicar identifies the code of values he writes about as 'macho', associating it with a conception of masculinity as essentially defined by aggressiveness.[5] His observations powerfully bring to mind that Tudor conception of robbery that saw it as a way in which a man showed his 'manhood'.

It is clear that for the young McVicar, becoming a criminal, and perhaps especially an armed robber, provided a solution to certain sharply pressing problems that had more to do with identity than anything else. We can catch a glimpse of a similar process at work in the case of John Clavell, over three hundred years earlier. In Chapter Twelve, I quoted Clavell's account of his youthful fantasies about becoming a robber, and how he had once considered it to be the only 'course' that had anything about it that was 'brave or good'.[6] Elsewhere, and more vaguely, he refers to the need to discourage those prospective robbers

> that yet sinne onely in intent,
> Conceiving that it is a gentle course,
> Not to be discommended . . . [7]

This was how he had once viewed it himself, of course. For Clavell, a gentleman born, only 'a gentle course', or something that he identified as such, could even begin to answer his problem of what to make of himself. The same was doubtless true for Richard Hals.

Clavell's youthful sense that robbery was 'a gentle course' is one indicator of the extent to which, even as he embarked on a career of calculated transgression, he could draw on much more cultural support for his choice, and a very much wider sympathy, than was available to McVicar in the 1950s. In early seventeenth-century England, many people viewed highway robbers with indulgence and even with admiration. The act of committing robbery was popularly considered to show courage, and men who seized with reckless violence on other people's goods were felt to be behaving 'manfully', in a way that asserted their masculinity. Closely bound up with such notions is the view of robbery embraced by the young Clavell, which saw it as a pursuit that a man of good family might engage in without loss of honour. During the Renaissance, as earlier, during the Middle Ages, the first mark of a gentleman was always that he should 'shew ... a more manly corage ... than others'.[8] Other marks of the gentleman were courtesy and generosity. On the face of it, these are unlikely attributes for a robber, but so strong was the association between robbery and gentility that the robber's life was quite often depicted as a sphere in which a gentleman, or a man who aspired to behave like one, might demonstrate these indispensable qualities.

Besides some glimpses of his own state of mind at the point when he first turned highwayman, Clavell offers us insights into those of his fellow robbers who, unlike himself, were born into non-gentle families.[9] His comments suggest that for men like these, an important attraction in becoming a highwayman was that they saw in it a way in which they might break through the barriers of rank. In Chapter Thirteen, I explored the mental world of the low-born robber by way of the published representations of the life and attitudes of James Hind, the one-time butcher who became a popular hero. By the time Adam Smith was assembling his thoughts on the prevention of crime, Hind's successors were commonly referred to, in an indicative phrase, as the 'gentlemen of the road'.[10] It is possible that Smith, as a Scotsman, knew very little about the historic traditions of the English mounted robbers. If he knew anything at all, he evidently considered it to be irrelevant to his argument. However, it is undoubtedly the case that, even in the later eighteenth century, the cult of the robber was continuing to exercise a powerful influence, at least on certain individuals. In 1774, ten years after Smith's lecture, the last of the truly colourful highwaymen ended his life at Tyburn. This was John Rann, commonly known as 'Sixteen-string Jack'. Rann, a former coachman, received his nickname from the ribbons he wore tied below the knees of his breeches. He affected a gorgeous style of dress altogether, frequently boasted in public that he was a highwayman, and protested if anyone treated him in a manner that he thought was unsuited to his dignity as a 'gentleman'.[11] Somehow, I feel it is unlikely that Rann would have been rescued from his self-destructive career by the prospect of employment in 'commerce' or 'manufactures'. To a temperament as exhibitionist as his, what was of most importance was the public presentation of the self, and the particular expressive possibilities that he found inherent in his self-chosen role of highwayman.

The most striking aspect of the cult of the robber is the way in which it was bound up with an English national myth. The notion that England was a nation full of robbers was certainly alive in the fourteenth century, since we find something like it in the great Latin preachers of the time, Bromyard and Brinton.[12] Neither of these, however, saw it as grounds for national self-congratulation. This particular view is first found expressed by Sir John Fortescue, in the later fifteenth century. For him, as we saw in Chapter One, the large numbers of his fellow-countrymen who were sent to the gallows for robbery provided evidence of native English courage. Moreover, he believed, apparently quite complacently, that only a very few Englishmen would consent to remain in poverty if they saw a chance to seize wealth by force from some other person.[13]

A very important element in this myth was the traditional history of the great English robbers of the past, with its 'evidence' that, as John Taylor the Water Poet put it in 1622, '*England* still hath bin a fruitfull Land / Of valiant *Thieves*'.[14] Of these the most popular has long been Robin Hood, whose legend has its roots in the medieval corpus of tales about outlaws. Another very famous legendary robber, who enjoyed a special vogue in the reign of Elizabeth, was Prince Harry, the Wild Prince, who, having proved his valour on the roads, afterwards became the conqueror king, Henry V.[15] Certain later robbers also found prominent places in the roll-call of heroes. James Hind, in particular, was remembered for a very long time, only to be eclipsed, eventually, by the rather less interesting figure of Turpin.

The myth that the English were a nation of heroic robbers and that this went to prove their commendable valour and aggressiveness is transparently a variant on the simpler and more comprehensible myth, still powerful in certain quarters, that characterises the English as exceptionally brave and tough.[16] What seems odd to a modern mind is the extent to which in social terms this variant form of the myth is blatantly anti-cohesive. Not to put too fine a point on it, it celebrates the English as a nation of rapacious contenders, disregardful of law and authority and prepared to use violence at will. George Schöpflin, in an interesting study, has described the function of national myths as being 'to strengthen collective solidarity'.[17] This may well be so – or normally so, at least – in the world of the modern nation state, and also in the modern minority ethnic or language community. But the myth of a nation of robbers can hardly fill such a role. It is unquestionably a national myth, but it is premodern: it developed before the modern ideology of patriotism, or service to the state or community.

Even as late as the mid-eighteenth century, some Englishmen were still taking pride in boasting to foreigners of the spirit displayed by their native highwaymen.[18] However, from the early decades of the seventeenth century, the myth is nearly always found in a modified form. Much more stress is laid on the English robber's outstanding 'courtesy', or as eighteenth-century writers sometimes have it, his 'humanity'. The English mounted robber, having decent instincts, will normally behave with civility; in particular, he will not kill you. Or not, at any rate, unless you resist.

At the root of the cult of the robber lay two somewhat divergent attitudes to robbery. From one viewpoint, robbery became acceptable when it was carried out in justified punishment or revenge. Sometimes the victim was a personal enemy, as the Sheriff of Nottingham is to Robin Hood. At other times the victim was representative of a class of social enemies, as the committee man is to Hind, or the lawyer to Turpin. A fairly late refinement on this was the more obviously ethical notion of robbing the rich for the sake of the poor.

The second attitude to robbery was, perhaps, the older of the two. This was the outlook that held that whoever the victim might be, there was nothing very much wrong with it. A man with the necessary strength and courage was entitled to take what he could, so long as certain rules were observed.[19] As time went on, however, those rules became stricter, to the point where the whole business became something of a contradiction in terms: to satisfy the requirements of the public, and maintain his own sense that he still has a place in the social order, the robber must never use actual violence. At this stage, we sense a growing unease about the whole cult and its associated myth. All the same, it was a myth of which the English long remained very tenacious. One of the latest expressions of it is found in the writings of Mary Wollstonecraft, a feminist and a radical, who nonetheless alludes with marked appreciation to the qualities of the English highwayman. Like Fortescue, three centuries earlier, she believed that robberies were rare in France. She also believed that when they did take place, they were 'almost always' accompanied by 'murder and cruelty', springing from cowardice and fear. In England, though, the highwayman shows his courage, and his respect for his victim's courage, by robbing with a certain 'humanity'.[20]

Among whom did the cult of the robber develop, and whom did the myth serve? Initially, the fighting aristocracy of the later Middle Ages and the officers of their households. It was fairly certainly a section of the latter, the yeomen servingmen, who were the original audience for the early tales of Robin Hood. But we can glimpse, too, a wider world of shiftless and lawless types, fighting-men, poachers, adventurers, who shared a set of heterodox values and thought of themselves as 'good fellows'. By the reign of Elizabeth, the cult of the robber had become a mass popular tradition, though its connections with the aristocracy, particularly the gentry, remained strong. For a very long time, the stereotypical robber was the impoverished young man from a gentle family. John Clavell fits quite neatly into what was felt to be a classic pattern. However, the cult of the robber flourished longest among certain proud, violent young men of common stock, for whom robbery was at once a proof of manhood and a passport to a kind of mimic gentility. The cult never left much space at all for either the actual or the imagined involvement of women, though readers interested in the literary manifestations and sparse historical records of the female robber will find this subject covered in Appendix A.

There were always critical voices raised against the glorification of robbers and robbery. Both during the Middle Ages and later, condemnation of such attitudes and the abuses that resulted from them was frequently expressed by men who were trained in the moral traditions of the preacher. Satirists and comic writers likewise found excellent scope in exposing the absurdities and contradictions that lay at the heart of the cult of the robber. The two most memorable literary highwaymen, Falstaff and Macheath, are both, in their different ways, figures of burlesque.

This notwithstanding, the cult of the robber and the myth of the English as a robber breed were influential for centuries in encouraging certain kinds of English male to commit robberies and to adopt an outlaw identity. It is fairly certain that, in earlier times, they affected the ways in which such offenders were typically treated by the legal system. As to their wider effects, these can only be a matter of conjecture. At worst, the cult of the robber functions by totally suppressing the rights of the victim, including his or her claim to any sort of imaginative sympathy. It legitimates unprovoked violence and a spirit of hard-hearted rapacity. However, at its best, it becomes associated with a very old myth of resistance and restitution. By going outside the law, which is viewed either as toothless or else as downright corrupt, the outlaw or highwayman takes to himself the power to set right injustices and to punish oppressors who otherwise cannot be touched.

APPENDIX A

The Female Robber

I am often asked if I have come across any cases of women who robbed on the highway. Many people, it seems, are hungry to hear about female highway robbers, and more than one recent popular book offers slanted or concocted stories to suit. The most colourful of these inventions is the legend of the 'wicked Lady Ferrers'. According to Peter Haining, in his book *The English Highwayman*, she was the historical original of the cross-dressing highwaywoman heroine of Magdalen King-Hall's novel *Life and Death of the Wicked Lady Skelton*, which was published in 1944 and filmed the following year as *The Wicked Lady*. In Haining's account, Lady Ferrers is a dashing counterpart to the highwayman of tradition – aristocratic, stylish, daring and doomed to a bad end. Haining supplies dates, details, place names, in what seems like a highly circumstantial report.[1] However, none of this is to be trusted. At the end of King-Hall's novel, she acknowledges a single source for her story of 'Lady Skelton'. It is Christina Hole's *Haunted England* (1940), which has a brief anecdote about a ghostly highwaywoman, said to haunt the neighbourhood of Markyate Cell, near Dunstable.[2] Here we have the truth. 'Wicked Lady Ferrers' is a figure of folklore, not history. She is interesting purely for what she tells us about women, violence and cross-dressing in the fantasies and hallucinations of English women and men of the twentieth century.

However, there are some documented cases from past centuries of women who committed robberies. There was even a Wicked Lady – wicked Lady Sandys – but of her, more in a moment. To begin with the earliest instances: James Buchanan Given found a few female robbers in legal records of the thirteenth century. These women robbed alongside their relatives – parents, children or brothers – or with their husbands or lovers.[3] Barbara A. Hanawalt, in her study of crime in the first half of the fourteenth century, gives brief details of a couple of cases where women were accused of taking part in a whole series of highway robberies. One robbed in company with her lover, the other belonged to a gang that included her husband. Hanawalt conjectures that the women may have functioned as decoys, to lull the suspicions of travellers. Certainly, there are examples of women playing that kind of role in some much later cases. Far fewer women than men were involved in this kind of crime. Hanawalt states that of what she terms bandit groups – associations of two or more charged with involvement in robberies and related crimes – only about five per cent of the members were women.[4]

The printed volumes of the Middlesex Sessions records running from 1549 to 1688 contain a bare handful of cases of women who were convicted of robbery with violence. Most of these women robbed in company with their husbands or some other male. In one case of 1564, a woman from London was hanged for robbing another woman on the highway at Hammersmith, then a rural village several miles outside the city. In 1620, a woman called Grace Jones was hanged for robbing a man in St John's Street, Clerkenwell, a district well known for its brothels and its thugs. Grace Jones's reputation was not of the sweetest; in 1617, she had done time in the house of correction.[5] The records show that it was much more common for women to break into houses than to rob on the streets and highways. This corroborates the evidence of George Wilkins, writing in 1607, who states that the 'mills' or professional housebreakers who operated in London routinely included women as well as men.[6]

If gentleman robbers were a recognised social phenomenon, it was highly unusual for well-born women to involve themselves in robbery. An exception was Susan, Lady Sandys, wife of Sir George Sandys, whose own career as a robber was briefly discussed in Chapter Nine. At the time of his execution, in March 1618, his wife and son were in jail as accomplices; this may mean only that they had been accessories after the fact. However, in January 1619, John Chamberlain, writing to his friend Dudley Carleton, recorded a titbit of gossip about 'a certain Lady Sands that hath don a robberie in her owne person', noting that her husband had been hanged for a similar crime 'about a yeare since'.[7] In July 1626, the couple's son, also named George, was tried and acquitted for the murder of a young woman. With him were acquitted 'Suzan Lady Sandes', his mother, and two men named James Jones and Edward Gent, all of whom were accused of harbouring him after the crime. A month later, George Sandys was on trial again, this time for a rape; Jones and Gent were tried as accomplices. The three were found guilty and sentenced to be hanged.[8] Their execution was the occasion for a very interesting broadside ballad. In it, Sandys is said to have boasted at his trial that he had repeatedly escaped being hanged for highway robbery and horse-stealing. The ballad recalls his notorious parents, ascribing to his mother full participation in his father's crimes, and describing the latter as a wastrel who

did live long time by stealing:
And with his wicked Lady wife,
did rob the highway side . . .

The ballad-maker clearly suspects that she may be the next to go to the gallows, observing:

Thus both the father and the sonne
did end their lives alike,
The Lady *yet* hath scapt that death . . . [my italics].[9]

The fact that Lady Sandys was twice tried as an accomplice makes it clear that the authorities believed her to be fully complicit in the crimes of her husband and son. Moreover, it is apparent from the ballad that the story that she had herself been an active robber was one that had stuck to her. It may have been pure gossip, but she obviously had the kind of reputation that made it plausible. However, it is noticeable that, like many other women robbers, her involvement in violent crime took place in the context of a delinquent family group.

Narcissus Luttrell's diary for 28 July 1692 records a case of two women who robbed in partnership. Meeting 'a gentlewoman of note, walking in the feilds near Richmond', they 'robb'd her of a gold watch, a pearl necklace and rings, stript all her cloathes, with holland shift, and left her naked bound'. Fortunately for her, a trooper came riding by, gave her his cloak, and galloped off to overtake and arrest the two footpads. In April of the following year, Luttrell notes that 'A list of 80 highwaymen is given to the cheife justice in order to their apprehension, among which are several women.' Highwaymen, for Luttrell, implied mounted robbers, as distinct from footpads. However, we never hear anything more of these female highwaymen, and in fact the names on the list may have included those of fences, informers, keepers of safe houses, and other accomplices.[10]

In his study of female crime during the eighteenth century, J. M. Beattie concluded that while women footpads were uncommon, women highwaymen were very rare indeed. Beattie notes that women were far less likely than men to acquire the skills that a mounted robber has to have, in horsemanship and the use of weapons. As a general rule, those women who were involved in robberies worked in conjunction with men, as decoys and lookouts. Prostitutes, in particular, were sometimes known to lure their customers to out-of-the-way places where their pimps might rob them. A much larger number of women were involved in burglary and housebreaking. Many of them worked in association with men, while others were closer to sneak-thieves than robbers, but there are a few records of women burglars who worked alone and used deliberate techniques for forcing

266

entry into houses. However, it does not appear that any of these women intentionally sought a violent confrontation with their victims, putting them in fear, as some burglars choose to do, and all robbers from the person – muggers, and, in the old days, highwaymen – necessarily do.[11]

Beattie cites only one record of a mounted woman robber, and this not from a court case but a report in the *Gentleman's Magazine* for 24 November 1735. This is the original account in full.

A Butcher was Robb'd in a very Gallant Manner by a Woman well mounted on a Side Saddle, &c. near *Rumford* in *Essex*. She presented a Pistol to him, and demanded his Money; he being amaz'd at her Behaviour told her, he did not know what she meant; when a Gentleman coming up, told him he was a Brute to deny the Lady's request, and if he did not gratify her Desire immediately, he wou'd Shoot him thro' the Head; so he gave her his Watch and 6 Guineas.

A woman highway robber would have had this advantage over a man, that it would have been easier for her to get close to travellers, who would not be expecting an attack from her. But a robber also needs to terrify the victims and assert dominance over them.[12] On this occasion, the butcher plainly could not believe that a woman would shoot him down, and it required the intervention of her male confederate to frighten him into parting with his valuables. The highwaywoman's nerve and 'Gallant Manner' were not enough to counteract the social conditioning that made any woman, even one pointing a pistol at him, into a non-threatening figure. In the end, her role in this affair doesn't amount to very much more than that of any other female decoy. Moreover, given the intriguing hints as to the robbers' apparent class position, the woman's good mount, the butcher's identifying her companion as a 'Gentleman' and the man's general manner of address to the unfortunate 'Brute' of a victim, it seems possible that the whole incident originated in an upper-class frolic. Whatever the case, and whoever she was, with her side-saddle and her male enforcer, she hardly matches up to the autonomous, evilly heroic, breeched-and-booted figure of the Wicked Lady.

There is an account, from the seventeenth century, of a gang of female highway robbers who are, in their own way, as full of swagger and daring as any romantic might wish. It occurs in a work of fiction: Richard Head's rambling picaresque novel *The English Rogue* (1665). The narrator, Meriton Latroon, a general-purpose crook and adventurer, who has previously been accepted into a band of highwaymen and has committed a couple of robberies, is held up on the road by a robber who bears the appearance of a well-armed and handsomely equipped gentleman. Meriton resists; they fight with pistols and swords; but Meriton overpowers and binds his opponent, only to find, when he frisks him for money, that the 'gentleman' is a woman. She takes Meriton to an inn, well hidden among trees, where she tells him the story of her life; later they are joined by two other female robbers in male disguise. In the original edition of the book, the episode ends here, though not before the narrator has dropped a strong hint that what follows next is a night of group sex.[13]

The English Rogue was a publishing sensation; over the next few years there were many reissues, and new material was added. Either Head himself or else his publisher and collaborator Francis Kirkman contributed two further chapters of Meriton's experiences with the female robbers. One of the two newcomers, who turn out to be sisters, tell him their history. The sexual encounters between Meriton and the women are mentioned directly, though not in any great detail. They spend the next morning carousing, and then, after a good dinner, they go out together to find someone to rob. This time only one of the women wears male clothing; the two others ride pillion, one behind her and one behind Meriton, in order to present an appearance of high respectability: a pair of married couples, travelling together. Together, they successfully take on and rob a group of four horsemen, having first lulled them thoroughly off guard by their pretence of being innocent travellers. They take back a considerable booty to their hideout, and return to their life of feasting, sex and heroic drinking. However, very soon the restless Meriton, exhausted by their sexual demands on him, resolves to move on.[14]

Did Head and Kirkman have any sources for these episodes besides their own licentious imaginations? It is hard to tell. *The English Rogue* incorporates many plagiarised passages; among the earlier works on which it draws are numerous criminal exposés and biographies, some of which have since been lost. Head may also have had some personal contacts with the underworld. Transvestite female robbers are not unheard of in the early modern period; there were several examples in the Netherlands.[15] But whether the episode is fiction or fictionalised reportage, the most interesting aspects of the highwaywomen in *The English Rogue* are the ways they are conceptualised and presented. They are, as we might say nowadays, thoroughly male-identified. One of them sings a drinking song in which she alludes to herself and her companions as 'Sons of the blade'.[16] In conversation, they show themselves thoroughly contemptuous of women. 'One said, She would not be a meer Woman for the whole universe, and wondered that man, so noble and rational a Soul, should so unman himself in his voluntary inslaving himself to a Womans will'.[17] Their view of themselves is endorsed by Meriton, who when he leaves them gives a poem to the highwaywoman whom he had first met. In it, he praises her for having shown, through her courage and readiness to fight, that she deserves to be ranked alongside men. He contrasts her favourably with those mere 'shadoes' of men whose sole claim to manhood is the fact that they can sexually service a woman.[18] The logic is clear: if, as the widespread assumption had it, a man establishes his manhood through acts of violence, including robbery, then a woman who lives a robber's life equally shows herself to be 'really' a man.

Until she is overcome by a resolute male, like Meriton, after which, of course, she becomes sexually available to him. Sexual freedom is part of the highwaywomen's ethos. The second of the two drinking songs they sing includes the couplet 'That woman sure no joy can find / Who to one man is only joyned.' The song praises their life for its 'liberty' and 'freedome'.[19] But Head's characters should not be mistaken for early liberationists. They are simply conforming to a Restoration stereotype. A woman with more than ordinary spirit is almost certain to disregard the ordinary rules for women's sexual behaviour.[20]

Though Meriton calls his highwaywoman a 'Female *heroe*',[21] she remains no more than a foil to the real hero, himself. He proves his own superiority, first by defeating her in a fight, then by sexually satisfying three voracious women, and finally when he abandons them. For in doing this, he proves that he, at least, has not 'inslav[ed] himself to a woman's will'. The common opinion in seventeenth-century England was that the female was by nature more lustful than the male; while chastity in women was conventionally prized, it was also held to be continually at risk because of women's unruly sexual appetites. This was believed to be one of the ways in which women in general were inherently inferior to men.[22] In accordance with these ideas, a man who showed himself unable to control his own desires was unlikely to be regarded as a stud or a great seducer; instead, he was felt to be weak, even womanish, and was often jeered.[23] Meriton's ability to ride away again is a final proof of his masculine superiority.

A broadside ballad of about 1690 tells a condensed and stylised version of the same story. In *The Female Frollick*, 'a young Gentlewoman' dresses herself in men's clothes, buys a mare and some pistols and rides out 'upon the Pad'. She single-handedly conducts a whole series of hold-ups, including a stage-coach – 'a Fifty-pound Jobb' – before she makes the same mistake as Head's female robber, and tries to hold up a highwayman. She is less valiant than the woman in *The English Rogue*, for when he prepares to resist her, she flees, only to be pursued, captured, searched and, when he discovers her sex, raped. However, the ballad concludes jauntily that

> she had no cause to complain.
> Tho' with her he did what he pleased,
> he gave her the Money again.

This is a made-up story, not a news ballad. It may have been inspired by *The English Rogue*, or it may testify independently to much the same attitudes and fantasies. Several of the highwaywoman's victims belong to unpopular social groups: a tailor, a miller, a Quaker, an exciseman. The ballad is a variant on the old theme of the robber as the scourge of hypocrites and the covertly dishonest. Since the robber in this case is a woman, the victims are doubly exposed as cowards and fools. Only the real highway robber is man enough to overcome her, whereupon he shows his masculinity further by imposing his sexual authority, and the magnanimity expected of a robber hero when he leaves her with her winnings. The rape, brutal as it is, is partly intended to clinch a joke. The highwaywoman has 'asked for it', not only by exceeding the limits of modest female behaviour, but also by demanding, in the traditional shout of the highway robber, that her victims 'Stand!' There is a pun here: 'to stand' also meant 'to have an erection'. By implication, her wilting victims are sexual failures as well as cowards. Only the highwayman matches up in every way to the challenge she presents to his prowess.[24]

Another ballad of the late seventeenth century features a female robber of a very different kind. It is possible, though not certain, that it is a news ballad, founded upon some actual incident. The story it tells is summarised in the title of the broadside:

A New Ballad of Three Merry Butchers and Ten High-Way Men, how three Butchers went to pay *Five Hundred* Pounds away, and hearing a Woman crying in a Wood, went to relieve her, and was there set upon by these Ten High-Way Men, and how only stout *Johnson* fought with them all, who kill'd Eight of the Ten, and last was kill'd by the Woman whom he went to save out of the Wood.[25]

The woman in the ballad is almost the antithesis of the heroic robber of tradition. She has no honour; she lures the unfortunate Johnson into ambush by appealing to his chivalrous instincts, and follows this by attacking him from behind while he is occupied in fighting the two surviving male robbers. Nor does she respect the convention, which had become firmly established during the seventeenth century, that the well-conducted English robber took pains to avoid murder. She represents a very different image of the female robber, conceived as crueller than the male, and inclined to cowardly subterfuge.[26] The unquestioned hero of the story is the victim, Johnson, 'the bravest Butcher that ever England won'. The final stanza tells how his murderer, who is never given a name, was captured, hanged and ignominiously gibbeted 'At the place where she did Johnson that great and mighty wrong'.

Captain Alexander Smith's *Complete History of the Highwaymen*, published in the second decade of the eighteenth century, incorporates a couple of what are supposed to be true reports of celebrated women robbers. But here, once again, we are certainly dealing with fiction. Smith is an unreliable source at best; he plagiarises widely, which is perhaps excusable in a compilation text, but he also treats his originals very cavalierly. Most of his chapter on the famous Moll Cutpurse is extracted from a book about her published in 1662.[27] But he has inserted a whole new passage in which she is credited with a career as a highway robber during the Civil War. Smith's Moll, who rides around dressed as a man and armed with pistols, is a version of the swaggering highwaywoman of *The English Rogue*. However, although Moll Cutpurse certainly existed, and was a prominent figure in the London underworld for many years, there is no evidence at all that she ever committed any robberies. And by the time the Civil War broke out, she was certainly well over fifty – an unlikely age to gallop about the countryside holding up travellers.[28] Smith's other cross-dressing highwaywoman, Joan Bracey, turns out when examined to be just as much of an invention.[29] It seems that, just like nowadays, dashing female robbers in male disguise were part of what the 'true crime' public wanted; but it's also apparent that authentic material was not to be had.

APPENDIX B

Maid Marian

Maid Marian is a relatively late arrival in the Robin Hood legend. There is no trace of her in the fifteenth-century narratives or the one surviving fifteenth-century play-text. The earliest reference to her occurs in 1509, in the churchwardens' accounts of Kingston upon Thames in Surrey, where her name is linked with that of Robin Hood as a character in the summertime role playing. She seems to have been a May Lady figure, and the role was evidently played by a woman. Very soon after, when it became fashionable for the Robin Hood performers to give displays of morris dancing, Maid Marian began to be known as a character dancer in the morris side. From now on, in Kingston and in other places, the role was normally performed by a male in drag, and there is some evidence that it came to be expected that the performance would be heavily burlesqued.[1]

A romantic Maid Marian emerges, or perhaps re-emerges, in the last decade of the century, in a group of plays written for the London stage. The anonymous *George a Greene, the Pinner of Wakefield* is based on a Robin Hood ballad. Maid Marian makes an appearance as Robin Hood's 'leman', or sweetheart.[2] In George Peele's *Edward I*, Lluellen, Prince of Wales, hard-pressed by Edward's forces, adopts the life of an outlaw and robber. He masquerades, whimsically, as Robin Hood, and his followers take on the roles of other members of the band. Lady Elinor, Lluellen's betrothed, becomes Maid Marian.[3] Well born and courtly, devoted to her outlaw lover, she may well have helped to suggest Munday and Chettle's Maid Marian in the two *Robert, Earl of Huntington* plays, which were written just a few years later, in 1598. In these plays, which are discussed more fully in Chapter Eleven, Robin Hood is an earl, and Marian his aristocratic betrothed.[4]

Just as she had no place in the medieval metrical tales, Maid Marian is almost entirely excluded from the narrative tradition represented by the broadside ballads. A couple of the later ballads mention her name, but the

272

only one in which she has a real part to play is a rather feeble late seventeenth-century effort, which derives from the *Huntington* plays rather than from the older corpus of stories about a yeoman robber. Once again, Maid Marian is a noblewoman, and Robin is her lover, the earl of Huntington. After he is forced to go to the greenwood, she follows him, disguised as a page. When the lovers meet, they fail to recognise each other, since Robin is also disguised. They fight with sword and buckler, rather improbably, for 'At least an hour or more', before Robin invites her to join his band, and she suddenly recognises him by his voice.[5] The great ballad editor, Francis James Child, thought that Marian belonged essentially to the festival tradition, and that until this piece was composed for the broadside market, 'no one thought of putting more of her than her name into a ballad'. He rejected rather peremptorily a piece of evidence to the contrary: an allusion to Maid Marian in an eclogue, or pastoral poem, by the minor poet Alexander Barclay.[6] This was written in about 1514; that is, only a few years after the very first mention of Maid Marian, in the churchwardens' accounts of Kingston upon Thames. One of Barclay's shepherds says to another: 'Yet would I gladly heare some mery fit / Of Maide Marian, or els of Robin Hood.'[7] A 'fit' is a section of a long rhyming narrative or song; so the reference implies the existence of at least one tale, existing in the early sixteenth century but now lost, about Maid Marian's adventures.

What might an early Tudor Maid Marian have been like, and what might have been the content of such a tale? There is a surviving text, hitherto neglected by Robin Hood specialists, that, although it doesn't mention Maid Marian, does represent an outlaw's woman within the familiar trappings of the greenwood legend. This is the verse dialogue of *The Nutbrown Maid*, first printed in 1502. A poor squire comes secretly to tell his sweetheart, 'the Nutbrowne maide', that he has been made an outlaw and must go alone to the greenwood. She says she will accompany him. He warns her that she will get a bad reputation. But she asserts that there is no shame in 'feithful love'. He reminds her of what the greenwood life is like:

> For ye must there in your hande bere
> A bowe, redy to drawe,
> And as a theef thus must ye live,
> Ever in drede and awe . . .

Undaunted, she says that she will help him hunt for game. He tells her that he will be pursued, and that she will be no use in helping him defend himself. She admits that women make poor fighters, but that if he were put in fear by his enemies,

> I wolde withstonde, with bowe in hande,
> To greve them as I might,
> And you to save, as wimen have
> From deth many one . . .

Likewise, she dismisses the hardships of the outlaw's life, the lack of shelter and food. She reminds him that he is a famous archer, and that they cannot starve while living in the forest among the deer. He says that if she comes with him, she must cut her hair short, 'up by your ere', and shorten her kirtle to the knee. Finally, he tells her that he has another mistress already within the forest, whom he loves more than her; but still she says that she will go with him. At this point, in a twist that probably delighted a romantic reader of the time, but that strikes a modern as rather sickening, the squire reveals that he hasn't been outlawed at all; it has all been a test of her love and fidelity. He is actually the heir to an earldom, and having proved that she really loves him, he will arrange to marry her forthwith.[8]

The Nutbrown Maid shows that at the end of the Middle Ages it was already possible to imagine a place for the outlaw's woman within the framework of the legend. Just like the outlaw himself, she has her conventional attributes: the mannish short hair and kirtle, the bow. Her presence changes the greenwood: depending on how you look at it, it becomes a site of faithful love, or of sexual licence. *The Nutbrown Maid* handles these matters delicately, as befits its romantic tone. However, it is noticeable that in addition to the loyal Nutbrown Maid, the poem is haunted by the image of a second woman, the paramour in the wood. The poem focuses on the former, but it cannot exclude the latter, probably because she already had too potent an existence as a stereotype. At any rate, in the mid-sixteenth-century *Playe of Robyn Hoode*, a text written for performance at summer festivals, the unnamed 'lady', a Maid Marian figure, is hailed by Friar Tuck as

> a trul of trust,
> To serve a frier at his lust,
> A prycker, a prauncer, a terer of sheetes,
> A wagger of ballockes when other men slepes.[9]

It is quite possible that the lost early Tudor tale or tales of Maid Marian were bawdy, or at least that they contained bawdy elements. Certainly, in Elizabethan England, Maid Marian's loose ways were semi-proverbial.[10] This would help to explain why texts have not survived. On the other hand, the evidence of *The Nutbrown Maid* shows us that nearly a century before Munday and Chettle wrote the *Huntington* plays, it was already possible to imagine the outlaw's woman in terms of a heroine of romance.

However, if the outlaw's drama is one of violent conflict and revenge, hers is a drama of faithfulness and love in the teeth of misfortune: love to the point of absolute self-abnegation. She exists only for and with her outlaw lover.

APPENDIX C

Social Bandits

The concept of the 'social bandit' was originated by Eric Hobsbawm more than forty years ago, and developed and defended by him in a series of books and articles.[1] The most detailed statement of his theories appears in his book *Bandits*, first published in 1969 and three times reissued in revised and expanded editions, most recently in 2000. According to Hobsbawm, the social bandit is a robber who conforms to a certain code of behaviour and who in consequence has the support, moral and practical, of the community of which he (very occasionally she) is a member. In its pure form, social banditry is supposed to be a phenomenon of peasant societies only. Hobsbawm is at pains to stress that the true social bandit, who is always a peasant, should not be confused with the superficially similar but distinct figure of the gentleman robber, nor with urban criminals such as highwaymen.

Among social bandits proper, he distinguishes several types. The first, and the only one relevant to the themes of this book, is what he calls the 'noble robber', whose archetype is Robin Hood. The 'noble robber' is the champion of his people. Hobsbawm assigns him various attributes, but the indispensable core of his activities involves 'social redistribution' – he steals from the rich and distributes his plunder to the poor – together with a deep concern for justice and the righting of wrongs. Other elements listed by Hobsbawm as belonging to what he calls 'the "image" of the noble robber' include being driven outside the law as a result of injustice or the application of unfair laws, and killing only 'in self-defence or just revenge'. Hobsbawm makes very large claims for social banditry, calling it 'one of the most universal social phenomena known to history', a statement that seems liable to conflict with his emphasis on the importance of the peasant community as the matrix of the true social bandit. In addition, in one of his most obviously contentious observations, he describes it as 'amazingly uniform', a claim that is rather undermined by the material he assembles in his book, in which he finds evidence of social banditry in a range of quite diverse activities and social movements.[2]

Hobsbawm's concept of the social bandit has been taken up and modified by Graham Seal, in his book *The Outlaw Legend* (1996). Seal's proposed aim is to combine a Hobsbawmian socio-historical approach with a folklorist's attention to the processes of transmission and cultural shaping in investigating what he calls the 'outlaw hero' in Britain, North America and Australia. The characteristics of Seal's outlaw hero are very similar to those of Hobsbawm's noble robber. His chief departure from the Hobsbawmian model of the social bandit is that he does not define the outlaw hero as primarily a phenomenon of peasant societies. Instead, he states that such heroes appear as a result of 'serious social, economic and political tensions' between different communities and social groups. This enables him to relate his theories closely to the careers and legends of robbers like Jesse James and Ned Kelly, whose societies were not in any sense traditional peasant communities.

Seal follows Hobsbawm, and perhaps goes somewhat beyond him, in describing the stereotype of the outlaw hero as a 'cultural constant', available across the world and in all periods.[3] Both theorists insist on the power of the image to influence the behaviour of real bandits in historically known societies, while Hobsbawm, in particular, maintains that the 'good' robber, who acts at all times on principles of justice and magnanimity, is something more than a figment of fantasy or myth. In addition, both regard the dream of the Robin Hood figure as a necessary one, so that in all cultures those who feel themselves oppressed are liable to co-opt existing bandits or representatives of similar lawless types and tailor their reputations to fit the pattern. This, according to Hobsbawm, is the reason why the attributes that, in his view, primarily belong to the noble peasant robber are sometimes found attached to out-and-out criminals like highwaymen.[4]

This appendix is not the place for a detailed discussion either of Hobsbawm's thesis or Seal's related one. Here I am concerned with the narrower question of how far their theories are borne out by the surviving traditions of real and legendary robber heroes in England. Apart from continually referring to Robin Hood as the ideal type of the 'noble robber', Hobsbawm himself has relatively little to say about the presence, or putative presence, of social banditry in England. Moreover, in the new edition of his book, he has added a note that for the purposes of his argument, Robin Hood is, as he puts it, 'myth', not history.[5] However, in a passage that has remained unchanged from earlier editions he asserts that in England there is 'no record of actual social bandits after, say, the early seventeenth century'.[6] He does not provide any references for this statement, and it is hard to know what records he has in mind.

It might be quite pleasant to think that pre-seventeenth-century England harboured a breed of social bandits, primitive peasant rebels, driven to prey on their betters by a burning sense of injustice. However, if any such existed, they have left no obvious traces either in legend or historical record. The noble robbers of medieval stories are figures like Fouke and Gamelyn, whose nobility of behaviour springs from their knightly blood; or, at a lower social level, Robin Hood, no peasant farmer but a proud yeoman archer. Nowhere in the early tales is Robin presented as operating with the support, let alone on behalf, of a peasant community. Moreover, we might note that when the rebel leader John Ball mentioned the figurative 'Hobbe Robbyoure', Hob (or Robert) the Robber, in the letters that he sent out in 1381 at the time of the Peasants' Revolt, it was not to hail him as an ally or even a kindred spirit, but to stigmatise him as worthy of punishment.[7] In *A Geste of Robyn Hode*, those who show themselves most in sympathy with the values of the forest outlaw are right-thinking aristocrats, like the knight and the King. In England, the cult of the robber has its roots, not in peasant protest, but in aristocratic codes of behaviour. And if justice is a central theme in the outlaw legends, well, aristocrats, as well as peasants, may have their grievances, and their experiences of oppression, and their dreams of revenge and of forcing restitution.

The characteristics of Hobsbawm's social bandit and Seal's outlaw hero are supposed to be uniform, constant over time and place. However, it is very noticeable that in England, the attributes that were traditionally associated with the heroic robber, and the legendary tales that became attached to his reputation, evolved and changed over time, in ways that it has been part of the purpose of this book to chart. Considered in relation to the English traditions about heroic robbers and outlaws, Hobsbawm's and Seal's concepts of the noble robber and outlaw hero appear syncretised, rigid and ahistorical. The characteristics that are supposed to make up these stereotypes are never all of them present together in any single English hero, nor are they all found at once in any one period. For example, while the medieval texts, just like Hobsbawm and Seal, stress the personal experience of injustice as the compulsion that drives the hero to become a bandit, by the Renaissance the emphasis is on economic causes: the archetypal robber is now a prodigal heir, or else a younger brother with no patrimony.[8]

According to Hobsbawm and Seal, one of the attributes that marks out the 'noble robber' and 'outlaw hero' is the fact that they are reluctant to kill.[9] In England, it was not until the early seventeenth century that the avoidance of bloodshed became a settled part of the image of the popular robber hero. This development, which apparently accompanied changes in the practices of mounted robbers in real life, seems to have happened as an accommodation to changing attitudes in a society that was less and less willing to tolerate serious random violence, or to view its practitioners with even limited indulgence.[10] As a general rule, the greenwood outlaw of legend is a far more casually violent figure than the heroic highwayman of later centuries.

As for the theme of social redistribution, that, as I explained in Chapter Five, enters into the Robin Hood tradition at quite a late date. Moreover, it does not originate in popular tales, but emerges gradually over the course of the sixteenth century in the works of various writers on English history.[11] The best explanation as to why this took place is that they were struggling to give a morally palatable account of a popular hero who in origin was little more than a witty and generous robber. It was not before the later seventeenth century, when the motif of stealing from the rich to give to the poor had become fully incorporated in the popular legend of Robin Hood, that it first begins to be also attached to the names of certain highwaymen. There is no evidence that any English robber or outlaw actually engaged in a systematic project of redistribution of property, although robbers were traditionally open-handed, and undoubtedly needed to be so, to make sure of the loyalty of those who might otherwise have impeached them.[12]

Observing that some of the motifs that he identified as making up the image of his noble robber are found associated with highwaymen in some eighteenth-century accounts, Hobsbawm takes this as showing a deep need on the part of the public to believe in the existence of social bandits, a need that in his view resulted in the idealisation of more or less inappropriate substitutes. Seal develops a similar line of argument in greater detail, paying special attention to the ballad literature about Dick Turpin. He points out that although in many ways the historical Turpin was unpromising material for hero status, he nevertheless fell heir to a corpus of robber tales and motifs that depicted the highwayman as robbing unpopular social types, and above all as giving generously to the poor out of the loot that he took from the rich.[13]

There can be no doubt that in most societies there is always an eager audience for stories of resistance to oppression, the outwitting of malice or greed, and the succour and vindication of innocence and righteousness. These were certainly among the most important satisfactions offered by the tales of outlaws and highwaymen. In addition, the example of the Folville brothers in the fourteenth century shows that, on occasion, the careers and exploits of historical bandits might be reshaped both in written and oral traditions to conform more closely to the patterns found in legend: in this case, a pattern of violent resistance to misappropriation and injustice.[14] A similar process took place with certain later robbers: for example, the Royalist highwayman Hind, who, during the Interregnum, was portrayed in popular fiction as a scourge to the Parliamentarians and a benefactor to the poor.[15] However, these two cases alone are enough to show by their differences that the stereotype of the righteous robber and the elements of his legend were far from being permanently fixed. Instead, they were continually, if often very gradually, going through change, to accommodate altered social and political conditions and new cultural preoccupations.

To sum up: I do not believe that the eighteenth-century Turpin of the street ballads, or any other legendary English highway robber, acquired his characteristics, or some of them, in conformity to some universal, unchanging stereotype of the noble robber. Nor do I believe, by way of alternative, that the English highwaymen heroes were modelled on some ancient image of the ideal robber that had endured without change from the days of Robin Hood (whenever those may be said to have been). Instead, I believe that the popular highwayman heroes of the eighteenth century and, indeed, very much earlier, were all of them manifestations of a tradition that, under the pressure of social change, had passed through many centuries of slow mutation. This tradition carried along with it many ancient motifs and stories, but though it might be said to be backward-looking, it was never fossilised; it was continually undergoing adaptation, losing elements, transforming elements, and sometimes gaining new ones. It is certainly true that it was always in process of co-opting and shaping the images and legends of real robbers. It was probably also the case that some historical robbers consciously behaved, at least at times, in ways that corresponded to the image of the robber hero as they themselves had received it. Seal's idea that what he calls the 'outlaw hero tradition' functions as a 'cultural script' is one of his most interesting suggestions.[16]

During the final decade of the eighteenth century, the traditions of representation of the English robber began to develop in a new direction, one to which, for reasons of space, and because it runs at something of a tangent to my main themes, I have paid very little attention. In these years, with revolution in the air, the figures of the outlaw and robber heroes began to be reconstructed to accord with new and radical ideas. So in 1795 Joseph Ritson, the first great anthologist of Robin Hood, in the 'Life' of the hero with which he prefaced his collection, hailed him as a freedom fighter against tyranny and champion of the common people, a powerful reinterpretation of the legend that has found echoes ever since.[17] The year before had seen the publication of *Caleb Williams*, a novel by the anarchist William Godwin. In one episode, Godwin introduces a robber gang, whose captain defiantly declares, 'Our profession is the profession of justice.' Godwin is careful to establish the point that this is the character's view, not his own; however, he portrays his robber chief as a principled and generous man, and very much as a primitive rebel.[18] One way of reading

Hobsbawm's *Bandits* is to see it as a late and glittering successor in this kind of radical tradition, and as exemplifying one of the more recent forms in which English culture has continued to pursue its very long love affair with the figure of the robber.

Chronology

Eleventh Century

1066   Death of King Edward the Confessor. The Norman invasion of England. Duke William of Normandy is crowned King William I of England.

before 1070   Hereward, an English thane, outlawed under King Edward, returns from exile abroad.

1070   Hereward and his men join an invading army of Danes in sacking the town and monastery of Peterborough.

1071   Hereward plays an important role in defending the Isle of Ely against the besieging Normans.

Twelfth Century

after 1109   Richard, a monk of Ely, writes the *Gesta Herwardi*.

about 1139   Geoffrey Gaimar composes *L'Estoire des Engleis*.

1200   The Marcher lord Fouke Fitz Waryn revolts after King John denies him Whittington Castle, which Fouke claims as part of his inheritance.

Thirteenth Century

1203   Fouke and his followers are pardoned.

1204   Whittington Castle is restored to Fouke.

1246   A Latin letter sent by the English clergy to Pope Innocent IV protests that if he persists in demanding that they send him half their income, they will have to disband their households and send away the well-born laymen whom they retain in service. Such men are certain to become robbers, 'since they would not be able to dig and would be ashamed to beg' – the earliest explicit statement to the effect that men of gentle birth could be expected to view robbery as less disgraceful than begging.

about 1249 The chronicler Matthew Paris describes how after the Norman invasion the English nobles took to the woods as robbers, 'being ashamed to beg'.

about 1280 Very approximate date of composition of lost Anglo-French verse romance about Fouke Fitz Waryn.

1285 The Statute of Winchester: ordains the institution of the hue and cry, or pursuit of thieves, robbers and murderers.

Fourteenth Century

1304 Institution of trailbaston courts.

about 1305 *The Outlaw's Song* (poem in Anglo-French).

about 1317 A Franciscan preacher composes the manual called *Fasciculus Morum*. This contains the earliest reference to the belief that the English, more specifically the English gentry, were particularly given to robbery, and disinclined to admit that there was anything wrong with it.

about 1325 The extant prose Anglo-French romance about Fouke Fitz Waryn is redacted from the metrical version at some point between now and about 1340.

1326 Sir Roger Bellers, a Leicestershire magnate, is murdered by a gang that includes Eustace Folville and two of his brothers.

1330 The Dominican preacher John Bromyard has begun work on his *Summa Praedicantium*, a vast preaching manual in Latin, which contains many references to criminals and crime. He finally completes it in about 1348.

1331 The Folville brothers and their associates kidnap Sir Richard Willoughby and hold him to ransom.

about 1340 Very approximate date of composition of *The Tale of Gamelyn*, the earliest surviving outlaw tale in English.

about 1377 William Langland revises his poem *Piers Plowman* and includes in it references to 'rymes of Robyn Hood' and 'Folvyles lawes'.

about 1395 Geoffrey Chaucer composes 'The Friar's Tale' as part of *The Canterbury Tales*.

Fifteenth Century

1411 Prince Henry, eldest son of King Henry IV, falls out with his father. This is the period to which the later legends of the 'Wild Prince' allude.

1413 Prince Henry succeeds to the throne and rules as Henry V.

1427 Earliest record of the performance of a Robin Hood play.

about 1450 Earliest likely date for the manuscript of *Robin Hood and the Monk*, the oldest surviving text of a Robin Hood metrical tale.

1471 At some point between now and 1476, Sir John Fortescue writes his treatise *The Governance of England*. This contains a passage arguing that the superior courage of the English, when compared to the French and the Scots, is demonstrated by the Englishman's propensity to robbery.

about 1475   Date of the manuscript of the earliest surviving Robin Hood play.

1485   Henry Tudor is crowned as King Henry VII, the first Tudor king.

1492   Earliest possible date for the first print publication of *A Gest of Robyn Hode*. (The component tales are older.)

about 1497   An anonymous Venetian diplomat reports that there are more thieves and robbers in England than anywhere else in the world. The most unsafe place of all is London.

about 1500   Date of the manuscript of the metrical tale of *Robin Hood and the Potter*.

Sixteenth Century

1509   Accession of Henry VIII.
Earliest reference to Maid Marian, as a May-game character at Kingston upon Thames.

winter 1513–14   Composition and first performance of *Youth* (allegorical play). Youth is led astray by the highway robber Riot. Contains a very early allusion to the custom of allowing condemned criminals to speak from the gallows.

1514   Composition and first performance of *Hyckescorner* (allegorical play).

1515   Henry VIII and Catherine of Aragon ride out maying to Shooters Hill and feast with 'Robin Hood' and his men.

1516   Thomas More's Latin work *Utopia* is published. It includes an attempt to account for the causes of property crime.

1531   Publication of *The Book named The Governor* by Sir Thomas Elyot. Contains a passage deploring the tendency of the nobility and gentry to sympathise with offenders who have committed certain kinds of violent offence, including robbery.

1547   A statute is passed removing from highway robbers and some burglars the right to claim benefit of clergy.

1551   Ralph Robinson publishes the first English translation of More's *Utopia*.

1552   *A Manifest Detection of Diceplay*: first detailed account of the criminal networks of London.

1558   Accession of Elizabeth I.

about 1560   Publication of the May-game play of *Robin Hood and the Potter*.

1568   *The Contention Between Liberality and Prodigality* (allegorical play). Revived in 1601.

1569   Richard Grafton, *Chronicle at Large*: first source to describe Robin Hood as a nobleman.

1576   Execution of George Mannington at Cambridge Castle. The ballad called 'Mannington's Repentance' is written for the occasion, possibly by Mannington himself.

1580 Robert Hitchcock includes a passage in his *A Politic Plat for the honour of the Prince* in which he declares that any man of spirit will always prefer to rob rather than beg.

1584 George Whetstone's *A Mirour for Magestrates of Cyties* describes how well-dressed highwaymen associate on equal terms with landed gentlemen in fashionable London eating houses.

1587 William Harrison comments on the prevalence of robbery in England in the second edition of *The Description of England*.

Thomas Underdowne translates the ancient romance of the *Aethiopica* by Helidorus.

about 1587 *The Famous Victories of Henry the Fifth* (play).

1588 Thomas Lodge turns *The Tale of Gamelyn* into the romance *Rosalynde*. It is published in 1590.

1589 The second edition of William Warner's *Albions England* contains a passage on Robin Hood which for the first time states explicitly that he stole from the rich to give to the poor.

1592 Robert Greene, *The Blacke Bookes Messenger. Laying open the Life and Death of Ned Browne*. Earliest example of criminal 'life'. Fiction.

about 1593 William Shakespeare writes *The Two Gentlemen of Verona*.

1595 The highwayman Luke Hutton, imprisoned in Newgate, writes his verse 'repentance'.

1596 Probable date of publication of Hutton's *The Black Dog of Newgate*, an exposé of the crooked practices of jailers. Hutton is later hanged at York.

The Jesuit Robert Parsons comments on the number of robbers in England, notes that many are gentlemen's sons, and suggests some remedies.

about 1597 Shakespeare writes *King Henry IV, Parts I* and *II*.

1598 Anthony Munday and others write two linked plays about Robin Hood: *The Downfall of Robert, Earl of Huntington* and *The Death of Robert, Earl of Huntington*. Robin Hood and Maid Marian are depicted as a pair of aristocratic lovers.

1599 Shakespeare responds with *As You Like It*.

Munday and others write *Sir John Oldcastle*, a history play set in the reign of Henry V.

Ben Jonson satirises the fashion for cultivating the company of highwaymen in his comedy *Every Man out of his Humour*.

Seventeenth Century

1603 Death of Elizabeth I. The dynasty of the Tudor monarchs gives way to the Stuarts, with the accession of James I.

Gamaliel Ratsey, an impoverished gentleman, who has served

as a soldier in Ireland, returns to England and embarks on a career as a highway robber.

1605 Ratsey and two associates are executed at Bedford. Two pamphlets, *The Life and Death of Gamaliel Ratsey* and *Ratseis Ghost*, purport to give an account of his life and exploits.

1612 Publication of *The Life, Apprehension, Arraignment, and Execution of Charles Courtney*.

1613 The satirist George Wither writes scathingly about the prevalent admiration for highway robbers and pirates.

1618 Sir George Sandys is executed for highway robbery. The following year, there is gossip about his widow, who is rumoured to have become a robber herself.

1622 John Taylor 'the Water Poet' looks back light-heartedly on the famous English robbers of the past in his verse pamphlet *An arrant Thief*.

1625 Accession of Charles I.

1626 John Clavell is condemned for robbery. He is reprieved from execution, but left in jail.

1628 Clavell, now pardoned and released from jail, publishes *A Recantation of an Ill Led Life*.

1633 Philip Massinger's comedy *The Guardian* is licensed for the theatre. It contains the earliest explicit reference to the idea that English robbers are superior to those of the Continent in showing themselves exceptionally humane.

1642 Outbreak of the English Civil War.

1649 Execution of Charles I.

1650 The radical visionary Abiezer Coppe publishes his *Fiery Flying Roll*, in which he imagines God returning to the world as a highwayman, expropriating the wealth of the rich and distributing it among the poor.

1651 Oliver Cromwell defeats Charles II at the battle of Worcester. James Hind, a former highwayman turned Royalist soldier, escapes from the field. He is still at large when *Hinds Ramble* appears, a collection of apocryphal tales of his adventures, but shortly after, he is captured and imprisoned in Newgate. Publications about him flood from the presses.

1652 *The English Gusman*, the longest and best of the fictional accounts of Hind's career, is published in January. Later that year, Hind is taken to Worcester and executed for high treason.

1654 Beginning of the process of systematising and extending the previously small-scale practice of transporting convicted criminals to the colonies.

1660 Restoration of Charles II.

1663 Richard Hals, a distant cousin of Sir Ralph Verney, is arrested for robbery. His relatives negotiate a pardon.

1665 First edition of Richard Head's novel *The English Rogue*. The book includes a couple of highwayman episodes, one of which involves a gang of women robbers.

1670 The executions for highway robbery of Claude and Louis Du Vall (or 'Lewis Deval') are followed by the publication of a couple of pamphlet 'lives'.

1685 After two further escapes from the gallows, Hals is executed for a robbery.

1692 'An Act for encourageing the apprehending of Highway Men' puts on a statutory footing the system of offering rewards for the capture of highwaymen, and immunity to robbers who testify against their accomplices.

Eighteenth Century

1701 *Hanging, Not Punishment Enough, for Murtherers, High-way Men, and House-Breakers.*

1707 First performance of George Farquhar's comedy *The Beaux' Stratagem.*

1713 Publication of the first two volumes of Captain Alexander Smith's *Complete History of the Highwaymen.* The third volume followed in 1714.

Jonathan Wild begins his career as a thief-taker.

1714 Wild sets up as a 'finder' of stolen property.

1718 Parliament passes an act which further systematises the practice of transportation and puts it on a statutory footing.

1721 George I appoints Sir Robert Walpole as Prime Minister and Chancellor of the Exchequer.

1722 March: execution of the highwayman Benjamin Childe. Two pamphlet 'lives' follow, one incorporating an autobiographical statement by Childe.

May: execution of John Hawkins and George Sympson for robbing the Bristol Mail. Their accomplice Ralph Wilson, who has won immunity by giving evidence against them, justifies himself in a printed account of the gang's activities.

December: publication of Defoe's novel *Colonel Jack.*

1724 The burglar Jack Sheppard escapes from jail four times this year. Two of these escapes are made from Newgate. He is finally recaptured on 31 October and hanged on 16 November.

1725 Execution of Jonathan Wild. His methods of doing business are exposed in numerous publications.

1726 A Swiss visitor, César de Saussure, writes a letter describing the polite behaviour shown by some English mounted robbers.

1728 First season of *The Beggar's Opera* by John Gay.

1734 Richard ('Dick') Turpin takes part with at least six others in an attack and burglary at a farmhouse in the parish of Barking. Similar attacks are made elsewhere, some of them very violent.

1735   In February, several of the gang of housebreakers to which Turpin belongs are arrested. Other arrests follow later in the year. Turpin himself evades capture and turns highwayman.

      A case of a mounted woman robber is reported in the press.

1737   Turpin shoots and kills a gamekeeper's assistant who tries to arrest him in Epping Forest.

about 1738   A story goes round that a gentleman whom Turpin had once robbed ran into him at the races, and the two had a bet together in friendly fashion. The Frenchman Jean Bernard Le Blanc, who records the tale in a letter home, is intrigued and shocked by English attitudes to highway robbers.

1739   Turpin is hanged at York for horse-stealing.

1750   Execution of James Maclaine, a robber who catches the sympathy of some fashionable London ladies.

1761   Execution for robbery of Isaac Darkin, who spends part of his time in prison reading *The Beggar's Opera*.

1794   *Caleb Williams*, a novel by the radical William Godwin.

1795   Execution of Jerry Abershaw, the last mounted highway robber to achieve popular fame.

Nineteenth Century

1805   Institution of mounted police patrol round London.

1808   First appearance, in a chapbook, of the story of Turpin's ride to York.

1830   Publication of the novel *Paul Clifford* by Edward Lytton Bulwer.

1831   Last mounted highway robbery recorded.

1834   *Rookwood. A Romance* by William Harrison Ainsworth. First appearance in the Turpin legend of his famous horse, Black Bess.

1837   Accession of Queen Victoria.

      Charles Dickens's 'Newgate' novel, *Oliver Twist*, begins to be published in serial form.

1839   Publication of Ainsworth's *Jack Sheppard*.

1841   Dickens adds a preface to the third edition of *Oliver Twist* condemning romanticised treatments of criminal life in fiction, and distancing his novel from the work of Ainsworth and Bulwer. Publication in serial form of Dickens's novel *Barnaby Rudge*.

about 1853   The essayist Thomas De Quincey looks back nostalgically on the lost days of the highwaymen.

Twentieth Century

1906   Publication of Alfred Noyes's narrative poem, *The Highwayman*.

Select Bibliography

Ainsworth, William Harrison, *Rookwood. A Romance*, 3 vols, London, Richard Bentley, 1834

The Authentic Trial, and Memoirs of Isaac Darkin, Oxford, R. Baldwin and W. Jackson [1761]

Barlow, Derek, *Dick Turpin and the Gregory Gang*, London, Phillimore, 1973

Beattie, J. M., *Crime and the Courts in England, 1660–1800*, Oxford, Clarendon Press, 1986

Bellamy, J. G., 'The Coterel Gang: an Anatomy of a Band of Fourteenth-century Criminals', *English Historical Review*, vol. 79 (1964), pp. 698–717

Bellamy, John, *Crime and Public Order in England in the Later Middle Ages*, London, Routledge & Kegan Paul, 1973

Bulwer, Edward, *Paul Clifford*, 3 vols, London, Henry Colburn and Richard Bentley, 1830

Burgess, Glyn S., *Two Medieval Outlaws: Eustace the Monk and Fouke Fitz Waryn*, Cambridge, Brewer, 1997

Child, Francis James (ed.), *The English and Scottish Popular Ballads*, 5 vols, New York, Dover, 1965

Childe, Benjamin, *A Narrative of the Life of Mr. Benjamin Childe*, London, T. Payne, 1722

Clavell, John, *A Recantation of An Ill Led Life*, 3rd edn, London, 1634, reprinted in facsimile in *John Clavell 1601–1643*, by John Pafford: see under Pafford for details.

Cockburn, J. S. (ed.), *Crime in England 1550–1800*, London, Methuen, 1977

The Contention Between Liberality and Prodigality, ed. W. W. Greg, Oxford, Malone Society, 1913

Defoe, Daniel, *Colonel Jack*, ed. Samuel Holt Monk, Oxford University Press, 1970

Dickens, Charles, *Barnaby Rudge*, Everyman's Library, London, Dent, 1950, repr. 1972

Dickens, Charles, *Oliver Twist*, ed. Fred Kaplan, Norton Critical Edition, New York, W. W. Norton, 1993

Dobson, R. B., and Taylor, J. (eds), *Rymes of Robyn Hood. An Introduction to the English Outlaw*, revised edn, Stroud, Sutton Publishing, 1997

F[idge], G[eorge], *The English Gusman; or the History of that Unparallel'd Thief James Hind*, London, 1652

Faller, Lincoln B., *Turned to account. The forms and functions of criminal biography in late seventeenth- and early eighteenth-century England*, Cambridge University Press, 1987

The Famous Victories of Henry the Fifth, ed. Geoffrey Bullough in *Narrative and Dramatic Sources of Shakespeare*, vol. 4, London, Routledge & Kegan Paul, 1962

Farquhar, George, *The Beaux' Stratagem*, ed. Charles N. Fifer, Regents Restoration Drama Series, London, Edward Arnold, 1977

Fielding, Henry, *An Enquiry Into the Causes of the Late Increase of Robbers*, ed. Malvin R. Zirker, Middletown, Connecticut, Wesleyan University Press, 1988

Fortescue, Sir John, *The Governance of England*, ed. Charles Plummer, Oxford, Clarendon Press, 1885

Fouke le Fitz Waryn, ed. E. J. Hathaway, P. T. Ricketts, C. A. Robson and A. D. Wilshere, Oxford, Anglo-Norman Text Society, 1975

Gay, John, *The Beggar's Opera*, ed. John Fuller in *Dramatic Works*, vol. 2, Oxford, Clarendon Press, 1983

Gesta Herwardi, ed. Thomas Duffus Hardy and Charles Trice Martin, in *Lestorie des Engles*, by Geffrei Gaimar, vol. 1, Rolls Series, London, HMSO, 1888

Greene, Robert, *The Blacke Bookes Messenger*, ed. G. B. Harrison, Bodley Head Quartos, London, John Lane, 1924

Hanawalt, Barbara A., 'Ballads and Bandits. Fourteenth-Century Outlaws and the Robin Hood Poems' in *Chaucer's England*, ed. Barbara A. Hanawalt, Minneapolis, University of Minnesota Press, 1992

Hanawalt, Barbara A., *Crime and Conflict in English Communities 1300–1348*, Cambridge, Massachusetts, Harvard University Press, 1979

Harper, Charles G., *Half-Hours with the Highwaymen*, 2 vols, London, Chapman and Hall, 1908

Harrison, William, *The Description of England*, ed. Georges Edelen, New York, Dover, 1994

Hay, Douglas, Linebaugh, Peter, Thompson, E. P., and others (eds), *Albion's Fatal Tree. Crime and Society in Eighteenth-Century England*, London, Allen Lane, 1975

Head, Richard, and Kirkman, Francis, *The English Rogue described, in the Life of Meriton Latroon*, London, George Routledge, 1928

Christopher Hill, *Liberty Against the Law. Some Seventeenth-Century Controversies*, London, Allen Lane, 1996

Hobsbawm, Eric, *Bandits*, revised edn, London, Weidenfeld & Nicolson, 2000

Holt, J. C., *Robin Hood*, revised edn, London, Thames & Hudson, 1989

Johnston, Alexandra F., 'The Robin Hood of the Records' in *Playing Robin Hood. The Legend as Performance in Five Centuries*, ed. Lois Potter, Newark, University of Delaware Press, 1998

Jonson, Ben, *Every Man out of his Humour*, ed. C. H. Herford, Percy and Evelyn Simpson, in *Works*, vol. 3, Oxford, Clarendon Press, 1927

Judges, A. V. (ed.), *The Elizabethan Underworld*, London, Routledge, 1930

Keen, Maurice, *The Outlaws of Medieval Legend*, revised paperback edn, London, Routledge & Kegan Paul, 1987

Knight, Stephen, *Robin Hood. A Complete Study of the English Outlaw*, Oxford, Blackwell, 1994

The Life and Death of Gamaliel Ratsey and *Ratseis Ghost*, London, 1605; facs. repr. London, Shakespeare Association, 1935

The Life, Apprehension, Arraignment, and Execution of Charles Courtney, London, 1612

The Life of Deval, London, 1669 [1670]

Linebaugh, Peter, *The London Hanged. Crime and Civil Society in the Eighteenth Century*, London, Penguin, 1993

Lives of the Most Remarkable Criminals, ed. Arthur L. Hayward, London, Routledge, 1927

Luttrell, Narcissus, *A Brief Historical Relation of State Affairs from September 1678 to April 1714*, 6 vols, Oxford University Press, 1857

The Malefactor's Register; or, the Newgate and Tyburn Calendar, 5 vols, London, Alexander Hogg, [1779]

Mandeville, Bernard, *An Enquiry into the Causes of the Frequent Executions at Tyburn* (1725), ed. Malvin R. Zirker, Augustan Reprint Society No. 105, Los Angeles, University of California, 1964

A manifest detection of the moste vyle and detestable use of Diceplay, London, Abraham Vele, [1552]

More, Thomas, *Complete Works*, Vol. 4, *Utopia*, ed. Edward Surtz and J. H. Hexter, New Haven, Yale University Press, 1965

More, Thomas, *Utopia*, translated by Ralph Robinson, ed. J. Rawson Lumby, Cambridge University Press, 1885

Munday, Anthony, and Chettle, Henry, *The Huntingdon Plays. A Critical Edition of The Downfall and The Death of Robert, Earl of Huntingdon*, ed. John Carney Meagher, New York, Garland, 1980

Munday, Anthony, Drayton, Michael, and others, *Sir John Oldcastle*, ed. C. F. Tucker Brooke, in *The Shakespeare Apocrypha*, Oxford, Clarendon Press, 1908

Noyes, Alfred, 'The Highwayman' in *The Oxford Book of Narrative Verse*, ed. Iona and Peter Opie, Oxford University Press, 1988

Pafford, John, *John Clavell 1601–1643. Highwayman, Author, Lawyer, Doctor*, Oxford, Leopard's Head Press, 1993

Peterson, Spiro (ed.), *The Counterfeit Lady and other criminal fiction of seventeenth-century England*, New York, Doubleday, 1961

Pope, Walter, *The Memoires of Monsieur Du Vall*, London, 1670

Rowley, Samuel, *When you see me, you know me*, ed. F. P. Wilson, Oxford, Malone Society, 1952

Seal, Graham, *The Outlaw Legend. A Cultural Tradition in Britain, America and Australia*, Cambridge University Press, 1996

Shakespeare, William, *As You Like It*, ed. Agnes Latham, The Arden Shakespeare, London, Methuen, 1975

Shakespeare, William, *King Henry IV, Part I*, ed. A. R. Humphreys, The Arden Shakespeare, London, Methuen, 1966

Shakespeare, William, *King Henry IV, Part II*, ed. A. R. Humphreys, The Arden Shakespeare, London, Methuen, 1966

Shakespeare, William, *The Two Gentlemen of Verona*, ed. Clifford Leech, The Arden Shakespeare, London, Methuen, 1972

Smith, Alexander, *A Complete History of the Lives and Robberies of the most notorious Highwaymen*, London, George Routledge, 1926

Stones, E. L. G., 'The Folvilles of Ashby-Folville, Leicestershire, and their associates in crime, 1326–1347', *Transactions of the Royal Historical Society*, 5th series, vol. 7 (1957), pp. 117–36

Summerson, Henry, 'The Criminal Underworld of Medieval England', *Journal of Legal History*, vol. 17, no. 3 (December 1996), pp. 197–224

The Tale of Gamelyn, ed. W. W. Skeat in *The Complete Works of Geoffrey Chaucer*, 6 vols, Oxford, Clarendon Press, 1894 (introduction, vol. III; text, vol. IV)

Trailbaston, ed. Isabel S. T. Aspin in *Anglo–Norman Political Songs*, Oxford, Anglo Norman Text Society, 1953

Two Tudor Interludes: Youth and Hick Scorner, ed. Ian Lancashire, Manchester University Press, 1980

Verney, Margaret M., *Memoirs of the Verney Family*, Vol. 4, London, Longmans, Green, 1899

Villette, John, *The Annals of Newgate; or, Malefactor's Register*, 4 vols, London, J. Wenman, 1776

Whetstone, George, *A Mirour for Magestrates of Cyties*, London, 1584

Wiles, David, *The Early Plays of Robin Hood*, Cambridge, Brewer, 1981

Wilson, Ralph, *A Full and Impartial Account Of all the Robberies Committed by John Hawkins, George Sympson . . . and their Companions*, 3rd edn, London, J. Peele, [1722]

Notes

ONE: INTRODUCTION: THE CULT OF THE ROBBER

1 Jean Bernard Le Blanc, *Letters on the English and French Nations. Translated from the Original French*, 2 vols (London, J. Brindley and others, 1747), II, pp. 292–3.

2 See Sir Edward Coke, *The Third Part of the Institutes of the Laws of England* (London, 1644), pp. 68–9 [cap. xvi]; and see above, epigraph.

3 Sir John Fortescue, *The Governance of England*, ed. Charles Plummer (Oxford, Clarendon Press, 1885), pp. 141–2 [chap. XIII; see also chap. XII].

4 Thomas More, *Complete Works*, vol. 4, *Utopia*, ed. Edward Surtz and J. H. Hexter (New Haven, Yale University Press, 1965), pp. 60–9; quotations on pp. 62, ll. 12, 22, 26–7; 64, ll. 18–9; 68, ll. 23–4.

5 Thomas More, *Utopia*, translated by Ralph Robinson, ed. J. Rawson Lumby (Cambridge University Press, 1885), pp. 30, 35.

6 For the Folvilles, see Chapter Two, nn. 9, 22. For other well-born gangsters, see R. H. Hilton, *A Medieval Society. The West Midlands at the End of the Thirteenth Century* (Cambridge University Press, 1983 [first publ. 1966]), pp. 254–8; John Bellamy, *Crime and Public Order in England in the Later Middle Ages* (London, Routledge & Kegan Paul, 1973), pp. 45–9, 72–82; James Buchanan Given, *Society and Homicide in Thirteenth-Century England* (Stanford University Press, 1977), pp. 122–4; Barbara A. Hanawalt, *Crime and Conflict in English Communities 1300–1348* (Cambridge, Massachusetts, Harvard University Press, 1979), pp. 141–3, 202, 208, 216.

7 William Harrison, *The Description of England*, ed. Georges Edelen (New York, Dover, 1994), pp. 192–3. Passage added in second edition.

8 [Richard Head], *The English Rogue Described in the Life of Meriton Latroon* (London, Henry Marsh, 1665), sigs Ff$_3$v–Ff$_4$r [chap. xxvi].

9 Robert Hitchcock, *A Politic Plat for the honour of the Prince*, in *Social England Illustrated. A Collection of XVIIth Century Tracts*, intr. Andrew Lang, English Garner Series (Westminster, Archibald Constable, 1903), pp. 86–7.

10 Thomas Wilson, *A Discourse Upon Usury*, introduced by R. H. Tawney

(London, G. Bell, 1925), p. 205; see also Robert Parsons, quoted in Chapter Nine, p. 101 and n. 1.

11 Margaret M. Verney, *Memoirs of the Verney Family*, vol. 4 (London, Longmans, Green, 1899), p. 282. The date is 1679. Original has 'T'is' for "Tis'.

12 George Wither, *Abuses Stript and Whipt. Or Satirical Essayes* (London, 1613), sigs P₁r–v (Lib. 2, Satyr 2). Original has no comma after '*pitty*'.

13 Philip Henslowe, *Henslowe's Diary*, ed. R. A. Foakes and R. T. Rickert (Cambridge University Press, 1961), p. 216; see also William Kemp, *Nine Daies Wonder* (1600), ed. G. B. Harrison, Bodley Head Quartos (London, The Bodley Head, 1923), p. 20.

14 Christopher Hill, *Liberty Against the Law. Some Seventeenth-Century Controversies* (London, Allen Lane, 1996), p. 4.

15 John Clavell, *A Recantation of An Ill Led Life*, 3rd edn (London, 1634), reprinted in facsimile in John Pafford, *John Clavell 1601–1643. Highwayman, Author, Lawyer, Doctor* (Oxford, Leopard's Head Press, 1993), pp. 7–8. For inn servants lionising highwaymen, see also Thomas Middleton (with Ben Jonson and John Fletcher?), *The Widow*, ed. A. H. Bullen, in *The Works of Thomas Middleton*, 8 vols (London, John C. Nimmo, 1885), V, III i 22–37.

16 John Gay, *The Beggar's Opera*, ed. John Fuller, in *Dramatic Works*, vol. 2 (Oxford, Clarendon Press, 1983), I viii 30–1.

17 Harrison, *The Description of England*, ed. Edelen, p. 114; Ruth Kelso, 'Sixteenth-Century Definitions of the Gentleman in England', *Journal of English and Germanic Philology*, vol. 24 (1925), p. 380; Guy Miege, 'The Present State of Great Britain: An Eighteenth-Century Self-Portrait', in *Aristocratic Government and Society in Eighteenth-Century England. The Foundations of Stability*, ed. Daniel A. Baugh (New York, Franklin Watts, 1975), p. 46; Daniel Defoe, *The Compleat English Gentleman*, ed. Karl D. Bülbring (London, David Nutt, 1890), pp. 47, 48.

18 Clavell, *A Recantation*, pp. 6–8, 16–17, 23; see also Ben Jonson, *Every Man out of his Humour*, ed. C. H. Herford, Percy and Evelyn Simpson, in *Works*, vol. 3 (Oxford, Clarendon Press, 1927), IV v 36–55, V iii 61–74, also under characters, 'Shift' (p. 426).

19 *Annales de Burton* in *Annales Monastici*, vol. 1, ed. Henry Richards Luard, Rolls Series (London, Longmans etc. 1864), p. 281; Matthew Paris, *Chronica Majora*, ed. Henry Richards Luard, 7 vols, Rolls Series (London, HMSO, 1872–1883), IV, p. 583; Johannis de Trokelowe, *Chronica et Annales Monasterii S. Albani*, ed. Henry Thomas Riley, Rolls Series (London, Longmans etc., 1866), p. 93.

20 Bellamy, *Crime and Public Order*, pp. 42–5.

21 Harrison, *The Description of England*, p. 193; see also pp. 119, 239. Note also Henry Brinklow, *Complaynt of Roderyck Mors . . . unto the parliament howse of England*, ed. J. Meadows Cowper (London, Early English Text Society, 1874), pp. 44–5, 40–1.

22 For the most detailed and reliable account of Turpin's career, see Derek Barlow, *Dick Turpin and the Gregory Gang* (London, Phillimore, 1973).

23 John Taylor the Water Poet, *All the Workes* (London 1630, facs. repr.

Menston, Scolar Press, 1973), sig. Ll₄r. Original has 'cowne' for 'towne', and no comma after *'Tucke'*.

TWO: ROBBERY IN THE GREENWOOD

1 *Trailbaston*, ed. Isabel S. T. Aspin, in *Anglo-Norman Political Songs* (Oxford, Anglo Norman Text Society, 1953), pp. 67–78; quotations from stanzas 7, 24, 21, 9, 22, 4, 19. For an enlightening account of the trailbaston courts and criminal law procedure, including outlawry, see R. B. Pugh (ed.), *Wiltshire Gaol Delivery and Trailbaston Trials 1275–1306* (Devizes, Wiltshire Record Society, 1978), pp. 5–28; for conditions in medieval jails, see Ralph B. Pugh, *Imprisonment in Medieval England* (Cambridge University Press, 1968), esp. pp. 180–1; for outlawry, see also Bellamy, *Crime and Public Order*, pp. 104–6; for pardons, see Bellamy, op. cit., pp. 85–7, 191–8, and see also J. G. Bellamy, *The Criminal Trial in Later Medieval England. Felony before the courts from Edward I to the Sixteenth Century* (Stroud, Sutton Publishing, 1998), pp. 137–48.

2 *Trailbaston*, ed. Aspin, in *Anglo-Norman Political Songs*, stanzas 5, 14, 5. For the *locus amoenus*, see Ernst Robert Curtius, *European Literature and the Latin Middle Ages*, trans. Willard R. Trask (London, Routledge & Kegan Paul, 1979 [first publ. 1953]), pp. 195–200.

3 *Trailbaston*, ed. Aspin, in *Anglo-Norman Political Songs*, stanza 13.

4 For the mss. of *The Outlaw's Song* (*Trailbaston*) and *Fouke le Fitz Waryn*, see E. J. Hathaway, P. T. Ricketts, C. A. Robson and A. D. Wilshere (eds), *Fouke le Fitz Waryn* (Oxford, Anglo-Norman Text Society, 1975), pp. xxxvii–xliv; Aspin (ed.), *Anglo-Norman Political Songs*, pp. 24–5, 67.

5 *The Harley Lyrics. The Middle English Lyrics of Ms. Harley 2253*, ed. G. L. Brook, 2nd edn (Manchester University Press, 1956), pp. 43–4, 62–3.

6 Compare the late fifteenth-century lyric 'I muste go walke the woodes so wyld'; see Chapter Eleven, p. 133 and n. 6.

7 Henry of Knighton, *Chronicle*, ed. Joseph Rawson Lumby, 2 vols, Rolls Series (London, HMSO, 1889, 1895), I, pp. 460–1.

8 *Trailbaston*, ed. Aspin, in *Anglo-Norman Political Songs*, stanzas 9, 10.

9 The Willoughby kidnapping and related events are studied in detail in E. L. G. Stones, 'The Folvilles of Ashby-Folville, Leicestershire, and their associates in crime, 1326–1347', *Transactions of the Royal Historical Society*, 5th series, vol. 7 (1957), pp. 117–36, and J. G. Bellamy, 'The Coterel Gang: an Anatomy of a Band of Fourteenth-century Criminals', *English Historical Review*, vol. 79 (1964), pp. 698–717. For the sums taken from Willoughby, see Stones, op. cit., p. 122. A mark was the value of two-thirds of £1 sterling.

10 Bellamy, 'The Coterel Gang', p. 700; Stones, 'The Folvilles of Ashby-Folville', pp. 118–20; *Calendar of the Patent Rolls 1327–1330* (London, HMSO, 1891), p. 70.

11 Knighton, *Chronicle*, I, pp. 432–3.

12 *Trailbaston*, ed. Aspin, in *Anglo-Norman Political Songs*, stanza 12, ll. 45–7.

13 Stones, 'The Folvilles of Ashby-Folville', p. 120; *Calendar of the Patent Rolls 1327–1330* (London, HMSO, 1891), p. 10.

14 Stones, 'The Folvilles of Ashby-Folville', pp. 120–1; *Calendar of the Patent Rolls 1327–1330*, p. 373.

15 Barbara A. Hanawalt, 'Ballads and Bandits. Fourteenth-Century Outlaws and the Robin Hood Poems', in *Chaucer's England*, ed. Barbara A. Hanawalt (Minneapolis, University of Minnesota Press, 1992), p. 158.

16 Bellamy, 'The Coterel Gang', p. 708.

17 *Year Books of the Reign of King Edward III*, Years XIV and XV, ed. and trans. Luke Owen Pike, Rolls Series (London, HMSO, 1889), pp. 258–63; quotation on p. 259.

18 Bellamy, 'The Coterel Gang', pp. 700, 707, 702.

19 Stones, 'The Folvilles of Ashby-Folville', p. 124.

20 *Rotuli Parliamentorum* 6 vols (London, 1767–1777), II, p. 201; see also pp. 136, 165.

21 Stones, 'The Folvilles of Ashby-Folville', pp. 117, 129–30.

22 William Langland, *Piers Plowman*, B text, ed. W. W. Skeat (London, Early English Text Society, 1869), Passus xix, ll. 239–41. Original has 'recoeure'. See R. H. Bowers, ' "Foleuyles Lawes" ("Piers Plowman", C. XXII. 247)' in *Notes and Queries*, ser. viii, September, 1961, pp. 327–8.

23 Langland, *Piers Plowman*, Passus v, ll. 469–84.

24 Ibid., Passus vi ll. 25–37; see also Thomas Wimbledon, *Sermon: Redde Rationem Villicationis Tue*, ed. Ione Kemp Knight (Pittsburgh, Duquesne University Press, 1967), p. 63; G. R. Owst, *Literature and Pulpit in Medieval England*, revised edition (New York, Barnes & Noble, 1966), pp. 549–54.

25 *Dives and Pauper*, ed. Priscilla Heath Barnum, vol. 1, parts i and ii (London, Early English Text Society, 1976 and 1980), part ii, p. 144 [Commandment vii cap. vi].

26 Bellamy, *Crime and Public Order*, p. 66; Philippe Contamine, *War in the Middle Ages*, trans. Michael Jones (Oxford, Basil Blackwell, 1986), pp. 260, 265–6, 299; Philippa C. Maddern, *Violence and Social Order. East Anglia 1422–1442* (Oxford, Clarendon Press, 1992), p. 80.

THREE: THE OUTLAW DISPOSSESSED

1 *Flores Historiarum*, ed. Henry Richards Luard, 3 vols, Rolls Series (London, HMSO, 1890), II, p. 14, and see also p. 2; for date and authorship, see Richard Vaughan, *Matthew Paris* (Cambridge University Press, 1958), pp. 37–41, 102–3. With 'ashamed to beg, ignorant of how to dig' compare *The Gospel of Luke*, chap. 16 v. 3 (Vulgate).

2 Only in late texts written for the broadside market is Robin Hood given a nephew or cousin, Gamwell, or Gamble Gold, who in one ballad is identified with Will Scarlet. See *Robin Hood Newly Revived* and *The Bold Pedlar and Robin Hood* in *The English and Scottish Popular Ballads*, ed. Francis James Child, 5 vols (New York, Dover, 1965 [first publ. 1882–98]), III, pp. 144–50, 154–5 [Child nos 128 and 132].

3 Bellamy, *Crime and Public Order*, p. 71; Given, *Society and Homicide*, pp. 126–7; Hanawalt, *Crime and Conflict*, pp. 192–4; Hanawalt, 'Ballads and Bandits', p. 158.

4 See also Matthew Paris, *Chronica Majora*, ed. Luard, IV, p. 583; *Annales de Burton* in *Annales Monastici*, ed. Luard, I, p. 281.

5 St Thomas Aquinas, *Summa Theologiae. Latin text and English translation*, 61 vols (London, Blackfriars, 1964–80), XXXVIII, pp. 80–3 (2a 2ae, qu. 66, art. 7); note *The Book of Proverbs*, chap. 6 v. 30 (Vulgate); and see also *Dives and Pauper*, ed. Barnum, vol. i, part ii, pp. 141–4 (Commandment vii cap. vi); Edward Surtz and J. H. Hexter (eds), *The Complete Works of St. Thomas More*, vol IV: *Utopia*, pp. 332–3, note to 66/21.

6 William of Malmesbury, *De Gestis Regum Anglorum and Historiae Novellae*, ed. William Stubbs, 2 vols, Rolls Series (London, HMSO, 1889), II, § 252, p. 311. William's account is as much legend as fact: compare *The Anglo Saxon Chronicle*, trans. G. N. Garmonsway, Everyman's University Library (London, Dent, 1972), pp. 206–8.

7 *The Anglo Saxon Chronicle*, trans. Garmonsway, pp. 205, 208; *Two of the Saxon Chronicles Parallel*, ed. Charles Plummer, 2 vols (Oxford, Clarendon Press, 1892, 1899), I, pp. 205, 208.

8 *Gesta Herwardi*, ed. Thomas Duffus Hardy and Charles Trice Martin, in *Lestorie des Engles*, by Geffrei Gaimar, vol. 1, Rolls Series (London, HMSO, 1888), pp. 340–3. For a note on the date and authorship of the *Gesta Herwardi*, see E. O. Blake (ed.), *Liber Eliensis*, Camden Society, 3rd series, vol. 92 (London, Royal Historical Society, 1962), pp. xxxiv–xxxvi.

9 *Gesta*, pp. 394–6; Geffrei Gaimar, *L'Estoire des Engleis*, ed. Alexander Bell (Oxford, Anglo-Norman Text Society, 1960), ll. 5551, 5563–4.

10 For Fouke Fitzwarin, see below, n. 19; *A Gest of Robyn Hode*, ed. R. B. Dobson and J. Taylor in *Rymes of Robyn Hood. An Introduction to the English Outlaw*, revised edn (Stroud, Sutton Publishing, 1997), pp. 71–112, stanzas 202–4, 282–300, 347–8.

11 See n. 7 above; Hugh Candidus, *Chronicle*, ed. W. T. Mellows (London, Friends of Peterborough Cathedral, 1949), pp. 77–9; *Domesday Book*, general editor John Morris, vol. 31: Lincolnshire (Chichester, Phillimore, 1986), part 1, 8:34, part 2, CK:48.

12 William of Malmesbury, *De Gestis Pontificorum Anglorum*, ed. N. E. S. A. Hamilton, Rolls Series (London, HMSO, 1870), p. 420 (Book V, § 264).

13 Maurice Keen, *Chivalry* (New Haven, Yale University Press, 1984), pp. 154, 230–1.

14 Maurice Keen, *The Laws of War in the Late Middle Ages* (London, Routledge & Kegan Paul, 1965), pp. 65–6, 69, 81, 139–140.

15 Stones, 'The Folvilles of Ashby-Folville', pp. 120–1, 128, 129.

16 William of Malmesbury, *Chronicle of the Kings of England*, trans. J. A. Giles, (London, Bohn, 1847), pp. 253–7, 271–7.

17 *Gesta*, pp. 376, 384–9. For *Robin Hood and the Potter*, see below, Chapter Five, pp. 56–7 and n. 36, also p. 61.

18 *Gesta*, pp. 372–3. For stories of Robin Hood saving men from execution, see below, Chapter Eleven, p. 136 and n. 21.

19 *Fouke le Fitz Waryn*, ed. Hathaway *et al.*, pp. 48 l. 33–50 l. 15. For a third-century Roman analogue to this tale, see Dio Cassius, *Roman History*, Book 77, 10.

20 William of Malmesbury, *Chronicle of the Kings of England*, trans. Giles, pp. 114, 129; see also Stith Thompson, *Motif-Index of Folk Literature*, 6 vols (Copenhagen, Rosenkilde and Bagger, 1955–1958), K2357, K2357.1.

21 R. M. Wilson, *The Lost Literature of Medieval England*, 2nd edn, revised (London, Methuen, 1970), pp. 113–15; *Liber Eliensis*, ed. Blake, p. 188.

22 For Jack Sheppard see Chapter Eighteen, p. 241 and n. 32. For three earlier robbers whose escapes helped to bring them popular renown, see *A new ballade, shewing the cruell robberies and lewde lyfe of Phillip Collins*, ed. Andrew Clark, in *The Shirburn Ballads 1585–1616* (Oxford, Clarendon Press, 1907), pp. 130–3; *The Life, Apprehensio[n], Arraignement, and Execution of Char[les] Courtney* (London, 1612); *Hannams Last farewell to the World* (London, 1656); *The English Villain: or the Grand Thief. Being a full Relation of the desperate Life, and deserved Death of . . . Richard Hanam* (London, [1656]); *The witty Rogue Arraigned, Condemned, & Executed. Or, The History of that incomparable Thief Richard Hainam* (London, 1656). Note also Jonson, *Every Man out of his Humour*, ed. Herford and Simpson, in *Works*, vol. 3, IV v 45–7.

23 *Gesta*, p. 393; *Fouke le Fitz Waryn*, p. 32 ll. 4–9; Katharine M. Briggs, *The Folklore of the Cotswolds* (London, Batsford, 1974), p. 102. See also Alan Macfarlane, *The Justice and the Mare's Ale. Law and disorder in seventeenth-century England* (Oxford, Basil Blackwell, 1981), p. 171.

24 Charles G. Harper, *Half-Hours with the Highwaymen*, 2 vols (London, Chapman & Hall, 1908), vol. I, p. 77; and see also below, Chapter Eighteen, p. 239 and nn. 20, 21, p. 240 and n. 27, p. 248 and n. 58; note Thompson, *Motif-Index*, F989.17.

25 *Gesta*, pp. 403–4; *Domesday Book*, ed. John Morris, vol. 23: Warwickshire, (Chichester, Phillimore, 1976), 16:26, 48; Gaimar, *L'Estoire des Engleis*, ll. 5599–694; *A Gest of Robyn Hode*, stanzas 451–5, and *Robin Hood's Death*, both ed. Dobson and Taylor in *Rymes of Robyn Hood*, pp. 111–12, 133–9. On the death by treachery motif, note the comments of Eric Hobsbawm in *Bandits*, revised edn (London, Weidenfeld & Nicolson, 2000), pp. 47, 55-6. For an ancient analogue, see Dio Cassius, *Roman History*, Book 77, 10. See also below, Chapter Fourteen, p. 195 and nn. 52, 53.

26 Maurice Keen, *The Outlaws of Medieval Legend*, revised paperback edn (London, Routledge & Kegan Paul, 1987 [first publ. 1961]), pp. 31, 36.

27 John Hayward, 'Hereward the Outlaw', *Journal of Medieval History*, vol. 14 (1988), p. 302.

28 *Gesta*, pp. 340–1.

29 Gaimar, *L'Estoire des Engleis*, l. 5465.

30 Tim Lundgren, 'The Robin Hood Ballads and the English Outlaw Tradition', *Southern Folklore*, vol. 53 (1996), pp. 225–32; *Two of the Saxon Chronicles Parallel*, ed. Plummer, I, p. 187; see also *The Anglo Saxon Chronicle*, trans. Garmonsway, p. 187.

31 Hathaway *et al.* (eds), *Fouke le Fitz Waryn*, pp. ix, xix–xxvi, xxxv, xxxvii.

32 Ibid., p. xxxiii.

33 Ibid., pp. xxvii–xxix; Glyn S. Burgess, *Two Medieval Outlaws: Eustace the Monk and Fouke Fitz Waryn* (Cambridge, Brewer, 1997), pp. 92–107.

34 *Fouke le Fitz Waryn*, pp. 26 l. 27–27 l. 34, 30 ll. 29–31, 43 ll. 6–8.

35 Keen, *The Laws of War*, pp. 65, 72–3 and 73 n. 1, 139–140; see also above, Chapter Two, p. 22 and n. 25; *Fouke le Fitz Waryn*, pp. 24 l. 26–25 l. 1.

36 *Fouke le Fitz Waryn*, pp. 30 l. 32–32 l. 3.

37 See above, n. 19. Quotation from *Fouke le Fitz Waryn*, p. 49 l. 36. On pardons, note Francis Bacon, 'Of Revenge', in *Essayes or Counsels, Civill and Morall* (1625) [many editions]; Coke, *The Third Part of the Institutes of the Laws of England*, p. 233 [cap. cv].

38 *Fouke le Fitz Waryn*, p. 57 ll. 22–35.

39 Ibid., p. 59 ll.5–10, 25–35; *The Acts of the Apostles*, chap. 9 vv. 3–9; Aquinas, *Summa Theologiae*, XXXV, pp. 82–3 (2a2ae, qu 40, art 1); see also Contamine, *War in the Middle Ages*, pp. 266–8.

FOUR: 'I WIL BE JUSTICE THIS DAY'

1 *Fasciculus Morum. A Fourteenth-Century Preacher's Handbook*, ed. Siegfried Wenzel (University Park, Pennsylvania State University Press, 1989), p. 340.

2 *Oxford English Dictionary*, 2nd edn, ed. J. A. Simpson and E. S. C. Weiner, (Oxford University Press, 1989), s. v. shavaldour, rifler[1], rifle *v.*[1]; Frances A. Foster, 'Some English Words from the "Fasciculus Morum" ', in *Essays and Studies in Honor of Carleton Brown*, (New York University Press, 1940), pp. 154–6.

3 *A Gest of Robyn Hode*, ed. Dobson and Taylor in *Rymes of Robyn Hood*, stanzas 15, 19, 86–124, 212–60, 8–9, 271.

4 *The Tale of Gamelyn*, ed. W. W. Skeat, in *The Complete Works of Geoffrey Chaucer*, 6 vols (Oxford, Clarendon Press, 1894), IV, pp. 645–67. For Skeat's introduction, see vol. III, pp. 399–405.

5 See Edgar F. Shannon, Jr, 'Mediaeval Law in *The Tale of Gamelyn*', *Speculum*, vol. 26, no. 3 (July, 1951), pp. 458–9.

6 W. R. J. Barron, *English Medieval Romance* (London, Longman, 1987), pp. 84, 217, 218; Keen, *The Outlaws of Medieval Legend*, p. 90.

7 *Gamelyn*, ll. 107–108. Original has no comma after 'gadeling'.

8 Richard Grafton, *A Chronicle at large and meere History of the affayres of Englande and Kinges of the same* (London, 1569), p. 85; William Warner, *The First and Second Parts of Albions England*, 2nd edn (London, 1589), p. 118 [sig. R₁v] [Book V, chap. 27]; Anthony Munday and Henry Chettle, *The Huntingdon Plays. A Critical Edition of The Downfall and The Death of Robert, Earl of Huntingdon*, ed. John Carney Meagher (New York, Garland, 1980); Martin Parker, *A True Tale of Robin Hood*, ed. Child, in *The English and Scottish Popular Ballads*, III, pp. 227–233, stanza 3 [Child no. 154].

9 *Gamelyn*, ll. 1–2, 169–70, 289–90, 341–2, 769–70.

10 The Luttrell Psalter, Lincolnshire, first half of fourteenth century, fol. 207. See Janet Backhouse, *Medieval Rural Life in the Luttrell Psalter* (London, British Library, 2000), pp. 12, 13.

11 *Gamelyn*, l. 314.

12 Ibid., ll. 449, 516.

13 Ibid., ll. 505–8.

14 Ibid., ll. 627–9, 637–44; *A Gest of Robyn Hode*, stanzas 6–7, 17–19, 25–40, 191–3, 209–60, 387–94.

15 *Gamelyn*, ll. 663–4.

16 Ibid., ll. 693–4.

17 Ibid., l. 729.

18 Shannon, 'Mediaeval Law in *The Tale of Gamelyn*', pp. 460–1.

19 *Gamelyn*, ll. 779–82. Original has no comma after 'priours'.

20 Ibid., ll. 821–2, 825–6. Original has no commas after 'Gamelyn' and 'day', and no semi-colon after 'dore'.

21 Ibid., l. 876.

22 Ibid., l. 885; Bartlett Jere Whiting and Helen Wescott Whiting, *Proverbs, Sentences and Proverbial Phrases from English Writings Mainly Before 1500* (Cambridge, Massachusetts, Harvard University Press, 1968), P448, see also P302; B639.

23 Pugh (ed.), *Wiltshire Gaol Delivery and Trailbaston Trials*, p. 28; Maddern, *Violence and Social Order*, pp. 74, 132, 231.

24 *Gamelyn*, ll. 888–9, 894.

25 Bellamy, *Crime and Public Order*, pp. 86–7.

26 Richard W. Kaeuper, 'An Historian's Reading of *The Tale of Gamelyn*', *Medium Aevum*, vol. 52, no. 1 (1983), p. 57; John Scattergood, '*The Tale of Gamelyn*: The Noble Robber as Provincial Hero', in *Readings in Medieval English Romance*, ed. Carol M. Meale (Cambridge, Brewer, 1994), p. 170. For a case of a Roman bandit who conducted a mock trial of a captured centurion, see the passage in Dio Cassius cited above in Chapter Three, n. 19.

27 See Chapter Three, pp. 35–6 and n. 37.

28 *Trailbaston* in *Anglo-Norman Political Songs*, ed. Aspin, p. 70, stanza 9, l. 4.

29 *Select Cases in the Court of King's Bench under Edward III*, vol. 5, ed. G. O. Sayles (London, Selden Society, vol. 76, 1957), pp. 93–5; J. R. Maddicott, 'The birth and setting of the ballads of Robin Hood', *English Historical Review*, vol. 93 (April, 1978), pp. 284–5.

30 Wimbledon, *Sermon: Redde Rationem Villicationis Tue*, ed. Knight, p. 85, see also p. 86; Owst, *Literature and Pulpit*, pp. 293, 316–7, 338–49; note also Henry de Bracton, *De Legibus et Consuetudinibus Angliae*, ed. George E. Woodbine, trans. Samuel E. Thorne, 4 vols (Cambridge, Massachusetts, Harvard University Press, 1968–77), II, pp. 21–2.

31 *Gamelyn*, l. 896.

32 Aquinas, *Summa Theologiae*, XXXVII, pp. 12–13, 18–19 (2a 2ae, qu 57, art 4, obj 1, qu 58, art. 1); *Fasciculus Morum*, ed. Wenzel, pp. 498–9; Bracton, *De Legibus*, II, p. 23. The principle is cited by Hobbes: see Thomas Hobbes, *Leviathan, or The Matter, Forme, & Power of a Common-wealth Ecclesiasticall and Civill* (1651), with an essay by W. G. Pogson Smith (Oxford, Clarendon Press, 1909, repr. 1952), p. 110 (Part I, chap. xv).

33 Bracton, *De Legibus*, II, p. 20; see also Aquinas, *Summa Theologiae*, XXXVII, pp. 36–7, 70–1 (2a 2ae, qu 58, art 6; qu 60, art 2).

34 Owst, *Literature and Pulpit*, p. 175, n. 2; note also Thomas More, *The Workes . . . in the Englysh tonge*, 2 vols (London, 1557, facs. repr. London, Scolar Press, 1978), I, p. 199 [*A Dialogue of Images*, Book II, chap. xi].

35 John de Bromyard, *Summa Praedicantium*, Nuremberg, 1518, fol. CXVIIr, cols a–b (Fi, Falsitas 41); see also fol. XLIXr, col. b (Ciiii, Civitas 4). For Bromyard's dates, see Leonard E. Boyle, 'The Date of the *Summa Praedicantium* of John Bromyard', *Speculum*, vol. 48, no. 3 (July, 1973), pp. 533–7.

36 *The Sermons of Thomas Brinton, Bishop of Rochester (1373–1389)*, ed. Sister Mary Aquinas Devlin, 2 vols, Camden Society, 3rd series (London, 1954), I, p. 92, II, pp. 246–7; see n. 22 above.

37 Brinton, *Sermons*, II, p. 390; see also Bromyard, *Summa Praedicantium*, fol. XLIXr, col. b (Ciiii, Civitas 4).

38 Devlin (ed.), *The Sermons of Thomas Brinton*, I, pp. ix–x.

39 Brinton, *Sermons*, II, p. 247.

40 Stones, 'The Folvilles of Ashby-Folville', p. 121.

41 Bromyard, *Summa Praedicantium*, fol. CXIIIv, cols a, b (Fi, Falsitas 11).

42 Ibid, fol. XCIv, col. a (Dxii, Dominatio 9).

43 *Fasciculus Morum*, ed. Wenzel, pp. 188–9, 530–1; *Jacob's Well*, ed. Arthur Brandeis (London, Early English Text Society, 1900), p. 201; see also above, Chapter Two, p. 22 and n. 23.

44 Dan Michel, *Ayenbite of Inwyt* (1340), ed. Richard Morris (London, Early English Text Society, 1866), pp. 30, 38–9; *Fasciculus Morum*, ed. Wenzel, pp. 120–3, 336–9; *Middle English Sermons*, ed. Woodburn O. Ross (London, Early English Text Society, 1940), pp. 51, 123–4; *Jacob's Well*, ed. Brandeis, pp. 91, 129.

45 Bromyard, *Summa Praedicantium*, fols. CXVv, col. a–CXVIr, col. a (Fi, Falsitas 29–32); see also Owst, *Literature and Pulpit*, pp. 45–6.

FIVE: THE ROBIN HOOD TRADITION

1 For various attempts and critical surveys of attempts to identify the personnel of the Robin Hood stories, see Dobson and Taylor (eds), *Rymes of Robyn Hood*, pp. 11–17, xvi–xxii, xxix–xxxiii; Maddicott, 'The birth and setting of the ballads of Robin Hood'; John Bellamy, *Robin Hood: an historical enquiry* (London, Croom Helm, 1985); J. C. Holt, *Robin Hood*, revised edn (London, Thames & Hudson, 1989), esp. chaps 3, 4 and 8; Stephen Knight, *Robin Hood. A Complete Study of the English Outlaw* (Oxford, Blackwell, 1994), pp. 22–32.

2 See Chapter One, p. 12 and n. 23.

3 John Major, *Historia Maioris Britanniae* (Paris, 1521), Book IV, Cap. ii, fol. LVv.

4 *A Gest of Robyn Hode*, ed. Dobson and Taylor, in *Rymes of Robyn Hood*, stanzas 21–143, 206–280, esp. 210, and 456.

5 Grafton, *A Chronicle at large*, p. 84 [sig. H₁v]. Grafton's account was closely followed by John Stow in *The Chronicles of England* (London, 1580), p. 218; see also Michael Drayton, *Poly-Olbion*, ed. J. William Hebel in *Works*, vol. 4 (Oxford, Shakespeare Head Press, 1961), p. 530 [Song XXVI].

6 William Warner, *The First and Second Parts of Albions England*, 2nd edn (London, 1589), p. 118 [sig. R₁v] [Book V, chap. 27]. For some later manifestations of this theme, see above, Chapter One, p. 12 and n. 23; Martin Parker, *A True Tale of Robin Hood* (1632), ed. Child, in *The English and Scottish Popular Ballads*, III, pp. 227–33, esp. stanzas 51–3 [Child no. 154]; Dobson and Taylor (eds), *Rymes of Robyn Hood*, p. 290.

7 See Appendix C, and books and articles listed there under n. 1.

8 Joseph Falaky Nagy, 'The Paradoxes of Robin Hood', *Folklore*, vol. 91 (2, 1980), pp. 199, 205–6; see also Jeffery L. Singman, *Robin Hood. The Shaping of the Legend* (Westport, Connecticut, Greenwood Press, 1998), pp. 36, 41.

9 Langland, *Piers Plowman*, B text, ed. Skeat, Passus v, ll. 401–2.

10 *Dives and Pauper*, ed. Barnum, i, part 1, p. 189 (Commandment i cap. li); note also Hugh Latimer, *Sermons* (Cambridge, Parker Society, 1844), p. 208.

11 Knight, *Robin Hood*, p. 35; Child (ed.), *The English and Scottish Popular Ballads*, III, p. 41, fn.

12 Dobson and Taylor (eds), *Rymes of Robin Hood*, p. 114.

13 Texts in *Rymes of Robyn Hood*, ed. Dobson and Taylor, pp. 203–19.

14 David Wiles, *The Early Plays of Robin Hood* (Cambridge, Brewer, 1981); Alexandra F. Johnston, 'The Robin Hood of the Records', in *Playing Robin Hood. The Legend as Performance in Five Centuries*, ed. Lois Potter (Newark, University of Delaware Press, 1998); and see below, n. 33.

15 Philip Stubbes, *The Anatomie of Abuses*, ed. F. J. Furnivall, 2 parts (London, New Shakspere Society, 1877–1882), pp. 146–8; quotation on p. 148 and see nn. 13, 14; see also Johnston, 'The Robin Hood of the Records', pp. 37–9; Wiles, *The Early Plays of Robin Hood*, pp. 14–15.

16 Wiles, *The Early Plays of Robin Hood*, passim, especially pp. 26–7.

17 'Robin Hood Newly Revived', ed. Child, in *The English and Scottish Popular Ballads*, III, pp. 144–7 [Child no. 128]; see also 'Robin Hood and the Butcher', version B, III, 118–120 [Child no. 122]; Wiles, *The Early Plays of Robin Hood*, p. 41.

18 Wiles, *The Early Plays of Robin Hood*, p. 17.

19 *Robin Hood and the Monk*, ed. Dobson and Taylor, in *Rymes of Robyn Hood*, pp. 113–22, stanza 3; Wiles, *The Early Plays of Robin Hood*, p. 4.

20 *Rymes of Robyn Hood*, ed. Dobson and Taylor, pp. 115, 125, 161, 180, and see also pp. 141, 159.

21 See Chapter Eleven, n. 6; *The Nutbrown Maid* in *Early English Lyrics*, ed. E. K. Chambers and F. Sidgwick (London, A. H. Bullen, 1907), p. 41, ll. 169–176; *Hary's Wallace*, ed. Matthew P. McDiarmid, 2 vols (Edinburgh, Scottish Text Society, 1968, 1969), I, p. 73 (Book V, ll. 1–6).

22 Child (ed.), *The English and Scottish Popular Ballads*, III, p. 41, fn.

23 Wiles, *The Early Plays of Robin Hood*, pp. 4, 64–6.

24 *Paston Letters and Papers of the Fifteenth Century*, ed. Norman Davis, Part 1 (Oxford, Clarendon Press, 1971), p. 461.

25 Edward Halle, *The Union of the Two Noble Families of Lancaster and York* (1550; facs. repr. Menston, Scolar Press, 1970), reign of Henry VIII, fol. VIv, ll. 3–12. Robyn emended from 'Rokyn'.

26 Wiles, *The Early Plays of Robin Hood*, pp. 6, 23–4; Johnston, 'The Robin Hood of the Records', pp. 28–9, 32–5.

27 Halle, *The Union of the Two Noble Families of Lancaster and York*, reign of Henry VIII, fols. LVIv l. 33–LVIIr l. 22.

28 *A Gest of Robyn Hode*, stanzas 371–417.

29 See Chapter Eight, p. 92 and n. 29.

30 See for example Halle, *The Union of the Two Noble Families of Lancaster and York*, reign of Henry VIII, fols. VIIv l. 42–VIIIr l. 1.

31 *Paston Letters and Papers*, ed. Davis, Part 1, pp. 128, 132, 396, 437–8, 535; for Paston's reputation as a ladies' man, and his abortive marriage negotiations, see H. S. Bennett, *The Pastons and their England. Studies in an Age of Transition* (Cambridge University Press, 1970 [first publ. 1922; 2nd edn, revised, 1932]), pp. 36–9. For medieval ideas of the duration of youth, see Ian Lancashire (ed.), *Two Tudor Interludes* (Manchester University Press, 1980), pp. 49, 90 n. 203.

32 For quotation, see Latimer, *Sermons*, p. 208. For references to the Robin Hood games as the province of the young, see Wiles, *The Early Robin Hood Plays*, p. 7; Johnston, 'The Robin Hood of the Records', pp. 29–30; Singman, *Robin Hood. The Shaping of the Legend*, p. 85.

33 Richard Robinson, *The Auncient Order, Societie, and Unitie Laudable, of Prince Arthure, and his knightly Armory of the Round Table. With a Threefold Assertion frendly in favour and furtherance of English Archery at this day* (London, 1583), sig. L₄v; note also Richard Niccolls, *Londons Artillery, briefly containing the noble practise of that wothie* [sic] *Societie* (London, 1616), p. 87.

34 *The Statutes of the Realm*, 3 Henry VIII c. 3; 33 Henry VIII c. 6; 13 Eliz. c. 14.

35 David Crook, 'Some further evidence concerning the dating of the origins of the legend of Robin Hood', *English Historical Review*, vol. 99 (1984), pp. 530–4; Holt, *Robin Hood*, pp. 187–90; Andrew Ayton, 'Military Service and the Development of the Robin Hood Legend in the Fourteenth Century', *Nottingham Medieval Studies*, vol. 36, (1992), pp. 126–147; Dobson and Taylor (eds), *Rymes of Robyn Hood*, pp. xxi–xxii, xxx–xxxi.

36 *Robin Hood and the Potter*, ed. Dobson and Taylor, in *Rymes of Robyn Hood*, pp. 123–32.

37 *Robin Hood and the Monk*, ed. Dobson and Taylor, in *Rymes of Robyn Hood*, pp. 113–22; quotation from stanza 52.

38 See also *A Gest of Robyn Hode*, stanzas 8–10, 62–6, 206, 235–52, 271; Knight, *Robin Hood*, p. 35.

39 William Caxton, *The Golden Legend*, ed. F. S. Ellis, 7 vols, The Temple Classics (London, Dent, 1900), V, p. 107.

40 *Robin Hood and the Monk*, stanza 82.

41 See Chapter Three, pp. 27–8, p. 30 and n. 19, pp. 35–6.

42 See Keen, *Chivalry*, chapters I–IV passim. For the phrase 'gentlemen of birth' see Holt, *Robin Hood*, p. 119.

43 Dobson and Taylor (eds), *Rymes of Robyn Hood*, p. 34; see also E. K. Chambers, *English Literature at the Close of the Middle Ages* (Oxford, Clarendon Press, 1945, 2nd imp., corr., 1947), p. 136.

44 Dobson and Taylor (eds), *Rymes of Robyn Hood*, pp. 33–6, and see also pp. xxxv–xxxvi; Holt, *Robin Hood*, pp. 116–28.

45 *A Gest of Robyn Hode*, stanzas 81, 224, 222, 377; see also stanza 14.

46 *Robin Hood and the Potter*, stanzas 22, 24, 25.

47 *Rymes of Robyn Hood*, ed. Dobson and Taylor, pp. 215–19.

48 Johnston, 'The Robin Hood of the Records', pp. 28–9.

49 See Chapter Three, p. 30 and n. 17; *Li Romans de Witasse Le Moine*, ed. Denis Joseph Conlon (Chapel Hill, University of North Carolina Press, 1972), pp. 67–9, ll. 1072–1141; *Hary's Wallace*, ed. McDiarmid, I, pp. 121–3 (Book VI, ll. 429–75).

50 *Robin Hood and the Potter*, stanzas 22, 23. Original reads 'yeme[n]rey'.

51 Dobson and Taylor (eds), *Rymes of Robyn Hood*, p. 125.

52 *Robin Hood and the Monk*, stanza 27; *A Gest of Robyn Hode*, stanzas 427–30.

53 Keen, *The Outlaws of Medieval Legend*, pp. 145–73; this book was first published in 1961. See also R. H. Hilton, 'The Origins of Robin Hood', in *Peasants, Knights and Heretics: Studies in Mediaeval English Social History*, ed. R. H. Hilton (Cambridge University Press, 1976), pp. 221–35 [article first published in 1958].

54 Keen, *The Outlaws of Medieval Legend*, pp. xiii–xvi; this passage was added in the first revised edition in 1977.

55 See Chapter Four, pp. 37–8 and nn. 1, 3.

56 See above, p. 60 and n. 44.

57 Holt, *Robin Hood*, pp. 109–28.

58 R. B. Dobson and J. Taylor, 'Review Article. "Robin Hood of Barnesdale: A Fellow Thou Has Long Sought"', in *Northern History*, vol. 19 (1983), pp. 217–19; quotation on p. 217.

SIX: GOOD FELLOWS AND SWORN BROTHERS

1 *Robin Hood and the Monk*, ed. Dobson and Taylor, in *Rymes of Robyn Hood*, quotations from stanzas 5 and 12.

2 See Philippa Maddern, 'Honour among the Pastons: gender and integrity in fifteenth-century English provincial society', *Journal of Medieval History*, vol. 14, no. 4 (December 1988), p. 358; Maddern, *Violence and Social Order*, p. 171; Julian Pitt-Rivers, 'Honour and Social Status', in *Honour and Shame. The Values of Mediterranean Society*, ed. J. G. Peristiany (London, Weidenfeld & Nicolson, 1965), pp. 25, 33; Julian Pitt-Rivers, 'Honor', in *International Encyclopaedia of the Social Sciences*, ed. David L. Stills, 17 vols, (New York, The Free Press, 1968), VI, p. 508.

3 Maddern, *Violence and Social Order*, pp. 86, 234.

4 *English Economic History: Select Documents*, ed. A. E. Bland, P. A. Brown and R. H. Tawney (London, G. Bell, 1914), p. 147.

5 Bellamy, *Crime and Public Order*, p. 55; Maddern, *Violence and Social Order*, pp. 104, 128.

6 *Robin Hood and the Monk*, stanza 33, see also stanza 51.

7 Ibid., stanzas 77, 79, 80.

8 *Middle English Dictionary*, s. v. fĕlau(e n., 1. (a), 2. (a), 5. (c), 6. (a), 11; see also *Oxford English Dictionary*, s. v. fellow, *sb.*, especially 1. a., 2. a., 5. a.

9 *Robin Hood and the Monk*, stanzas 87–9.

10 *Middle English Dictionary*, s. v. bĭnden v., 6a. (b), (c); 7b. (a), (c); see also *Oxford English Dictionary*, s. v. bind, *v.*, 18., 21; bond, *sb.*[2] and *a.*, 3. Note also *The Interlude of Youth*, ed. Ian Lancashire in *Two Tudor Interludes*, ll. 710–15 and fn. to l. 714.

11 Holt, *Robin Hood*, p. 30.

12 See Chapter One, p. 4 and n. 4.

13 Contamine, *War in the Middle Ages*, pp. 151–2.

14 See Chapter One, p. 4 and n. 4, pp. 10–11 and nn. 19, 20; Chapter Four, p. 49 and nn. 41, 42; note also Chapter Two, p. 20 and n. 18.

15 Holt, *Robin Hood*, p. 113.

16 See Chapter Three, p. 30 and n. 21, and Hayward, 'Hereward the Outlaw', p. 303.

17 See Chapter Three, p. 33 and n. 31, and Louis Brandin, 'Nouvelles Recherches sur *Fouke Fitz Warin*', *Romania*, vol. 55 (1929), pp. 17–44.

18 See Chapter Four, p. 48.

19 See Chapter Four, p. 39.

20 See Chapter Two, p. 20 and Stones, 'The Folvilles of Ashby-Folville', p. 129.

21 See Chapter Four, pp. 41, 44.

22 Dobson and Taylor, 'Review Article. "Robin Hood of Barnesdale: A Fellow Thou Has Long Sought"', p. 219; *A Gest of Robyn Hode*, ed. Dobson and Taylor, in *Rymes of Robyn Hood*, stanzas 433–50.

23 *Adam Bell, Clim of the Clough, and William of Cloudesly*, ed. Dobson and Taylor, in *Rymes of Robyn Hood*, stanza 4.

24 Grafton, *Chronicle At Large*, 1569, p. 85; Holt, *Robin Hood*, p. 44; *Early English Prose Romances*, ed. William J. Thoms, new edn, revised (London, George Routledge, no date), pp. 547–8; *Robin Hood's Progress to Nottingham*, ed. Child, in *The English and Scottish Popular Ballads*, III, pp. 175–7 [Child no. 139].

25 *A Gest of Robyn Hode*, stanzas 433–5.

26 Ibid., stanzas 436–7.

27 Ibid., stanzas 6, 7, 12–15; in stanza 14, Dobson and Taylor follow 'shawe' with a semi-colon.

28 Douglas Gray, 'The Robin Hood Poems', *Poetica*, vol. 18 (1984), pp. 20, 27, 30, 37; Richard Tardif, 'The "Mistery" of Robin Hood: a New Social Context for the Texts', in *Robin Hood. An Anthology of Scholarship and Criticism*, ed. Stephen Knight (Cambridge, D. S. Brewer, 1999), p. 358; Edwin Davenport, 'The Representation of Robin Hood in Elizabethan Drama: *George a Greene*

and *Edward I*', in *Playing Robin Hood*, ed. Potter, pp. 46–7; Singman, *Robin Hood. The Shaping of the Legend*, pp. 36–7, 154. Professor Singman's book only came to my attention in the final stages of revising these chapters on Robin Hood. His comments on 'yeomanry' as a key concept in these texts and on its connections with the idea of 'fellowship' are of considerable interest: see especially pp. 34–8.

29 Bromyard, *Summa Praedicantium*, fol. CXVv, col. b (Fi, Falsitas 29).

30 Owst, *Literature and Pulpit*, pp. 45–6.

31 Singman, *Robin Hood. The Shaping of the Legend*, p. 43, and see Davenport, cited above, n. 28.

32 *Rymes of Robyn Hood*, ed. Dobson and Taylor, p. 218.

33 William Caxton, trans., *The History of Reynard the Fox*, ed. N. F. Blake (London, Early English Text Society, 1970), p. 33, ll. 34–6 [chap xvi]. Punctuation modernised.

34 Maurice Keen, 'Brotherhood in Arms', *History*, vol. 47 (1962), pp. 1–17; K. B. McFarlane, 'A Business-partnership in War and Administration, 1421–1445', *English Historical Review*, vol. 78 (April, 1963), pp. 290–310.

35 *Sir Ferumbras*, ed. Sidney J. Herrtage (London, Early English Text Society, 1879), l. 277; punctuation slightly modernised. See also *King Horn*, ed. Jennifer Fellows in *Of Love and Chivalry: An Anthology of Middle English Romance*, Everyman's Library (London, Dent, 1993), ll. 998, 1091, and note ll. 284, 577, 1293; Robert [Mannyng] of Brunne, *Handlyng Synne*, ed. Frederick J. Furnivall, Part 1 (London, Early English Text Society, 1901), l. 2247; Geoffrey Chaucer, 'The Knight's Tale' in *The Canterbury Tales*, in *The Riverside Chaucer*, ed. Larry D. Benson, 3rd edn (Oxford University Press, 1987), ll. 1192, 1194, 1200, and see note to ll. 1191–1208 on pp. 830–1; *An Alphabet of Tales. An English Fifteenth Century Translation of the Alphabetum Narrationum of Etienne de Besançon*, ed. Mary Macleod Banks, Part 1 (London, Early English Text Society, 1904), p. 40, l. 20; compare p. 39, ll. 10–11.

36 Chaucer, 'The Pardoner's Tale', in *The Riverside Chaucer*, ed. Benson, ll. 696–704, quotation from l. 704.

37 *Fasciculus Morum*, ed. Wenzel, pp. 420–3; *Middle English Sermons*, ed. Ross, pp. 63–5. Note the character of 'Felawshyp' in *Everyman*, ed. A. C. Cawley (Manchester University Press, 1961), ll. 205–312.

38 *Amis and Amiloun*, ed. Fellows in *Of Love and Chivalry: An Anthology of Middle English Romance*, ll. 145–56, quotation from l. 149.

39 Note Keen's comments in 'Brotherhood in Arms', p. 17.

40 *Adam Bell, Clim of the Clough, and William of Cloudesly*, stanza 4; see also stanzas 8, 9, 10.

41 *Gamelyn*, ll. 409–10, see also l. 450; ll. 607–8.

42 *A Gest of Robyn Hode*, stanzas 169–173.

43 Clavell, *A Recantation of An Ill Led Life*, sig. C₃r, p. 8; see below, Chapter Twelve, p. 151 and n. 13; see also Chapter Seven, p. 82 and n. 20.

SEVEN: GUESTS AT ROBIN HOOD'S TABLE

1 Chaucer, 'The Knight's Tale', in *The Riverside Chaucer*, ed. Benson, ll. 1129–61, 1583, 1604–5; note also 1191–1200.
2 Chaucer, 'The Friar's Tale', in *The Riverside Chaucer*, ed. Benson, ll. 1379–86.
3 *A Gest of Robyn Hode*, ed. Dobson and Taylor in *Rymes of Robyn Hood*, stanzas 14, 284.
4 Janette Richardson, 'Hunter and Prey: Functional Imagery in "The Friar's Tale"', in *Chaucer's Mind and Art*, ed. A. C. Cawley (Edinburgh, Oliver & Boyd, 1969), p. 159; Helen Cooper, *Oxford Guides to Chaucer: The Canterbury Tales* (Oxford, Clarendon Press, 1989), p. 174.
5 J. C. Holt, 'The Origins and Audience of the Ballads of Robin Hood', in *Peasants, Knights and Heretics: Studies in Mediaeval English Social History*, ed. R. H. Hilton (Cambridge University Press, 1976), p. 247 and n. 43; Dobson and Taylor (eds), *Rymes of Robyn Hood*, p. 35; Holt, *Robin Hood*, pp. 120–2.
6 George E. Morris, 'A Ryme of Robyn Hode', *Modern Language Review*, vol. 43, no. 4 (October, 1948), pp. 507–8.
7 Chaucer, 'The Friar's Tale', ll. 1524, 1527–8.
8 Mroczowski, '"The Friar's Tale" and its Pulpit Background', in *English Studies Today, Second Series*, ed. G. A. Bonnard (Bern, Francke Verlag, 1961), pp. 107–20; Siegfried Wenzel, 'Chaucer and the Language of Contemporary Preaching', *Studies in Philology*, vol. 73, no. 2 (April, 1976), pp. 142–3; Cooper, *Oxford Guides to Chaucer: The Canterbury Tales*, p. 168. For analogues to the tale see especially Archer Taylor, 'The Devil and the Advocate', *Papers of the Modern Language Association of America*, vol. 36 (1921), pp. 35–59; Owst, *Literature and Pulpit*, pp. 162–3; Peter Nicholson, 'The Analogues of Chaucer's *Friar's Tale*', *English Language Notes*, vol. 17 (December 1979), pp. 93–8.
9 Compare Robin Hood's claim to be collecting road tolls: see Chapter Eight, p. 98 and n. 51. From much later periods, compare Thomas Middleton's conceit of highway robbers as 'landlords' collecting 'rents' from their 'tenants', the travellers: *The Black Book* (1604), ed. Bullen in *The Works of Thomas Middleton*, VIII, p. 20; and various slang terms for highway robbery mentioned in *The Annals of Newgate; or, Malefactor's Register* by John Villette, 4 vols (London, J. Wenman, 1776), I, p. 63 ('collecting money on the high way'), II, p. 201 ('to raise contributions on the road'), IV, p. 379 ('to levy contributions on the public').
10 Chaucer, 'The Friar's Tale', l. 1413; Earle Birney, '"After His Ymage": The Central Ironies of the "Friar's Tale"', *Mediaeval Studies*, vol. 21 (1959), pp. 24–5; Richardson, 'Hunter and Prey: Functional Imagery in "The Friar's Tale"', pp. 160–1; Benson (ed.), *The Riverside Chaucer*, p. 876, note to 'The Friar's Tale', l. 1413.
11 Skeat, *The Complete Works of Geoffrey Chaucer*, III, p. 399; Donald B. Sands (ed.), *Middle English Verse Romances* (New York, Holt, Rinehart & Winston, 1966), p. 154. Stephen Knight and Thomas H. Ohlgren make some interesting comments regarding its appropriateness as a tale for the Cook in the introduction to their edition of *The Tale of Gamelyn* (1997) in *TEAMS*

Middle English Texts, ed. Russell Peck, Consortium for the Teaching of the Middle Ages & University of Rochester <http://www.lib.rochester.edu/camelot/teams/gamint.htm> [accessed on 9 June, 1999].

12 See Chapter Two, p. 17 and n. 7.

13 Clavell, *A Recantation of an Ill Led Life*, p. 12; note also the Turpin anecdote recounted by Le Blanc, quoted at the start of Chapter One (p. 1 and n. 1).

14 *A Gest of Robyn Hode*, stanzas 27, 67–78, quotations from stanzas 27, 68, 70.

15 Keen, *The Outlaws of Medieval Legend*, pp. 136–7; Holt, *Robin Hood*, pp. 123–4. A different interpretation of the themes of livery and fellowship in this poem has been offered by Thomas H. Ohlgren in his essay 'The "Marchaunt" of Sherwood: Mercantile Ideology in *A Gest of Robyn Hode*', in *Robin Hood in Popular Culture. Violence, Trangression, and Justice*, ed. Thomas Hahn (Cambridge, D. S. Brewer, 2000). I regret that this essay only came into my hands as I was making the final revisions to this book. Briefly, Ohlgren argues that the organisation of the outlaw band in *A Gest* is patterned on that of a guild of merchants or craftsmen. He suggests that Robin Hood was a hero for guildsmen, and even that the poem was commissioned by a specific guild for recitation at one of their feasts. I find his arguments interesting but ultimately unpersuasive. If Robin Hood does resemble a merchant, which, in one or two respects, may be arguably the case, he is a parody merchant, just as Little John, when he measures out the cloth for the knight's livery, certainly becomes a parody draper (as Much the miller's son points out). Neither Robin nor Little John can be contained or wholly explained within these categories. As for the resemblances between the outlaw band and a guild, these show the persistence in medieval life of certain sorts of organisational principle. Craft guilds, leagues of knights and even monastic orders were all organised along somewhat similar lines.

16 *Middle English Dictionary*, s. v. liverē, n. (3), 4. (d); *Oxford English Dictionary*, s. v. livery, *sb*. 2. a, note citations under 1386, 1389, 1480; Keen, 'Brotherhood in Arms', pp. 13, 15.

17 Keen, 'Brotherhood in Arms', pp. 7–8; see also Keen, *Chivalry*, pp. 179–84, 187–90, 196–8.

18 Note Singman's comments in *Robin Hood. The Shaping of the Legend*, p. 38.

19 Clavell, *A Recantation of An Ill Led Life*, p. 39. For twentieth-century American armed robbers and their predilection for a 'partnership' model of professional relationship over a hierarchical one, see Werner J. Einstadter, 'The Social Organization of Armed Robbery', *Social Problems*, vol. 17 (Summer, 1969), pp. 65–74; see also Everett DeBaun, 'The Heist. The Theory and Practice of Armed Robbery', *Harper's Magazine*, vol. 200, no. 1197 (February, 1950), p. 72.

20 G[eorge] F[idge], *The English Gusman; or the History of that Unparallel'd Thief James Hind* (London, 1652), p. 4 [sig. B₃v].

21 See Chapter Five, p. 61 and n. 46.

22 *A Gest of Robyn Hode*, stanzas 197–8, quotation from stanza 197; Keen, *Chivalry*, p. 14; Contadine, *War in the Middle Ages*, pp. 253–4.

23 *Li Romans de Witasse Le Moine*, ed. Conlon, p. 64, ll. 930–53; pp. 85–6, ll. 1746–77; Dobson and Taylor (eds), *Rymes of Robyn Hood*, p. 76.

24 *A Gest of Robyn Hode*, stanza 229.

25 A similar point is made by Gray, in 'The Robin Hood Poems', p. 27.

26 *A Gest of Robyn Hode*, stanzas 376–83, quotation from stanza 378.

27 See Chapter Six, pp. 71–2 and n. 32.

28 George Peele, *Edward I*, ed. Frank S. Hook, in *Life and Works*, vol. 2 (New Haven, Yale University Press, 1961), ll. 1842, 1848–52, 1858–61.

29 *A Gest of Robyn Hode*, stanzas 418–22, quotation from stanza 427.

30 Robin's role as a tester is commented on by Nagy in 'The Paradoxes of Robin Hood', pp. 204–5, and Gray, 'The Robin Hood Poems', p. 27.

31 *A Gest of Robyn Hode*, stanzas 72–4, quotation from stanza 74.

32 Dobson and Taylor (eds), *Rymes of Robyn Hood*, p. 32.

33 *A Gest of Robyn Hode*, stanza 144.

34 Thomas Fuller, *The History of the Worthies of England* (London, 1662), p. 320 [sig.Sss₃r].

EIGHT: THE RISE OF THE LONDON UNDERWORLD

1 *A Relation of the Island of England*, trans. Charlotte Augusta Sneyd (London, Camden Society, 1847), p. 34.

2 See Chapter Four, p. 47 and nn. 35, 36.

3 See Chapter One, pp. 2–3 and n. 3.

4 See Chapter One, p. 1 and n. 1, p. 6 and n. 7, pp. 7–8 and n. 10, p. 12 and n. 23; Chapter Nine, p. 101 and n. 1; Chapter Twelve, p. 155 and n. 27. See also *A Foreign View of England in the Reigns of George I & George II. The Letters of Monsieur César de Saussure to his family*, ed. Madame Van Muyden (London, John Murray, 1902), pp. 127, 131; Jacobite report of 1728 quoted by Frank McLynn in *Crime and Punishment in Eighteenth-century England* (Oxford University Press, 1991 [first publ. 1989]), p. 57.

5 Peter Clark and Paul Slack, *English Towns in Transition, 1500–1700* (London, Oxford University Press, 1976), pp. 63, 83; F. J. Fisher, 'The Development of London as a Centre of Conspicuous Consumption in the Sixteenth and Seventeenth Centuries', in *Essays in Economic History*, vol. 2, ed. E. M. Carus-Wilson (London, Edward Arnold, 1962), pp. 197–8; see also F. J. Fisher, 'London as an "Engine of economic growth"', in *The Early Modern Town. A Reader*, ed. Peter Clark (London, Longman, 1976), p. 205.

6 A. V. Judges (ed.), *The Elizabethan Underworld* (London, George Routledge, 1930), pp. xlviii–li; Valerie Pearl, *London and the Outbreak of the Puritan Revolution. City Government and National Politics, 1625–43* (London, Oxford University Press, 1961), pp. 23–9.

7 Donald Rumbelow, *I Spy Blue. The Police and Crime in the City of London from Elizabeth I to Victoria* (London, Macmillan, 1971), pp. 27–32; see also Judges (ed.), *The Elizabethan Underworld*, pp. xlvi–xlviii, 520 n. 28, 521 n. 1.

8 Fisher, 'The Development of London as a Centre of Conspicuous Consumption in the Sixteenth and Seventeenth Centuries'; Fisher, 'London as an "Engine of economic growth"'.

9 Henry Summerson, 'The Criminal Underworld of Medieval England', *Journal of Legal History*, vol. 17, no. 3 (December, 1996), esp. pp. 200–1, 208–10; see also Bellamy, *Crime and Public Order*, pp. 59–60.

10 For an early reference (1575) to highway robbers using pistols, see Historical Manuscripts Commission, *Catalogue of the Manuscripts of the Marquis of Salisbury*, vol. 2 (London, HMSO, 1888), p. 123.

11 Clavell, *A Recantation of an Ill Led Life*, p. 35.

12 J. A. Sharpe, *Crime in seventeenth-century England. A county study* (Cambridge University Press, 1983), pp. 105, 213; J. M. Beattie, *Crime and the Courts in England, 1660–1800* (Oxford, Clarendon Press, 1986), p. 158–9; see also J. S. Cockburn, 'The Nature and Incidence of Crime in England 1559–1625', in *Crime in England 1550–1800*, ed. J. S. Cockburn (London, Methuen, 1977), p. 65.

13 Narcissus Luttrell, *A Brief Historical Relation of State Affairs from September 1678 to April 1714*, 6 vols (Oxford University Press, 1857), IV, p. 695; IV, pp. 106, 394, 557, 651; II, pp. 95–6, III, p. 18; II, p. 347; III, p. 187; II, p. 613; III, p. 21; III, p. 130; II, p. 642; III, p. 73, see also IV, p. 392; III, p. 266; III, p. 432, IV, pp. 313, 679; II, p. 632; IV, p. 419; II, p. 639; III, p. 21, IV; p. 602; III, pp. 278, 114; see also p. 378. The existing volumes of Luttrell's diary run from 1678 to 1714, but before 1690 he gives details of only two highway robberies, and after 1700 his interest in recording them seems to wane sharply. For Luttrell's use of newsletters, see Henry L. Snyder, 'Newsletters and newspapers: the circulation of news in Britain in the 17th and 18th centuries', paper given at the 63rd General Conference of the International Federation of Library Associations and Institutions, 1997 <http://www.ifla.org/IV/ifla63/63snyh.htm> [accessed on 8 August 2000].

14 Richard Head (ascribed), *Jackson's Recantation*, ed. Spiro Peterson, in *The Counterfeit Lady and other criminal fiction of seventeenth-century England* (New York, Doubleday, 1961), pp. 171–2.

15 See Robert Greene, *The Blacke Bookes Messenger*, ed. G. B. Harrison, Bodley Head Quartos (London, John Lane, 1924), p. 14.

16 Ralph Wilson, *A Full and Impartial Account Of all the Robberies Committed by John Hawkins, George Sympson . . . and their Companions*, 3rd edn (London, J. Peele, no date [1st edn, 1722]), p. 10.

17 Luttrell, *A Brief Historical Relation of State Affairs*, III, p. 531 [28 September 1695].

18 I am assuming that the 1598 broadside ballad about Hutton is reasonably accurate, at least about the place of his execution; see *Luke Huttons lamentation*, ed. Herbert L. Collman, in *Ballads and Broadsides chiefly of the Elizabethan Period* (Oxford, The Roxburghe Club, 1912), pp. 159–61. Hutton was certainly imprisoned for a while in London's Newgate prison, and later remanded to York; see M. A. Shaaber, 'Luke Hutton's Repentance', in *The Library Chronicle*, vol. 21, 2 (Spring, 1955), p. 66. For Ratsey, see below, Chapter Nine, pp. 113–16 and n. 52.

19 Ian Lancashire (ed.), *Two Tudor Interludes: Youth and Hick Scorner* (Manchester University Press, 1980), pp. 17–24.

20 *Youth*, ed. Lancashire, in *Two Tudor Interludes*, ll. 57–8, 207, 757–8, 227–68.

21 More, *Utopia*, ed. Surtz and Hexter, p. 68, ll. 28–31.

22 R. B. Outhwaite, *Inflation in Tudor and Early Stuart England*, Studies in Economic History (London, Macmillan, 1969), pp. 9–13; John Burnett, *A History of the Cost of Living* (Harmondsworth, Penguin, 1969), p. 60; see also John Pound, *Poverty and Vagrancy in Tudor England*, Seminar Studies in History (London, Longman, 1971), pp. 5–7, 9, 11–13.

23 For a brief overview of critical opinion, see Lancashire (ed.), *Two Tudor Interludes*, pp. 58–9, 65–6 and nn. 241, 254–6.

24 *Hick Scorner*, ed. Lancashire, in *Two Tudor Interludes*, ll. 167–76, 801–10, 707–8.

25 Note the 'wyld roge' encountered by Thomas Harman in the 1560s; see Harman, *A Caveat or Warening for Commen Cursetors*, ed. Edward Viles and F. J. Furnivall (London, Early English Text Society, 1869), p. 42.

26 *Hick Scorner*, ed. Lancashire, ll. 186, 231, 218, 255–6, 264–6, 227–8, 267–8, 236.

27 Ibid., ll. 301–400; quotations from ll. 366, 369.

28 Ibid., ll. 410–18; 542–3; see above, Chapter Five, p. 55 and n. 27.

29 Ralph B. Pugh, 'Some Reflections of a Medieval Criminologist', *Proceedings of the British Academy*, vol. 59 (1973), p. 19; see also Lancashire (ed.), *Two Tudor Interludes*, p. 192, note to l. 388. There are numerous references to Shooters Hill in the later literature of highway robbery. For a description of the spot, see Edward Hasted, *The History and Topographical Survey of the County of Kent*, 2nd edn, 12 vols (Canterbury, 1797–1801; facs. repr. East Ardsley, Wakefield, E. P. Publishing, 1972), I, pp. 456–7.

30 *Hick Scorner*, ed. Lancashire, in *Two Tudor Interludes*, ll. 650–84; quotation from l. 682.

31 Ibid., ll. 822–4.

32 *A manifest detection of the moste vyle and detestable use of Diceplay* (London, Abraham Vele, [1552]). Sometimes ascribed to a certain 'Gilbert Walker', of whom nothing is known: see Judges (ed.), *The Elizabethan Underworld*, p. 492.

33 *A manifest detection*, esp. sigs $B_3v–B_5r$, $D_5r–D_7r$.

34 Ibid., sigs B_4v, D_6r.

35 John Palsgrave, *Lesclarcissement de la Langue Francoyse* (London, 1530; facs. repr. Menston, Scolar Press, 1969), fol. CCC. LXVIII; Robert Copland, *The hye way to the Spyttell hous* (London, no date [c. 1536]), sig. E_3v; Harman, *Caveat*, passim, esp. pp. 82–7.

36 A handful of terms used by dice cheaters were recorded a few years earlier, in 1545, by Roger Ascham: see Roger Ascham, *Toxophilus*, ed. William Aldis Wright, in *The English Works of Roger Ascham* (Cambridge University Press, 1904), pp. 25–6. Most of these terms are also found in *A manifest detection*.

37 *A manifest detection*, sigs C_4r, D_1r, D_6v, C_6r; Harman, *Caveat*, p. 86; John Awdeley, *The Fraternitye of Vacabondes*, ed. Edward Viles and F. J. Furnivall (London, Early English Text Society, 1869 [same volume as Harman's *Caveat*]), p. 4.

38 *A manifest detection*, sigs $B_4v–B_5r$; David W. Maurer, *The Big Con. The Classic Story of the Confidence Man and the Confidence Trick* (London, Century, 1999 [first publ. 1940]), p. 249; David W. Maurer, *Whiz Mob. A Correlation of the*

Technical Argot of Pickpockets with Their Behavior Pattern (New Haven, College & University Press, 1964 [first publ. 1955]), pp. 52–4.

39 *A manifest detection*, sig. A₁v.

40 Ibid., sig. D₆r.

41 Ibid., sigs B₃v, B₅r. Sutherland's 'professional thief' denied that argot was ever used for the purpose of secret communication: see *The Professional Thief By A Professional Thief* (University of Chicago Press, 1937, 8th imp., 1961), ed. Edwin H. Sutherland, p. 18. However, David W. Maurer states that it was sometimes used for exactly this purpose in the 'short con' games, many of which work on similar lines to the practices described in *A manifest detection*: see *The Big Con*, p. 248. See also Maurer, *Whiz Mob*, pp. 53–4, on pickpocket teams using argot in the presence of victims.

42 *The Professional Thief*, ed. Sutherland, pp. 16–7; Maurer, *The Big Con*, pp. 247–50; David W. Maurer 'The Argot of the Dice Gambler', *Annals of the American Academy of Political and Social Science*, vol. 269 (May, 1950), pp. 118–19; Maurer, *Whiz Mob*, p. 53. For the reported views of an eighteenth-century pickpocket, who regarded the use of argot as an index of trustworthiness in the people with whom she worked, see P. Linebaugh, 'The Ordinary of Newgate and His *Account*', in *Crime in England, 1550–1800*, ed. Cockburn, p. 265.

43 Roger Prior, 'The Life of George Wilkins', *Shakespeare Survey*, vol. 25 (1972), pp. 137–52; Mark Eccles, 'George Wilkins', *Notes and Queries*, vol. 220 (June 1975), pp. 250–2.

44 *A manifest detection*, sigs D₃v–D₅r; Awdeley, *The Fraternitye of Vacabondes*, ed. Viles and Furnivall, pp. 7–11; Robert Greene, *A Notable Discouery of Coosnage*, ed. G. B. Harrison, Bodley Head Quartos (London, John Lane, 1923), pp. 17–34; *The Professional Thief*, ed. Sutherland, pp. 62–6, 67–8; Maurer, *The Big Con*, pp. 222–5, 229–33, 237–9.

45 Robert Greene, *The Second and last part of Conny-catching*, ed. G. B. Harrison, Bodley Head Quartos (London, John Lane, 1923), pp. 29–37; T[homas] D[ekker] and George Wilkins, *Iests to make you Merie: With the Coniuring vp of Cock Watt (the walking Spirit of Newgate) To tell Tales*, ed. A. B. Grosart, in *The Non-Dramatic Works of Thomas Dekker*, vol. 2 (London, 1885), pp. 326–9, 332–4; *The Professional Thief*, ed. Sutherland, pp. 44–6; Maurer, *Whiz Mob*, chapter 5 and passim. For Wilkins's authorship of the 'Cock Wat' section of *Iests to make you Merie*, see M. T. Jones-Davies, *Un Peintre de la Vie Londonienne: Thomas Dekker (c. 1572–1632)*, 2 vols (Paris, Didier, 1958), II, 377.

46 For 'stall', see Greene, *A Notable Discouery of Coosnage*, p. 39; Greene, *The Second . . . part of Conny-catching*, pp. 31–2; compare *The Professional Thief*, ed. Sutherland, p. 45; Maurer, *Whiz Mob*, p. 58 and passim. For 'cousin', see *A manifest detection*, sigs C₃r, C₅v, C₆r; compare Maurer, *Whiz Mob*, p. 108. For 'flat', see Ascham, *Toxophilus*, ed. Wright, p. 25; *A manifest detection*, sigs A₁v, C₁v; compare Maurer, 'The Argot of the Dice Gambler', p. 122 (s. v. 'brick').

47 See the remarks of J. A. Sharpe in *Crime in seventeenth-century England*, pp. 113–4; also the same author's *Crime in Early Modern England, 1550–1750*

(London, Longman, 1984), pp. 118–20; Cockburn, 'The Nature and Incidence of Crime in England 1559–1625', pp. 63–4. There is an interesting discussion of professional crime in Elizabethan London by Ian W. Archer in *The Pursuit of Stability. Social Relations in Elizabethan London* (Cambridge University Press, 1991), pp. 204–15.

48 *A manifest detection*, sigs D_5v–D_6r; Maurer, *Whiz Mob*, pp. 29–30, see also p. 26, and chapter 9; Sutherland (ed.), *The Professional Thief*, pp. 218–20, 227, and chapters 4, 5.

49 *A manifest detection*, sigs B_4v, B_4r; see also John Cowell, *The Interpreter* (Cambridge, 1607; facs. repr. Menston, Scolar Press, 1972), s. v. 'Escheate', 'Escheatour'.

50 *A manifest detection*, sig. B_4v.

51 *Robin Hood and the Potter*, stanzas 5, 11–13; see also *The Play of Robin Hood and the Potter*, pp. 216–8; both ed. Dobson and Taylor in *Rymes of Robyn Hood*. Note also *Wisdom Who Is Christ*, ed. Mark Eccles, in *The Macro Plays* (London, Early English Text Society, 1969), ll. 802–4.

52 *A manifest detection*, sigs B_3v, B_5r. Original has full stop after 'Maydenhead'.

53 Greene, *The Blacke Bookes Messenger*, pp. 13–6, quotation on p. 13. For Pieres de Brubyle, see above, Chapter Three, p. 35 and n. 36.

54 See Chapter Twelve.

55 Luke Hutton, *The Black Dog of Newgate*, ed. Judges, in *The Elizabethan Underworld*; Shaaber, 'Luke Hutton's Repentance', pp. 65–82; see also E. D. Pendry, *Elizabethan Prisons and Prison Scenes*, 2 vols (University of Salzburg, 1974), I, pp. 121–7, 130–1.

NINE: GENTLEMEN THIEVES IN VELVET COATS

1 R[obert] P[arsons], *The Jesuit's Memorial for the Intended Reformation of England, Under their First Popish Prince*, intr. Edward Gee (London, 1690), pp. 210–11; compare the comments by Harrison cited in Chapter One, p. 6 and n. 7.

2 J. S. Cockburn, 'The Nature and Incidence of Crime in England 1559–1625: A Preliminary Survey', in *Crime in England 1550–1800*, ed. J. S. Cockburn (London, Methuen, 1977), p. 65; Frank Aydelotte, *Elizabethan Rogues and Vagabonds* (Oxford, Clarendon Press, 1913), p. 99; see also *Middlesex County Records*, 4 vols, ed. John Cordy Jeaffreson (London, Greater London Council, 1972–5 [first published 1886–92]), I (1549–1603), pp. 25, 32, 38–9, 43, 46, 89, 172, 185, 201–2, 224–5, 229 (2), 242, 249–50, 261, 263–4.

3 Sharpe, *Crime in seventeenth-century England*, p. 105.

4 F. G. Emmison, *Elizabethan Life: Disorder* (Chelmsford, Essex County Council, 1970), p. 277.

5 *Calendar of State Papers. Domestic. 1611–1618*, p. 527, see also p. 391; *County of Middlesex: Calendar to the Sessions Records*, n. s., ed. William Le Hardy, 4 vols (London, Clerk of the Peace, 1935–1941), III, pp. 306–7; see also IV, p. 190; John Chamberlain, *Letters*, ed. Norman Egbert McClure, 2 vols (Philadelphia, American Philosophical Society, 1939), II, pp. 147, 205;

Middlesex County Records, ed. John Cordy Jeaffreson, vol. 3 (Clerkenwell, Middlesex County Records Society, 1888), p. 11; see also vol. 2 (1887), p. 149; *The life and death of Mr George Sandys* in *A Pepysian Garland. Black-Letter Broadside Ballads of the years 1595–1639*, ed. Hyder E. Rollins (Cambridge, Massachusetts, Harvard University Press, 1971 [first publ. 1922]), pp. 248–255. Chamberlain says that Sir George was 'cousen german to Sir Edwin and the rest of that house' (p. 147).

6 For Clavell, see Chapter Twelve.

7 Bellamy, *The Criminal Trial in Later Medieval England*, pp. 137–48; see also Joel Samaha, *Law and Order in Historical Perspective. The Case of Elizabethan Essex* (New York, Academic Press, 1974), pp. 58–9; Sharpe, *Crime in seventeenth-century England*, p. 147.

8 See Chapter Four, pp. 47–8 and nn. 36 and 37.

9 Brinklow, *Complaynt of Roderyck Mors*, ed. Cowper, p. 45.

10 Edward Coke, *The Third Part of the Institutes of the Laws of England* (London, 1648), p. 233 [cap. cv].

11 Ben Jonson, *Poems*, ed. George Burke Johnston (London, Routledge & Kegan Paul, 1954, repr. 1971), p. 9 [Epigramme no. VIII]; for other satires on the pardon system, see Thomas Lupton, *All for Money* (1577), ed. Edgar T. Schell and J. D. Schuchter, in *English Morality Plays and Moral Interludes* (New York, Holt, Rinehart & Winston, 1969), ll. 923–43, 976–1018; Richard Brome, *The Court Begger*, in *Dramatic Works*, vol. 1 (London, John Pearson, 1873), p. 188. See Sharpe, *Crime in seventeenth-century England*, p. 147. Note also George Whetstone, *Promos and Cassandra*, ed. Geoffrey Bullough, in *Narrative and Dramatic Sources of Shakespeare*, vol. 2 (London, Routledge & Kegan Paul, 1958), pp. 442–513, Part I, II vi, p. 456: the Hangman speaks of his fear of pardons, which, as he says, don't come for poor prisoners but for 'cutters', highwaymen or armed bullies, whose clothes are usually good ones. The clothes of executed victims were the hangman's perquisites. For a good account of how the system worked during the eighteenth century, including the part played by patronage, see Douglas Hay, 'Property, Authority and the Criminal Law', in *Albion's Fatal Tree. Crime and Society in Eighteenth-Century England*, ed. Douglas Hay and others (London, Allen Lane, 1975), pp. 44–9.

12 George Farquhar, *The Beaux' Stratagem*, ed. Charles N. Fifer, Regents Restoration Drama Series (London, Edward Arnold, 1977), V ii 165–6; note also *The Life . . . of Charles Courtney*, pp. 15f. [sigs C₄r–v]; *The Life and Death of Mal Cutpurse* (1662), in *Counterfeit Ladies*, ed. Janet Todd and Elizabeth Spearing (London, William Pickering, 1994), pp. 22, 64; Head, *Jackson's Recantation*, ed. Peterson, in *The Counterfeit Lady and other criminal fiction*, p. 154.

13 G[eorge] F[idge], *The English Gusman*, p. 43 (sig. G₃r). This section of *The English Gusman* was plainly reprinted from a news pamphlet, apparently now lost.

14 *In God's Name. Examples of Preaching in England 1534–1662*, ed. John Chandos (London, Hutchinson, 1971), p. 32.

15 Sir Thomas Elyot, *The Book named The Governor*, ed. S. E. Lehmberg, Everyman's Library (London, Dent, 1962), pp. 119–20.

16 *A Hundred Merry Tales and Other English Jestbooks of the Fifteenth and Sixteenth Centuries*, ed. P. M. Zall (Lincoln, Nebraska, University of Nebraska Press, 1963), pp. 108–9; Brinklow, *Complaynt of Roderyck Mors*, p. 45; Lawrence Stone, *The Crisis of the Aristocracy 1558–1641* (Oxford, Clarendon Press, 1965), pp. 229–30; Sharpe, *Crime in seventeenth-century England*, p. 147. This was still very much the case in the eighteenth century; see Hay, 'Property, Authority and the Criminal Law', in *Albion's Fatal Tree*, p. 47.

17 Note also *Nice Wanton*, ed. Glynne Wickham, in *English Moral Interludes*, Everyman's University Library (London, Dent, 1976), ll. 352–3; and see above, Chapter One, pp. 6–7 and n. 8.

18 *A Handful of Pleasant Delights*, ed. Hyder E. Rollins (New York, Dover, 1965; edn first publ. 1924), pp. 65–8, 118–22; quotations from pp. 67 (ll. 1965–6), p. 65 (l. 1922), p. 67 (l. 1971).

19 *The Shirburn Ballads 1585–1616*, ed. Andrew Clark (Oxford, Clarendon Press, 1907), pp. 20–4, quotation from stanza 3.

20 Clavell, *A Recantation of an Ill Led Life*, p. 7.

21 Coke, *Third Part of the Institutes*, p. 68 [cap. xvi].

22 Samuel Rowlands, *The Knave of Clubbs* (1611), in *Works*, ed. S. J. Herrtage, 3 vols (Glasgow, Hunterian Club, 1880), II, pp. 42–3 [sigs $F_1v–F_2r$]; Clavell, *A Recantation of an Ill Led Life*, p. 31; *A Second Discovery of Hind's Exploits* (London, 1651), p. 3 [sig. A_5r]; G[eorge] F[idge], *The English Gusman*, p. 14 [C_4v]; William Cavendish, *A Pleasante & merrye Humor off a Roge*, in *Dramatic Works*, ed. Lynn Hulse (Oxford, Malone Society, 1996), ll. 552–5; Head, *Jackson's Recantation*, ed. Peterson, p. 161; Alexander Smith, *A Complete History of the Lives and Robberies of the most notorious Highwaymen* (London, George Routledge, 1926), p. 27.

23 Verney, *Memoirs of the Verney Family*, IV, p. 285.

24 For an example, see John Evelyn, *Diary*, ed. E. S. de Beer, 6 vols (Oxford, Clarendon Press, 1955), III, p. 73 (10 and 12 July 1652). However, in spite of Evelyn's professed unwillingness 'to hang the fellow', his robber was convicted and sentenced to death: see *Middlesex County Records*, ed. Jeaffreson, III, p. 209. For a fictional instance of a victim's expressing a repugnance towards prosecution, see Daniel Defoe, *Colonel Jack*, ed. Samuel Holt Monk (Oxford University Press, 1970), p. 84; for similar cases, see also Thomas Middleton, *Your Five Gallants*, ed. Bullen, in *Works*, III, III ii 54–70; *Hinds Elder Brother, or the Master Thief Discovered* (London, 1651), pp. 6–7 [sigs $A_4v–B_1r$]. Note also the irritated comments of two magistrates from widely separated periods: the Elizabethan Edward Hext, in Aydelotte, *Elizabethan Rogues and Vagabonds*, p. 169, and Henry Fielding in *An Enquiry Into the Causes of the Late Increase of Robbers*, ed. Malvin R. Zirker (Middletown, Connecticut, Wesleyan University Press, 1988), pp. 154–7 [Sect. VIII]; see also Thomas Fuller, 'The true Gentleman', in *The Holy State and the Profane State*, ed. Maximilian Graff Walten, 2 vols (Cambridge, 1642, facs. repr. New York, Columbia University Press, 1938) II, pp. 151–2 [Book II, Chapter 24]. In 1750, Horace Walpole was, as he himself reported in a letter, 'honorably mentioned in a grub ballad' for not appearing in evidence against the highwayman James Maclaine, who had robbed him and narrowly

missed killing him with a bullet. (Maclaine was condemned anyway, on other evidence.) See Horace Walpole, *Correspondence*, ed. W. S. Lewis and others, 48 vols (London, Oxford University Press, 1937–1983), vol. 20, p. 188; and see also vol. 13, p. 23; vol. 40, pp. 63–5.

25 Harman, *Caveat*, ed. Viles and Furnivall, p. 29.

26 See Chapter Three, pp. 24–5 and nn. 1, 4. For further examples besides Hitchcock, cited in Chapter One, p. 7 and n. 9, and Wilson, cited below, reference in n. 29, see John Skelton, *Magnificence*, ed. Paula Neuss (Manchester University Press, 1980), ll. 2041–3; *The Cashiered Soldier* (1643), quoted in Harper, *Half-Hours with the Highwaymen*, I, p. 65; William Lee, *Daniel Defoe: His Life, and recently discovered writings: extending from 1716 to 1729*, 3 vols (London, John Camden Hotten, 1869), II, p. 517 [*Applebee's Journal*, May 5, 1722]. Note also *The Life and Death of Gamaliel Ratsey*, quoted on p. 114, reference in n. 55 below.

27 Owst, *Literature and Pulpit*, p. 45; *Hick Scorner*, ed. Lancashire, ll. 558–9; W. Wager, *The Longer Thou Livest*, ed. R. Mark Benbow, in *The Longer Thou Livest and Enough Is as Good as a Feast* (London, Edward Arnold, 1968), l. 688.

28 See Chapter One, p. 5 and n. 5, p. 7 and n. 9.

29 Robert Wilson, *The Three Ladies of London*, ed. W. Carew Hazlitt, in *Dodsley's Old Plays*, vol. 6 (London, Reeves & Turner, 1874), p. 352.

30 S[amuel] R[id], *Martin Markall, Beadle of Bridewell*, ed. Judges, in *The Elizabethan Underworld*, pp. 415–6. For 'gentleman thief' as a synonym for highway robber, see also Robert Cary, *Memoirs*, ed. G. H. Powell, The King's Classics (London, De la More Press, 1905), p. 58; Defoe, *Colonel Jack*, ed. Monk, p. 62.

31 *The Contention Between Liberality and Prodigality*, ed. W. W. Greg (Oxford, Malone Society, 1913).

32 See Mildred Campbell, *The English Yeoman Under Elizabeth and the Early Stuarts* (London, Merlin Press, 1983 [first publ. 1942]), esp. chapter II. In *The Contention Between Liberality and Prodigality*, Tenacity is expressly called a yeoman at V v 1266.

33 Thomas Smith, *De Republica Anglorum* (London, 1583; facs. repr. Menston, Scolar Press, 1970), p. 30.

34 George Whetstone, *A Mirour for Magestrates of Cyties* (London, 1584), sigs H₃v–H₄r; see also John Taylor the Water Poet, *All the Workes*, sig. Rr₁r (*Wit and Mirth*, no. 75); Francis Thynne, *Emblemes and Epigrammes*, ed. F. J. Furnivall (London, Early English Text Society, 1876), p. 47. Note also Durazzo's comments on his ward Caldoro in *The Guardian*, by Philip Massinger, ed. Philip Edwards and Colin Gibson, in vol. 4 of *The Plays and Poems of Philip Massinger*, 5 vols (Oxford, Clarendon Press, 1976), I i 49–53.

35 Hugh Latimer, *Sermons*, ed. George Elwes Corrie (Cambridge, Parker Society, 1844), p. 431; Thomas Becon, *The Catechism with other pieces*, ed. John Ayre (Cambridge, Parker Society, 1844), p. 373; Thomas Wilson, *The State of England, Anno Dom. 1600*, ed. F. J. Fisher (London, Camden Society, 1936), p. 28.

36 *The Contention Between Liberality and Prodigality*, ed. Greg, ll. 349–50.

37 See Chapter One, p. 6 and n. 7; *The Famous Victories of Henry the Fifth*, l. 11, cited in Chapter Ten, pp. 117–18 and n. 3; Mannington, *A sorrowful Sonet*, ed. Rollins in *A Handful of Pleasant Delights*, l. 1928; Middleton, *The Phoenix*, ed. Bullen in *Works*, I, III i 59–60, 64–70.

38 Grafton, *A Chronicle at large*, pp. 85 [sig. H$_2$r], 84 [sig. H$_1$v].

39 See Chapter Five, p. 52 and n. 6.

40 See Chapter Four, p. 38 and n. 5; Chapter Six, p. 68.

41 See Joan Thirsk, 'Younger Sons in the Seventeenth Century', *History*, vol. 54, no. 182 (October 1969), pp. 358–77.

42 John Earle, *Microcosmography*, ed. Harold Osborne (London, University Tutorial Press, no date), p. 23; note also William Sprigge quoted by Michael McKeon in *The Origins of the English Novel, 1600–1740* (Baltimore, Johns Hopkins University Press, 1987), pp. 227–8.

43 Stone, *Crisis of the Aristocracy*, pp. 211–13.

44 I. M., *A Health to the Gentlemanly Profession of Serving-Men* (London, 1598; facs. repr. London, Shakespeare Association, 1931), sigs I$_3$v–I$_4$r; see also Mark Thornton Burnett, *Masters and Servants in the English Renaissance Drama and Culture* (Houndmills, Macmillan, 1997), pp. 176–8.

45 Burnett, *Masters and Servants in the English Renaissance Drama and Culture*, pp. 40–2.

46 Earle, *Microcosmography*, ed. Osborne, p. 51.

47 Whetstone, *A Mirour for Magestrates of Cyties*, sig. H$_2$r.

48 Smith, *De Republica Anglorum*, p. 27. Note I. M., *A Health to the Gentlemanly Profession of Serving-Men*, sigs D$_3$v–D$_4$v; and see below, Chapter Thirteen, p. 171 and n. 38.

49 Verney, *Memoirs of the Verney Family*, IV, pp. 289, 292–317, quotations on pp. 295, 300, 301, 303, 307, 310; see also vol. 1, ed. Frances Parthenope Verney (London, Longmans, 1892), pp. 201–2.

50 Clavell, *A Recantation of an Ill Led Life*, p. 16.

51 William Shakespeare, *King Henry IV, Part I*, ed. A. R. Humphreys, The Arden Shakespeare (London, Methuen, 1966), IV ii 28.

52 *The Life and Death of Gamaliel Ratsey* and *Ratseis Ghost* (London, 1605; facs. repr. London, Shakespeare Association, 1935). A small amount of what appears to be more or less authentic biographical information about Ratsey may be found in the *Life and Death*, sigs A$_2$r–A$_3$r, E$_2$r. There are no other sources.

53 *Life and Death*, sig. A$_2$v.

54 Ibid., sigs E$_2$v–F$_3$v; Shaaber, 'Luke Hutton's Repentance', pp. 73–81. In 1612, *Ratseys repentance* was itself plagiarised; *Courtneis repentance*, in *The Life, Apprehensio[n], Arraignement, and Execution of Char[les] Courtney* (sigs D$_2$r–D$_3$v), is simply a cut-down version of the earlier poem, with a few minor changes.

55 *Life and Death*, sig. C$_1$v; note also sig. C$_3$r and *Ratseis Ghost*, sigs A$_4$v, C$_3$r.

56 *Ratseis Ghost*, sig. D$_2$r; see also *Life and Death*, sig. B$_3$r.

57 *Ratseis Ghost*, sig. C$_3$v.

58 Ibid., sigs D$_4$r–v; note also sig. D$_2$r.

59 Becon, *The Catechism*, ed. Ayre, pp. 104–8. This is all traditional Christian teaching: compare *Dives and Pauper*, ed. Barnum, I, ii, pp. 136, 153–4, 159–60, 195–7, 202–8 [Commandment vii, caps iv, x, xii, xxiv, xxvi, xxvii, xxviii].

60 *The Oxford Dictionary of English Proverbs*, 3rd edn, ed. F. P. Wilson (Oxford, Clarendon Press, 1970), p. 175 [Tilley D 182]; see also *Ratseis Ghost*, sig. B₄v.

61 *Life and Death*, sigs B₁v, E₁v.

62 *Ratseis Ghost*, sigs A₃v, D₂r, C₃r; see also sig. C₁v; *Life and Death*, sigs D₃r, A₃v.

63 *Ratseis Ghost*, sigs F₂v–F₃r, quotation on sig. F₃r.

TEN: FALSTAFF AND THE WILD PRINCE

1 A forgotten robber of legend who had a vogue in popular entertainment in the mid-1590s was 'Bellin Dun' or 'Bellendon', the subject of a lost play, ballad and 'chronicle' narrative: see Henslowe, *Diary*, ed. Foakes and Rickert, p. 21; Hyder E. Rollins, 'An Analytical Index to the Ballad-Entries in the Registers of the Company of Stationers of London', *Studies in Philology*, vol. 21, 1 (January, 1924), pp. 23–4.

2 John Stow, *The Chronicles of England* (1580), excerpted in *Narrative and Dramatic Sources of Shakespeare*, vol. 4, ed. Geoffrey Bullough (London, Routledge & Kegan Paul, 1962), p. 219; see also Humphreys, (ed.), *King Henry IV, Part I*, pp. xxix–xxx.

3 *The Famous Victories of Henry the Fifth*, ed. Geoffrey Bullough, in *Narrative and Dramatic Sources of Shakespeare*, IV pp. 299–343, ll. 9–10, 11, 23–4, 22, 26–7.

4 Ibid., ll. 86, 41–2, 88, 89, 93–4.

5 Ibid., ll. 329, 460, 468–74.

6 Ibid., ll. 683–6. In l. 686, original speech prefix reads 'L. ambo.'

7 William Shakespeare, *King Richard II*, ed. Peter Ure, The Arden Shakespeare (London, Methuen, 1966), V iii 8–12.

8 See *OED*, s. v. support, *v.*, 2. a.

9 Stone, *The Crisis of the Aristocracy*, pp. 229–30.

10 William Empson, 'Falstaff and Mr Dover Wilson', in *Shakespeare, Henry IV Parts I and II. A casebook*, ed. G. K. Hunter (London, Macmillan, 1970), pp. 137–9 [essay first published in 1953].

11 Shakespeare, *King Henry IV, Part I*, ed. Humphreys, I ii 28–9, 31, 96.

12 Ibid., ll. 22, 23–9.

13 Ibid., l. 14.

14 See Chapter Four, pp. 37–8 and nn. 1, 2. For 'roberdesmen' see 5 Edward III, c. 14; 7 Richard II, c. 5. 'High lawyer' is first found in Greene's *A Notable Discouery of Coosnage* (1591), ed. Harrison, p. 38. For 'good fellow', see below, nn. 29, 30. See *OED* s. v. cutter, *sb¹*, 3. a; Nicholas, 2. b.

15 'Forester' is sometimes used at this time as a synonym for 'outlaw': see Chapter Eleven, p. 138 and n. 29; Thomas Heywood, *The Four Prentices of London*, ed. Mary Ann Weber Gasior (New York, Garland, 1980), ll. 797, 806. For 'dame Dianaes knyght', with the meaning 'a banished man', see William Baldwin, George Ferrers and others, *The Mirror for Magistrates*, ed. Lily B. Campbell (Cambridge University Press, 1938), p. 107 ['Lord Mowbray', l. 161].

16 *OED* s. v. countenance, *sb.*, I. 2, 5; II. 8; III. 9, 10.

17 See Chapter Eight, p. 98 and n. 52.

18 Note the remarks of Thomas Dekker, in *The Belman of London* [1608]: see *The Guls Hornbook and the Belman of London in Two Parts*, The Temple Classics (London, Dent, 1941), p. 112 ('Of cheating Lawe').

19 *King Henry IV, Part I*, I ii 80–1.

20 Ibid., ll. 30–8.

21 Ibid., ll. 56–60. For the social status of hangmen, see Arthur Griffiths, *The Chronicles of Newgate* (London, Bracken Books, 1987; facs. of edn of 1884), pp. 173–4, and note Fielding, *An Enquiry into the Causes of the Late Increase of Robbers*, ed. Zirker, p. 153.

22 *King Henry IV, Part I*, I ii 66–9.

23 David Loades, *The Tudor Court*, revised edn (Bangor, Headstart History, 1992), pp. 133–47; Stone, *The Crisis of the Aristocracy*, pp. 402–49.

24 *King Henry IV, Part I*, I ii 103–4, 120–4, 134, 151–2.

25 Ibid., ll. 135–7.

26 *OED* s. v. honesty, *sb.* I. 1, 3. d.

27 *King Henry IV, Part I*, I ii 111–13.

28 *A Hundred Merry Tales*, ed. Zall, p. 79.

29 Whetstone, *A Mirour for Magestrates of Cyties*, sig. K₁r–v; Thomas Heywood, *The first part of King Edward the fourth* [ed. R. H. Shepherd], in *Dramatic Works*, vol. 1 (New York, Russell & Russell, 1964 [edn first publ. 1874]), pp. 41–2; Thomas Heywood, *The Four Prentices of London*, ed. Gasior, ll. 444, 675; Middleton, *The Black Book*, ed. Bullen, in *Works*, VIII, p. 30; Thomas Middleton, *A Trick to Catch the Old One*, ed. G. J. Watson, New Mermaids (London, Ernest Benn, 1968), II i 18–20; note also *The Famous Victories of Henry the Fifth*, ed. Bullough, l. 161; Samuel Rowley, *When you see me, you know me*, ed. F. P. Wilson (Oxford, Malone Society, 1952), l. 1121–2, 1284; Massinger, *The Guardian*, ed. Edwards and Gibson, V iii 24, V iv 186.

30 Anthony Munday, Michael Drayton and others, *Sir John Oldcastle*, ed. C. F. Tucker Brooke, in *The Shakespeare Apocrypha* (Oxford, Clarendon Press, 1908), I ii 163–5, III iv 44–9. Compare Heywood, *The first part of King Edward the fourth* [ed. Shepherd], pp. 41–2.

31 Smith, *De Republica Anglorum*, p. 29; see above, Chapter One, pp. 5 and n. 5, 7 and n. 9; Chapter Nine, pp. 105–7 and nn. 25, 29; see also Dekker, *The Belman of London*, p. 142 ('The High Law'); compare *King Henry IV, Part I*, II iv 125–8.

32 *King Henry IV, Part I*, II i 72–3, 74–81.

33 Ibid., I ii 150; compare II i 69.

34 Ibid., II iv 6–21, see also II iv 273–5; William Shakespeare, *King Henry IV, Part II*, ed. A. R. Humphreys, The Arden Shakespeare (London, Methuen, 1966), V iii 60–7. For gentlemen and drinking, note also Robert Burton, *The Anatomy of Melancholy*, 3 vols, ed. Thomas C. Faulkner, Nicolas K. Kiessling, Rhonda L. Blair (Oxford, Clarendon Press, 1989–94), I, p. 222, ll. 16–28 [1. ii. ii. 2]; Bülbring (ed.), *The Compleat English Gentleman* by Defoe, p. lxxxi. For Falstaff on sherris-sack, see *King Henry IV, Part II*, IV iii 85–123. Elizabeth A. Foyster's study *Manhood in Early Modern England. Honour, Sex and*

Marriage (London, Longman, 1999), came to my attention after this chapter was written; see pp. 40–1 for her comments on manhood and drinking.

35 *King Henry IV, Part I*, I iii 29–63; quotations from ll. 44, 62. Note Stone in *The Crisis of the Aristocracy*, pp. 239, 265, on changing attitudes to warfare among the Elizabethan aristocracy.

36 *King Henry IV, Part I*, II iii 1–35, quotation in l. 15.

37 Ibid., III ii 4–128; quotations in ll. 125, 128, 65; see also I i 77–89.

38 Ibid., II iv 494–7, 540–1.

39 *King Henry IV, Part II*, V i 34–46. The parallel between Davy and Falstaff is noted by Harry Levin in 'Falstaff's Encore', *Shakespeare Quarterly*, vol. 32, 1 (1981), p. 16.

40 *King Henry IV, Part II*, V iii 132–3, V v 7–8.

41 Ibid., V v 10–13, 73–6; see also V i 28–9, iii 125–7.

42 See Chapter Nine, p. 115 and n. 60; *King Henry IV, Part I*, I ii 119.

43 *King Henry IV, Part II*, II iv 523–35; see also III iii 50–8, 78–80, 95–101, 154–169.

44 Note *King Henry IV, Part II*, IV v 190–1; see the comments of Barbara Everett, 'The Fatness of Falstaff: Shakespeare and Character', *Proceedings of the British Academy*, vol. 76 (1991), p. 122.

45 *King Henry IV, Part II*, IV v 19–176.

46 Munday and others, *Sir John Oldcastle*, ed. Tucker Brooke, in *The Shakespeare Apocrypha*, III iv 69–70, 62–5, 117–8.

47 See Chapter One, p. 12 and n. 23; Smith, *A Complete History of the Lives and Robberies of the most notorious Highwaymen*, p. 13.

48 Thomas Nashe, *Christs Teares Over Jerusalem* (London, 1593; facs. repr. Menston, Scolar Press, 1970), pp. 29, 28v.

49 *King Henry IV, Part I*, II ii 85, 86–7, 81–2, 86.

50 J. S. Cockburn, *A History of English Assizes 1558–1714* (Cambridge University Press, 1972), pp. 112–3; Cynthia Herrup, *The Common Peace. Participation and the Criminal Law in Seventeenth-Century England* (Cambridge University Press, 1989), pp. 100–1.

51 *King Henry IV, Part II*, II i 108–9.

52 Note *King Henry IV, Part I*, III ii 26–7; V ii 16–17.

53 See Chapter Twelve, p. 149 and n. 5. Clavell's statement is a piece of insincerity, but that does not invalidate the principle.

54 Clavell, *A Recantation of an Ill Led Life*, p. 7; C. G. Cruikshank, *Elizabeth's Army* (Oxford, Clarendon Press, 1966), pp. 26–9.

55 Rowley, *When you see me, You know me*, ed. Wilson, ll. 1062–1178, 1358–85; quotations from ll. 1099, 1370–1.

56 *King Henry IV, Part I*, IV ii 11–48, V iii 36–8 and see fn.; *King Henry IV, Part II*, III ii 81–286.

57 *King Henry IV, Part I*, I ii 2–12.

58 *The Oxford Dictionary of English Proverbs*, ed. Wilson, p. 928 [Tilley S 33].

59 See Chapter Four, p. 49 and n. 44; *The Prayer-Book of Queen Elizabeth 1559* (London, Griffith Farran, no date), p. 119.

60 *King Henry IV, Part I*, I ii 92–3; III iii 4–5; V iv 162–4; Jonson, *Every Man out of his Humour*, V iii 64–7, 69–71; see also IV v. In relation to Shift, the

pretended highwayman, compare the lying swaggerers described by Clavell in *A Recantation of an Ill Led Life*, p. 23.

61 *King Henry IV, Part I*, I ii 88–95; see also III iii 9–10; George Gascoigne, *The Glasse of Governement . . . and other poems*, ed. John W. Cunliffe (Cambridge University Press, 1910), p. 86, see also p. 87; *Luke Huttons lamentation*, ed. Collman, in *Ballads and Broadsides*, p. 159; see also the speech of the First Hackster in Whetstone, *Promos and Cassandra*, ed. Bullough, Part I, II vii (p. 457).

62 *King Henry IV, Part I*, V i 134–5.

63 William Shakespeare, *King Henry V*, ed. John H. Walter, The Arden Shakespeare (London, Methuen, 1974), II iii 41–3. See *King Henry IV, Part I*, II iv 310–12; III iii 24–49, 75–7; *King Henry IV, Part II*, II ii 71–80; II iv 263, 326–7, 329–331.

64 *King Henry V*, II iii 9–10; *The Gospel of Luke*, chap. 16 v. 22 [Bishops' Bible, 1568]; Sir Thomas Malory, *Le Morte D'Arthur*, intr. John Lawlor, 2 vols (Harmondsworth, Penguin, 1969), II, p. 519 [Caxton's text, Book XXXI, chaps 6, 7].

ELEVEN: OUTLAWS IN ARCADIA

1 William Shakespeare, *The Two Gentlemen of Verona*, ed. Clifford Leech, The Arden Shakespeare (London, Methuen, 1972), IV i, quotations from ll. 37, 39–40, 71–3.

2 Ibid., l. 36.

3 See Chapter Five, n. 5.

4 *The Two Gentlemen of Verona*, IV i 2, 44–6.

5 Ibid., V iv 1–12; see Chapter Two, pp. 16–17 and n. 5.

6 *Unpublished Poems from the Blage manuscript* by Sir Thomas Wyatt and his circle, ed. Kenneth Muir, (Liverpool University Press, 1961), pp. 26–8; quotations from ll. 1, 5, 71–2; text corrected by H. A. Mason in *Editing Wyatt: An Examination of Collected Poems of Sir Thomas Wyatt together with suggestions for an improved edition* (Cambridge Quarterly, 1972), pp. 47, 53.

7 *The Two Gentlemen of Verona*, V iv 2, 3. Leech's edition has no comma after 'shadowy'.

8 F. P. Wilson and G. K. Hunter, *English Drama 1485–1585* (Oxford, Clarendon Press, 1986), pp. 118–19.

9 Heliodorus, *An Aethiopian History*, trans. Thomas Underdowne, intr. George Saintsbury (London, Chapman & Dodd, no date), pp. 8, 9, 10, 11, etc. [Book I].

10 Ibid., pp. 28, 38–9, 11–12, 175–6 [Books I, VII].

11 Ibid., pp. 54, 28–30 [Books II, I].

12 *Fouke le Fitz Waryn*, p. 30, ll. 20–2.

13 *The Two Gentlemen of Verona*, V iv 16–17.

14 Ibid., ll. 138, 154–5. For *The Tale of Gamelyn*, see Chapter Four, p. 44 and n. 24.

15 *Trailbaston*, ed. Aspin, in *Anglo-Norman Political Songs*, p. 72, stanza 21, l. 82; 'I muste go walke the woodes so wyld', ll. 6–8 (see above, n. 6).

16 Johnston, 'The Robin Hood of the Records', p. 39.

17 See above, n. 6, and Chapter Five, n. 21.

18 *Robin Hood and the Monk*, ed. Dobson and Taylor, in *Rymes of Robyn Hood*, stanzas 1, 2.

19 *Trailbaston*, ed. Aspin, in *Anglo-Norman Political Songs*, p. 69, stanza 5, ll. 17, 18.

20 *Robin Hood and Allen a Dale*, ed. Dobson and Taylor, in *Rymes of Robyn Hood*, pp. 172–5 [Child no. 138]; note the traces of an older analogue in a late sixteenth-century ms. 'life' of Robin Hood, see *Early English Prose Romances*, ed. Thoms, p. 548.

21 *Robin Hood Rescuing Three Squires*, see also *Robin Hood Rescuing Will Stutly*, and *Robin Hood and the Beggar, I*, all ed. Child, in *The English and Scottish Popular Ballads*, III, pp. 177–87, 155–8 [Child nos. 140, 141, 133]; see also Munday and Chettle, *The Downfall of Robert, Earl of Huntington*, ed. Meagher, in *The Huntingdon Plays*, ll. 798–999 [scene v]. Some form of the rescue from the gallows story was known as the subject of Robin Hood plays as early as the late 1530s: see Sir Richard Morison, quoted in Knight, *Robin Hood*, p. 273.

22 See Chapter Three, p. 30 and n. 18; *Gesta Herwardi*, pp. 349–53.

23 Warner, *Albions England*, 2nd edn, pp. 118–19 [sigs R_1v-R_2r].

24 Knight, *Robin Hood*, pp. 135–6.

25 See Chapter Five, p. 54 and n. 18, p. 55 and n. 27. For feasting in summer bowers, see Stubbes, *The Anatomie of Abuses*, ed. Furnivall, p. 147; Michael Drayton, *Poems* (London, 1619; facs. repr. Menston, Scolar Press, 1969), p. 468 [*The Ninth Eglogue*].

26 See Chapter Five, p. 54.

27 Thomas Lodge, *Rosalynde*, ed. Bullough, in *Narrative and Dramatic Sources of Shakespeare*, II, pp. 158–256; quotation on p. 196.

28 For a succinct account of Arcadia, see Peter V. Marinelli, *Pastoral* (London, Methuen, 1971), chaps 3, 4. See also Sir Philip Sidney, *The Old Arcadia*, ed. Katharine Duncan-Jones (Oxford University Press, 1985), pp. 4, 50; Thomas Heywood, *An Apology for Actors* (London, 1612; facs. repr. New York, Johnson Reprint Society, 1972), sig. F_4r.

29 Lodge, *Rosalynde*, pp. 197, 199, 200, 201, etc.

30 Sir Philip Sidney, *The Lady of May*, ed. Katherine Duncan-Jones, in *Major Works* (Oxford University Press, 1989), ll. 120–3, 163, 188, 197.

31 *OED*, s. v. prowl, *v.*, 1 a, 2 b, c; prowler.

32 Lodge, *Rosalynde*, p. 222.

33 Ibid., p. 203.

34 Edward Arber, *A Transcript of the Registers of the Company of Stationers of London, 1554–1640*, 5 vols (London, 1875–7, Birmingham, 1894), II, p. 649.

35 Munday and Chettle, *The Downfall of Robert, Earl of Huntington*, ed. Meagher, in *The Huntingdon Plays*, ll. 1366–81 [scene viii]. For another 'pastoral' moment, see also ll. 1490–5 [scene x]. For the early development of the 'Maid Marian' figure, see Appendix B.

36 See above, n. 21.

37 Munday and Chettle, *The Downfall of Robert, Earl of Huntington*, ll. 1349–55; quotation from l. 1355 [scene viii].

38 Note Parker, *A True Tale of Robin Hood*, ed. Child, in *The English and Scottish Popular Ballads*, III, pp. 227–33, stanzas 15–18 [Child no. 154].

39 See Chapter Nine, pp. 109, 114–15.

40 Munday and Chettle, *The Downfall of Robert, Earl of Huntington*, ll. 1357–8 [scene viii].

41 Ibid., ll. 2080–207 [scene xiii].

42 Munday and Chettle, *The Death of Robert, Earl of Huntington*, ed. Meagher, in *The Huntingdon Plays*, ll. 316–7 [scene iii].

43 William Shakespeare, *As You Like It*, ed. Agnes Latham, The Arden Shakespeare (London, Methuen, 1975), I i 114–19.

44 Ovid, *Metamorphoses*, I, ll. 89–112.

45 Harry Levin, *The Myth of the Golden Age in the Renaissance* (London, Faber & Faber, 1970), esp. pp. 13–25, 42–4; see also Marinelli, *Pastoral*, chaps 2, 3.

46 *As You Like It*, I i 1–2, 85–7.

47 Ibid., II iii 31–3.

48 Hesiod, *Works and Days*, l. 184; Ovid, *Metamorphoses*, Book I, l. 145.

49 *As You Like It*, II vii 107–9.

50 Thomas Heywood burlesques outlaws of this type in *The Four Prentices of London*, ed. Gasior, ll. 304–14, 444–854. The episode includes some direct parody of the outlaw scenes in *The Two Gentlemen of Verona*.

51 *As You Like It*, II i 5–11; see also II v 6–8; II vii 174–93.

52 Ibid., II i 21–66; quotations from ll. 22, 23, 61.

53 Sidney, *The Lady of May*, ll. 223–5; Francis Bacon, *The Advancement of Learning*, ed. Brian Vickers, in *The Major Works* (Oxford University Press, 1996), p. 150 [I. vi. 7].

54 *As You Like It*, II i 15–17.

55 Ibid., l. 64; note also IV i 17.

56 Ibid., IV ii 3–4; St Augustine, *Civitas Dei*, Book IV chap. iv.

57 See Chapter Two, p. 17 and n. 8; 'I muste go walke the woodes so wyld', ll. 73, 74 (see above, n. 6).

58 Ovid, *Metamorphoses*, I. l. 144.

59 For a couple of cases in point, see Alfred, Lord Tennyson, *The Foresters*, in *Poems and Plays*, ed. T. Herbert Warren, rev. Frederick Page (London, Oxford University Press, 1971); Alfred Noyes, *Robin Hood. A Play in Five Acts* (Edinburgh, Blackwood, 1926). For Tennyson's *The Foresters* and its stage history, see Knight, *Robin Hood*, pp. 197–201; Lois Potter, 'The Apotheosis of Maid Marian: Tennyson's *The Foresters* and the Nineteenth Century Theater', in *Playing Robin Hood*, ed. Potter.

60 Ben Jonson, *The Sad Shepherd*, ed. C. H. Herford, Percy and Evelyn Simpson, in *Works*, vol. 7 (Oxford, Clarendon Press, 1941).

61 See Appendix C, n. 17. For discussions of this development see Holt, *Robin Hood*, pp. 183, 185; Knight, *Robin Hood*, pp. 154–8.

62 For texts, see Child, *The English and Scottish Popular Ballads*, vol. III; *Robin*

Hood: The Forresters Manuscript. BL Add. MS 71158, ed. Stephen Knight (Cambridge, D. S. Brewer, 1998).

63 *Historical Manuscripts Commission. Twelfth Report, Appendix, Part I. The Manuscripts of the Earl Cowper, K. G., preserved at Melbourne Hall, Derbyshire*. vol. 1 (London, HMSO, 1888), p. 282.

64 Clavell, *A Recantation of an Ill Led Life*, p. 28.

65 *Captain Hind's Progress and Ramble*, ed. J. W. Ebsworth, in *The Roxburghe Ballads*, ed. William Chappell and J. W. Ebsworth, 8 vols (London, Ballad Society, 1871–95), VII, pp. 642–7.

TWELVE: THE ROBBER REPENTANT: CLAVELL'S *RECANTATION*

1 Pafford, *John Clavell, 1601–43. Highwayman, Author, Lawyer, Doctor*, pp. 27–32, 25, 125–34, 139–140; [John Clavell], *The Soddered Citizen*, ed. John Henry Pyle Pafford and W. W. Greg, Malone Society, 1935 [1936].

2 Pafford, *John Clavell*, pp. 2–3, 16–24, 32, 282–9.

3 [Clavell], *The Soddered Citizen*, ll. 2807–11 (quoted), 2816–23; Pafford, *John Clavell*, pp. 129, 138.

4 The closest stage parallel is the character of Tom Lurcher in John Fletcher's *The Night-Walker* (c. 1611). There is an early forerunner in the character of Thrasibulus in Thomas Lodge and Robert Greene's *A Looking Glass for London and England* (late 1580s). Otherwise, Thomas Middleton's city comedies abound in financial sharks of Mountain's stamp, as well as in ruined young gentlemen living by their wits and sometimes by dishonest means, including robbery (see *Your Five Gallants* and *A Mad World, My Masters*, both written between 1604 and 1607).

5 Clavell, *A Recantation of An Ill Led Life*, 1634 edn (repr. in facs. in Pafford, *John Clavell*), p. 2; Pafford, *John Clavell*, pp. 278–9.

6 Clavell, *A Recantation*, p. 45.

7 [Clavell], *The Soddered Citizen*, ll. 1–12; compare Clavell, *A Recantation*, p. 1.

8 Clavell, *A Recantation*, p. 13.

9 Ben Jonson, *Bartholomew Fair*, ed. E. A. Horsman (London, Methuen, 1960), II iv 66–7, 69 70. Note also Benjamin Childe, *A Narrative of the Life of Mr. Benjamin Childe . . . Executed . . . for Robbing the Bristol Mail* (London, T. Payne, 1722), pp. 20–1.

10 John Fletcher and William Shakespeare, *The Two Noble Kinsmen*, ed. G. R. Proudfoot (London, Edward Arnold, 1970).

11 See for example Gascoigne, *The Glasse of Governement*, ed. Cunliffe, p. 72; Shakespeare, *King Henry IV, Part I*, ed. Humphreys, II iv 6–7; Anon., *The Puritaine Widdow*, ed. C. F. Tucker Brooke, in *The Shakespeare Apocrypha* (Oxford, Clarendon Press, 1908), I ii 143–7; Farquhar, *The Beaux' Stratagem*, ed. Fifer, III iii 34–40. For a rare Jacobean reference to the swearing of brotherhood between gentlemen, see Thomas Middleton (with Ben Jonson and John Fletcher?), *The Widow*, ed. Bullen, in *Works*, V, I ii 219–20.

12 Samuel Rowlands, 'False Knaves will never be true', in *More Knaves yet? The Knaves of Spades and Diamonds* (London, [1613]) ed. Herrtage, in *Works*, II,

pp. 15–16 [sig. C₁r–v]; *Fasciculus Morum*, ed. Wenzel, pp. 420–3. In Richard Head's fictional version of the life of one Jackson, a highwayman hanged in 1674, he represents him as swearing brotherhood with one of his confederates; see Head, *Jackson's Recantation*, ed. Peterson, in *The Counterfeit Lady and other criminal fiction*, pp. 150, 153.

13 Clavell, *A Recantation*, sig. C₃r, pp. 8–9, 10.

14 Smith, *A Complete History of the . . . Highwaymen*, pp. 188–9; 'Damnation' expanded from 'D—tion'. For a reference to footpads binding themselves by oaths, see Luttrell, *A Brief Historical Relation of State Affairs*, II, p. 642 [17 December 1692]. For an eighteenth-century highwayman's lack of confidence in oaths, see *Lives of the Most Remarkable Criminals* (1735), ed. Arthur L. Hayward (London, George Routledge, 1927), pp. 48–9; see also Villette, *The Annals of Newgate*, I, p. 42. For an eighteenth-century highwayman, Paul Lewis, who refused to break his oath, see Villette, *The Annals of Newgate*, IV, p. 101.

15 Clavell, *A Recantation*, pp. 24–5, quotation on p. 25; Harrison, *The Description of England*, pp. 238, 398–9, passages added in 2nd edn, 1587; *The Life . . . of Charles Courtney*, p. 5 [sig. B₃r]. For inn servants tipping off highway robbers, see also Frank Aydelotte, *Elizabethan Rogues and Vagabonds*, p. 100; Shakespeare, *King Henry IV, Part I*, II i 46–95; *The Life and Death of Gamaliel Ratsey*, sig. C₂r; *Ratseis Ghost*, sig. B₂v; G[eorge] F[idge], *The English Gusman*, p. 33 [sig. F₂r]. For highway robbers with inside knowledge, see Luttrell, *A Brief Historical Relation of State Affairs*, II, p. 642, IV, p. 427.

16 Clavell, *A Recantation*, pp. 29–30, 26–7, 6, 10, 28, quotation on p. 28.

17 Ibid., pp. 6, 17; see above, Chapter Eight, p. 98 and n. 52, pp. 99, 100.

18 Clavell, *A Recantation*, pp. 28–9; quotation on p. 29.

19 Shakespeare, *King Henry IV, Part I*, I ii 26, 29.

20 Wilson, *A Full and Impartial Account Of all the Robberies Committed by John Hawkins, George Sympson . . . and their Companions*, 3rd edn, pp. 8, 10, 18, 17; note also p. 28.

21 Clavell, *A Recantation*, p. 29; see also p. 37; J. S. Farmer and W. E. Henley, *Slang and Its Analogues* (1890), repr. in facs. as *A Dictionary of Slang*, 2 vols (Ware, Wordsworth, 1987), s. v. kill-calf (or -cow), *subs.*, and compare *OED*, s. v. kill-cow, *sb.* and *a.*; Harrison, *The Description of England*, p. 238.

22 *Lives of the Most Remarkable Criminals*, p. 69, and note also Villette, *The Annals of Newgate*, I, p. 69. Beattie discusses the use of brutality by footpads as contrasted (generally) with the behaviour of mounted robbers in *Crime and the Courts in England, 1660–1800*, pp. 150–2; for some foreign views of the contrasting behaviour of the two sorts of robber, see Leon Radzinowicz, *A History of English Criminal Law and its Administration from 1750*, vol. 1: The movement for reform (London, Stevens, 1948), p. 706 and nn. 47, 48. There are various references to brutal robbings and even murders by footpads in Luttrell, *A Brief Historical Relation of State Affairs*: see II, pp. 151–2, 524, III, pp. 28, 43, IV, pp. 581, 585, VI, p. 492. See also the broadside ballads, *Another Bloody murther committed neere Ware* (March 1633), ed. William Chappell, in *The Roxburghe Ballads*, vol. 3 (Part 1), pp. 147–9; *Summers's frolic* (1694), ed.

Hyder Edward Rollins, in *The Pepys Ballads*, 8 vols (Cambridge, Massachusetts, Harvard University Press, 1929–32), VII, pp. 39–43, esp. stanzas 3, 4.

23 For the modus operandi of footpads, see further in Abraham de la Pryme, *Diary* (Durham, Surtees Society, 1870), pp. 76–7; A. P. Herbert, *Mr. Gay's London*, (London, Ernest Benn, 1948), pp. 99–101, 110–11; Fielding, *An Enquiry into the Causes of the Late Increase of Robbers*, ed. Zirker, p. 159; and note also G[eorge] F[idge], *The English Gusman*, p. [12], [sig. C₃v]. For footpads working in the evening or at night, see Luttrell, *A Brief Historical Relation*, V, p. 220, VI, p. 492; Herbert, in the place cited; Fielding, in the place cited.

24 Evelyn, *Diary*, ed. de Beer, III, pp. 69–70 (23 June 1652).

25 Clavell, *A Recantation*, pp. 31–2; Pafford, *John Clavell*, p. 27.

26 *The Life ... of Charles Courtney*, p. 5 [sig. B₃r]. Note also *Luke Huttons lamentation*, ed. Collman, in *Ballads and Broadsides*, p. 160 (line 7); Munday, Drayton and others, *Sir John Oldcastle*, ed. Tucker Brooke, in *The Shakespeare Apocrypha*, III iv 81–92.

27 Fynes Moryson, *An Itinerary Containing His Ten Yeeres Travell*, 4 vols (Glasgow, James MacLehose and Sons, 1907–8), III, p. 408; Sharpe, *Crime in seventeenth-century England*, p. 106. Note also the comments of Macfarlane in *The Justice and the Mare's Ale*, p. 186.

28 See Chapter Five, p. 57 and n. 37; Chapter One, pp. 2–3 and n. 3.

29 Massinger, *The Guardian*, ed. Edwards and Gibson in vol. 4 of *Plays and Poems*, V iii 7–12; quotation from l. 11.

30 Henry Fielding, *The History of Tom Jones A Foundling*, ed. Fredson Bowers, 2 vols (Oxford, Clarendon Press, 1974), II, p. 681 [Book xii, chap. xiv]. Note Defoe, *Colonel Jack*, ed. Monk, p. 185 (quoted below, Chapter Fourteen, p. 183), and see also Radzinowicz, *A History of English Criminal Law*, I, p. 705 n. 42, p. 706 n. 48, pp. 708–9; Paul Langford, *Englishness Identified. Manners and Character 1650–1850* (Oxford University Press, 2000), p. 145.

31 Le Blanc, *Letters on the English and French Nations*, II, p. 296.

32 Luttrell, *A Brief Relation*, IV, pp. 313; 392, see also 395; 537, see also 610; 602; 679. Luttrell mentions a number of murders committed in the course of robberies, but it is not always clear whether the assailants were mounted highwaymen or footpads. I have listed only those where he specifies that the assailants were highwaymen. Note IV, p. 557, where it is apparent that for Luttrell, the difference between highwaymen and footpads was that the former were always mounted.

33 Ibid., II, pp. 120, 200, 323, 633; III, pp. 289–90, see also 317; 537.

34 *Robbery Rewarded*, ed. Hyder Edward Rollins, in *The Pack of Autolycus* (Cambridge, Massachusetts, Harvard University Press, 1927, reissued 1969), pp. 168–71, stanza 8; Daniel Defoe, *Moll Flanders*, ed. G. A. Starr, Oxford World's Classics (Oxford University Press, 1998), pp. 279–80; see also *The Confession of the Four High-Way-Men* (London, 1674), pp. 3–4; Richard Head, *The English Rogue* (1665), sig. Ccc₅v [Chapter xxxiii]; Gay, *The Beggar's Opera*, ed. Fuller, I iv 25–9; and see below, Chapter Nineteen, p. 251 and n. 5.

35 Mary Wollstonecraft, *An Historical and Moral View of the French Revolution*

(1794), in *Works*, ed. Janet Todd and Marilyn Butler, vol. 6 (London, William Pickering, 1989), p. 232.

36 Parker, *A True Tale of Robin Hood*, ed. Child, in *The English and Scottish Popular Ballads*, III, p. 232, stanzas 108–10, 116. In l. 3 of stanza 116 I have followed the variant reading: see notes on p. 233.

37 Clavell, *A Recantation*, pp. 10–11, 1; compare the story in Harman, *Caveat*, ed. Viles and Furnivall, pp. 30–1.

38 *The Life and Death of Gamaliel Ratsey*, sigs C_3r–D_1v, D_4r; *Ratseis Ghost*, sigs C_3r–v, E_2v–E_3r. Many similar tales were later told of James Hind; see for example G[eorge] F[idge], *The English Gusman*, pp. 4–5, 12, 18, 21–2, 22, 23–4, 26–7, 29–30, 33–4 [sigs B_3v–B_4r, C_3v, D_2v, D_4r–v, D_4v, E_1r–v, E_2v–E_3r, E_4r–v, F_2r–v]. See also 'George's Confession', stanza 3, in *The Life and Death of George of Oxford*, in *The Pepys Ballads*, ed. W. G. Day, 5 vols (Cambridge, Brewer, 1987), vol. II, p. 150; Farquhar, *The Beaux' Stratagem*, ed. Fifer, II ii 77–82; *Lives of the Most Remarkable Criminals*, pp. 111–12, 426, 517; Johann Wilhelm von Archenholz, *A Picture of England containing a Description of the Laws, Customs and Manners of England. Translated from the French* (Dublin, P. Byrne, 1790), p. 182; and see below, Chapter Thirteen, p. 178 and n. 65; Chapter Fourteen, p. 186 and n. 18; p. 187 and nn. 22, 23.

39 Clavell, *A Recantation*, p. 2; note Luttrell, *A Brief Historical Relation of State Affairs*, II, p. 613.

40 27 Eliz. c. 13 (1585).

41 Clavell, *A Recantation*, pp. 32–3, 30–1.

42 Ibid., pp. 33–4, 12. For the hue and cry, see below, Chapter Fourteen, pp. 193–4 and n. 44.

43 Clavell, *A Recantation*, p. 35; *The Life . . . of Charles Courtney*, pp. 5–6 [sigs B_3r–v].

44 Clavell, *A Recantation*, pp. 36–7.

45 Ibid., pp. 38–41, 12. For highwaymen insisting that their horses should receive special feeding, see also Thomas Middleton, *The Phoenix*, ed. Bullen, in *Works*, I, I iv 32–5. Some highwaymen are said to have fed their horses on meat: see the broadside ballad *The High-way Hector* (London, early 1640s [British Library C. 22. f. 6 (124)]), end of stanza 1; G[eorge] F[idge], *The English Gusman*, p. 5 [sig. B_4r] (marginal note); Barlow, *Dick Turpin and the Gregory Gang*, pp. 447–8.

46 Clavell, *A Recantation*, pp. 10, 9; Pafford, *John Clavell*, pp. 24–7. On another reformed highwayman's view of the non-binding nature of robbers' oaths, see Wilson, *A Full and Impartial Account*, 3rd edn, p. 24.

47 Clavell, *A Recantation*, sigs B_1v–B_2r, pp. 7, 46, 47 (quotation on p. 7); note p. 9.

48 [Clavell], *The Soddered Citizen*, ll. 2818–9.

49 Pafford, *John Clavell*, pp. 286–7, 32–3, 39–41, 161, 214–19, 221–2.

50 Stone, *The Crisis of the Aristocracy*, pp. 656–9; Ann Jennalie Cook, *Making a Match. Courtship in Shakespeare and his Society* (Princeton University Press, 1991), pp. 19–27; David Lindley, *The Trials of Frances Howard. Fact and Fiction at the Court of King James* (London, Routledge, 1993), pp. 22–3; see

also Alan Macfarlane, *Marriage and Love in England. Modes of Reproduction 1300–1840* (Oxford, Basil Blackwell, 1986), pp. 211–12.

51 Pafford, *John Clavell*, p. 191.

52 Ibid., pp. 16, 263.

THIRTEEN: KNIGHTS OF THE ROAD

1 *The true and perfect Relation Of the taking of Captain James Hind* (London, 1651 [ms. date November 14]), pp. 1–2, 4 [sigs A₂r–v, A₃v]; G[eorge] F[idge], *Hind's Ramble, or, The Description of his manner and course of life* (London, 1651 [ms. date 27 October]), p. 41 [sig. C₆r]; *The Declaration of Captain James Hind* (London, 1651 [ms. date 18 November]), p. 4 (sig. A₃v).

2 *The Trial of Captain James Hind* (London, 1651 [ms. date 15 December]), pp. 4, 8 [sigs A₂r, A₄v]; *Wit for Mony. Being a full Relation of the Life, Actions, merry Conceits, and pretty Pranks of Captain James Hind* (London, 1652), sigs D₄r–v; 'An Act of General Pardon and Oblivion', 24 February 1651/2, in *Acts and Ordinances of the Interregnum*, ed. C. H. Firth and R. S. Rait, 3 vols (London, HMSO, 1911), II, pp. 565–77; *No Jest Like a True Jest* (London, 1674), reprinted in *Historical and Biographical Tracts*, vol. 2 (Westminster, George Smeeton, 1820), sig. G₂v [chap. xvi].

3 Quotation from G[eorge] F[idge], *The English Gusman*, p. 5 [sig. B₄r].

4 *The . . . Relation Of the taking of Captain James Hind*, p. 6 [sig. A₄v].

5 G[eorge] F[idge], *Hind's Ramble*, p. 41 [sig. C₆r].

6 *The . . . Relation Of the taking of Captain James Hind*, p. 5 [sig. A₄r]. Original reads 'full fed-fees'.

7 *The Declaration of Captain James Hind* (London, 1651 [ms. date 18 November]), p. 2 [sig. A₂v]. This and the *Relation* were both published by G. Horton.

8 *The . . . Relation Of the taking of Captain James Hind*, p. 6 [sig. A₄v].

9 G[eorge] F[idge], *Hind's Ramble*, pp. 18–20 [sigs B₂v–B₃v]. The story of Hind and the committee man is also found in G[eorge] F[idge], *The English Gusman*, pp. 27–8 [sigs E₃r–v]; *Wit for Mony*, sigs B₆v–B₇r; *No Jest like a true Jest*, sigs F₁r–v [chap. xii]; the ballad *Captain Hind's Progress & Ramble* (see above, Chapter Eleven, n. 65); and is mentioned in *The Life and Death of Mal Cutpurse* (1662), ed. Todd and Spearing, in *Counterfeit Ladies*, p. 66.

10 G[eorge] F[idge], *The English Gusman*, pp. [16]–17 [sigs D₁v–D₂r]. The British Library (Thomason Collection) copy of this book bears the ms. date 10 January.

11 See Richard Holworthy, *Discoveries in the Diocesan Registry, Wells, Somerset* (Wells, Somerset Diocesan Registry [1927]), no pagination, case of Joan Tyrrye, 1555; Robert Pitcairn, *Criminal Trials in Scotland 1488–1624*, 3 vols (Edinburgh, William Tait, 1833), I, ii, p. 51; *The Brideling, Sadling and Ryding, of a rich Churle in Hampshire* (1595), ed. [extract] by Barbara Rosen in *Witchcraft in England, 1558–1618* (Amherst, University of Massachusetts Press, 1991 [first published, as *Witchcraft: The Stratford-upon-Avon library 6*, in 1969]), p. 218; *Trial, Confession and Execution of Isobel Inch, John Stewart,*

Margaret Barclay & Isobel Crawford, For witchcraft at Irvine anno 1618 (Ardrossan, A. Guthrie [1855?]), p. 9.

12 Thompson, *Motif-Index of Folk Literature*, F348.5.2. See Katharine M. Briggs, *A Dictionary of British Folk-Tales in the English Language*, 2 parts (London, Routledge, 1991; first publ. 1970–1), Part A, vol. i, pp. 577–9; Part B, vol. i, pp. 271–2.

13 See for example Briggs, *A Dictionary of British Folk-Tales*, Part A, vol. i, pp. 195–7.

14 Eric Hobsbawm, *Bandits*, rev. edn (London, Weidenfeld & Nicolson, 2000), pp. 57–8.

15 *The Trial of Captain James Hind*, p. 4 [sig. A$_2$v].

16 G[eorge] F[idge], *The English Gusman*, p. 1 [sig. B$_2$r]; O. M. Meades, *The Adventures of Captain James Hind of Chipping Norton, the Oxfordshire Highwayman* (Chipping Norton, O. M. Meades, 1985), p. 11.

17 G[eorge] F[idge], *The English Gusman*, pp. 1–2 [sigs B$_2$r–v]; J. S., *An Excellent Comedy Called, The Prince of Priggs Revels* (London, 1651 [ms. date 11 November]), p. 7 [sig. B$_1$r]; *A Second Discovery of Hind's Exploits* (London, 1651 [ms. date 19 November]), sig. A$_3$r. A reference to *Hind's Exploits* in *The . . . Relation Of the taking of Captain James Hind*, p. 6 [sig. A$_4$v], shows that its publication must have occurred before 14 November.

18 Passage quoted more fully in Chapter One: see pp. 9–10 and n. 15.

19 G[eorge] F[idge], *The English Gusman*, p. [3], sig. B$_3$r.

20 Smith, *De Republica Anglorum*, p. 28.

21 See Chapter Nine, p. 111 and n. 47.

22 G[eorge] F[idge], *The English Gusman*, pp. [6]–7, 9–10, 17, 19–20, 24 [sigs B$_4$v–C$_1$r, C$_2$r–v, D$_2$r, D$_3$r–v, E$_1$v].

23 Clavell, *A Recantation of An Ill Led Life*, p. 39, and note also p. 13; see also above, Chapter Seven, pp. 81–2. For some further examples, see Harman, *Caveat*, ed. Viles and Furnivall, pp. 30–31; *The Life and Death of Gamaliel Ratsey*, sigs C$_1$r–v, C$_4$r, D$_1$r–v; Luttrell, *A Brief Historical Relation of State Affairs*, VI, p. 3; Villette, *The Annals of Newgate*, I, pp. 14–16; Barlow, *Dick Turpin and the Gregory Gang*, p. 265.

24 Luttrell, *A Brief Historical Relation of State Affairs*, II, p. 617; note also Villette, *The Annals of Newgate*, I, p. 15.

25 Fuller, *The Holy State and the Profane State*, ed. Walten, II, p. 150 [Book II, chap. 24].

26 See Chapter Nine, p. 107 and n. 30; see also Defoe, *Colonel Jack*, ed. Monk, p. 67; Lincoln B. Faller, *Crime and Defoe. A New Kind of Writing* (Cambridge University Press, 1993), p. 170 n. 6.

27 See Chapter Ten, p. 124 and n. 32.

28 Jonson, *Every Man out of his Humour*, ed. Herford and Simpson, IV v 39–41.

29 G[eorge] F[idge], *The English Gusman*, pp. 4, 5, 25 [sigs B$_3$v, B$_4$r, E$_2$r].

30 See above, p. 163 and n. 2.

31 More, *Utopia*, trans. Robinson, ed. Lumby, p. 29, note also pp. 81–2.

32 Burton, *The Anatomy of Melancholy*, ed. Faulkner, Kiessling, Blair, II, p. 68, ll. 6–10 [II ii iv 1]; see also *An Homily Against Idleness* (1563), ed. J. Griffiths, in *The Two Books of Homilies appointed to be read in Churches* (Oxford

University Press, 1859), p. 516; George Chapman, Ben Jonson and John Marston, *Eastward Ho*, ed. R. W. Van Fossen (Manchester University Press, 1979), I i 138.

33 Henry Peacham, *The Compleat Gentleman* (London, 1622, facs. repr. Amsterdam, Theatrum Obis Terrarum, 1968), p. 10.

34 *An Humble Request to the Ministers of Both Universities and to all Lawyers in every Inns-A-Court*, ed. George H. Sabine, in *The Works of Gerrard Winstanley* (Ithaca, New York, Cornell University Press, 1941), p. 432.

35 Smith, *De Republica Anglorum*, p. 27.

36 George Chapman, *May-day*, ed. Thomas Marc Parrott, in *The Plays of George Chapman: The Comedies*, vol. 1, I i 415–6; note also Burton, *The Anatomy of Melancholy*, ed. Faulkner, Kiessling, Blair, I, p. 348, ll. 3–13 [I ii iv 6].

37 Smith, *De Republica Anglorum*, p. 29.

38 Greene, *The Blacke Bookes Messenger*, ed. Harrison, p. 25; note also *A manifest detection of Diceplay*, sigs A_2r, B_3r; Whetstone, *A Mirour for Magestrates of Cyties*, sigs H_1v–H_2r.

39 Harper, *Half-Hours with the Highwaymen*, I, p. 65. Harper says that these lines are taken from '*The Cashiered Soldier*, a tract published in 1643'. I have been unable to trace a copy of this publication. It sounds like a broadside ballad. Original has no punctuation after 'base' in line 2. I have taken out a dash after 'theft' in the same line.

40 Clavell, *A Recantation of An Ill Led Life*, p. 16; Sir Thomas Culpeper, *The Necessity of Abating Usury Re-asserted* (London, 1670), p. 28; 'To the Memory of Captain James Hind' in *A General History of the Lives and Adventures of the Most Famous Highwaymen*, by 'Capt. Charles Johnson' (London, J. Janeway, 1734), p. 90, stanza IX; Gay, *The Beggar's Opera*, ed. Fuller, II iv 123–6.

41 See Chapter One, p. 10 and nn. 15, 16, 17; G[eorge] F[idge], *The English Gusman*, p. 24 [sig. E_1v]; Anon., *The Puritaine Widdow*, ed. Tucker Brooke, in *The Shakespeare Apocrypha*, p. 221: see 'Captain Idle, a Highway-man', in 'The Actors Names', and see also I ii 141–150, iv 11–18; Verney, *Memoirs*, IV, p. 296; [Head], *Jackson's Recantation*, ed. Peterson in *The Counterfeit Lady*, p. 162; Farquhar, *The Beaux' Stratagem*, ed. Fifer, II ii 129–131, 133, III ii 54, 76–123; Henry Fielding, *Amelia*, ed. Martin C. Battestin (Oxford, Clarendon Press, 1983), pp. 95–8 [Book II, chap. ix].

42 Clavell, *A Recantation of An Ill Led Life*, p. 6. For an early occurrence of 'knight of the road', see Head, *The English Rogue* (1665), sig. Ff₃v [chap. xxvi]. Note also 'knight o' th' Blade', in *Hinds Elder Brother* (1652), sig. B_3v; 'Knights of the padd', in *Robbery Rewarded* (1674), ed. Hyder Edward Rollins in *The Pack of Autolycus* (Cambridge, Massachusetts, Harvard University Press, 1927), p. 169; 'Knights of the High-Padd', in *The High-way Mans Advice To his Brethren*, ed. Rollins, in *The Pepys Ballads*, III, p. 127, and see also p. 128. The parallel term 'Gentlemen of the Road' is first found in 1683: see below, p. 173 and n. 46.

43 See Chapter Four, p. 39 and n. 8; Chapter Nine, p. 109 and nn. 38, 39; Chapter Eleven, p. 139.

44 For Claude Du Vall, see Chapter Fourteen, p. 187 and n. 23, p. 189 and n. 27; also *Devol's last Farewel*, ed. J. W. Ebsworth, in *Bagford Ballads*, 2 vols (Hertford, Ballad Society, 1878), I, pp. 14–16. For an account of Whitney see

Lincoln Faller, 'King William, "K.J.," and James Whitney: The Several Lives and Affiliations of a Jacobite Robber', *Eighteenth Century Life*, n. s., vol. 12, no. 3 (November 1988), pp. 88–104. Butchers as a trade were exceptionally well represented among highway robbers; for a discussion of this phenomenon in the eighteenth century, see Peter Linebaugh, *The London Hanged. Crime and Civil Society in the Eighteenth Century* (London, Penguin, 1993 [first publ. 1991]), pp. 184–92.

45 Fuller, *The Holy State and the Profane State*, ed. Walten, II, p. 416 [Book V, chap. 14]; Samuel Butler, *Characters and Passages from Note-books*, ed. A. R. Waller (Cambridge University Press, 1908), p. 227.

46 J. M., *The Traveller's Guide, and, the Country's Safety* (London, 1683), sigs A₃r–v. See also 'On a Pretender to Gentility, suspected to be a Highway-man', in *Westminster Drolleries, Both Parts, of 1671, 1672*, ed. J. Woodfall Ebsworth (Boston, Lincs., R. Roberts, 1875), p. 59 [Part I, 1671].

47 See above, p. 164 and n. 6.

48 *The Life . . . of Charles Courtney*, p. 5 [sig. B₃r].

49 Gerrard Winstanley, *A New-Year's Gift for the Parliament and Army* (1650), ed. Christopher Hill, in *The Law of Freedom and other Writings* (Harmondsworth, Penguin, 1973), p. 170.

50 *OED*, s. v. bumpkin.

51 See Chapter Nine, pp. 108–9; Chapter Ten, p. 128.

52 P. R. Newman, *The Old Service. Royalist regimental colonels and the Civil War, 1642–46* (Manchester University Press, 1993), chap. 2; Brian Manning, *The English People and the English Revolution*, 2nd edn (London, Bookmarks, 1991), pp. 320–4, 330–7, 350–8.

53 Abiezer Coppe, *A Fiery Flying Roll*, ed. Andrew Hopton, in *Selected Writings* (London, Aporia Press, 1987), pp. 25, 21 [chaps II, I]. Coppe and the Ranters are discussed by Norman Cohn in *The Pursuit of the Millenium. Revolutionary Millenarians and Mystical Anarchists of the Middle Ages* (London, Paladin, 1970 [first publ. 1957]), pp. 287–330; A. L. Morton, *The World of the Ranters* (London, Lawrence and Wishart, 1970), chap. 4; Christopher Hill, *The World Turned Upside Down. Radical Ideas During the English Revolution* (Harmondsworth, Penguin, 1975 [first publ. 1972]), chap. 9; Nigel Smith (ed.), *A Collection of Ranter Writings from the 17th Century* (London, Junction Books, 1983), pp. 7–38; J. C. Davis, *Fear, Myth and History. The Ranters and the historians* (Cambridge University Press, 1986), esp. pp. 48–57; Christopher Hill, 'The Lost Ranters? A critique of J. C. Davis', *History Workshop*, Issue 24 (Autumn, 1987), pp. 134–40.

54 Coppe, *A Fiery Flying Roll*, ed. Hopton, pp. 37–8 [*A Second Fiery Flying Roule*, chap. II]. I am grateful to Catie Gill for drawing my attention to this passage. For the biblical verse quoted by Coppe, see *First Epistle to the Thessalonians* chap. 5, v. 2; *Second Epistle of Peter*, chap. 3, v. 10; *Revelation*, chap. 3, v. 3, chap. 16, v. 15; and see also *The Gospel of Matthew*, chap. 24, vv. 42–44; *The Gospel of Luke*, chap. 12, vv. 39–40 [Authorised Version].

55 'Capt. Charles Johnson', *A General History of the Lives and Adventures of the Most Famous Highwaymen*, p. 90, stanza IV.

56 Smith, *A Complete History of the . . . Highwaymen*, p. 216, note also p. 52.

57 *The Gospel of Luke*, chap. 1, v. 53 [Authorised Version, 1611].

58 *The Penitent Highway-man*, ed. Rollins, in *The Pepys Ballads*, VII, p. 202.

59 Harper, *Half-Hours with the Highwaymen*, II, pp. 234–6 [from a broadside by J. Pitts, Seven Dials]. For further examples of Turpin's being transformed into a quasi-Robin Hood, see Linebaugh, *The London Hanged*, pp. 203–5; Seal, *The Outlaw Legend*, pp. 55, 60, 61; and see below, Chapter Nineteen, p. 253 and nn. 9, 11.

60 Christopher Hill, *The English Bible and the Seventeenth-Century Revolution* (London, Penguin, 1994 [first published 1993]), pp. 443–6; *Liberty Against the Law*, pp. 221–2.

61 For evidence of the readership of the late seventeenth-century chapbook, see Margaret Spufford, *Small Books and Pleasant Histories. Popular fiction and its readership in seventeenth-century England* (London, Methuen, 1981), especially chap. III.

62 McLynn, *Crime and Punishment in Eighteenth-century England*, p. 60.

63 *The Whole Life and History of Benjamin Child, Lately Executed for Robbing the Bristol Mail* (London, A. Moore, 1722), pp. 26, 3–4.

64 Benjamin Childe, *A Narrative of the Life of Mr. Benjamin Childe*, (London, T. Payne, 1722).

65 *The Ordinary of Newgate, His Account of the Behaviour, Confession, and Dying Words, of the Malefactors Who were Executed at Tyburn On Wednesday the 7th of April, 1742*, p. 13; Linebaugh, *The London Hanged*, p. 187. For some reason Linebaugh states that this incident happened on Putney Heath; but Walden is absolutely precise in locating it in Suffolk.

66 *The Life of Deval* (London, 1669 [70]), pp. 5–6 [A₃r–v]. On the two Du Valls, see Gordon S. Maxwell, *Highwayman's Heath. The story in fact and fiction of Hounslow Heath in Middlesex* (Hounslow, Heritage Publications, 1994 [first publ. 1935]), p. 163. The odd thing about these two presumed brothers is that though each was the subject of a pamphlet 'life', and though they were sentenced and executed on the same dates, neither of these pamphlets has anything to say about the existence of the other Du Vall.

67 G[eorge] F[idge], *The English Gusman*, pp. [2–3] [sigs B₂v–B₃r].

FOURTEEN: 'THE PROFESSION IS GROWN SCANDALOUS'

1 *Lives of the Most Remarkable Criminals*, ed. Hayward, pp. 362–3.

2 Villette, *The Annals of Newgate*, I, pp. 14–16; III, pp. 220–61; IV, pp. 96–103; quotation on p. 102.

3 *Lives of the Most Remarkable Criminals*, pp. 205–7; quotations on p. 206.

4 *Lives of the Most Remarkable Criminals*, pp. 56–7; Wilson, *A Full and Impartial Account Of all the Robberies Committed by John Hawkins, George Sympson . . . and their Companions*, 3rd edn, pp. 10–11, 15–16. With Wright's views on robbing the rich compare Hobbes, *Leviathan*, ed. Pogson Smith, pp. 237–8 [Part 2, chap. 27].

5 Villette, *The Annals of Newgate*, I, p. 147; see also Lincoln B. Faller, *Turned to account. The forms and functions of criminal biography in late seventeenth- and*

early eighteenth-century England (Cambridge University Press, 1987), pp. 251–2, nn. 1, 4.

6 *The Flying Highwayman*, in *Later English Broadside Ballads*, ed. John Holloway and Joan Black (London, Routledge & Kegan Paul, 1975), pp. 103–4.

7 See Chapter One, p. 1 and n. 1.

8 Defoe, *Colonel Jack*, ed. Monk, p. 185. For similar eighteenth-century references, see above, Chapter Twelve, nn. 30 (Fielding), 35.

9 Radzinowicz, *A History of English Criminal Law*, I, pp. 706 n. 48, 708; Langford, *Englishness Identified*, p. 145.

10 See below, pp. 194–5, and n. 50; Gay, *The Beggar's Opera*, ed. Fuller, in *Dramatic Works*, II, I iii 24–5.

11 Lee, *Daniel Defoe: His Life, and recently discovered writings*, III, pp. 184–5 [*Applebee's Journal*, September 21, 1723].

12 Graham Seal, *The Outlaw Legend. A Cultural Tradition in Britain, America and Australia* (Cambridge University Press, 1996); see esp. pp. 11, 17–18, 8, 2, 179. See above, Chapter Twelve, pp. 155–6. For a more detailed critique of Seal's theories, see Appendix C.

13 Walpole, *Correspondence*, ed. Lewis and others, vol. 40, pp. 63–5, quotation on p. 64; note — Allen, *An Account of the Behaviour of Mr. James Maclaine, From the Time of his Condemnation To the Day of his Execution* (London, J. Noon and A. Millar, 1750), p. 16. For other eighteenth-century robbers with similar scruples, see *Lives of the Most Remarkable Criminals*, p. 552; *The Authentic Trial, and Memoirs of Isaac Darkin* (Oxford, R. Baldwin and W. Jackson, [1761]) p. 26.

14 The two are directly identified by Massinger in his play *The Guardian* (1633); see above, Chapter Twelve, p. 156 and n. 29.

15 *A Gest of Robyn Hode*, ed. Dobson and Taylor, in *Rymes of Robyn Hood*, stanza 2; see above, Chapter Five, pp. 59–60; Chapter Seven, p. 86; Chapter Three, p. 34 and n. 34; Chapter Four, p. 42 and n. 15.

16 *A Gest of Robyn Hode*, stanza 231; see Holt, *Robin Hood*, pp. 125–6.

17 On courtesy see Anna Bryson, *From Courtesy to Civility. Changing Codes of Conduct in Early Modern England* (Oxford, Clarendon Press, 1998), esp. pp. 58–60, 64–6. On politeness, see Lawrence E. Klein, *Shaftesbury and the culture of politeness. Moral discourse and cultural politics in early eighteenth-century England* (Cambridge University Press, 1994), pp. 3–8; Lawrence E. Klein, 'Politeness for plebes. Consumption and social identity in early eighteenth-century England', in *The Consumption of Culture 1600–1800. Image, Object, Text*, ed. Ann Bermingham and John Brewer (London, Routledge, 1995); Philip Carter, *Men and the Emergence of Polite Society, Britain 1660–1800* (Harlow, Longman, 2000).

18 De Saussure, *Letters*, p. 128.

19 See for instance Herbert, *Mr. Gay's London*, pp. 55, 73, 84–9, 126–7; *The Malefactor's Register; or, the Newgate and Tyburn Calendar*, 5 vols (London, Alexander Hogg [1779]), II, p. 298; *Lives of the Most Remarkable Criminals*, p. 55, and see also p. 110; Le Blanc, *Letters on the English and French Nations*, II,

p. 296; Walpole, *Correspondence*, ed. Lewis and others, vol. 24, p. 47; Beattie, *Crime and the Courts*, p. 152.

20 *Lives of the Most Remarkable Criminals*, pp. 110, 517; von Archenholz, *A Picture of England*, p. 182; Beattie, *Crime and the Courts*, pp. 152–4; McLynn, *Crime and Punishment in Eighteenth-Century England*, pp. 60–2; and see the case of 'Civil John', below, n. 22.

21 *A Gest of Robyn Hode*, stanzas 256–7.

22 *Lives of the Most Remarkable Criminals,* pp. 425–7.

23 [Walter Pope], *The Memoires of Monsieur Du Vall* (London, 1670), pp. 8–9. In the original, the passage in square brackets appears as an afterthought in the middle of the paragraph that follows the story. As this is something of a blemish on a lively piece of story-telling, I have taken the liberty of inserting it in a rather more sensible position.

24 Farquhar, *The Beaux' Stratagem*, ed. Fifer, IV ii 143–5; V ii 133–9; note also II ii 78–82. With Gibbet's words to Mrs Sullen compare Herbert, *Mr. Gay's London*, p. 73. For instances of highwaymen represented as giving special treatment to women, see Francis Kirkman, *The English Rogue: Continued in the Life of Meriton Latroon, and other Extravagants. The Third Part* (London, 1671), pp. 225–6 [sigs Q_1r–v; chap. xvi]; Smith, *A Complete History of the . . . Highwaymen*, p. 27; *Lives of the Most Remarkable Criminals*, p. 517; Villette, *The Annals of Newgate*, I, pp. 47, 148.

25 *The Female Tatler*, ed. Fidelis Morgan, Everyman's Library (London, Dent, 1992), p. 40 [Wednesday 10 August to Friday 12 August].

26 *Sir Thomas Overbury his Wife with Additions of New Characters, and many other Witty Conceits never before Printed. The sixteenth Impression* (London, 1638), sig. Q_6v; note also George Farquhar, *The Recruiting Officer*, ed. Michael Shugrue (London, Edward Arnold, 1966), V ii 12–14.

27 [Pope], *Memoires of Du Vall*, p. 12; see also pp. 14–16; Samuel Butler, 'To the Happy Memory of the Most Renowned Du-Val. A Pindaric Ode', in *Poetical Works*, 2 vols (London, Bell & Daldy, no date), II, pp. 252–8, stanzas ix, x.

28 *The Life and Death of George of Oxford*, in *The Pepys Ballads*, Day, II, p. 150; see also Child, *The English and Scottish Popular Ballads*, IV, pp. 141–2. For the use of silken ropes in executions, see *The Diary of Samuel Pepys*, ed. Robert Latham and William Matthews, 11 vols (London, Bell, 1970–83), IV, p. 60 and n. 1 [27 February 1663].

29 Walpole, *Correspondence*, ed. Lewis and others, vol. 20, pp. 168–9, 184; *A Complete History of James Maclean, the Gentleman Highwayman* (London, Charles Corbett [1750]); Harper, *Half-Hours with the Highwaymen*, II, pp. 271–300. For a reproduction of the print, see plate section.

30 Defoe, *Colonel Jack*, pp. 62, 59.

31 Ibid., pp. 3, 62, 67, 64.

32 Ibid., pp. 60–1.

33 Chaucer, 'The Parson's Tale', in *The Riverside Chaucer*, ed. Benson, ll. 601–3; Burton, *The Anatomy of Melancholy*, ed. Faulkner, Kiessling, Blair, II, p. 138, ll. 20–5 [2. iii. ii. 1]; Henry Peacham, quoted in Chapter Thirteen above, p. 170 and n. 33; Defoe, *The Compleat English Gentleman*, ed. Bülbring, p. 239; E. P. Thompson, *Whigs and Hunters. The Origin of the Black Act* (London,

Penguin, 1990 [first publ. 1975]), p. 126, n. 2; *Oxford Dictionary of English Proverbs*, 3rd edn, ed. Wilson, p. 792 [Tilley A 4, and see also 'Swear like a lord, To' (unnumbered)]; note Shakespeare, *King Henry IV, Part I*, ed. Humphreys, III i 240–50; see also above, Chapter Ten, pp. 124–5 and n. 34.

34 Defoe has more to say on these themes in *The Compleat English Gentleman*, ed. Bülbring, pp. 21, 232–6. On attitudes to swearing, note *Charges to the Grand Jury 1689–1803*, ed. Georges Lamoine, Camden Fourth Series vol. 43 (London, Royal Historical Society, 1992), pp. 94–6; see also pp. 215–16, 233–4, 285, 295, 298–9, 333–4.

35 Daniel Defoe, *The Life and Strange Surprizing Adventures of Robinson Crusoe*, ed. J. Donald Crowley (London, Oxford University Press, 1972), pp. 4–5; Daniel Defoe, *The Complete English Tradesman in familiar letters*, 2 vols (London, Charles Rivington, 1727; facs. repr. Augustus M. Kelley, New York, 1969), II, p. 106 [chap. III].

36 Defoe, *Colonel Jack*, pp. 60, 61–2, 67, 81.

37 Ibid., pp. 155–6; note Lee, *Daniel Defoe: His Life, and recently discovered writings*, II, p. 517.

38 For Defoe on the gentleman tradesman, see esp. *The Complete English Tradesman*, I, pp. 304–319 [Letter XXII]; note also I, pp. 86, 92 [Letter VIII] on the tradesman and good manners; II, pp. 28–52 [Chapter I] on the tradesman and honesty. See further Michael Shinagel, *Daniel Defoe and Middle-Class Gentility* (Cambridge, Massachusetts, Harvard University Press, 1968).

39 Defoe, *The Complete English Tradesman*, I, pp. 315, 304 [Letter XXII].

40 Peter Earle, *The Making of the English Middle Class. Business, Society and Family Life in London, 1660–1730* (London, Methuen, 1991 [first publ. 1989], pp. 5–13; Roy Porter, *England in the Eighteenth Century* (London, Folio Society, 1998), pp. 50–3, 69–73, 76–80; Paul Langford, *A Polite and Commercial People. England 1727–1783* (Oxford, Clarendon Press, 1989), chap. 3; Nicholas Rogers, 'Money, land and lineage: the big bourgeoisie of Hanoverian London', *Social History*, vol. 4, no. 3 (October 1979), pp. 437–54; P. J. Corfield, 'Class by Name and Number in Eighteenth-Century Britain', *History*, vol. 72, no. 234 (February 1987), pp. 42–3, 53–6, 60; Lawrence Stone, 'Social Mobility in England, 1500–1700', *Past and Present*, no. 33 (1966), pp. 52–4; Defoe, *The Compleat English Gentleman*, ed. Bülbring, pp. 257–68. For Defoe on this topic, see also n. 38 above. For a fairly early statement of the view that the gentleman's son who went into trade still retained his right of birth, see Fuller, 'The Younger Brother', in *The Holy State and the Profane State* (1642), ed. Walten, II, pp. 48–9 [Book I, chap. 15].

41 *Hanging, Not Punishment Enough, for Murtherers, High way Men, and House Breakers* (London, A. Baldwin, 1701), p. 1, see also p. 6; note the complaints of some Bristol merchants in 1723, quoted by Beattie in *Crime and the Courts in England 1660–1800*, p. 148 and n. 18.

42 The famous jail-breaker Jack Sheppard was a notable recipient of the popular sympathy: see [Daniel Defoe?], *A Narrative of all the Robberies, Escapes, &c. of John Sheppard*, in Defoe, *Freebooters and Buccaneers. Novels of Adventure and Piracy* (New York, The Dial Press, 1935), 'The King of Pirates', p. 225; Lee,

Daniel Defoe: His Life, and recently discovered writings, III, p. 329 [*Applebee's Journal*, November 7, 1724].

43 See Chapter One, p. 1 and n. 1.

44 13 Edward I, c. 1, 2, 4, 5 [The Statute of Winchester, 1285]; 28 Edward III, c. 11; 27 Elizabeth c. 13; 29 Charles II, c. 7, s. 5; Bellamy, *Crime and Public Order*, p. 93; Smith, *De Republica Anglorum*, pp. 71–2; Harrison, *The Description of England*, ed. Edelen, pp. 194–5 [passage added in edition of 1587]; Herrup, *The Common Peace*, pp. 70–2; John Styles, 'Print and Policing: Crime Advertising in Eighteenth-Century Provincial England', in *Policing and Prosecution in Britain 1750–1850*, ed. Douglas Hay and Francis Snyder (Oxford, Clarendon Press, 1989), esp. pp. 56, 72–3, 82–6, 111. On the vestigial survival of the hue and cry in the eighteenth century, see also Leon Radzinowicz, *A History of English Criminal Law and its Administration from 1750*, vol. 2: The clash between private initiative and public interest in the enforcement of the law (London, Stevens, 1956), pp. 27, 37; Beattie, *Crime and the Courts*, pp. 36–7.

45 Radzinowicz, *A History of English Criminal Law*, II, pp. 87–8; Beattie, *Crime and the Courts*, p. 51; see also Luttrell, *A Brief Historical Relation of State Affairs*, I, pp. 86, 248, 323, 336, 432, 558. For one eighteenth-century commentator who did indeed see the system of 'king's evidences' and private thief-takers as intrinsically dishonourable, see Radzinowicz, op. cit., pp. 54–5.

46 4 William and Mary, c. 8.

47 Beattie, *Crime and the Courts*, pp. 35–9; see also Herrup, *The Common Peace*, pp. 88–9.

48 Smith, *De Republica Anglorum*, p. 71; see also Beattie, *Crime and the Courts*, pp. 36–7. On the ordinary subject's powers of arrest, see Bellamy, *Crime and Public Order*, pp. 102–3; J. H. Baker, 'Criminal Courts and Procedure at Common Law 1550–1800', in *Crime in England 1550–1800*, ed. Cockburn, p. 32.

49 See Chapter Nine, p. 105 and n. 24.

50 Beattie, *Crime and the Courts*, pp. 366–9; see also Radzinowicz, *A History of English Criminal Law*, II, pp. 43–5.

51 Carey, *Memoirs*, ed. Powell, p. 58. For the date at which this incident took place, see George MacDonald Fraser, *The Steel Bonnets. The Story of the Anglo-Scottish Border Reivers* (London, Pan Books, 1974 [first published in 1971]), p. 281.

52 *The true and perfect Relation Of the taking of Captain James Hind*, p. 2.

53 *The Life and Death of Gamaliel Ratsey*, sigs E₁v–E₂r; *Ratseis Ghost*, sig. F₂v.

54 Wilson, *A Full and Impartial Account Of all the Robberies Committed by John Hawkins, George Sympson . . . and their Companions*, 3rd edn, pp. 8–9.

55 Beattie, *Crime and the Courts*, pp. 368–9. For cases in point, see Herbert, *Mr. Gay's London*, pp. 80–3, 110–14; Gerald Howson, *Thief-Taker General. The Rise and Fall of Jonathan Wild* (London, Hutchinson, 1970), pp. 19, 139, 140–1, 213, 216, 243, 246–7 [William Field] and pp. 190, 195–201 [John Dyer]; for Dyer see also *Lives of the Most Remarkable Criminals*, pp. 121–3, 124–5, 136, 502.

56 Wilson, *A Full and Impartial Account*, pp. 19–24, quotations on p. 24.

57 Le Blanc, *Letters on the English and French Nations*, II, pp. 296–7; Radzinowicz, *A History of English Criminal Law*, I, p. 725–6, and nn. 55, 56, 57; Leon Radzinowicz, *A History of English Criminal Law and its Administration from 1750*, vol. 3: Cross-currents in the movement for the reform of the police (London, Stevens, 1956), pp. 2, 91 and n. 13, 311–12, 347, 358–9, 420, 424–5, 447, 539–52; see also David Philips, ' "A New Engine of Power and Authority": The Institutionalization of Law-Enforcement in England 1780–1830', in *Crime and the Law. The Social History of Crime in Western Europe since 1500*, ed. V. A. C. Gatrell, Bruce Lenman and Geoffrey Parker (London, Europa Publications, 1980), esp. pp. 155–6, 161–2, 167–9, 172–4, 187.

58 For an instructive example of how one such reward was carved up, see Howson, *Thief-Taker General*, pp. 200–1.

59 Beattie, *Crime and the Courts*, p. 156.

60 Beattie, *Crime and the Courts*, pp. 55–9, 260, 468; Radzinowicz, *A History of English Criminal Law*, II, pp. 23, 317, 326–32; Philip Rawlings, *Drunks, Whores and Idle Apprentices. Criminal biographies of the eighteenth century* (London, Routledge, 1992), pp. 108–9, n. 52; Ruth Paley, 'Thief-takers in London in the Age of the McDaniel Gang, c. 1745–1754', in *Policing and Prosecution in Britain 1750–1850*, ed. Hay and Snyder.

61 The best account of Wild's career remains that by Gerald Howson, *Thief-Taker General* (1970). See also Lucy Moore, *The Thieves' Opera. The Remarkable Lives and Deaths of Jonathan Wild, Thief-Taker, and Jack Sheppard, House-Breaker* (London, Viking, 1997).

62 [Daniel Defoe?], *The Life and Actions of Jonathan Wild*, in Defoe, *Freebooters and Buccaneers. Novels of Adventure and Piracy*, 'The King of Pirates', pp. 231–75. There is an excellent bibliography of Wild material in Howson, *Thief-Taker General*, pp. 317–21.

63 Henry Fielding, *Jonathan Wild*, ed. A. R. Humphreys, Everyman's Library (London, Dent, 1973). See also William Robert Irwin, *The Making of Jonathan Wild. A study in the literary method of Henry Fielding* (Hamden, Connecticut, Archon Books, 1966 [first published 1941]).

64 See Chapter Eighteen, pp. 241–2 and n. 36.

FIFTEEN: 'WHY ARE THE LAWS LEVELL'D AT US?'

1 William Eben Schultz, *Gay's Beggar's Opera. Its content, history and influence* (New Haven, Yale University Press, 1923), pp. 5, 7–8, 10, 63–97.

2 See Schultz, *Gay's Beggar's Opera*, pp. 139–53; 'The Beggar's Opera, the Burlesque, and Italian Opera', by Arthur V. Berger, in *Music and Letters*, vol. xvii, no. 2 (April, 1936), pp. 93–105; Peter Elfed Lewis, *John Gay: The Beggar's Opera* (London, Edward Arnold, 1976), chap. 2: '*The Beggar's Opera* as Opera and Anti-opera'.

3 Gay, *The Beggar's Opera*, ed. Fuller, in *Dramatic Works*, II, II iii 5.

4 Ibid., III xvi 9–10, 16–17.

5 See Elyot, *The Book named The Governor*, ed. Lehmberg, p. 77; Sir John

Davies, *Orchestra*, ed. Douglas Brooks-Davies, in *Silver Poets of the Sixteenth Century*, The Everyman Library (London, Dent, 1992), especially stanzas 17–21, 33, 96, 109–10.

6 Gay, *The Beggar's Opera*, III xvii 12–17. Original is in italics.

7 The tune specified for dance and song is one called 'Lumps of Pudding', and there is a dance already set to it in the great country dance manual of the time, John Playford's *Dancing Master*: see [John Playford,] *The Dancing-Master: Vol. the First. Or, Directions for Dancing Country Dances*, 17th edn (London, W. Pearson for John Young, 1721), p. 251. This dance, though, is one in which the couples remain with the same partners throughout, which doesn't seem to fit either the words of the song or the spirit of the scene. However, these eighteenth-century country dances were seldom fixed by tradition; as Cecil J. Sharp pointed out long ago, anyone with a knowledge of the various steps and figures and a feel for fitting them to music could make up a dance at will. See Cecil J. Sharp, *The Country Dance Book*, Part II, 3rd edn (London, Novello, 1927), pp. 7–8. For an example of a Playford dance in which the dancers move from partner to partner, see *The Hemp-Dresser* (also called *The London Gentlewoman*), in *The Dancing-Master*, p. 60.

8 Gay, *The Beggar's Opera*, I i Stage Direction, 9–10.

9 Ibid., I x 40, 40–1; iv 25–9; III ii 21–2.

10 Ibid., I viii 31.

11 See Wilkins, *Iests to make you Merie*, p. 334; Butler, *Characters*, ed. Waller, p. 227; Defoe, *Colonel Jack*, ed. Monk, pp. 62, 67.

12 Gay, *The Beggar's Opera*, I xiii 12; II ii 14, 20–1; ix 18, 58; III iv 16. Compare Defoe's use of the expression 'man of honour' in *The Compleat English Gentleman*, ed. Bülbring, p. 48.

13 Bernard Mandeville, *The Fable of the Bees: or, Private Vices, Publick Benefits*, ed. F. B. Kaye, 2 vols (Oxford, Clarendon Press, 1924), I, p. 275.

14 Gay, *The Beggar's Opera*, I xi 6; II ii 12–13.

15 See Farquhar, *The Beaux' Stratagem*, ed. Fifer, III ii 91–2; Defoe, *Moll Flanders*, ed. Starr, p. 305.

16 For robbers and gambling, see Wilson, *A Full and Impartial Account Of all the Robberies Committed by John Hawkins, George Sympson … and their Companions*, 3rd edn, pp. 2, 3, 4, 5, 10; Fielding, *An Enquiry into the Causes of the Late Increase of Robbers*, ed. Zirker, p. 92.

17 Gay, *The Beggar's Opera*, I iv 49–51.

18 Ibid., III iv Stage Direction.

19 Ibid., II iv 124–5; III iv 17–24; I iv 53–5; see also III ii 12–20.

20 Ibid., II i 18.

21 Ibid., III iv 35–6. This may have been a current catchphrase: see *Lives of the Most Remarkable Criminals*, p. 174, where it is said to have been an expression in use among the Waltham Blacks.

22 Gay, *The Beggar's Opera*, III iv 4–5, 16–17.

23 Mandeville, *The Fable of the Bees*, ed. Kaye, I, p. 230.

24 Gay, *The Beggar's Opera*, I i 7–8.

25 Eveline Cruickshanks, 'The Political Management of Sir Robert Walpole, 1720–42', in *Britain in the Age of Walpole*, ed. Jeremy Black (Houndmills,

Basingstoke, Macmillan, 1984); H. T. Dickinson, *Walpole and the Whig Supremacy* (London, English Universities Press, 1973), esp. chaps 5, 8, 10.

26 *A Key To The Beggar's Opera In A Letter To Caleb Danvers, Esq* (1728), ed. J. V. Guerinot and Rodney D. Jilg, in *Contexts 1: The Beggar's Opera* (Hamden, Connecticut, Archon Books, 1976), pp. 83–92; Schultz, *Gay's Beggar's Opera*, chap. XVII, esp. pp. 195–7; Peter Lewis (ed.), *The Beggar's Opera* by John Gay (Edinburgh, Oliver & Boyd, 1973), pp. 16–17; J. A. Downie, 'Walpole, "the Poet's Foe" ', in *Britain in the Age of Walpole*, ed. Black, p. 171; J. A. Downie, 'Gay's Politics', in *John Gay and the Scriblerians*, ed. Peter Lewis and Nigel Wood (London, Vision Press, 1988), pp. 53–4; David Nokes, *John Gay. A Profession of Friendship* (Oxford University Press, 1995), pp. 433–6.

27 *A Key To The Beggar's Opera*, ed. Guerinot and Jilg, in *Contexts 1: The Beggar's Opera*, pp. 88–9.

28 See Chapter Nine, p. 103 and n. 14, pp. 114–15 and nn. 58, 59; see also Chapter Thirteen, p. 164 and n. 6.

29 Butler, *Characters*, ed. Waller, p. 3.

30 John Gay, *Letters*, ed. C. F. Burgess (Oxford, Clarendon Press, 1966), p. 45; compare Thompson, *Whigs and Hunters*, p. 217 and n. 1; *Harlequin Sheppard* (1724), ed. Guerinot and Jilg, in *Contexts 1: The Beggar's Opera*, pp. 24–6. See also Richard Steele, *The Englishman. A Political Journal*, ed. Rae Blanchard (Oxford, Clarendon Press, 1955), pp. 191–3 [23 January 1714]; Smith, *A Complete History of the ... Highwaymen*, pp. 212–13.

31 See Chapter Four, p. 46 and n. 30; cf. Lupton, *All for Money*, ed. Schell and Schuchter, in *English Morality Plays and Moral Interludes*, esp. ll. 885–1312.

32 Gay, *The Beggar's Opera*, III xvi 24–6. This is another Mandevillian sentiment; see *The Fable of the Bees*, I, pp. 23–4.

33 *The Authentic Trial, and Memoirs of Isaac Darkin*, pp. 4, 6–7, 26 (quotation on p. 26); *The Malefactor's Register*, IV, pp. 191–8, quotation on p. 197.

34 *Contexts 1: The Beggar's Opera*, ed. Guerinot and Jilg, pp. 118–55; Schultz, *Gay's Beggar's Opera*, pp. 226–65; Radzinowicz, *A History of English Criminal Law*, III, pp. 19–21; Daniel Defoe, *Augusta Triumphans*, p. 34 and *Second Thoughts are Best*, pp. 9–10, in *Novels and Miscellaneous Works*, vol. 18 (Oxford, Thomas Tegg, 1841), where they are separately paginated; Le Blanc, *Letters*, pp. 294–5; Samuel Johnson, *Prefaces, Biographical and Critical, to the Works of the English Poets*, vol. 8 (London, J. Nichols, 1781), 'Gay', pp. 19–21. For Dickens's views, see below, Chapter Eighteen, p. 244 and n. 45.

35 *The Authentic Trial, and Memoirs of Isaac Darkin*, p. 28.

36 James Boswell, *London Journal 1762–1763*, ed. Frederick A. Pottle (London, Heinemann, 1950), pp. 263–4.

37 Gay, *The Beggar's Opera*, I xiii 39; II ii 33; iv 28; III xvii 19; *Contexts 1: The Beggar's Opera*, ed. Guerinot and Jilg, pp. 119–20.

38 *Contexts 1: The Beggar's Opera*, ed. Guerinot and Jilg, p. 155.

39 Gay, *The Beggar's Opera*, I iv 41–3; xi 6–7.

40 Ibid., III xiv 4–6.

41 Ibid., II ii 28–9; see also I iv 38–41; III vi 35–8.

42 See Chapter Nine, pp. 115–16.

43 Pafford, *John Clavell*, pp. 25–6.

44 Childe, *A Narrative of the Life of Mr. Benjamin Childe*, pp. 15–22; quotation on p. 20.

45 Thomas Middleton (with Ben Jonson and John Fletcher?), *The Widow*, ed. Bullen, in *Works*, V, III i 28–30. Original is in italics.

46 Gay, *The Beggar's Opera*, II i 9–12; Hobbes, *Leviathan*, Part I, chap. XIII. For Hobbes's pervasive influence on *The Beggar's Opera*, see Ian Donaldson, *The World Upside-Down. Comedy from Jonson to Fielding* (Oxford, Clarendon Press, 1970), pp. 175–8; Lewis (ed.), *The Beggar's Opera*, pp. 18–20.

47 Gay, *The Beggar's Opera*, II i 13–20, 22–3; see above, Chapter Thirteen, pp. 173–7.

48 Gay, *The Beggar's Opera*, II i 24–30; see above, Chapter Nine, p. 109 and n. 39, p. 114 and n. 58. Note Mandeville, *The Fable of the Bees*, I, pp. 87, 103.

49 Gay, *The Beggar's Opera*, II ii 44–52. Original is in italics.

SIXTEEN: THE SHADOW OF TYBURN

1 Smith, *De Republica Anglorum*, pp. 85, 86. 'i' in 'haultie' supplied; see also Harrison, *The Description of England*, ed. Edelen, p. 187.

2 Le Blanc, *Letters on the English and French Nations*, II, p. 294.

3 Coke, *The Third Part of the Institutes of the Laws of England*, pp. 68–9 [cap xiv]. This apparently dates from a judicial ruling in 1348; see Alan Harding, *A Social History of English Law* (Harmondsworth, Penguin, 1966), p. 83.

4 The traditional verse was Psalm 51, verse 1; in Latin, of course. See *OED* s. v. neck-verse, citation dated 1607.

5 I Edward VI, c. 12. The provisions in this act for removing benefit of clergy from robbers and murderers had previously been enacted in 4 Henry VIII, c. 2 and 23 Henry VIII, c. 1, but in each case they had been allowed to lapse. For the history of benefit of clergy, see also Bellamy, *The Criminal Trial in Later Medieval England*, pp. 134–7; J. M. Beattie, *Crime and the Courts in England 1660–1800* (Oxford, Clarendon Press, 1986), pp. 141–6.

6 Cynthia B. Herrup, *The Common Peace. Participation and the criminal law in seventeenth-century England* (Cambridge University Press, 1987), p. 167; see also J. S. Cockburn, *A History of English Assizes, 1558–1714* (Cambridge University Press, 1972), pp. 128–9.

7 James C. Oldham, 'On Pleading the Belly: A History of the Jury of Matrons', *Criminal Justice History*, vol. 6 (1985), pp. 1–64; see also Beattie, *Crime and the Courts in England*, pp. 430–1.

8 Carl Bridenbaugh, *Vexed and Troubled Englishmen 1590–1642* (Oxford, Clarendon Press, 1968), p. 380.

9 See Chapter Nine, pp. 100–2 and nn. 1, 7, 10–12; Bellamy, *The Criminal Trial in Later Medieval England*, pp. 143–4; Cockburn, *A History of English Assizes*, pp. 129–30; Beattie, *Crime and the Courts in England*, pp. 470–83, 500–6, 431; Abbot Emerson Smith, *Colonists in Bondage. White Servitude and Convict Labor in America, 1607–1776* (Chapel Hill, University of North Carolina

Press, 1947), chaps 5, 6; John Gay, *Polly*, ed. John Fuller, in *Dramatic Works*, vol. 2 (Oxford, Clarendon Press, 1983).

10 See Chapter One, pp. 2–3 and n. 3; P[arsons], *The Jesuit's Memorial*, pp. 211, 212–13, 253; quotation on p. 211; see also Whetstone, *A Mirour for Magestrates of Cyties*, sig. K₃v; Sir Thomas Chaloner, quoted by Cockburn in *Crime in England, 1550–1800*, p. 49.

11 Thomas Platter, *Travels in England 1599*, ed. and trans. Clare Williams (London, Jonathan Cape, 1937), p. 174; note also More, *Utopia*, p. 60, l. 10.

12 Paul Hentzner, *Travels in England During the Reign of Queen Elizabeth*, trans. Horace Walpole (London, Edward Jeffery, 1797), pp. 63–4.

13 See E. H. Sugden, *A Topographical Dictionary to the Works of Shakespeare and his fellow Dramatists* (Manchester University Press, 1925), s. v. Tyburn, Thomas (Saint) A Waterings.

14 Jeaffreson (ed.), *Middlesex County Records*, II, pp. xvi–xvii, xx–xxi.

15 Philip Jenkins, 'From Gallows to Prison? The Execution Rate in Early Modern England', *Criminal Justice History*, vol. 7 (1986), pp. 54, 55–6, 56, 57.

16 De Saussure, *Letters*, p. 127.

17 Jenkins, 'From Gallows to Prison? The Execution Rate in Early Modern England', pp. 51–71; Jeaffreson (ed.), *Middlesex County Records*, III, pp. xvii–xxi; Sharpe, *Crime in seventeenth-century England*, p. 144; V. A. C. Gatrell, *The Hanging Tree. Execution and the English People 1770–1868* (Oxford University Press, 1994), pp. 6–7, 616.

18 Beattie, *Crime and the Courts in England*, p. 514; John Howard, *The State of the Prisons*, Everyman's Library (London, Dent, 1929), p. 290; see also Radzinowicz, *A History of English Criminal Law*, I, pp. 145–6 and n. 26.

19 *The Oxford Dictionary of English Proverbs*, ed. Wilson, p. 350 (Tilley W 232); Bromyard, *Summa Praedicantium*, fol. CXLIIr, col. a (Giii, Gratia 27); see also Verney, *Memoirs of the Verney Family*, IV, p. 290.

20 More, *The Workes . . . in the Englysh tonge*, II, p. 1407, F (Latin on p. 1406, C–D) [*A godly instruccion . . . by sir Thomas More knyght, whyle he was prisoner in the towre of london*, 1534]; Bernard Mandeville, *An Enquiry into the Causes of the Frequent Executions at Tyburn* (1725), ed. Malvin R. Zirker, Augustan Reprint Society No. 105 (Los Angeles, University of California, 1964), p. 37 (original has 'awry' for 'a wry'); Wilkins, *Iests to make you Merie*, p. 309.

21 Clavell, *A Recantation of an Ill Led Life*, p. 17. For 'going to heaven in a string', see Greene, *The Second and last part of Conny-catching*, ed. Harrison, p. 19; William Cavendish, *A Pleasante & merrye Humor off a Roge*, ed. Lynn Hulse, in *Dramatic Works* (Oxford, Malone Society, 1996), l. 929.

22 Defoe, *Moll Flanders*, ed. Starr, p. 301.

23 Clavell, *A Recantation of an Ill Led Life*, p. 17.

24 Gatrell, *The Hanging Tree*, esp. chaps 2, 3.

25 *Calendar of State Papers and Manuscripts Relating to English Affairs Existing in the Archives and Collections of Venice*, ed. Allan B. Hinds, vol. 15, 1617–1619, (London, HMSO, 1909), pp. 135–6; 'so as' corrected from 'as as' in the original.

26 Platter, *Travels in England*, p. 174; see also *Memoirs Of the Right Villanous J[ohn] H[all], The Late Famous and Notorious Robber, Penn'd from his own*

Mouth some time before his Death, 4th edn, 'with large Additions', (London, H. Hills, 1708), p. 19; Henri Misson, *Memoirs and Observations in his Travels over England*, trans. John Ozell (London, D. Browne and others, 1719), p. 123; Béat Louis de Muralt, *Letters describing the Character and Customs of the English and French Nations*, 2nd edn (London, Tho. Edlin & N. Prevost, 1726), p. 44; de Saussure, *Letters*, p. 125; *The Authentic Trial, and Memoirs of Isaac Darkin*, p. 28.

27 Thomas Nashe, *The Vnfortunate Traueller. or, The life of Iacke Wilton* (London, 1594, facs. repr. Menston, Scolar Press, 1971), sig. I₃r.

28 *The Speech and Confession of Mr Richard Hannam* (London, 1656), title page and sigs A₂r, A₄v; *The witty Rogue Arraigned, Condemned, & Executed. Or, The History Of that incomparable Thief Richard Hainam* (London, 1656), sigs A₃r, A₃v, and p. 47 [sig. G₄r]; Barlow, *Dick Turpin and the Gregory Gang*, p. 427.

29 *Memoirs Of the Right Villanous J[ohn] H[all]*, p. 19; note also John Heywood, *The fifth hundred of Epigrams* (1562), no. 12, in John Heywood, *The Proverbs, Epigrams and Miscellanies*, ed. John S. Farmer (London, Early English Drama Society, 1906), p. 241; More and Wilkins quoted on pp. 215–16, references in n. 20 above.

30 Radzinowicz, *A History of English Criminal Law*, I, pp. 194–5 and nn. 4, 5, 6; Peter Linebaugh, 'The Tyburn Riot Against the Surgeons', in *Albion's Fatal Tree. Crime and Society in Eighteenth-Century England*, ed. Douglas Hay and others (London, Allen Lane, 1975), pp. 103–4.

31 Whetstone, *Promos and Cassandra*, ed. Bullough, in *Narrative and Dramatic Sources of Shakespeare*, II, pp. 456–8 [Part I, Act II, sc. vii].

32 De Saussure, *Letters*, p. 125; see also Mandeville, *An Enquiry into the Causes of the Frequent Executions at Tyburn*, pp. 24–5; Samuel Richardson, *Letters Written To and For Particular Friends, On the most Important Occasions* (London, C. Rivington and others, 1741), p. 241. By 1708, the traditional hymn was 'the Two last [?first] Staves of the 51st *Psalm*' (*Memoirs Of . . . J[ohn] H[all]*, p. 6, see also p. 18). This tradition was probably ancient. Sir Thomas More repeated Psalm 51 on the scaffold in 1535: see R. W. Chambers, *Thomas More* (London, Jonathan Cape, 1948 [first publ. 1935]), p. 348. So, in 1601, did the Earl of Essex: see Lucinda McCray Beier, 'The Good Death in Seventeenth-Century England', in *Death, Ritual and Bereavement*, ed. Ralph Houlbrooke (London, Routledge, 1989), pp. 60–1. The first verse of this psalm was often used as the 'neck-verse'; see above, n. 4.

33 *Calendar of State Papers: Venetian*, ed. Hinds, XV, p. 135; see also David Cressy, *Birth, Marriage, and Death. Ritual, Religion, and the Life-Cycle in Tudor and Stuart England* (Oxford University Press, 1997), p. 438; John Brand, *Observations on the Popular Antiquities of Great Britain*, edited and enlarged by Sir Henry Ellis, 3 vols (London, Bohn, 1849–55), II, pp. 251–3.

34 Note *Memoirs Of the Right Villanous J[ohn] H[all]*, p. 18.

35 P. Linebaugh, 'The Ordinary of Newgate and His *Account*', in *Crime in England, 1550–1800*, ed. Cockburn. Linebaugh says little about the seventeenth-century 'Accounts'. For the date at which they began to appear regularly, see Rawlings, *Drunks, Whores and Idle Apprentices*, pp. 114–15, and see further pp. 4–5; also Faller, *Turned to account*, p. 327.

36 De Muralt, *Letters*, p. 72. For the date at which de Muralt's letters were written, see Radzinowicz, *A History of English Criminal Law*, I, p. 699, n. 5.

37 For a reference to the Ordinary travelling in the cart with the condemned prisoner, see *The Triumph of Truth: in an Exact and Impartial Relation of the Life and Conversation of Colonel James Turner* (1664), ed. Peterson, in *The Counterfeit Lady*, p. 127. But in *Memoirs Of . . . J[ohn] H[all]*, p. 18, it appears that by that date (1708) the Ordinary customarily rejoined them at the gallows.

38 *Lives of the Most Remarkable Criminals* (1735), ed. Hayward, p. 146; note also pp. 221–2.

39 Wilkins, *Iests to make you Merie*, p. 309.

40 Martin Ingram, *Church Courts, Sex and Marriage in England 1570–1640* (Cambridge University Press, 1987), p. 54.

41 *Youth*, ed. Lancashire, in *Two Tudor Interludes*, ll. 253–7; see also George Gascoigne, *The Steele Glas* (1576), ed. Edward Arber (Westminster, Constable, 1901), p. 55. See also Thomas Draxe, *Bibliotheca Scholastica Instructissima. Or, A Treasurie of ancient Adagies* (London, 1616), ed. Max Förster, in 'Das Elisabethanische Sprichwort Nach Th. Draxe's *Treasurie of Ancient Adagies* (1616)', *Anglia*, vol. 42 (1918), p. 413 (no. 2112: 'The Gallous is the cut-purses pulpit'); Robert Greene, *A Disputation, Betweene a Hee Connycatcher, and a Shee Conny-catcher*, ed. G. B. Harrison, Bodley Head Quartos (London, John Lane, 1923), p. 36.

42 Whetstone, *Promos and Cassandra*, p. 457 [Part I, Act II, sc. vii].

43 For examples, see Peter Moor, *The Apprentice's Warning Piece* (1641), ed. Chandos, in *In God's Name*, pp. 384–7; Childe, *A Narrative of the Life of Mr. Benjamin Childe* (1722), pp. 27–31; *Lives of the Most Remarkable Criminals*, ed. Hayward, pp. 437–8.

44 For examples see *Lives of the Most Remarkable Criminals*, pp. 159, 373.

45 Greene, *A Disputation*, ed. Harrison, p. 36. Original has a comma after 'make', instead of a question mark, and a small 't' for 'that'. Note also the First Hackster's speech in Whetstone's *Promos and Cassandra*: see above, n. 42.

46 *Lives of the Most Remarkable Criminals*, p. 503; for other examples, see pp. 116, 397, 473. The commonness of this claim was also noted by Bernard Mandeville in *The Fable of the Bees* (edn of 1723); see *The Fable of the Bees or Private Vices, Publick Benefits*, ed. F. B. Kaye, 2 vols (Oxford, Clarendon Press, 1924), I, p. 225 [Remark (T.)].

47 *The Triumph of Truth*, ed. Peterson, in *The Counterfeit Lady*, pp. 127–8.

48 *The Diary of Samuel Pepys*, ed. Latham and Matthews, V, p. 23 [21 January 1664].

49 Moor, *The Apprentice's Warning Piece*, ed. Chandos, in *In God's Name*, p. 385; de Saussure, *Letters*, p. 125. However, Luttrell reports that the highway robber James Whitney, who made a great display of his penitence, 'was an hour and halfe in the cart before turn'd off.' Whitney, like Turner, was probably hoping for a reprieve; he had pretended to have knowledge of a plot to assassinate William III (*A Brief Historical Relation of State Affairs*, III, p. 27, see also pp. 24, 26). For the practice of bribing the hangman to delay the

execution, see *The Whole Life and History of Benjamin Child, Lately Executed for Robbing the Bristol Mail* (London, A. Moore, 1722), p. 29.

50 Luttrell, *A Brief Historical Relation of State Affairs*, V, p. 623; for Smith's nickname, see Lee, *Daniel Defoe: His Life, and recently discovered writings*, II, p. 431 (*Applebee's Journal*, 16 September 1721); *The Complete Newgate Calendar*, ed. J. L. Rayner and G. T. Crook, 5 vols (London, Navarre Society, 1926), II, p. 182; Radzinowicz, *A History of English Criminal Law*, I, p. 176 and n. 48. Note Cavendish, *A Pleasante & merrye Humor off a Roge*, in *Dramatic Works*, ed. Hulse, ll. 1023–1065.

51 Jonathan Swift, *Poetical Works*, ed. Herbert Davis (London, Oxford University Press, 1967), p. 312; *The Speech and Confession of Mr Richard Hannam* (ms. date 18 June), pp. 6–7 [sigs A$_3$v–A$_4$r]; *Hannams Last farewell to the World* (ms. date 19 June), pp. 13–14 [sigs B$_4$r–v]; *The witty Rogue Arraigned, Condemned, & Executed. Or, The History Of that incomparable Thief Richard Hainam. . . . Together with his Speech at the place of Execution* (ms. date 25 June), pp. 46–7 [sigs G$_3$v–G$_4$r]. See also Radzinowicz, *A History of English Criminal Law*, I, pp. 180–1, nn. 62, 63.

52 *Memoirs Of . . . J[ohn] H[all]*, pp. 18–19, quotations on p. 18.

53 Whetstone, *Promos and Cassandra*, p. 458 [Part I, Act II, sc. vii].

54 De Muralt calls them 'Elogies' (elegies), and says that at most executions, 'four or five Thieves are generally honour'd with' them (*Letters*, p. 43).

55 Arber, *A Transcript of the Registers of the Company of Stationers of London*, II, p. 304; see above, Chapter Nine, n. 18.

56 *Luke Huttons lamentation*, ed. Collman, in *Ballads and Broadsides*, p. 159; *The Pepys Ballads*, ed. Rollins, VI, p. 326; see also p. 322.

57 H[enry] P[arrot], *Cures for the itch* (London, 1626), sig. A$_2$v; note also Taylor, *All the Workes*, sig. Ll$_3$v.

58 Nashe, *The Unfortunate Traueller*, sig. I$_3$r; Chapman, Jonson and Marston, *Eastward Ho*, ed. Van Fossen, V iii 62–4, v 9–21, 30–129, quotations from v 45–6, 122–3.

59 This serves as preface to his pamphlet of the same title; see above, Chapter Eight, n. 55.

60 *Luke Huttons lamentation*, ed. Collman, in *Ballads and Broadsides*, pp. 159, 160. Italics not in original.

61 *A Handful of Pleasant Delights*, ed. Rollins, pp. 65, 67, ll. 1917–8, 1987.

SEVENTEEN: 'DYING LIKE A HEROE'

1 Harrison, *The Description of England*, ed. Edelen, p. 187; passage added in 2nd edn.

2 *Luke Huttons lamentation*, ed. Collman in *Ballads and Broadsides*, p. 160.

3 Gay, *The Beggar's Opera*, ed. Fuller, III xiii 16–17, xv 15, 17; Mandeville, *An Enquiry into the Causes of the Frequent Executions at Tyburn*, p. 23, see also pp. 34–5; de Muralt, *Letters*, p. 44.

4 Mandeville, *An Enquiry into the Causes of the Frequent Executions at Tyburn*, pp. 23–4.

5 *Memoirs Of . . . J[ohn] H[all]*, p. 6; note also de Muralt, *Letters*, p. 43; *Hanging, Not Punishment Enough*, p. 21; Fielding, *An Enquiry Into the Causes of the late Increase of Robbers*, ed. Zirker, p. 167; *The Authentic Trial, and Memoirs of Isaac Darkin*, p. 27. On the authorship of *Memoirs Of . . . J[ohn] H[all]*, see Faller, *Turned to account*, pp. 218–19.

6 Misson, *Memoirs and Observations*, p. 124. For the date at which Misson's book was written, see pp. 216, 319.

7 *The witty Rogue Arraigned, Condemned, & Executed,* p. 46 [sig G₃r]. For a later example see *The Authentic Trial, and Memoirs of Isaac Darkin*, p. 28.

8 See Whetstone, *Promos and Cassandra*, p. 456 [Part I, Act II, sc. vi]; Shakespeare, *King Henry IV, Part I*, ed. Humphreys, I ii 70–1.

9 *Hannams Last farewell to the World* (London, 1656), sig. A₈v; *The Speech and Confession of Mr Richard Hannam*, sig. A₄v; *The witty Rogue Arraigned, Condemned, & Executed*, sig. A₃v.

10 *Memoirs Of . . . J[ohn] H[all]*, p. 18 (original has 'a spruce' for 'as spruce'); [Daniel Defoe], *Street Robberies, consider'd . . . Written by a Converted Thief* (London, J. Roberts, [1728]), p. 52; Misson, *Memoirs and Observations*, p. 124.

11 William Shakespeare, *Measure for Measure*, ed. J. W. Lever, The Arden Shakespeare (London, Methuen, 1965), III i 81–4; note also William Shakespeare, *Antony and Cleopatra*, ed. M. R. Ridley, The Arden Shakespeare (London, Methuen, 1965), IV xiv 99–101.

12 For the latter idea, see William Drummond of Hawthornden, *A Cypresse Grove*, in *Poems and Prose*, ed. Robert H. MacDonald (Edinburgh, Scottish Academic Press, 1976), pp. 163–4.

13 For an example, see Gatrell, *The Hanging Tree*, p. 35.

14 Swift, *Poetical Works*, ed. Davis, p. 312, see l. 5; Linebaugh, 'The Tyburn Riot Against the Surgeons', in *Albion's Fatal Tree*, ed. Hay and others, pp. 112–14. For men's wedding clothes in the eighteenth century, see C. Willett Cunnington and Phillis Cunnington, *Handbook of English Costume in the Eighteenth Century*, revised edn (London, Faber & Faber, 1972), pp. 72, 82, 217–18.

15 Brand, *Popular Antiquities*, ed. Ellis, II, p. 283, note also p. 284; Pepys, *Diary*, ed. Latham and Matthews, I, p. 24 [20 January 1660].

16 For strewing flowers at maiden funerals, see Sir William Waad in 1603, quoted by Christina Hole in *English Home-Life 1500 to 1800* (London, Batsford, 1947), p. 75; Brand, *Popular Antiquities*, ed. Ellis, II, pp. 304, 311–12; William Shakespeare, *Hamlet*, ed. Harold Jenkins, The Arden Shakespeare, V i 226; note also Gatrell, *The Hanging Tree*, pp. 88–9, n. 113.

17 Brand, *Popular Antiquities*, ed. Ellis, II, p. 283 n. 1; Gatrell, *The Hanging Tree*, pp. 86–7, see also p. 290.

18 *Revelation*, chap. 3, vv. 4, 5, 18, chap. 4, v. 4, chap. 7, vv. 9, 13, 14, chap. 19, v. 8.

19 Misson, *Memoirs and Observations*, p. 124.

20 See de Muralt quoted on p. 225, reference in n. 3 above; below, nn. 21, 22, 45; Mandeville, *An Enquiry into the Causes of the Frequent Executions at Tyburn*, p. 29; Fielding, *An Enquiry Into the Causes of the late Increase of Robbers*, p. 167.

21 Verney, *Memoirs of the Verney Family*, IV, p. 291.

22 De Muralt, *Letters*, p. 42.

23 Shakespeare, *King Henry IV, Part I*, II iv 490–1.

24 Mandeville, *An Enquiry into the Causes of the Frequent Executions at Tyburn*, pp. 34, 37; Fielding, *An Enquiry Into the Causes of the late Increase of Robbers*, p. 168.

25 Sir John Reresby, *Memoirs and Travels*, ed. Albert Ivatt (London, Kegan Paul etc., 1904), p. 228; note also *The Malefactor's Register*, V, p. 135.

26 Verney, *Memoirs of the Verney Family*, IV, p. 291.

27 Chamberlain, *Letters*, ed. McClure, I, p. 50.

28 Richardson, *Letters . . . On the most Important Occasions*, pp. 239, 240.

29 Swift, *Poetical Works*, ed. Davis, pp. 312–13.

30 Luttrell, *A Brief Historical Relation of State Affairs*, III, p. 345; *The Oxford Dictionary of English Proverbs*, ed. Wilson, p. 186 (Tilley S 381). A similar story is told of Jerry Abershaw; see Harper, *Half-Hours with the Highwaymen*, II, p. 369.

31 William Roper, *The Mirrour of Vertue in Worldly Greatnes or the Life of Sir Thomas More Knight*, The King's Classics (London, Alexander Moring, 1903), p. 101; Halle, *The Union of the Two Noble Families of Lancaster and York*, reign of Henry VIII, fol. CCXXVIIv, ll. xv–xxxix.

32 Cavendish, *A Pleasante & merrye Humor off a Roge*, in *Dramatic Works*, ed. Hulse, ll. 881–1021; see also [William Cavendish], Duke of Newcastle, *The Triumphant Widow, or the Medley of Humours. A Comedy* (London, 1677), pp. 91–3 [Act V]. For the scene in *The Triumphant Widow*, Cavendish rehashed the equivalent scene in *A Pleasante & merrye Humor off a Roge*, and the dialogue is very similar.

33 De Muralt, *Letters*, pp. 42–3.

34 See Chapter Nine, p. 116, and *Ratseis Ghost*, sig. F₃r.

35 *The Diary of Samuel Pepys*, ed. Latham and Matthews, V, pp. 23, 10, 11 [21 and 10 January 1664].

36 *The Letters of John Wilmot, Earl of Rochester*, ed. Jeremy Treglown (Oxford, Basil Blackwell, 1985 [first published 1980]), p. 134.

37 See Chapter One, p. 8 and n. 12; John Stephens, *Essayes and Characters Ironicall, and Instructive*, 2nd impression (London, 1615), p. 400 [Character xxi. A Pandar]. See also below, nn. 40, 41; Thomas Deloney, *A most sweet Song of an English-Merchant*, in *The Works of Thomas Deloney*, ed. Francis Oscar Mann (Oxford, Clarendon Press, 1912), p. 486, l. 29; James Shirley, *The Wedding*, ed. Sister Martin Flavin (New York, Garland, 1980), IV iii 132–5.

38 Bromyard, *Summa Praedicantium*, fol. LXVr, col. a (Cxii, Compassio 2).

39 Gay, *The Beggar's Opera*, I iv 13–20; original is in italics; I iv 11–12.

40 Cavendish, *A Pleasante & merrye Humor off a Roge*, in *Dramatic Works*, ed. Hulse, ll. 921–3; see also Cavendish, *The Triumphant Widow*, p. 92 [Act V].

41 Swift, *Poetical Works*, ed. Davis, p. 312, l. 8; note also Richard Head, *The English Rogue* (1665), sigs. Ccc₅v–Ccc₆r [chap. xxxiii]; *The Life of Deval*, p. 5.

42 James Boswell, 'On Executions', in *Boswell's Column*, ed. Margery Bailey (London, William Kimber, 1951), p. 347.

43 Gay, *The Beggar's Opera*, I xii 1–9.

44 See R. H., *The Royal Pastime of Cock-fighting* (London, D. Brown, 1709; facs. repr. Liss, Hampshire, Spur Publications, 1973), esp. sigs C_2r–C_3v, 1–3, 5–9, 29–30.

45 [Defoe], *Street Robberies, consider'd*, p. 52. 'God Damn' expanded from 'G—d D—mn'. Original has 'thr' for 'the'.

46 Francis Grose, *A Classical Dictionary of the Vulgar Tongue*, 3rd edn [1796], ed. Eric Partridge (London, Routledge & Kegan Paul, 1963 [edn first publ. in 1931], s. v. 'game', 'dunghill'. See also Linebaugh, *The London Hanged*, p. 210.

47 Misson, *Memoirs and Observations*, pp. 123–4; de Muralt, *Letters*, p. 73; de Saussure, *Letters*, pp. 126–7.

48 Fielding, *The History of Tom Jones*, II, p. 681.

49 Verney, *Memoirs of the Verney Family*, IV, p. 291; *Ratseis Ghost*, sig. F_2v. For hanging as a death that brings shame, see also Chapter One, p. 8 and n. 12; Chapter Sixteen, p. 220 and n. 46, p. 221 and n. 52; Greene, *The Blacke Bookes Messenger*, ed. Harrison, p. 31; *The Life and Death of George of Oxford*, in *The Pepys Ballads*, ed. Day, II, p. 150; Defoe, *Moll Flanders*, p. 302.

50 Clavell, *A Recantation of an Ill Led Life*, p. 17.

51 John Cowell, *The Interpreter* (Cambridge, 1607, facs. repr. Menston, Scolar Press, 1972), s. v. 'Corruption of blood'; Edward Coke, *The First Part of the Institutes of the Lawes of England. Or, A Commentarie upon Littleton*, 2nd edn, corrected (London, 1629), pp. 8r, 392r [Lib. 1, cap. i, sect. 1; Lib. 3, cap. 13, sect. 747]; Coke, *The Third Part of the Institutes of the Laws of England*, pp. 47, 233, 240–1 [caps. vi, cv, cvi].

EIGHTEEN: 'GIVE ME A HIGHWAYMAN': THE AGE OF NOSTALGIA

1 Edward Walford, *Greater London: A Narrative of its History, its People and its Places*, 2 vols (London, Cassell, 1882?), II, p. 316; Harper, *Half-Hours with the Highwaymen*, II, pp. 361–9.

2 J. J. Tobias, *Crime and Industrial Society in the Nineteenth Century* (Harmondsworth, Penguin, 1972; first publ. 1967), pp. 221, 230, 268; Beattie, *Crime and the Courts in England 1660–1800*, pp. 160–1; see also V. A. C. Gatrell, 'The Decline of Theft and Violence in Victorian and Edwardian England', in *Crime and the Law. The Social History of Crime in Western Europe since 1500*, ed. V. A. C. Gatrell, Bruce Lenman and Geoffrey Parker (London, Europa Publications, 1980), p. 317; McLynn, *Crime and Punishment in Eighteenth-century England*, pp. 81–2.

3 Gatrell, in the place cited in the previous note.

4 [Edward Bulwer], *Paul Clifford*, 3 vols (London, Henry Colburn & Richard Bentley, 1830), II, p. 190.

5 Ibid., I, p. 277.

6 Ibid., II, p. 226.

7 Ibid., III, pp. 146–7.

8 Ibid., III, chap. ii; Barlow, *Dick Turpin and the Gregory Gang*, pp. 280–1;

Arabian Nights' Entertainments, ed. Robert L. Mack (Oxford University Press, 1995), pp. 764–87.

9 For a key to the political satire in *Paul Clifford*, see Keith Hollingsworth, *The Newgate Novel, 1830–1847. Bulwer, Ainsworth, Dickens, & Thackeray* (Detroit, Wayne State University Press, 1963), pp. 73–7.

10 Bulwer, *Paul Clifford*, III, pp. 278–9; see also Edward Bulwer Lytton, *Paul Clifford* (London, Routledge, 1848?), pp. vii–viii [Preface to the edition of 1840].

11 Bulwer, *Paul Clifford*, I, pp. 19, 23.

12 Ibid., III, pp. 277–81; II, pp. 145–7, quotations on p. 146.

13 William Godwin, *Caleb Williams*, ed. David McCracken (Oxford University Press, 1982), pp. 216, 226.

14 Bulwer, *Paul Clifford*, II, p. 121, see also p. 189.

15 Hollingsworth, *The Newgate Novel*, p. 81.

16 William Harrison Ainsworth, *Rookwood. A Romance* (London, Routledge, 1856?), p. xxxiii [Preface to the edition of 1849].

17 [William Harrison Ainsworth], *Rookwood. A Romance*, 3 vols (London, Richard Bentley, 1834), I, pp. 220–3.

18 Beattie, *Crime and the Courts in England*, pp. 135–9; see also pp. 111–12.

19 Ainsworth, *Rookwood*, II, p. 314; III, pp. 159–60, 240–1.

20 Barlow, *Dick Turpin and the Gregory Gang*, pp. 442–9; note Daniel Defoe, *A Tour Through the Whole Island of Great Britain*, 2 vols, intr. G. D. H. Cole and D. C. Browning, Everyman's Library (London, Dent, 1962), I, pp. 104–5; S. M. Ellis, *William Harrison Ainsworth and his friends*, 2 vols (London, John Lane, 1911), I, pp. 244–6; see also Leigh Hunt, 'Thieves, Ancient and Modern', in *The Indicator and the Companion, A Miscellany for the fields and the fire-side. . . . in Two Parts* (London, Edward Moxon, 1840), I, p. 41 [essay first published in *The Indicator*, 22 December 1819 to 5 January 1820].

21 For later street ballads about Turpin and Black Bess, see below, n. 29. Although Ainsworth was the first to give Turpin's horse the name of 'Black Bess', by which she has been known to tradition ever since, Charles G. Harper pointed out that a burlesque ballad of 1825, by Horace Smith, already credits Turpin with the ownership of a 'black mare' who is called 'Bess' (*Half-Hours with the Highwaymen*, II, pp. 229–31).

22 Ainsworth, *Rookwood*, III, p. 333; see also p. 160.

23 Ibid., II, p. 353.

24 Ibid., III, p. 463.

25 Hollingsworth, *The Newgate Novel*, p. 105.

26 Barlow, *Dick Turpin and the Gregory Gang*.

27 See for example Graham Seal, *The Outlaw Legend. A Cultural Tradition in Britain, America and Australia* (Cambridge University Press, 1996), pp. 61–2.

28 Hollingsworth, *The Newgate Novel*, pp. 105–6; Harper, *Half-Hours with the Highwaymen*, II, pp. 226–9.

29 *The Common Muse. An Anthology of Popular British Ballad Poetry XVth–XXth Century*, ed. Vivian de Sola Pinto and Allan Edwin Rodway (London, Chatto & Windus, 1957), pp. 160–1; Seal, *The Outlaw Legend*, pp. 60–1.

30 Harper, *Half-Hours with the Highwaymen*, II, p. 226.

31 G. P. R. James, *The Robber: A Tale* (London, Simms & M'Intyre, 1851), esp. pp. 12–16, 43–7, 68–70, 175, 274 [chaps II, VI, IX, XXIII, XXXV].

32 The best short account of Sheppard's career is in Howson, *Thief-Taker General. The Rise and Fall of Jonathan Wild*, pp. 207–26; see also [Daniel Defoe?], *The History of the Remarkable Life of John Sheppard* and *A Narrative of all the Robberies, Escapes, &c. of John Sheppard* (both 1724), in Defoe, *Freebooters and Buccaneers. Novels of Adventure and Piracy*, 'The King of Pirates', pp. 167–227; Arthur Griffiths, *Chronicles of Newgate*, pp. 183–7; Christopher Hibbert, *The Road to Tyburn. The Story of Jack Sheppard and the Eighteenth Century Underworld* (London, Longmans, Green & Co, 1957); Moore, *The Thieves' Opera*.

33 Hollingsworth, *The Newgate Novel*, pp. 131, 138–40.

34 Ibid., pp. 141–5, 158–61.

35 26 October 1839, p. 803; quoted by Hollingsworth in *The Newgate Novel*, p. 142.

36 W[illiam] Harrison Ainsworth, *Jack Sheppard. A Romance*, 3 vols (London, Richard Bentley, 1839), esp. Book III.

37 Ainsworth, *Rookwood*, II, pp. 307–8.

38 Laman Blanchard, 'Memoir of William Harrison Ainsworth', in *Rookwood. A Romance* (London, Routledge, 1856?), p. xvi; originally published in the *Mirror*, 1842.

39 Ainsworth, *Rookwood*, II, pp. 311–12; for 'tobyman', etc., see *Lexicon Balatronicum. A Dictionary of Buckish Slang, University Wit, and Pickpocket Eloquence* (London, C. Chappel, 1811), s. v. toby lay, cracksman, sneak; *Oxford English Dictionary*, s. v. toby, *sb.*[2].

40 Bulwer, *Paul Clifford*, III, pp. 38, 244.

41 See William Harrison cited in Chapter One, p. 6 and n. 7; Richard Grafton cited in Chapter Nine, p. 109 and n. 38. For housebreakers who gained some popular fame, see *The Life, Apprehensio[n], Arraignment, and Execution of Char[les] Courtney* (London, 1612); *The English Villain: or the Grand Thief. Being a full Relation of the desperate Life, and deserved Death of . . . Richard Hanam* (London, [1656]); *The witty Rogue Arraigned, Condemned, & Executed. Or, The History of that incomparable Thief Richard Hainam* (London, 1656); and, of course, Jack Sheppard himself.

42 Charles Dickens, *Oliver Twist*, ed. Fred Kaplan, Norton Critical Edition (New York, W. W. Norton, 1993), p. x.

43 See for example the review of *Oliver Twist* in the *Quarterly Review*, vol. LXIV, no. 127 (June, 1839), pp. 92, 97, 101.

44 Hollingsworth, *The Newgate Novel*, pp. 129, 158–9.

45 Dickens, *Oliver Twist*, ed. Caplan, p. 4.

46 Ibid., pp. 4–5.

47 Bulwer, *Paul Clifford*, I, pp. 276–7; III, pp. 34–6.

48 Ibid., III, p. 24; Ainsworth, *Rookwood*, I, pp. 208, 219–20.

49 I am indebted to Marion Shaw for suggesting this connection.

50 Dickens, *Oliver Twist*, p. 138 [chap. XIX].

51 Dickens, *Oliver Twist*, esp. pp. 134, 151–4, 169–70, 259–60 [chaps XIX, XXII, XXV, XXXIX].

52 Charles Dickens, *Barnaby Rudge*, Everyman's Library (London, Dent, 1950, repr. 1972), pp. 4–6 (quotation on p. 6), 27–9, 48–50 [chaps I, III, VI].

53 Ibid., p. 65 [chap. VIII].

54 Thomas De Quincey, 'Travelling in England in Old Days', in *Collected Writings*, ed. David Masson, 14 vols (Edinburgh, Adam & Charles Black, 1889–90), I, pp. 280–2.

55 De Quincey, 'At Manchester Grammar School', in *Collected Writings*, ed. Masson, I, pp. 389, 390; note *Posthumous Works*, ed. Alexander H. Japp, 2 vols (London, William Heinemann, 1891, 1893), I, pp. 320–1.

56 Robert Louis Stevenson, 'A Gossip on Romance', in *Memories and Portraits*, ed. Edmund Gosse in *Works*, vol. IX (London, Cassell etc., 1907), pp. 146–7.

57 J. R. Hammond, *A Robert Louis Stevenson Chronology* (Houndmills, Basingstoke, Macmillan, 1997), p. 44; Robert Louis Stevenson, *The Great North Road*, chapter VIII, in *Works*, vol. XVIII, ed. Edmund Gosse (London, Cassell etc., 1907), pp. 380–5.

58 R. D. Blackmore, *Lorna Doone* (London, Penguin, 1994 [first publ. 1869]); for Faggus and Winny, see esp. pp. 77–84, 90–1, 94–5, 316, 561–6, 656 [chaps X, XI, XII, XXXIX, LXIV–LXV, LXXV]. For Faggus and his horse in West Country folk legend, see Briggs, *A Dictionary of British Folk-Tales*, Part B, vol. ii, pp. 46–47.

59 Blackmore, *Lorna Doone*, pp. 92–4 [chap. XII].

60 Ibid., p. 379 [chap. XLVI].

61 Alfred Noyes, 'The Highwayman', in *The Oxford Book of Narrative Verse*, ed. Iona and Peter Opie (Oxford University Press, 1988), pp. 341–4, and see note on pp. 398–9.

62 Ibid., ll. 7–9. For Dickens on 'the attractions of dress' in relation to the literary highway robber, see above, p. 245, and n. 46.

63 Noyes, 'The Highwayman', ll. 23, 16, 18.

64 Ibid., ll. 85, 30.

NINETEEN: THE TURPIN LEGEND

1 Barlow, *Dick Turpin and the Gregory Gang*, Book Two; see esp. pp. 87–9.

2 Ibid., Book Five, especially chaps 1, 2, 6.

3 See Chapter Two, p. 23; Chapter Thirteen, pp. 166–7.

4 See Chapter Twelve, pp. 156–7.

5 *Turpin's Rant*, stanza 5 [Bodleian Library, Harding B. 22 (304)]; see Bodleian Library Broadside Ballads, Bodleian Library, University of Oxford, 1999 <http://www.bodley.ox.ac.uk/ballads/ballads.htm> [accessed on 1 November 2000].

6 Barlow, *Dick Turpin and the Gregory Gang*, pp. 284, 288, 291–3, 301, 304.

7 Note *The Famous Victories of Henry the Fifth*, quoted in Chapter Ten, p. 118 and n. 5.

8 Barlow, *Dick Turpin and the Gregory Gang*, Book Six.

9 Ibid., pp. 311, 314, 261.

10 *The Life and Death of Gamaliel Ratsey*, sigs C₃v–D₂r; G[eorge] F[idge], *The English Gusman*, p. 22 [sig. D₄v].

11 *Turpen's Appeal to the Judge in his defence*, early nineteenth-century street ballad, given in full by Harper, *Half-Hours with the Highwaymen*, II, pp. 234–6 (see also above, Chapter Thirteen, p. 176); Seal, *The Outlaw Legend*, pp. 60, 61, 74; Barlow, *Dick Turpin and the Gregory Gang*, p. 315.

12 Barlow, *Dick Turpin and the Gregory Gang*, pp. 309–10; note that Barlow's text reads '*place.* [new paragraph] *Place!*', which is an obvious error, though possibly faithful to his original, which I have not checked.

13 G[eorge] F[idge], *The English Gusman*, p. 31 [sig. F₁r].

14 *Turpin's Rant*, stanza 4; comma after 'Store' conjectural (original hard to read).

15 William Chappell, *The Ballad Literature and Popular Music of the Olden Time*, 2 vols (New York, Dover, 1965 [first published 1859]), II, p. 662. For other (more corrupt) versions of *Turpin's Valour*, see W. H. Logan, *A Pedlar's Pack of Ballads and Songs* (Edinburgh, William Paterson, 1869), pp. 118–21; Seal, *The Outlaw Legend*, pp. 57–9.

16 See Chapter Two, p. 23.

17 Chappell, *Popular Music of the Olden Time*, II, p. 663.

18 See Chapter One, pp. 2–3 and n. 3.

19 See Chapter Thirteen, pp. 172–3 and n. 45.

20 Ellis, *William Harrison Ainsworth and his friends*, I, pp. 20, 22; Ainsworth, *Rookwood* (London, George Routledge, 1856?), p. xxxvii [Preface to the edition of 1849].

21 [William Harrison Ainsworth,] *Rookwood*, 3 vols (London, Richard Bentley, 1834), III, pp. 240–3.

22 Defoe, *A Tour Through the Whole Island of Great Britain*, I, pp. 104–5; Ellis, *William Harrison Ainsworth and his friends*, I, p. 245.

23 Barlow, *Dick Turpin and the Gregory Gang*, p. 447. For another Turpin alibi story, in the form of a comic ballad by Horace Smith, published in 1825, see Harper, *Half-Hours with the Highwaymen*, II, pp. 230–1. Here, the ride is from Hounslow Heath to Gloucester. This may have been purely parodic, or it may have been more or less closely founded on some lost popular tradition.

24 Christina Hole, *Traditions and Customs of Cheshire* (East Ardsley, Wakefield, S. R. Publishers, 1970 [first published 1937]), p. 199.

25 Jacqueline Simpson, *The Folklore of the Welsh Border* (London, Batsford, 1976), p. 50.

26 Roy Palmer, *The Folklore of Warwickshire* (London, Batsford, 1976), pp. 30, 77; Harper, *Half-Hours with the Highwaymen*, II, pp. 236–8.

27 Harper, *Half-Hours with the Highwaymen*, II, p. 236.

28 Note Ainsworth, *Rookwood*, III, pp. 239–40.

29 Ibid, III, pp. 240–1, 255–6, 280–2; and see above, Chapter Eighteen, p. 239.

30 See Chapter Eighteen, p. 240.

31 Note Seal, *The Outlaw Legend*, pp. 61–2.

TWENTY: CONCLUSION

1 Adam Smith, *Lectures on Jurisprudence*, ed. R. L. Meek, D. D. Raphael and P. G. Stein (Oxford, Clarendon Press, 1978), p. 487. For the probable date and circumstances of delivery, see Introduction, pp. 7–9. The lecture has survived only in the form of notes taken down by a student who attended it. Moreover, it is likely that, although Smith composed it, it was delivered by another lecturer.

2 Ibid., pp 486–7.

3 Note the remarks of J. A. Sharpe in 'Crime and Delinquency in an Essex Parish 1600–1640' in *Crime in England 1550–1800*, ed. Cockburn, pp. 96–7; also in *Crime in Early Modern England*, pp. 94–5.

4 See Chapter Nine, pp. 111–12 and n. 49; and see Verney, *Memoirs of the Verney Family*, IV, p. 293.

5 John McVicar, *McVicar by Himself*, revised edn (London, Arrow, 1979), pp. 160–2, and see also pp. 132–3, 23–4; Eric Partridge, *A Dictionary of the Underworld* (Ware, Wordsworth, 1989 [first published 1950]), s. v. staunch.

6 See Chapter Twelve, p. 149 and n. 6.

7 Clavell, *A Recantation of an Ill Led Life*, p. 7.

8 Thomas Smith, *De Republica Anglorum*, p. 29.

9 See Chapter One, pp. 9–10 and n. 15.

10 For an early example of this, see Chapter Thirteen, p. 173 and n. 46.

11 *An Account of John Rann, Commonly called Sixteen String Jack* (London, T. Sabine; Lewis Tomlinson, 1774), pp. 6–7, 15–18, 22, and see also frontispiece, for the ribbons round his breeches; *The Life of John Rann, otherwise Sixteen Strings Jack* (London, Frederick Wheeler, 1884), pp. 12, 19, 21–23, 27, 29. (This second pamphlet life is either reprinted from, or very closely based on, an earlier publication that first appeared in 1774.)

12 See Chapter Four, p. 47 and nn. 35, 36.

13 See Chapter One, pp. 2–3 and n. 3.

14 See Chapter One, p. 12 and n. 23.

15 See Chapter Ten. For the phrase 'the wild prince' see William Shakespeare, *The Merry Wives of Windsor*, ed. H. J. Oliver, The Arden Shakespeare (London, Methuen, 1971), III ii 66–7, and cf. *King Henry IV, Part I*, V ii 70–1; *King Henry IV, Part II*, V ii 123–4, both ed. Humphries.

16 See for example Langford, *Englishness Identified*, pp. 46, 67–70, 142–3; Defoe, *The Complete English Tradesman*, I, p. 305 [chap. XXII].

17 George Schöpflin, 'The Functions of Myth and a Taxonomy of Myths', in *Myths and Nationhood*, ed. Geoffrey Hosking and George Schöpflin (London, Hurst, 1997), p. 25.

18 See Chapter One, p. 1 and n. 1.

19 This is, of course, very close to Thomas Hobbes's account of how matters were under 'the Law of Nature': see *Leviathan*, pp. 128–9 [Part 2, chap. 17], and *The Elements of Law*, ed. J. C. A. Gaskin (Oxford University Press, 1999 [first published 1994]), p. 104 [Part I, chap. XIX, section 2].

20 See Chapter Twelve, n. 35.

APPENDIX A: THE FEMALE ROBBER

1 Peter Haining, *The English Highwayman. A Legend Unmasked* (London, Robert Hale, 1991), pp. 120–4. See also Michael Billett, *Highwaymen and Outlaws* (London, Arms & Armour Press, 1997), p. 79.

2 Magdalen King-Hall, *Life and Death of the Wicked Lady Skelton* (London, Peter Davies, 1944); Christina Hole, *Haunted England. A Survey of English Ghost-lore* (London, Batsford, 1940), pp. 93–4.

3 Given, *Society and Homicide in Thirteenth-Century England*, pp. 126–7.

4 Hanawalt, *Crime and Conflict*, p. 88; see also Hanawalt, 'Ballads and Bandits', pp. 158, 172 nn. 18, 19, and for her definition of banditry, see pp. 156–7.

5 *Middlesex County Records*, ed. Jeaffreson, I, p. 66, II, p. 7, III, p. 74; *County of Middlesex. Calendar to the Sessions Records*, ed. Le Hardy, I, p. 142; *Middlesex County Records*, ed. Jeaffreson, I, p. 51; II, p. 156; *County of Middlesex. Calendar to the Sessions Records*, ed. Le Hardy, IV, p. 114. For a further case, this time in Essex, see above, Chapter Sixteen, p. 213 and n. 8.

6 Wilkins, *Iests to make you Merie*, p. 335.

7 See Chapter Nine, pp. 101–2 and n. 5. Quotation from Chamberlain, *Letters*, II, p. 205.

8 *Middlesex County Records*, ed. Jeaffreson, III, p. 11.

9 *The life and death of Mr George Sandys*, in *A Pepysian Garland*, ed. Rollins, pp. 248–55; quotations from stanzas 15, 16.

10 Luttrell, *A Brief Relation of State Affairs*, II, p. 524; III, p. 85. For the meaning of 'highwayman' in Luttrell, see above, Chapter Twelve, n. 32. Luttrell also notes a couple of executions of women convicted of robbery; see *A Brief Relation of State Affairs*, V, pp. 372, 547.

11 J. M. Beattie, 'The Criminality of Women in Eighteenth-Century England', *Journal of Social History*, vol. 8 (Summer 1975), pp. 89–92.

12 Note the remarks of Einstadter in 'The Social Organization of Armed Robbery', pp. 75–6.

13 [Richard Head], *The English Rogue Described in the Life of Meriton Latroon* (London, Henry Marsh, 1665), sigs Gg_4r–Gg_8v [chaps. xxix–xxx] [British Library shelf mark C.70.b.4].

14 The publishing history of *The English Rogue* is complex, and there is no critical edition. The additional material about the female robbers was incorporated in the text at latest by 1672. See [Richard Head and Francis Kirkman], *The English Rogue described, in the Life of Meriton Latroon* (London, Francis Kirkman, 1672), sigs S_2r–T_7v [chaps xxxiii–xxxvi] [British Library shelf mark 12614.c.21].

15 Rudolf M. Dekker and Lotte C. van de Pol, *The Tradition of Female Transvestism in Early Modern Europe* (London, Macmillan, 1989), pp. 35–7.

16 Head, *The English Rogue* (1672), sig. T_4v [chap. xxxvi].

17 Ibid., sig. T_5v [chap. xxxvi]. Original has no comma after 'Soul'.

18 Head, *The English Rogue* (1665), sig. Hh_2r [chap. xxxi]; see also 1672 edn, sig. V_1r [chap. xxxvii].

19 Head, *The English Rogue* (1672), sig. T_5r [chap. xxxvi].

20 Note the remarks of Rochester in *The Letters of John Wilmot, Earl of Rochester*,

ed. Jeremy Treglown (Oxford, Basil Blackwell, 1980), pp. 75–6; and see also C. L. Barber, *The Idea of Honour in the English Drama 1591–1700* (Göteborg, University of Gothenburg, 1957), pp. 302–5.

21 Head, *The English Rogue* (1665), sig. Hh₂r [chap. xxxi]; see also 1672 edn, sig. V₁r [chap. xxxvii].

22 Joseph Swetnam, *The Araignment of Lewde, idle, froward and unconstant Women*, (London, 1615), repr. in facs. in *Female Replies to Swetnam the Woman-Hater*, intr. Charles Butler (Bristol, Thoemmes Press, 1995), pp. 14–15; *Oxford Dictionary of English Proverbs*, ed. Wilson, pp. 907–8 [Tilley W 646]; Anne Laurence, *Women in England 1500–1760. A Social History* (London, Weidenfeld & Nicolson, 1994), pp. 66–7; David Lindley, *The Trials of Frances Howard. Fact and Fiction at the Court of King James* (London, Routledge, 1996, 1st publ. 1993), p. 103; Foyster, *Manhood in Early Modern England*, p. 29.

23 Alan Bray, *Homosexuality in Renaissance England* (London, Gay Men's Press, 1982), pp. 130–1; Foyster, *Manhood in Early Modern England*, pp. 55–8.

24 *The Pepys Ballads*, ed. Hyder Edward Rollins, 8 vols (Cambridge, Massachusetts, Harvard University Press, 1929–32), vol. V, pp. 291–3 [no. 330]; quotations from stanzas 2, 8, 18, 5, 15. For a late eighteenth-century text, see W. H. Logan, *A Pedlar's Pack of Ballads and Songs* (Edinburgh, William Paterson, 1869), pp. 123–6. See also the oral version collected by Alfred Williams in *Folk-Songs of the Upper Thames* (London, Duckworth, 1923), pp. 267–8.

25 *The Pepys Ballads*, ed. Day, II, p. 176. For oral versions see James Reeves, *The Idiom of the People: English Traditional Verse edited from the manuscripts of Cecil J. Sharp*, reprinted with corrections (London, Heinemann, 1958), pp. 215–16; Williams, *Folk-Songs of the Upper Thames*, pp. 275–6.

26 See John de Bromyard, *Summa Praedicantium*, 2 vols (Venice, 1586), II, fol. 92r [M xiii, Mundus 10] (relevant page missing from copy of 1518 edition in Cambridge University Library); [Daniel Defoe?], *An Account of the Cartoucheans in France*, in *Freebooters and Buccaneers. Novels of Adventure and Piracy*, by Daniel Defoe (New York, The Dial Press, 1935), 'The King of Pirates', pp. 130, 132, 147–8. A modus operandi for a woman robber that exploits masculine chivalry in a similar manner is described by Head in *The English Rogue*, 1665 edn, sigs Hh₁r–v [chap. xxxi]; see also 1672 edn, sigs. T₈r–v [chap. xxxvii].

27 Smith, *A Complete History of the . . . Highwaymen*, pp. 282–90; compare *The Life and Death of Mal Cutpurse* in *Counterfeit Ladies*, ed. Todd and Spearing. For Smith's generally cavalier way with his sources, see also Faller, *Turned to Account*, pp. 18–19, 170–1.

28 Smith, *A Complete History of the . . . Highwaymen*, p. 285. For the earliest record of Moll Cutpurse, see Mark Eccles, 'Mary Frith, the Roaring Girl', *Notes and Queries*, vol. 230 (March 1985), pp. 65–6.

29 Smith, *A Complete History of the . . . Highwaymen*, pp. 502–7; compare the pamphlet, currently untraceable, cited by Harper in *Half-Hours with the Highwaymen*, I, pp. 75–7.

APPENDIX B: MAID MARIAN

1 Wiles, *The Early Plays of Robin Hood*, pp. 21–4. For evidence of burlesque in Elizabethan performances of the role, see Thomas Nashe, *The Returne of the renowned Caualiero Pasquill . . . and his meeting with Marsorius*, ed. R. B. McKerrow in *Works*, 5 vols, revised by F. P. Wilson (Oxford, Blackwell, 1958, repr. 1966), I, p. 83; Nicholas Breton, *Pasquils Mistresse*, ed. Jean Robertson, in *Poems by Nicholas Breton* (*not hitherto reprinted*), (Liverpool University Press, 1952), p. 90; Breton, *Olde Mad-cappes new Gally-mawfrey*, ed. Robertson, in *Poems*, p. 120; Thomas Heywood, *The Iron Age*, ed. Arlene W. Weiner (New York, Garland, 1979), III i 17–21.

2 *The Comedy of George a Greene*, ed. F. W. Clarke and W. W. Greg (Malone Society, 1911), ll. 923–70, 1043, 1090–5, 1265–6 [scs xi, xii, xiii]; for the ballad, see *The Jolly Pinder of Wakefield*, ed. Dobson and Taylor, in *Rymes of Robyn Hood*, pp. 146–9 [Child no. 124].

3 Peele, *Edward I*, ed. Hook, in *Life and Works*, II, esp. ll. 1150–1206 (sc. 7).

4 See Chapter Eleven, pp. 139–41.

5 *Robin Hood and Maid Marian*, ed. Dobson and Taylor, in *Rymes of Robyn Hood*, pp. 176–8 [Child no. 150]. For references to Marian in broadside ballads, see *The English and Scottish Popular Ballads*, ed. Child, III, pp. 198, 209 [Child nos 145A, 147].

6 Child (ed.), *The English and Scottish Popular Ballads*, III, p. 218.

7 Alexander Barclay, *Fourth Eclogue*, quoted by Child in *The English and Scottish Popular Ballads*, III, p. 46, fn.

8 *Early English Lyrics*, ed. Chambers and Sidgwick, pp. 34–48, 334–6; quotations from ll. 20, 113, 125–8, 163–6, 219.

9 *Rymes of Robyn Hood*, ed. Dobson and Taylor, p. 214 and see n. 3.

10 *Misogonus*, ed. Lester E. Barber (New York, Garland, 1979), II ii 75–6; Gabriel Harvey, *Pierces Supererogation* (London, 1593, facs. repr. Menston, Scolar Press, 1970), pp. 145–6; Shakespeare, *King Henry IV, Part I*, ed. Humphreys, III iii 112–13; Nicholas Breton, *Wits Trenchmour*, in *Works*, ed. Alexander B. Grosart, 2 vols (1879; repr. in reduced facs., Hildesheim, Georg Olms, 1969), II, p. 17.

APPENDIX C: SOCIAL BANDITS

1 E. J. Hobsbawm, 'The Social Bandit', in *Primitive Rebels. Studies in Archaic Forms of Social Movement in the 19th and 20th Centuries*, 3rd edn (Manchester University Press, 1971 [first published 1959]); Eric Hobsbawm, *Bandits*, revised edn (London, Weidenfeld & Nicolson, 2000 [first published 1969; further edns 1972 and 1981]); Eric Hobsbawm, 'Social Bandits: Reply', *Comparative Studies in Society and History*, vol. 14 (1972), pp. 503–5 [answer to Anton Blok, 'The Peasant and the Brigand: Social Banditry Reconsidered', in the same issue]; E. J. Hobsbawm, 'Distinctions between Socio-Political and Other Forms of Crime: Social Criminality', *Bulletin of the Society for the Study of Labour History*, vol. 25, (1972), pp. 5–6; E. J. Hobsbawm, 'Social Banditry',

in *Rural Protest: Peasant Movements and Social Change*, ed. Henry A. Landsberger (London, Macmillan, 1974).

2 Hobsbawm, *Bandits*, pp. 19–21, 54–5, 141, 41–5, 106–7, 46–8, 171; quotations on pp. 171, 47, 21 (Page references here and below are to the 2000 edition.)

3 Graham Seal, *The Outlaw Legend. A Cultural Tradition in Britain, America and Australia* (Cambridge University Press, 1996), pp. 2–11, 179; quotations on pp. 11, 2.

4 Hobsbawm, *Bandits*, pp. 170, 46–7, 61–2, 22, 44–5, 141–5; Seal, *The Outlaw Legend*, pp. 15–18, 31, 64–5, 189–90, 197–8.

5 Hobsbawm, *Bandits*, p. 46.

6 Ibid., p. 22.

7 Richard Firth Greene, 'John Ball's Letters. Literary History and Historical Literature', in *Chaucer's England*, ed. Barbara A. Hanawalt (Minneapolis, University of Minnesota Press, 1992), pp. 193–4.

8 See Chapters Two, Three, Four, passim, Chapter Nine, pp. 107–11.

9 Hobsbawm, *Bandits*, pp. 47, 51–3; Seal, *The Outlaw Legend*, pp. 8, 192.

10 See Chapter Twelve, pp. 155–8.

11 See Chapter Five, pp. 51–2; Chapter Nine, p. 109.

12 See Chapter Thirteen, pp. 175–7 and nn. 55, 56, 58, 59; Chapter Twelve, pp. 150, 158 and n. 38.

13 Hobsbawm, *Bandits*, pp. 22, 44–5, 61; Seal, *The Outlaw Legend*, pp. 52–65.

14 See Chapter Two, pp. 17–23.

15 See Chapter Thirteen, pp. 164–6.

16 Seal, *The Outlaw Legend*, pp. 17–18, 48–9, 65, 183, quotations on p. 17; note also Hobsbawm, *Bandits*, p. 170.

17 Joseph Ritson, *Robin Hood, A Collection of all the Ancient Poems, Songs and Ballads*, 2 vols (London, T. Egerton & J. Johnson, 1795), I, pp. xi–xii.

18 William Godwin, *Caleb Williams*, ed. David McCracken (Oxford University Press, 1982), p. 216.

Index

Visual Basic® .NET

Black Book

Steven Holzner

President and CEO
Roland Elgey

Publisher
Al Valvano

Associate Publisher
Katherine R. Hartlove

Acquisitions Editor
Jawahara Saidullah

Product Marketing Manager
Jeff Johnson

Project Editor
Sean Tape

Technical Reviewer
Kourosh Ardestani

Production Coordinator
Wendy Littley

Cover Designer
Carla Schuder

CD-ROM Developer
Michelle McConnell

Visual Basic® .NET Black Book

Limits of Liability and Disclaimer of Warranty

The author and publisher of this book have used their best efforts in preparing the book and the programs contained in it. These efforts include the development, research, and testing of the theories and programs to determine their effectiveness. The author and publisher make no warranty of any kind, expressed or implied, with regard to these programs or the documentation contained in this book.

The author and publisher shall not be liable in the event of incidental or consequential damages in connection with, or arising out of, the furnishing, performance, or use of the programs, associated instructions, and/or claims of productivity gains.

Trademarks

Trademarked names appear throughout this book. Rather than list the names and entities that own the trademarks or insert a trademark symbol with each mention of the trademarked name, the publisher states that it is using the names for editorial purposes only and to the benefit of the trademark owner, with no intention of infringing upon that trademark.

The Coriolis Group, LLC
14455 N. Hayden Road
Suite 220
Scottsdale, Arizona 85260

(480) 483-0192
FAX (480) 483-0193
www.coriolis.com

Library of Congress Cataloging-in-Publication Data
Holzner, Steven.
    Visual Basic .NET black book / by Steven Holzner.
        p.   cm.
    Includes index.
    ISBN 1-57610-835-X
    1. Microsoft Visual BASIC.   2. BASIC (Computer program language)   I. Title.
QA76.73.B3 H6895   2001
005.2'768–dc21   2001047658
                                                                                            CIP

Printed in the United States of America
10   9   8   7   6   5   4   3   2   1

CORIOLIS